LONDON'S BOROUGHS AT 50

LONDON'S BOROUGHS AT 50

TONY TRAVERS

Biteback Publishing

First published in Great Britain in 2015 by
Biteback Publishing Ltd
Westminster Tower
3 Albert Embankment
London SE1 7SP
Copyright © Tony Travers 2015

Tony Travers has asserted his right under the Copyright, Designs and Patents Act 1988 to be identified as the author of this work.

ISBN 978-1-84954-919-6

10 9 8 7 6 5 4 3 2 1

A CIP catalogue record for this book is available from the British Library.

Set in Bulmer and DIN by Adrian McLaughlin

Printed and bound in Great Britain by
CPI Group (UK) Ltd, Croydon CR0 4YY

CONTENTS

APPENDICES

ACKNOWLEDGEMENTS

This book has been written with help from many people. Colleagues at the London School of Economics & Political Science (working within the Greater London Group and latterly LSE London) have been a source of ideas and inspiration in relation to government, planning, housing, the economy and transport. Christine Whitehead and Ian Gordon have contributed insights and opinions over many years, as has Patrick Dunleavy. Michael Hebbert (UCL) and Stephen Glaister (Imperial) have similarly provided inputs to subjects considered here. George Jones, a contributor to the LSE's Greater London Group research of the 1960s and 1970s, read manuscripts and provided advice. His epic understanding of London and local government cannot be underestimated. My colleagues in the LSE's government department, particularly Simon Hix and Nicole Boyce, have supported the process of writing.

Many London commentators and journalists have provided help with my understanding of contemporary London including Simon Jenkins (*Evening Standard* and *The Guardian*), Ben Rogers and Richard Brown (Centre for London), Patricia Brown (Central), Alexander Jan (Arup), Alexandra Jones and Andrew Carter (Centre for Cities), Tony Halmos (City of London), Tim Donovan (BBC), Simon Harris (ITV), Jerry Thomas and Andrew Cryan (Juniper) and Dave Hill (*The Guardian*).

All the London boroughs kindly responded to a request for historical information and also about their former leaders and chief executives. Officers at London Councils, particularly John O'Brien, Dick Sorabji and James

Odling-Smee, have provided immense help and support through the two years spent putting together the book. Many borough leaders and chief executives provided clarifications and comments on parts of the book relating to their authority. Barbara Salmon kindly managed the process of gathering questionnaire-based information from the thirty-two councils.

Thanks also go to Victoria Godden and Melissa Bond at Biteback for their kindly efficiency in ensuring the book was published in the boroughs' fiftieth year.

Books written by John Davis, Caroline Barron, Stephen Halliday, Ken Young, Patricia Garside, Jerry White and several of the individuals mentioned above have provided much of the historical background from which the boroughs' history has emerged.

However, the analysis and conclusions are those of the author alone.

PART 1

INTRODUCTION

CHAPTER 1

THE GROWTH OF LONDON AND ITS NEED FOR GOVERNMENT

1965

On 30 March 1965, the London County Council held its last meeting at County Hall on the South Bank of the Thames. A few hours earlier, the ashes of Herbert Morrison, the LCC's most famous leader, were scattered from a fireboat into the river near Westminster Bridge. Elsewhere in the capital, county, borough and district councils had already held their final meetings.[1] The old order of London's government was being swept away.

The year 1965 marked the border between post-war Britain and the 'Swinging Sixties'. A Labour government had been elected in 1964, following thirteen years of Conservative rule. Tory grandee leaders, most recently Harold Macmillan and Alec Douglas-Home, were replaced by the more meritocratic Harold Wilson. The period since 1945 had seen austerity, nationalisation, the creation of the welfare state, massive house-building programmes and the development of a 'Butskellite' political consensus. But, by the early 1960s, radical voices were calling for further changes in the way society functioned.

A series of political scandals during the early 1960s, notably the Profumo affair, helped create a climate that revealed establishment figures led rather different lives from those of the public at large. A 'satire boom' fed off the foibles and failures of the political class. By the mid-1960s, Britain was ripe for social and political change.

In his book *White Heat*, Dominic Sandbrook considers the 'end of an era'

---

1   Bernard Donoughue and G. W. Jones, *Herbert Morrison: Portrait of a Politician*, London: Weidenfeld & Nicolson, 1973, page 561

feeling that attended Sir Winston Churchill's funeral on 30 January 1965. The passing of Britain's great wartime leader was seen as a watershed for Britain. On both left and right, the prospect was national decline. Sandbrook quotes Patrick O'Donovan writing in *The Observer*:

> This [the funeral] was the last time that London would be capital of the world. This was an act of mourning for the imperial past. This marked the final act in Britain's greatness. This was a great gesture of self-pity, and after this the coldness of reality and the status of Scandinavia.[2]

London's fall from grace was part of this narrative. Having been the 'biggest city the world had ever known' and capital of an empire 'upon which the sun never set', it is easy to see how commentators thought London would fade as part of the 'orderly management of decline' envisaged by the British establishment at the time. Viewed from 2015, things look remarkably different. 'London' somehow managed to escape from 'Britain',[3] which itself has emerged into something far better than the crumbling Nordic museum that seemed likely in 1965.[4] Moreover, Scandinavia is now seen as a global exemplar of good government and human rights, and is widely admired.

In mid-1960s London, at the heart of British politics, the city's skyline was changing as if to signal a move not to decline, but to modernisation.[5] Tall buildings had started to appear through speculative office building and social housing programmes. Harold Macmillan's government had benefited from increasing affluence and change in Britain during the late 1950s and early 1960s. A desire

---

2   Dominic Sandbrook, *White Heat: A History of Britain in the Swinging Sixties*, London: Little, Brown, 2006 (extract taken from 2007 Abacus edition), page xv

3   See, for example, Janan Ganesh, 'Disunited Kingdom: London in a world of its own', *Financial Times*, 2 March 2015, or Aditya Chakrabortty, 'London's economic boom leaves rest of Britain behind', *The Guardian*, 23 October 2013

4   See Tom Kelly, 'Britain ousts the US as world's most influential nation: country tops rankings for "soft power"', *Daily Mail*, 18 November 2012, and Norma Cohen, OECD immigration destinations, 13 June 2013, *Financial Times* blog, http://blogs.ft.com/ftdata/2013/06/13/oecd-immigration-destinations (accessed 12 June 2015)

5   Roy Porter, *London: A Social History*, London: Penguin, 2000, pages 435–40

to achieve social and economic progress had created an enthusiasm for new modernist buildings. Massive home-building programmes were undertaken using new techniques such as system building. Modern architecture became a symbol of progress, though there have long been conflicting views about its benefits. As Edward Jones and Christopher Woodward have observed:

> [T]he good intentions of the Welfare State, coupled with watered-down allegiances to Le Corbusier's principles and the democratic building style of Sweden, were not enough to produce good architecture. The lack of coherent architectural models, combined with mad planning policies, resulted in a further deterioration in the quality of building in London ... the skyline of London is now a depressing spectacle of stubby, evenly distributed towers.[6]

More recently, a defender of twentieth-century modernism, Owen Hatherley, has written (partly, though not exclusively, of London):

> There is another modernism well worth rescuing from the dustbin of history and the blandishments of heritage ... Left modernisms of the 20th century continue to be *useful*: a potential index of ideas, successful or failed, tried, untried or broken on the wheel of the market or the state. Even in their ruinous condition, they can still offer a sense of possibility which decades of being told that 'There is No Alternative' has almost beaten out of us.[7]

This debate, or some of the structures that provoked it, will recur in the pages that follow. Before and immediately after 1965, many councils were replacing slums with superior (it was thought) homes in the sky. In central

---

6   Edward Jones and Christopher Woodward, *A Guide to the Architecture of London*, London: Weidenfeld & Nicolson, 1983, page 27

7   Owen Hatherley, *Militant Modernism*, Ropley: O Books/John Hunt Publishing, 2008, page 13

London, Centre Point and other architectural icons were reaching upwards. On 8 October 1965, the Post Office (now BT) Tower was opened by Prime Minister Harold Wilson, creating a permanent monument to the London of that year and to what Wilson himself described as the white heat of the technological revolution.[8]

London government reform, including the creation of today's boroughs, took place in the midst of all this upheaval. With hindsight, it is easy to see the reformed 'Greater London' governance arrangements as yet another element in the transformation of Britain that occurred in the 1960s. Yet the pressure to create a system of government that embraced most or all of the wider urban area of London had been evolving since the 1920s. Uncontrolled expansion between 1918 and 1939 had added hundreds of square miles of housing, high streets and industry to the area covered by the LCC.

LONDON'S GROWTH – A BRIEF HISTORY

'London' is an amorphous concept. The City of London, originally a Roman city, was long established as 'London'. But, as new and important settlements developed across the river in Southwark and in far-flung locations such as Westminster, it was not entirely clear if they were part of London or, more plausibly, places in their own right. The City sometimes established Southwark as part of its jurisdiction, though generally without voting rights. As Westminster and the City of London grew together along the Strand, a wider urban area developed. But the City resolutely retained its boundaries and powers. Counties and parishes developed government arrangements in the surrounding territory.

Elizabethan efforts to impose a green belt to contain the burgeoning sprawl that bulged around the Thames were unsuccessful. The city grew inexorably outwards. The coming of railways speeded this expansion. Towns and villages

---

8   Dominic Sandbrook, *White Heat: A History of Britain in the Swinging Sixties*, London: Little, Brown, 2006 (extract taken from Abacus 2007 edition), pages 44–6

that had been miles from London eventually found themselves embraced by brick and tarmac. A unique form of mega-city developed, with millions of small houses covering almost 800 square miles of land: larger than today's Greater London. London became a vast province of towns within a town.

Thus, St Mary's Church in Harrow, which can be seen from tall buildings in central London (and vice versa), once looked southwards over mile after mile of open countryside. Today, perhaps a million homes lie between the church and Centre Point at St Giles. St Giles's own church is 'in-the-Fields', or at least it used to be. However, a protected view that allows visitors to Richmond Park to see St Paul's Cathedral frames an image of the City within a long canopy of trees. No other global city entwines its rural history and urban present so deliberately.

The names of Underground and railway stations attest both to the city's history, but also to the efforts of the embraced territories to cling on to their pastoral origins. Harrow-on-the-Hill conjures up images of a rural idyll. Similarly – and there are many examples to choose from – Harringay Green Lanes, Stamford Brook, Parsons Green, Northfields, Southfields, Shepherd's Bush, Oakwood, and Ruislip Gardens all sound plaintively non-urban. Waltham Forest, a borough name chosen in 1965, implies a large expanse of trees. This is still partly true, but less so than in the distant past.

This historical preamble explains the unique composition of contemporary London. It is one of the world's largest and most successful cities, but it is also a patchwork of architecture, small settlements, trees and wildlife. The system of government that exists today is the product of two factors: the way the urban area of 'London' grew outwards; and the City of London's approach to protecting its boundaries.

Nothing can be understood about London without a grasp of the city's history. Although this book is about London's thirty-two post-1965 boroughs, their creation was a direct consequence of the City of London's government model, evolved over 1,000 years. In particular, the City's defence of its original territory set the stage for all that has followed, and, indeed, for the way Londoners think about their city.

THE CITY OF LONDON AND THE GROWTH
OF A METROPOLIS

The City was originally founded by the Romans, who left Britain in AD 410. By 450 or 460, English history descends into a period when the city was abandoned and its great Roman buildings fell into disrepair. The Anglo-Saxon settlement of London – or Lundenwic, as they called it – began during the seventh century, not on the site of the Romans' Londinium, but somewhat to the west, at contemporary Aldwych.[9] Later, King Alfred took London back within the Roman walls to make it easier to protect from Viking invaders. From this point onwards, meetings of the 'folkmoot' (a general assembly of citizens) took place, allowing all the people of the city a voice, though formal power rested with the Court of Hustings, which developed a 'Court of Aldermen' to perform administrative functions. The Court of Aldermen came, over time, to seek the support of a Court of Common Council as a way of broadening decision-making.[10]

King Alfred re-established London and attempted, though with little success, to impose a grid street plan on London. The establishment of the city's own government during the Anglo-Saxon settlement of England put in place the first building block of today's system of government. King Canute (1016–35) is believed to have built the first royal palace, and seat of national government, near to a church (a minster) to the west of the City of London. Westminster has been the centre of national government since the eleventh century, and has remained separate from the government of London in the City.[11] From here on, 'the City' is the centre of mercantile London, while 'Westminster' is the home of the national government.

The relationship between these two districts was not always easy.

---

9   Peter Ackroyd, *London: The Biography*, London: Chatto & Windus, 2000, pages 32–3

10   Derek Keene, 'Roots and Branches of Power, 1000–1300', *The London Journal*, Vol. 26, No. 1, 2001, pages 4–6

11   UK Parliament, 'Anglo-Saxon origins', History of the Parliamentary Estate, http://www.parliament.uk/about/living-heritage/building/palace/estatehistory/the-middle-ages/anglosaxon-royal-palace (accessed 5 May 2015)

Sir Laurence Gomme describes the ancient origins of the City and Westminster as being very different. The Dean of Westminster Abbey was, according to Dean Stanley, the 'shadowy head of a shadowy corporation' that was wholly separate from the City of London:

> [It was] a system of government [in the twelfth and thirteenth centuries] absolutely different from that of the [C]ity. The constitution of Westminster was based upon the English manorial system in its most complete form … [the City of] London was governed upon a system as unlike it as possible. The two systems were alongside of each other, but being drawn from different origins they developed in quite different fashion … We see in particular the lordship at the top of the Westminster system. We see in London the elected mayor, and we may well recall at this point the cry of the Londoners that they have no lord but their mayor. This Westminster evidence shows too that the constitution of London was built upon the government of the 'whole community', which not even the power and personal interest of Henry III could put on one side … The separation of Westminster from the [C]ity … emphasises the action of the sovereign most markedly.[12]

The City of London Corporation (that is, the local government of the City of London) as it operates today dates its earliest origins from around this point. Because the City's evolution comes to determine so much else about London government, these early stages can be seen as hugely important in setting the scene for developments during Norman, Plantagenet, Tudor and Victorian history. William the Conqueror decided to leave the City alone, granting it a charter to guarantee its freedoms.[13] The Tower of London, in neighbouring Tower Hamlets, was built to keep watch over the powerful, self-governing and taxpaying merchants of the City.

12 George Laurence Gomme, *The Governance of London*, London: T. Fisher Unwin, 1907, page 300

13 Peter Ackroyd, *London: The Biography*, London: Chatto & Windus, 2000, page 48

In the period after the granting of its charter, London's importance was stressed by it being the only city mentioned in Magna Carta, which stated 'the City of London shall have all its ancient liberties by land as well as by water'.[14] The office of Mayor of the City of London (established in 1189), later Lord Mayor, was entrusted with ensuring the provisions of the document were carried out. Dick Whittington became Lord Mayor in 1397.[15] Peter Ackroyd, in *London: The Biography*, suggests Magna Carta inaugurated the process of shifting London from being an independent city state towards becoming a national capital.[16] But it is the City's defence of its ancient 'square mile' boundaries that has had the most direct impact on the development of the wider city's government as London has grown.[17]

Between the eleventh and fifteenth centuries, as the historian Caroline Barron records, the City of London developed many of the livery companies and guilds that became part of its system of government. As the urban area surrounding London grew, Justices of the Peace and Sheriffs, who were appointed by the Crown within each shire, sustained the law and were responsible for a number of military functions. In the area surrounding London, the shire counties were Kent, Surrey, Berkshire, Middlesex, Buckinghamshire, Hertfordshire and Essex. Parish-based government evolved, mainly to administer the 1601 poor law.

The potential for London to spread far was constrained by travelling times. Roads were basic and carriages horse-drawn. Most people could travel no further than they could walk. London's geographical growth was, by today's standards, limited. Instead, population density increased to

---

14   George Laurence Gomme, *The Governance of London*, London: T. Fisher Unwin, 1907, page 362

15   Caroline Barron, *London in the Later Middle Ages*, Oxford: Oxford University Press, 2004, especially Chapter 8 and pages 232–3

16   Peter Ackroyd, *London: The Biography*, London: Chatto & Windus, 2000, page 48

17   William A. Robson, *The Government and Misgovernment of London*, London: George Allen & Unwin, 1939, Chapter 11

accommodate growth. In 1650, the population of the City of London was probably 150,000–200,000.[18] Today, it is just over 8,000.[19]

By the sixteenth century, Elizabeth I was so concerned with the sprawl of the city that her government attempted to prohibit further construction in its hinterland by an early form of green belt.[20] At this time, 'bills of mortality' were introduced to monitor deaths around London on a weekly basis – an early involvement by local government through parishes in public health. The parishes covered by these bills of mortality became the basis of the area of the 1855 Metropolitan Board of Works (MBW), and subsequently of the London County Council (LCC) and today's inner London.

By the time of Elizabeth's death in 1603, London had spread beyond the City and neighbouring Westminster in all directions. Her government's restrictions on development had had little effect, and the sprawl continued. Areas beyond the City were not governed by the City of London Corporation, although, from 1550 until 1899, part of today's Southwark (the historical ward of Bridge Without) was run from the City's Guildhall. Westminster, a settlement to the west of the City of London, had its own governance, administered by officers of the abbey and the Parish of St Margaret's. In other built-up areas close to the City and Westminster there was a limited kind of parish-based government, later to include poor law provision, funded by an early form of rates.

New players, in the shape of aristocratic estates, emerged into the story from the later seventeenth century. A number of families owned land between the City and Westminster and began to develop housing in places such as today's Covent Garden, Mayfair and Belgravia. These developments did not require planning permission. Simon Jenkins has described how, particularly during

---

18   Estimate derived from Christopher Chalklin, 'The Rise of the English Town', Prepared for the Economic History Society, Cambridge: Cambridge University Press, http://catdir.loc.gov/catdir/samples/cam031/2001269803.pdf (accessed 2 October 2015)

19   Office for National Statistics, *MYE2 Population Estimates for UK, England and Wales, Scotland and Northern Ireland, Mid-2014*, London: ONS, http://www.ons.gov.uk/ons/publications/re-reference-tables.html?edition=tcm%3A77-368259 (accessed 2 October 2015)

20   G. Topham Forrest, 'London One Hundred Years Hence', *Public Administration*, Vol. 4, No. 2, April 1926, pages 157-8

the eighteenth century, farmland was rapidly covered with elegant squares and thoroughfares.

A GROWING DEMAND FOR METROPOLITAN GOVERNMENT

From this point onwards, the great city sprawled across fields in what would today be Marylebone, Fitzrovia, north Lambeth and to Marble Arch and beyond. By 1820, London covered something close to today's Transport for London (TfL) Underground Zone 1, and was a city of 1.5 million people. But London's government did not expand to match this outward development. The City of London governed itself according to its historic traditions. By the start of the nineteenth century, there was a problem with the way London was run. The municipal corporations commissioners who reported in 1837 suggested there be a single metropolitan municipality that would, inevitably, consume the City. This proposal was given short shrift by the City of London Corporation, which wished to protect its ancient self-government and privileges. As a result, the growing urban area continued to be governed by county- and parish-based local authorities. Ad hoc boards and private companies came increasingly to have a role in delivering water, lighting, paving and other services.

Britain developed into the world's leading industrial economy. In the north of England and the Midlands, burgeoning cities such as Manchester, Liverpool, Sheffield and Birmingham successfully petitioned Parliament for the powers to create the elected corporations needed to provide their rapidly growing cities with government. But in the built-up area surrounding the ancient City of London, it proved harder to assert the need for a similar corporation. On the one hand, the City was unwilling to extend its boundaries to embrace the new, much bigger, London. On the other, the scale of London was such that a single corporation was seen by many politicians and reformers as inappropriate for such a massive urban agglomeration.

Every year that passed meant 'London' grew bigger and the need for city government increased. The Metropolitan Police Service was established in 1829, covering an area within a radius of 6–7 miles surrounding Charing Cross, and responsible to the Home Office. A number of writers have described with relish the random chaos of governmental institutions that developed in the city beyond the City. Writing in 1898, Sir Laurence Gomme summarised the nineteenth-century local government arrangements beyond the City boundaries in the following terms:

> [The local areas in London beyond the City] are marvellous productions. The ancient parishes with their civil powers, the districts formed by the [Metropolis Management] Act of 1855, the poor law areas, the Local Board of Health, all combine to produce a chaos ... not understood by any member of Her Majesty's government, and certainly not by the ordinary citizen ... The affairs of the county area are administered by the London County Council, the City of London Corporation, the Commissioners of Metropolitan Police (whose area extends beyond the county area), the School Board for London, the Metropolitan Asylums Board (whose area does not extend to the whole county), the Justices in Quarter Sessions, the Home Office with reference to the Metropolitan Police Courts (whose areas do not agree with the county), and the Thames Conservancy (whose area extends from Cricklade to Yantlet Creek).[21]

Gomme chose the unique district of Ely Place, Holborn, as an example of the minute subdivisions of London government that operated during the nineteenth century:

> [Ely Place,] an extra parochial jurisdiction of the Bishops of Ely when they had an Episcopal residence in London and to which Shakespeare alludes in a well-known passage in *Richard III*, still possesses its

---

21   G. Laurence Gomme, *London in the Reign of Victoria (1837–1897)*, London: Blackie & Son Limited, 1898, pages 189–90

commissioners of paving, still appoints its watchmen, the lineal successor of ancient 'Charley', who cries the hours four times a day, and
whose presence prevents any ordinary policeman having jurisdiction
within the 'liberty'.[22]

Complexity is not new to London. Throughout the nineteenth century, reformers struggled to make sense of the 'London government problem'. John Davis,
in his definitive study of the subject, boils it down to a number of key issues.

First, as outlined above, the City of London was serially resistant to reform
that threatened its boundaries and ancient privileges. Second, the parishes,
vestries and district boards (municipal units made up of smaller parishes) that
were empowered by the 1855 Metropolis Management Act were also unenthusiastic about most of the local government changes that were regularly
proposed. Third, there was a significant difference of opinion among reformers and politicians about the need for city-wide government in London.

The leading proponent of a centralised form of London government was
the sanitary reformer Edwin Chadwick, who believed that a powerful and
nationally appointed body was required to impose clean water, sewers and
public health on the vast and often filthy metropolis. Key supporters of the
existing form of super-local government included Joshua Toulmin Smith, who
campaigned to retain and strengthen the then-existing system of parishes and
district boards. It is worth noting that some vestries were 'open' and held elections, while others were 'close' and self-selecting. Only a few were properly
democratic, even by the standards of the time.[23]

By the middle of the nineteenth century, the civil parishes of London, which
were responsible for local government, often had populations bigger than
provincial cities. They may have been 'local', but the bigger parishes had
as many residents as the boroughs in 2015. St Pancras (in today's Camden)

---

22   Ibid., pages 200–201

23   See John Davis, *Reforming London: The London Government Problem, 1855–1900*, Oxford:
     Clarendon Press, 1988, Chapter 2

and Lambeth each had a population of about 150,000.[24] There were proposals for 'tenification': that is, creating ten large municipalities within London, based on parliamentary borough areas. But the notion of creating a series of Manchester- or Birmingham-style municipal corporations was bitterly opposed by localists, and, indeed, by the existing vestries.

The 1855 legislation, which had been triggered by a series of cholera epidemics during the 1840s and 1850s coupled with a growing realisation that the Thames was little more than an open sewer, created a classic London solution to the challenge of providing metropolitan government.[25] The MBW was created to deliver sewers, roads and other infrastructure for the city. Its chief engineer, Sir Joseph Bazalgette, was London's Haussmann.[26] But the 'Metropolitan Board of Works', as its name suggests, was not an elected council; rather it was operated by a joint committee of the City, vestries and district boards. Although well short of the powerful institution advocated by many reformers, it solved the London government problem without having to create an elected council.

The MBW, like the London Passenger Transport Board in the early to mid-twentieth century and the London Docklands Development Corporation in the late twentieth century (or, for that matter, a number of public bodies dominated by New York planner Robert Moses),[27] was an example of how single-purpose, unelected, city authorities can be highly effective in delivering infrastructure and urban redevelopment. A lack of democracy empowers individuals to drive forward change more quickly than would be possible if elected politicians were in charge. The indirect control of the MBW by the City, district board and parish members barely constrained Bazalgette as he constructed sewers, roads, bridges and embankments.

---

24   London County Council, *Statistical Abstract for London, 1901*, census tables, London: LCC, 1901

25   Stephen Halliday, *The Great Stink of London: Sir Joseph Bazalgette and the Cleansing of the Victorian Metropolis*, Stroud: Sutton Publishing Ltd, 1999, page xxii

26   George-Eugene Haussmann rebuilt Paris for Napoleon III in the mid-nineteenth century, see Willet Weeks, *The Man Who Made Paris Paris*, London: London House, 1999

27   See Robert A. Caro, *The Power Broker: Robert Moses and the Fall of New York*, New York: Vintage Books, 1975, pages 12–15

The fire brigade was also created by the MBW following a classic 'nothing ever changes' struggle between different arms of London and national government. In the early nineteenth century, parishes had been required by the government to provide fire engines, ladders and fire cocks. At this time, some private cover was offered by insurance companies.[28] A number of parish services were combined in 1833 to form the London Fire Engine Establishment.[29] Its concerns were mostly for property (not people) in the central area.

A big warehouse fire in Tooley Street, Southwark, in 1861 led to a demand for better fire protection. The Metropolitan Police Commissioner, Sir Richard Mayne, proposed that his force should take responsibility for a metropolitan fire brigade. The commissioner's proposed plan was, in the Home Secretary's (Sir George Grey's) view, far too costly. Instead, an arbitrary amount was determined by the government to fund a police-run brigade that would be funded partly by a rate precept, partly by the government and partly by insurance companies. This arrangement was then challenged by the City of London, which had its own police force. The City of London Corporation demanded that its police should run a separate City fire brigade. When this idea proved unacceptable to the government, the MBW was called upon to take over. It agreed to do so, and added the fire brigade to its empire.[30]

A second metropolitan authority was created in 1870. The London School Board (LSB) held its first elections on 29 November 1870. The legislation to introduce the board, driven through Parliament by William Gladstone and W. E. Forster, was controversial. The Church of England was opposed to state intervention in schooling, while Nonconformists and radicals opposed

---

28   G. Laurence Gomme, *London in the Reign of Victoria (1837–1897)*, London: Blackie & Son, 1898, page 56

29   London Fire Brigade, 'Early fire brigades', http://www.london-fire.gov.uk/early-fire-brigades-and-james-braidwood.asp (accessed 3 October 2015)

30   David Owen, *The Government of Victorian London, 1855–1889: The Metropolitan Board of Works, the Vestries and the City Corporation*, Cambridge MA and London: Harvard University Press, 1982, pages 128–9

a clerical monopoly.[31] These opponents were outweighed by the recognised need to tackle the scale of educational destitution in the great cities of Britain. The board was to be responsible for 'elementary education' – that is, the education of the lower classes. Its minimum content was prescribed by the Education Department and subject to inspection. Charles Dickens notably described the poor standards of schools in critiques such as *Our Mutual Friend* and *Hard Times*.

The board was the first city-wide elected local authority in London. Forster had originally intended to constitute the school board in much the same way as the MBW – that is, with district boards and parishes nominating members. But the legislation was amended in Parliament to make it directly elected. The capital was divided into ten electoral districts. The City, Southwark, Chelsea and Greenwich returned four members each. Lambeth, Tower Hamlets, Hackney and Westminster each returned five. Finsbury had six and Marylebone seven. The form of voting was unusual: each elector could cast as many votes as there were seats in the division. The voter could thus 'plump' all their votes for a single candidate, instead of spreading them throughout the list. The ballot was secret.

The quality of the board's membership is remarkable and suggestive of the growing importance of education in the capital. One of the initial members was Dr Elizabeth Garrett (later Elizabeth Garrett Anderson), the country's first female doctor,[32] whose name is commemorated in a wing at University College Hospital and a school in Islington. A number of Anglicans and Free Church members were elected, as were several MPs. The MPs included W. H. Smith, founder of the still-existing newsagency chain and future First Lord of the Admiralty. His lack of naval service before this latter role led him to be satirised by Gilbert and Sullivan in *HMS Pinafore*.[33] The first meeting of the LSB took place at the Guildhall by invitation of the City of London Corporation.[34]

---

31 Stuart Maclure, *A History of Education in London, 1870–1990*, London: Allen Lane, 1990, page 15

32 Ibid., page 18

33 Ibid., page 19

34 Ibid.

Both the LSB and the MBW were effective at delivering the services required of them. They provided a stepping stone between the fragmented, parish-based governance of the early-to-mid-nineteenth century, and the system that took shape between 1888 and 1899. In the cases of both the MBW and the LSB, parish and district board membership was considered, although by the time the School Board was created in 1870, a joint committee of indirectly elected members was deemed unacceptable. Nevertheless, the power of the local tier of London government to assert its parochial influence was still present well after the 1870 education reforms.

THE LONDON COUNTY COUNCIL

The MBW was a leading indicator of the 'bottom-heavy two-tier system' that has operated in London almost continuously since 1855. In 1888, with the MBW mired in accusations of corruption, legislation was introduced to replace it by the London County Council, which was a directly elected authority covering the same area. But the complex pattern of parishes, district boards and poor law guardians remained unreformed.

From 1888 to 1899, the long struggle to reform the 'local' tier of London government moved into a decisive stage. There was a growing acceptance from a number of vestries that reform would probably be their best chance of survival. The City of London found itself exposed to the risk that if there were a reform of the local level of London government, then it might be reduced to the status of (as it saw it) a district council. In the end, proposals put forward by the Kensington Vestry, one of the most powerful of the original parish-based municipal units, suggested a form of elected local borough, which the City saw as offering it the chance to survive largely unscathed. The 1899 legislation that reformed the vestries, district boards and poor law guardians created twenty-eight 'metropolitan boroughs' within the LCC area.

Parliament had, broadly, split along party lines on London government issues. Conservatives (generally styled 'Moderates' within the capital) were unenthusiastic about big government at either the metropolitan or local level. Liberals and later Labour ('Progressives' within London government) broadly favoured the creation of the LCC and new borough councils. Two books published in 1939 considered the operation of the metropolitan boroughs alongside the LCC in the forty years since 1899.

William Robson, in *The Government and Misgovernment of London*, argued that the post-1899 authorities had been created to undermine

> the interest and authority … the London County Council had aroused. It sought to strengthen and magnify the district councils to the greatest possible extent and to emphasise their independence of the larger body in subtle as well as obvious ways. Every device [that] might tend to divide the allegiance and confuse the loyalty of Londoners was imported to the bill [which created them]; while at the same time nothing was done to ensure coherent administration or give the London County Council power to override parochial views in the interests of the metropolitan community as a whole.[35]

Robson quoted A. G. Gardiner, who had observed: 'There was to be not one London, but thirty Birminghams,'[36] and also that the purpose of the 1899 reforms was:

> [T]o prevent the voice of London as a community from being heard on any subject affecting its common interest, and to substitute a chorus of sectional and competing interests … In order not to disturb the City, the measure of 1899 set up a system of new municipalities, which left London a mosaic of unreal and arbitrary cities, and its essential unity unrecognised.[37]

---

35   William A. Robson, *The Government and Misgovernment of London*, London: George Allen & Unwin, 1939, page 94

36   Ibid.

37   Ibid., page 96

The metropolitan boroughs often chose to exert influence on London Members of Parliament rather than on the LCC.[38]

Concluding his assault on the two-level system created by the 1888 and 1889 reforms, Robson stated:

> Twenty-eight autonomous authorities are responsible for providing such costly institutions as swimming baths, washhouses, public libraries etc.; yet no attempt is made to see that these are places in the most suitable locations in each district having regard to similar provision in neighbouring districts. There is no mutual consultation or common plan to determine the site of a swimming bath or a maternity and child welfare clinic, with the result that it is mere chance whether they are suitably placed or not.[39]

Also writing in 1939, Sir Gwilym Gibbon and Reginald Bell were less critical of the boroughs and their relationship with the LCC. Indeed, they concluded: 'The Council has grown greatly in stature and in girth compared with the City Corporation and the metropolitan borough councils.'[40] They added: 'It has always been felt by the borough councils as a whole that not enough has been done by Parliament in the way of decentralisation … There still remains a general desire among borough councils that more of the functions of the Council should be administered by them.'[41]

Gibbon and Bell accepted that

> at times there has been friction between the Council and the borough councils. This has been much less a matter of politics than of personalities and local traditions … A marked feature of recent years, however, is

---

38   Ibid., page 98

39   Ibid., page 363

40   Sir Gwilym Gibbon and Reginald W. Bell, *History of the London County Council, 1889–1939*, London: Macmillan & Co., 1939, page 591

41   Ibid., page 599

the general improvement in relations. A friendlier spirit has developed, and a greater readiness to bear with each other's difficulties.[42]

Notwithstanding such critical observations, the chaotic arrangements described by Gomme and nineteenth-century reformers were, after an extended and often bitter process, turned into a two-tier system of elected metropolitan authorities. The City of London survived as a city and county with its own police force and retaining its historic system of government. The arrangements enacted in 1888 and 1899 continued, substantially unreformed, until 1965. But the massive further geographical expansion of London after 1888 and 1899 meant voices were soon raised to propose further change. The LCC and the metropolitan boroughs operated in parallel within the same territory for sixty-six years, a period that saw the rapid growth of the metropolis outside their area. No other London government system has lasted as long. The MBW and parishes co-existed for thirty-three years, and the LCC with the parishes for eleven. The Greater London Council (GLC) and the post-1965 boroughs operated together for twenty-one years, followed by a fourteen-year 'interregnum' with no city-wide tier. The Greater London Authority (GLA) and the boroughs have, thus far, been together for about a quarter of the period of co-existence of the LCC and metropolitan boroughs.

THE COMING OF 'GREATER' LONDON

In considering contemporary London, it is easy to forget that most of its territory comprised open fields and villages as recently as 1850, and much of it remained so until the 1920s. However, to the east of the LCC, a major urban expansion had occurred even before it assumed the MBW's boundaries in 1888. Two county boroughs, similar to the corporations that had been created in other big cities across the country, were created in West Ham (1889) and

---

42   Ibid.

East Ham (1915), just across the River Lee from the easternmost metropolitan borough, Poplar. As the urban area of London continued to expand, places that had been free-standing towns and villages were gradually engulfed by the city.

All these places had their own, autonomous, local authorities before London crept out to them. County government, which had been reformed by the 1888 Local Government Act that created the LCC, operated in all the territory up to the LCC boundary, except in the county boroughs. Thus, Middlesex County Council, which covered the area to the north and north-west of the LCC, gradually filled up with houses and factories. Similarly, the northern parts of Kent and Surrey became urbanised, as did the west of Essex and south Hertfordshire.

The LCC area of 'London' had never, as was the case with other counties, been an ancient shire. The LCC came into being as a by-product of the reorganisation of the predominantly rural counties elsewhere in the country.[43] In some of the larger municipal boroughs within the counties surrounding London, there were pressures for greater autonomy, particularly in education. Many districts lobbied the government for 'excepted district' status, to allow them self-government over education. A number of the councils in the counties just outside London (such as Acton and Ilford) were bigger than metropolitan boroughs within the LCC area.

London was amorphous. By the 1920s, it was a vast province of houses, and continued to grow outwards without constraint. Observers became aware of the difficulty of generating a civic identity for such a large metropolis:

> The Londoner is often charged with lack of civic pride. The charge is untrue. Greater London, even the County of London, is too big to inspire much in the way of civic pride. It is too vast, the mind cannot grasp it; but the mind can and does grasp the importance and the glory of the Central Area ... Our planning has been in terms of a single building,

---

43   Gerald Rhodes, *The Government of London: The Struggle for Reform*, London: Weidenfeld & Nicolson, 1970, page 3

a single estate, perhaps a single parish, sometimes a borough, but seldom in regard to the requirements of London as a whole.[44]

Written during the Second World War, the 1944 *Greater London Plan* provides a planner's view of the way London grew. Although its author, Patrick Abercrombie, was concerned with the planning rather than the governance of the city, his analysis of the way London developed offers a useful insight into the challenges of providing such a large urban area with a system of government that could reasonably adapt to its rapid growth and scale. In particular, his plan considered the then-recently developed outer London area:

> In surveying the main features of the growth of Outer London, is any structure discernible in the apparently amorphous sprawl? One can discover old communities that still, in spite of accretions, retain their focal points, such as St Albans, Watford, Guildford, Kingston, Gravesend, Brentwood and others. One can find old communities that still remain more or less unchanged, as Hertford, Denham, Dorking or Epping. There are communities entirely new, as Letchworth, Welwyn Garden City and Becontree. There are others entirely overwhelmed, like Wembley, and finally there are vast areas of inchoate, incoherent housing, such as can be found to the south of Harrow, to the north of Hayes in Middlesex, to the south of the Kingston By-Pass, or around Hornchurch.
>
> Looked at in a more general way, there emerges a certain tendency towards concentric rings, which can be measured in terms of housing density. The central overcrowded urban mass of London is not confined within, but in places laps over the LCC boundary. Outside this mass are the fully developed suburbs, some within the County of London, but more without, containing on the whole tolerable densities. Next comes a zone with sufficient openness to have enabled attempts to be made to create a Green Belt, a zone in which the communities maintain some semblance

---

44   G. Topham Forrest, 'London One Hundred Years Hence', *Public Administration*, Vol. 4, No. 2, April 1926, pages 157, 173

of distinct individuality. Lastly, there is the outer zone in which communities old and new are still seen against an agricultural background.

This faint indication of structure calls for a decision. Is the structure to be maintained, revivified and strengthened in its present form? Are the dry bones of the valley once more to receive the call to stand and live? Or, on the other hand, is the skeleton to receive modification and alteration? Or, finally, is the shape so hopeless that only breaking up will meet the case? … What we now find before us is the combined result of two opposing trends. There has been an exodus of people moving from the centre, people moving out in a process of voluntary decentralisation of homes, if not of work, and at the same time the pull of London has caused an immigration from various parts of the country. The regional fringe has formed the meeting point of these two groups, who have there perforce formed uneasy settlements together.[45]

The *Greater London Plan* was written in the tone often adopted by grandee planners during the 1940s and 1950s. The growth of London that had occurred between the early nineteenth century and 1939 had randomly created a vast and unplanned town stretching for miles and miles. Abercrombie, in common with other experts, wanted to re-order the sprawl and impose greater harmony.

Looked at from the perspective of the inhabitants or civic leaders of, say, Croydon, Tottenham or Richmond, their local area was a distinct entity with its own local government. Croydon, like West Ham, had been given the status of a county borough as early as 1889. Tottenham and Richmond, in common with dozens of other municipal boroughs and urban districts in the counties of Middlesex, Essex, Kent and Surrey, had their own responsibility for council functions. These 'district' authorities had been created within the post-1889 counties, and, for a while until 1899, local government in the London area outside the LCC's boundaries was clearly superior and more democratic than the unreformed local tier inside the city.

---

45   Patrick Abercrombie, *Greater London Plan*, 1944, HMSO, pages 3–4

FURTHER STRUGGLE FOR REFORM

However, by the 1920s, pressure was once again building to reform London government so as to align metropolitan administrative capacity to the reality of the vast city that had accidentally evolved. London School of Economics academics, writing in 1970, summarised the issue by saying:

> The growth of London beyond the boundaries of the LCC in the twentieth century brought increasing problems for London's government. By 1914, places like Walthamstow and Leyton to the north-east and Acton and Willesden to the west and north, had grown to be indissolubly part of London's built-up area, and had demonstrated the artificial nature of the boundaries between London and Middlesex or Essex. This development brought pressures for action to be taken ... over a wider area than that of any existing local authorities. Between 1905 and 1920, for example, four official committees investigated various aspects of London's traffic problems and all concluded that there ought to be a single authority responsible for traffic and indeed transport services generally over an area at least as large as Greater London.[46]

In 1921, a Royal Commission was set up under Lord Ullswater to consider the government of Greater London. It was not unanimous: one set of commissioners proposed some redistribution of responsibilities within the existing system, but also believed there was no need for a London-wide authority. However, they recommended a statutory advisory committee for Greater London. A second group of commissioners proposed a central authority for Greater London, while a third group favoured a two-tier system with a Greater London authority and a number of county borough-type councils within it (close to the system eventually adopted in 1965). The conclusion of the majority of the commission that no changes were needed was reinforced

---

46   Gerald Rhodes, *The Government of London: The Struggle for Reform*, London: Weidenfeld & Nicolson, 1970, page 4

by the views of most of the local authorities in what was now called 'Greater London', who opposed reform. No action was taken on any of the Ullswater Commission's proposals.[47]

In the best traditions of London, a number of ad hoc solutions were found to the city's governance problems. A London and Home Counties Traffic Advisory Committee was set up in 1924 to advise the Minister of Transport about roads and traffic. In 1927, a Greater London Regional Planning Committee was initiated, though it had no powers to enforce any of its recommendations. The London Passenger Transport Board was created in 1933 to administer transport across a wide area surrounding London. For the time being, the establishment of such metropolitan institutions put off the day when a full reform of London government would be undertaken.[48]

Against all the odds, one major planning decision was taken during the 1930s which has had a lasting impact. The Greater London Regional Planning Committee proposed a green belt to control urban growth. The Town and Country Planning Act 1947 then allowed local authorities to designate green belt proposals in their development plans. Few London-related policies have ever been so effectively implemented, albeit this policy deliberately stopped things happening rather than facilitating development.

THE FINAL PUSH

From 1945 onwards, the need for post-war reconstruction and a desire to reform public services were seen as reasons for leaving the structure of local government unchanged. There was, however, an important challenge to this conservative approach. A wartime coalition White Paper proposed a commission to consider the organisation of local government outside London, including

---

47   *Report of the Royal Commission on Local Government in Greater London, 1957–60 (Cmnd 1164)*, London: HMSO, page 14

48   Gerald Rhodes, *The Government of London: The Struggle for Reform*, London: Weidenfeld & Nicolson, 1970, page 9

the creation or extension of county boroughs. In recognition of the problem of London and the wholly urban county of Middlesex, both were excluded from the scope of the proposed commission. It was further proposed that there should be a committee, chaired by Lord Reading, to consider the number, size and boundaries of the metropolitan boroughs within the LCC area. The new Labour government decided in 1946 that the Reading Committee should be wound up even before it could produce a report. In making his announcement about the Reading Committee, health minister Aneurin Bevan explained that it would be hard to look at only one aspect of London government rather than to consider the wider issues raised by the condition of metropolitan administration.[49]

Between 1945 and 1957, the established pattern of London government continued. A number of councils outside the LCC area, notably Ilford and Ealing, promoted private bills to acquire county borough status. The government's argument against them was always that it was wrong to consider them in isolation from the wider need for a review of London government. But this objection wore thin as successive governments failed to hold such a review. In 1954, when Ilford again and Luton for the fourth time promoted legislation to become county boroughs, the government acknowledged that something needed to be done, and soon.[50]

Academic experts and planners such as William Robson argued, as they had for some time, that there needed to be a Greater London authority and a consequent restructuring of local government within and around the capital.[51] But the possibility of reform was rendered insoluble by overlapping 'chicken-and-egg'-type problems. It was impossible to reform local government structures nationally, or even to create new county boroughs, without addressing the widely acknowledged inadequacy of London government's outer boundary. Middlesex, it was generally believed, could not alone be tackled unless London government were to be reformed. London's boundaries could not be

---

49   Ibid., pages 11–12

50   Ibid., page 18

51   See William A. Robson, *The Government and Misgovernment of London*, London: George Allen & Unwin, 1939 Chapter XIV

considered separately from the wider 'Greater London' area, which stretched well beyond Middlesex. The distribution of powers between the LCC and the metropolitan boroughs could not be tackled in isolation. Doing nothing was easier than doing everything.

On 29 July 1957, six months after the Suez Crisis had ended, the Macmillan government took action. Housing & Local Government Minister Henry Brooke, who had been a member of the LCC from 1945 to 1955 and leader of the Conservative opposition on the council, announced that a Royal Commission on London government would be created to consider the question of the possible reform of 'Greater London'. Chaired by a solicitor, Sir Edwin Herbert, it considered a far wider area than built-up London. There were 117 municipalities within a review area covering 840 square miles – a third larger than today's Greater London. The stage was set for the process that would lead to the establishment of the post-1965 London boroughs. But a huge struggle lay ahead before the new system could be born.

Royal Commissions were more popular as a means of examining important governmental problems in the 1950s and 1960s than they are today. They tend to act slowly and thoroughly, which is out of step with the way governments now want to work. The GLC, which emerged from the Herbert Commission, was unceremoniously abolished twenty-one years later, on the basis of little more than a government consultative paper. Nor was there a Royal Commission about the creation of the GLA in 2000. Back in the 1950s, governments were more willing to appoint a senior establishment figure and a set of commissioners to take several years to examine an administrative or governmental reform.

Herbert received very different evidence from two competitive groups of academics: the Greater London Group at the London School of Economics (LSE); and the Centre for Urban Studies at University College London (UCL). The LSE group, led by Professor William Robson, argued for a radical reform to the system of London government across the whole of the built-up metropolitan area around the existing version of 'London'. The UCL researchers preferred to leave the structure of local government largely unreformed, but also to advocate that central government took strong powers to co-ordinate metropolitan and regional policy and action.[52] Even the LSE academics in their study of reform conceded their UCL colleagues had gone further than the LSE team in examining socioeconomic (as opposed to service efficiency) arguments for particular sets of proposals. The UCL team concluded that the boundaries of the LCC corresponded to an area of 'distinct social identity', and that this coherence of identity provided a powerful reason to retain the LCC.[53]

With hindsight, the UCL researchers were correct about an important aspect of London's government, and one that proved fatal to the GLC. The boroughs that were to be created whose territory fell well beyond the LCC boundary generally had substantively different attitudes about, say, tall build-ings or council housing than the new authorities within the LCC area. The efforts of GLC politicians to build large housing estates and to move people from slums in inner London to leafy suburbs were to trigger significant oppo-sition from some of the new outer boroughs. Yet by the 2000s and 2010s, outer London came increasingly to have socioeconomic characteristics which resembled those of inner boroughs. As a result, the UCL view of the difference between the distinct social identity of inner boroughs and, by implication, the equivalent identities of outer ones is now far less important than in the 1960s.

THE BIRTH OF THE LONDON BOROUGHS

Herbert reported in 1960, proposing the creation of a 'Council for Greater London' and fifty-one Greater London Borough councils with popula-tions of between 100,000 and 250,000. The borough was to be 'the primary unit of local government in Greater London'. Many of the functions of the then-existing counties 'could be better performed by the Greater London

---

52   Donald L. Foley, *Governing the London Region: Reorganization and Planning in the 1960s*, Berkeley/Los Angeles/London: University of California Press, 1972, page 30

53   Gerald Rhodes, *The Government of London: The Struggle for Reform*, London: Weidenfeld & Nicolson, 1970, page 60

Boroughs'. The scale of operations of the boroughs 'must be big enough to attract first-rate people ... both as councillors and officials', and the resources of the borough 'must be sufficient to support the full range of borough services'. It followed that many existing councils would have to be reorganised.

The City of London was different. The Herbert Commission dryly noted: 'Logic has its limits and the position of the City lies outside them.' The commission went on:

> The City is, in some respects, a modern local authority with the powers
> of a metropolitan borough. It has also powers, ancient and modern, of
> its own ... Its wealth, its antiquity, the enormous part it has played in
> the history of the nation, its dignity, its traditions and its historical cer-
> emonial make the City of London an institution of national importance.

Herbert, and, indeed, the government, proposed to retain the City and give it all the powers of one of the new boroughs, plus a number unique to it.

The commission also opined: 'It may be that the Greater London Boroughs will find it desirable to have some form of joint committee ... covering the whole of the new area.' Thus, the London Boroughs Association (LBA) and, after a number of reforms and name changes, London Councils came into existence.

A number of Herbert's proposed boroughs – Newham, Merton and Harrow – exist today. Most did not get past this Royal Commission stage, although many formed the building blocks for subsequent mergers before the London Government Act 1963 was finally enacted. Herbert's borough of 'Finsbury, Holborn and Shoreditch' ended broken up in Islington, Camden and Hackney respectively, though Shoreditch briefly visited Tower Hamlets in the government's White Paper proposals. 'Banstead and Epsom & Ewell' and 'Esher and Walton & Weybridge' did not make it as boroughs because the government eventually chose to take them out of Greater London.

Some of the fifty-one proposed authorities included former district councils in what is today 'outer London' whose status would be much enhanced when they were liberated from their county council. Places such as Ilford had previously attempted to win county borough status and escape the clutches of Essex. A number, including Harrow, Twickenham and Wembley (in Middlesex), were 'excepted districts' within counties, providing education on behalf of the county. Many of the authorities in outer London were happy to become boroughs within the new Council for Greater London's area, because the new metropolitan authority was less powerful than the former counties. Uxbridge, Tottenham, Erith and Crayford were among those that supported the Royal Commission's proposals. Croydon and East Ham (both county boroughs) opposed reform, as did Middlesex County Council.

Within the LCC area (now inner London), Conservative boroughs including Kensington, Chelsea and Westminster were enthusiastic for the proposed reforms. Most Labour boroughs opposed them, except Fulham and Hackney, which supported change. Unsurprisingly, the LCC opposed its own demise, while many Labour boroughs within London supported the council's position. Labour accused the Conservatives (and not without reason) of wanting to expand 'London' and thus, by bringing in a number of affluent suburbs, make it more likely the Conservatives would win control of the new Council for Greater London. But Conservative-controlled Surrey County Council opposed reform and suggested, instead, the creation of a joint planning board of local authorities in the wider London area.

One of the earliest reviews of the new boroughs was published in 1961, four years before the new authorities started work. A pamphlet was based on a lecture by Professor William Robson, the LSE academic who had been so influential in pressing for 'Greater London' government and whose colleagues at the Greater London Group at the LSE had, along with the Centre for Urban Studies at UCL, provided much of the expert analysis for the Herbert Commission. Robson made his views public in the period between the publication of the Royal Commission's report and legislation being introduced to Parliament.

He concluded that his study of London led him to believe that 'many important functions, which urgently need to be carried out for the whole metropolis, are being neglected or carried out in a piecemeal fashion', and that 'second-tier authorities need strengthening'.[54] Robson made no secret of his own views, and explained how he and his LSE colleagues preferred powerful 'Greater London Boroughs', whose title was to include the word 'Greater', so as to stress these authorities' power: 'The adjective "Greater" applies not only to the area of London, but also to the powers and responsibilities of the author-ities concerned.' Robson wanted the name to be such that every citizen of the city 'will know he is a member of the Greater London community'.[55]

Robson was less convinced about the Royal Commission's desire to avoid the terms 'upper tier' and 'lower tier' of London government, which, in their view, conveyed the idea of superior and inferior authorities:

> They prefer to regard the distinction between Greater London Boroughs
> and the Council for Greater London as based on the difference between
> a narrower and wider area of administration. This is perhaps a little
> hypersensitive. Most theatres have three or four tiers of seats; but it
> is the lower tiers [that] contain the best and most expensive seats.[56]

Where the Herbert Commission proposed fifty-one boroughs, Robson wanted fewer. He and the LSE researchers proposed an average population of 350,000 to 450,000, leading to between twenty-five and thirty councils. The only smaller borough would be Watford, which had a well-defined boundary and would be left as a new authority with just 74,000 people. He suggested the Royal Commission might have decided to propose a smaller size to avoid upsetting the larger existing municipalities such as Croydon, Islington or Lewisham.[57]

The government published a White Paper in November 1961, which included a preference to call the new metropolitan authority the 'Greater London Council'. Henry Brooke, the Minister for Housing & Local Government, pro-posed there should be fewer, larger boroughs and that education should be run

---

54   W. A. Robson, *The Greater London Boroughs*, London: Greater London Group, 1961, page 5

55   Ibid., page 7

56   Ibid., page 8

57   Ibid., page 9

by the boroughs alone, except within the LCC area, where a single authority should take control. Herbert had suggested making education a joint responsibility of the GLC and the boroughs. At this point, thirty-four boroughs were proposed – fewer in number and thus bigger than those proposed by Herbert.

As the debate about the White Paper continued, ministers, under pressure from outer districts, gradually ruled out a number of proposed boroughs. Banstead, Caterham, Warlingham and Walton & Weybridge were excluded, as were Cheshunt, Esher, Staines and Sunbury-on-Thames. Parts of Hornchurch and Surbiton were taken out. Epsom & Ewell survived as part of London until the legislation reached its report stage in the House of Lords.

Commenting on the struggle between shire districts and the government over their place in London, *The Economist* commented:

> Dr Hill [now the Minister of Housing and Local Government] must not
> let himself be browbeaten by suburban witenagemots ... The Surrey
> Tories may dance in the streets because they still have sack and soke
> in Banstead ... [but] London's readjustment will not be advanced if
> Dr Hill's first action has to be to placate those of his political friends
> who make the loudest noise.

In fairness to Dr Hill, the more outer parts of the metropolitan area excluded from London, the less likely the smaller Greater London would be to vote Conservative.

In examining the government's proposals for new boroughs, LSE academics described the government's proposed 'Borough 27' (today's Hounslow) as:

> [A] funnel-shaped authority over 10 miles long from the Hammersmith/
> Chiswick boundary to the Thames at Staines with the A30 as its spine.
> But it was less easy to see what had led to the grouping in Borough
> 28 [Hillingdon]; it was almost as long from north to south as Borough 27
> but the main lines of communication ran across it.[58]

---

58 Gerald Rhodes, *The Government of London: The Struggle for Reform*, London: Weidenfeld
    & Nicolson, 1970, page 116

The White Paper proposed a series of conferences to be chaired by town clerks from outside London to consider the final composition of the proposed boroughs. These conferences faced a number of critical issues, and their decisions shaped the future government of London. The following is an edited section of Gerald Rhodes's book on the struggle for reform:

> The government had proposed to split Wandsworth … The main reasons were that it was very large … and an awkward shape. Moreover, its neighbour, Battersea, was small. It seemed an obviously sensible proposal, therefore, to add part of Wandsworth to Battersea. This the government had suggested, but unfortunately the result was to leave the remainder of Wandsworth as a separate borough 'without municipal buildings or any other of the basic equipment of public administration' … [T]he town clerks suggested a different borough grouping, but in doing so they rejected the views of both boroughs. Wandsworth did not want to be divided and Battersea simply wanted to take as much of Wandsworth as would bring it up to the required population size … To solve the problem, they suggested adding most of the eastern part of Wandsworth (i.e. Clapham and Streatham) to Lambeth, leaving the rest of Wandsworth to be joined to Battersea … However, the consequence of this suggestion was that there had to be a wholesale recasting of practically all the other boroughs in the area. In the government proposals, for example, Lambeth was to have been joined with Southwark. Now a new home had to be found for the latter.[59]

Thus, in a different version of history, Lambeth & Southwark would have been one of the new boroughs, Camberwell (including Bermondsey and Deptford) would have been another, and the new London Borough of Lewisham would have been Deptfordless and have no riverfront. It is remarkable how one period's modest administrative tidying-up can become the basis of another's day-to-day government.

---

59   Ibid., pages 147–8

Matters proved rather easier north of the river, though there were some creative suggestions for changes to the White Paper's proposals. The Borough of Chelsea came out with an ingenious proposal to combine Chelsea, South Kensington, Fulham and Knightsbridge into one borough. This approach was rejected because it meant splitting existing authorities. The proposal to merge Wembley and Willesden was fiercely opposed by both councils. But Wembley was considered too small to go it alone and would have had to be joined, if not to Willesden, then to Harrow. Neighbouring authorities opposed being joined to either Wembley or Willesden, so, in the end, the town clerks left the Wembley–Willesden borough (Brent) in place.

Summarising the efforts of the Herbert Commission, the government White Paper and the town clerks, Rhodes concluded:

> The metropolitan boroughs of 1899 were formed out of existing parish units of that date purely as the most convenient method … to hand. In 1962, the London Borough boundaries were drawn to form the most convenient administrative units out of the existing conglomeration of county boroughs, metropolitan and municipal boroughs, and urban districts. An attempt was made to do this with as much regard for criteria such as lines of communication and location of service centres as was possible given the limitations of size, of the need to amalgamate whole areas and, above all, of time within which the operation was carried out. But, when all is said, many of the groupings [that] finally emerged must be regarded mainly as marriages of administrative convenience. East Ham and West Ham; Hornsey, Tottenham and Wood Green; Ruislip-Northwood, Uxbridge, Hayes & Harlington and Yiewsley & West Drayton – they may form workable patterns for running education, welfare or public library services, but it would be hard to find any consistent reasons for the particular amalgamations [that] were finally accepted.[60]

---

60   Ibid., page 153

After extensive consultation about the White Paper, the government set about passing the legislation necessary to achieve reform. The London Government Bill was introduced in November 1962. It was pushed through by Conservative MPs and opposed by Labour. There were lengthy debates about the powers to be given to the GLC and the boroughs, and many proposed amendments about the precise configuration of the new boroughs. Any decision about the components of one borough had knock-on consequences for its neighbours. To make things even more difficult, the outer boundary of London was still not finally fixed.

One of the amendments put down by two opposition MPs (Eric Lubbock, Liberal victor of the Orpington by-election, and Labour MP for Dagenham, John Parker) proposed a single central London borough.[61] The government rejected the proposal on the grounds that it would be wrong to set up a borough purely based on the need for a planning function within the central area. A Conservative, Sir Hugh Lucas-Tooth, MP for Hendon, moved an amendment at the committee stage to make the GLC the sole planning authority for a smaller, core area of the centre. The Housing & Local Government Minister, Sir Keith Joseph, rejected it.

A large number of professional and other bodies played a part in shaping the final legislation. The (now 'Royal') Town Planning Institute and the Royal Institute of Chartered Surveyors lobbied about planning powers. But despite the momentous nature of the proposed change to the government of London, the public was not much interested. The Conservative MP for Beckenham, Philip Goodhart, remarked during the passage of the London Government Bill: 'I have been impressed by the lack of interest shown in my area ... since the beginning of this month. I have received more letters about the iniquities of the discrimination in the taxation on greyhound racing than on this topic.'[62]

In the end, there were to be thirty-two boroughs, not thirty-four. The City of London lived on once again.

---

61   W. A. Robson, *The Heart of Greater London: Proposals for a Policy*, London: Greater London Group/London School of Economics and Political Science, 1965

62   Hansard, HC Debates, Volume 654, London: HMSO, 20 February 1962, Column 286

CHAPTER 2

THE NEW BOROUGHS
AND THEIR
CONTEXT

Books written about London government and planning covering the period since 1965 have generally concentrated on plans for metropolitan, city-wide planning or on the central areas of London.[63] The creation and abolition of the GLC have been considered, yet there is no comprehensive history of the London boroughs. Much has been written about Ken Livingstone,[64] the GLC's final leader, while there are also publications analysing the creation of the GLA.[65] There have been a number of studies of planning or politics in particular boroughs,[66] and there have been books about the economy, planning, housing or development[67] that consider conditions in parts of London or use boroughs as an example. Some academics have

---

63   See, for example, Peter Hall, *London 2000*, London: Faber & Faber, 1963; Richard Rogers
     and Mark Fisher, *A New London: Two Views*, London: Penguin Books, 1992; or Bridget
     Rosewell, *Reinventing London*, London: London Publishing Partnership, 2013

64   See, for example, John Carvel, *Turn Again Livingstone*, London: Profile Books, 1999;
     or Andrew Hosken, *Ken: The Ups and Downs of Ken Livingstone*, London: Arcadia
     Books, 2008

65   See Ben Pimlott and Nirmala Rao, *Governing London*, Oxford: Oxford University
     Press, 2002; or Tony Travers, *The Politics of London: Governing an Ungovernable City*,
     Basingstoke: Palgrave Macmillan, 2004

66   See, for example, Stephen L. Elkin, *Politics and Land Use Planning: The London Experience*,
     Cambridge: Cambridge University Press, 1974; Paul Harrison, *Inside the Inner City: Life
     Under the Cutting Edge*, Harmondsworth: Penguin Books, 1983; or Andrew Glassberg,
     Representation and Urban Community, London: Macmillan Press, 1981

67   Nick Buck, Ian Gordon, Peter Hall, Michael Harloe and Mark Kleinman, *Working Capital:
     Life and Labour in Contemporary London*, London/New York: Routledge, 2002; or Patrick
     Dunleavy, *The Politics of Mass Housing in Britain, 1945–1975: A Study of Corporate Power
     and Professional Influence in the Welfare State*, Oxford: Clarendon, 1981

undertaken systematic examinations of aspects of planning in every borough,[68] but the number of boroughs has rendered detailed, comparative, analysis of how each has developed difficult.

Each of the boroughs has evolved a distinct entity. Political cultures differ from one to another, even when the same party is regularly in control. Some boroughs, for example Newham and Westminster, have never changed political control, while others, including Ealing and Richmond, have done so frequently. Labour groups in one borough have a different culture from others, even in neighbouring authorities. The same is true of Conservatives and Liberal Democrats.

This separateness is recognised in the next chapter of this book, which considers each of the thirty-two boroughs individually. Although the thirty-two authorities and the City collectively constitute a vast metropolis, their individual characteristics have led to different politics and policies. A sweep across the contemporary inner London skyline is instructive. Councils in Westminster and Kensington & Chelsea have largely rejected tall buildings, at least in central London. A scattering of 1960s medium-sized, shoebox-type blocks (many of them hotels built with subsidies) can be seen, but generally there is a four- or five-storey limit. Camden has adopted a similar policy, except at Centre Point and Euston. These exceptions date from the 1960s.

The City of London, apart from the Barbican estate, allowed only a single skyscraper before a post-1980s change of policy. It, like its neighbour Tower Hamlets, has latterly encouraged tall buildings. In the period since 2000, Hackney, Islington, Southwark, Lambeth and Wandsworth have been more willing to give permission for tall buildings around the edge of the central business district. Major new towers have been constructed (or are about to be) in locations such as the City Fringe (north and east of the City of London) and along the Thames. Latterly, Newham has started to create its own cluster of towers at Stratford. Lewisham (in the town centre), Redbridge (Ilford) and

---

68   Michael Hebbert, 'The Borough Effect in London's Geography' in *London: A New Metropolitan Geography*, Keith Hoggart and David R. Green (eds), London: Edward Arnold, 1991

Hackney (Woodberry Down) have been willing to see developers build at a height in neighbourhoods outside the city centre.

The economic and social condition of London in the early-to-mid-1960s gave rise to critical pressures that helped shape the fifty-year history of the thirty-two boroughs. The boroughs and the GLC took control almost exactly twenty years after the end of the Second World War, when Britain was changing rapidly. Although a Conservative government had originally appointed the Herbert Commission, broadly accepted the commission's proposals, and then legislated to enact them. It was a Labour government which was in power by the time the new councils started work.

Much has been written about the '60s, a decade when Britain threw off its curiously repressed approach (compared with a number of other European countries) to personal morality. Satire boomed. The Profumo scandal in 1963 allowed ordinary people to see how differently the rich and powerful lived. Between 1965 and 1968, legislation was passed that legalised prostitution, abortion and homosexuality. Race discrimination was made illegal. The changes made by Labour and sponsored by Home Secretary Roy Jenkins led to the creation of what its supporters called the 'civilised society', but its enemies labelled the 'permissive society'.[69] The historian David Kynaston observed of this period: 'The Profumo affair was one of the things that switched the English default position on politics from deference to scepticism, if not yet to cynicism.'[70] London flourished in many ways during the 1960s. Anti-establishment attitudes, liberation and fashion fused to produce 'Swinging London'.

The boroughs came into existence as this new world emerged. Although the local authorities were amalgamations of councils, which in many cases had their origins in the days of Victorian parish and vestry government, the world in which they operated was changing quickly. The modern signage and logos adopted by the new London boroughs reflected this shift to modernity.

---

69   Vernon Bogdanor, 'Roy Jenkins, Europe and the Civilised Society', lecture at Gresham College, 15 January 2013, http://www.gresham.ac.uk/lectures-and-events/roy-jenkins-europe-and-the-civilised-society (accessed 10 February 2015)

70   Vanessa Thorpe, 'Sex began 50 years ago, Larkin said. How has the Earth moved since 1963?', *The Observer*, 27 April 2013

Camden's decision to adopt a 'linked hands' logo or Westminster's definitive street signage, both of which are still in use in the city today, are reminders of the new London that was emerging at this time.

Yet the social and economic backdrop to the creation of the new London boroughs was less encouraging. The capital still bore the physical marks of a world war that had finished twenty years previously. There were hundreds of bombsites and soot-black public buildings, while many people lived in appalling housing conditions that are difficult to imagine today.

The population of Greater London, which had grown to 8.6 million in 1939, fell to about 7.6 million by 1965. Official projections made just after the boroughs were created suggested this total would fall to between 7.1 and 7.3 million by 1981.[71] The reduction was broadly seen as desirable by planners at the LCC and GLC, who, since the Abercrombie report in 1944, had come to accept that the capital needed to be made less congested and unpleasant to live in. The orderly management of decline, with the objective of the city eventually levelling off at a population closer to 6 million, was the broad planning consensus.

In the wider south-east region, where many Londoners moved to, the picture was different. Between 1961 and 1971 the Greater South East's population grew from 18.2 million to 19.5 million. New towns such as Harlow, Basingstoke and Milton Keynes took population from London – though, in doing so, they effectively became part of a growing metropolitan region still centred on the core of London.[72] A number of commentators lobbied for the creation of a wider, regional governance model to adapt to the reality of this wider super-region. Some still do.

Peter Hall, writing from an academic planner's perspective in 1963, outlined the findings of the Milner Holland report on housing in Greater London.[73] The report had been commissioned in 1963, following the

71   Greater London Council, *Greater London Development Plan Report of Studies*, London: GLC, undated, page 36

72   Peter Hall, *London 2001*, London: Unwin Hyman, 1989, pages 1–3

73   Sir Milner Holland, *Report of the Committee on Housing in Greater London (Cmd 2605)*, London: HMSO, 1965

publicity given to the activities in inner west and north London of notorious slum landlord Peter Rachman. Like Charles Dickens, Rachman has provided London with a word, derived from his name, to describe aspects of the city's sometimes dark soul. Rachmanism was one of the new boroughs' least attractive inheritances.

Hall observed slum housing was

> traditionally concentrated in the East End and in certain inner boroughs south of the Thames, like Southwark. In Stepney and Southwark, more than half the single family dwellings had no bath in 1961. Secondly, there are areas where the housing stock is better, but is overcrowded and ill adapted to the needs of its present occupants; these are the areas of multi-occupied big houses, which are chiefly in west and north London. While in the east the housing problem is getting better, Milner Holland found in the west it is all too often getting worse. Ranking the old metropolitan boroughs of London on a number of indices of housing stress, and then comparing the number of appearances in the table, the Milner Holland committee [was] able to produce an index of the intensity of the housing problem. Finsbury ranks worst, followed successively by Islington, Paddington, St Pancras, Hammersmith, Willesden, Kensington, Lambeth, and Stoke Newington. It is highly significant that these boroughs form a solid arc surrounding central London, but only (save for Lambeth) on its north and west sides. The real weight of the London housing problem ... is no longer concentrated in the East End; it is in London's west side.[74]

Milner Holland estimated there were 1,500 homeless families in Greater London, with a further 45,000 to 80,000 'concealed' households – that is, households sharing accommodation within existing single properties. Some 190,000 households were in urgent need of better housing and a further

---

74   Peter Hall, *London 2000*, London: Faber & Faber, 1963 [updated 1969], page 125

366,000–532,000 in less urgently deficient housing. In total, between 600,000 and 800,000 households, and thus between 1,800,000 and 2,400,000 people, were in need of housing improvement.[75] Much London housing lacked hot water, with 13 per cent not having an inside toilet.[76]

In the years immediately before 1965, the LCC had moved people out of the city to 'overspill' estates, in an attempt to reduce pressure within London itself. Peter Hall estimated there would be an 'overspill problem' (that is, a need to house this many people beyond London) of 2–3 million by 1981, unless much additional building were to be undertaken within the city.[77]

In Parliament, Lord Silkin responded to the Milner Holland report with an observation that, as with so much of the long history of London government, suggests there are near-permanent features of public policy:

> We have been slowly moving towards establishing two communities:
> the community who are benefiting from the affluent society and who
> are better housed and better off in every way, and the other community,
> the poor section, who are living on terms of insecurity and poverty and
> who are having to spend a disproportionate amount of their income in
> paying rent for wholly inadequate accommodation.[78]

Every word of this statement could have been made in 1896, when Charles Booth published his poverty mapping of London,[79] or, indeed, in 2015.

It is hard to comprehend fully the condition of slum housing in London in the 1950s and 1960s. Earl Jellicoe, a minister at the Ministry of

---

75   Ibid.

76   Donald L. Foley, *Governing the London Region: Reorganization and Planning in the 1960s*, Berkeley/Los Angeles/London: University of California Press, 1972, page 121

77   Ibid., page 125

78   Hansard, House of Lords Debate, Volume 264, London: HMSO, 29 March 1965, Columns 836–94

79   Danny Dorling, Richard Mitchell, Mary Shaw, Scott Orford, George Davey Smith, 'The Ghost of Christmas Past: health effects of poverty in London in 1896 and 1991', *BMJ*, 321:1547, 23 December 2000

Housing & Local Government, described slum properties at the time in the following terms:

> [B]asement areas used as common rubbish dumps, roofs used for garbage disposal, entrance halls bearing the marks, if I may use the term, of a common pissoir, with contraceptives strewn in the rickety Dickensian staircases, often with the plaster peeled off and the bare lattice boards exposed; broken window panes, exposed and danger-ous electrical fittings, and common lavatories and bathrooms of almost indescribable sordidness.[80]

From the Abercrombie report onwards, planners had been convinced London was burdened by old housing that was unfit for modern living.[81] The *Greater London Development Plan Report of Studies*, written in the period immedi-ately after 1965, stated: 'Of the total [houses in London] of 2.4 million, about 1,016,000 (43 per cent) were built before 1919, and 170,000 (7 per cent) were built before 1875. The obsolescence problem is in these houses.'[82]

The GLC report went on to explain that not all old houses were problem-atic, but that many were. The logic of planning at this time was that much of the old, slum, overcrowded housing should be knocked down and replaced with new homes.

Many of the post-1965 boroughs, particularly in parts of Greater London that developed rapidly during the nineteenth century, inherited these kinds of challenges. They also faced the plans of the Ministry of Transport to create a system of Ringways, which, if completed, would have left London with the kind of road system developed by Robert Moses in New York and by plan-ners in cities such as Birmingham and Glasgow.[83] In London:

---

80   Peter Hall, *London 2000*, London: Faber & Faber, 1963 [updated 1969], page 27

81   Patrick Abercrombie, *Greater London Plan 1944*, London: HMSO, 1945

82   Greater London Council, *Greater London Development Plan Report of Studies*, London: GLC, undated, page 5

83   Christopher Beanland, 'London: Roads To Nowhere', *The Independent*, 8 February 2011

There were to be four concentric ring roads. The North Circular and
the M25 were completed in the 1980s. But the innermost, Ringway 1
– dubbed the 'Motorway Box', even though it looked more like a parcel
the postman had squashed to fit through a letter box – was the real Trojan
Horse: four interconnected motorways that would have caused 100,000
people to be evicted, and changed the lives of millions of Londoners.
The North Cross Route was to slice from Harlesden to Hackney, the
South Cross Route from Clapham Junction to Kidbrooke. The two
parallel roads would be joined up by the West and East Cross Routes
to form one bulbous, eight-lane ring road.[84]

As the boroughs began their lives, the Ministry of Transport was stealthily
planning a sequence of road schemes that, together, would have added up to
the full system of Ringways. The newly created GLC was seen as an innovative agent to help achieve the ministry's objectives. A number of boroughs,
including Westminster, Kensington & Chelsea, Hammersmith & Fulham,
Redbridge and Islington lined up to fight the government and the GLC. In the
1970 GLC elections, eighty candidates from the newly formed Homes Before
Roads Party ran in twenty-seven out of thirty-two boroughs. Although none
won, the expression of substantial opposition was clear.[85]

Peter Hall summed up the risks that were being taken in the following terms:

> Today, in the early '60s, we stand on a critical watershed in the history of
> planning in London. For the first time in decades, the money is being made
> available for major road building: £10 million a year over the next ten years
> in the LCC area alone. In the late '60s, as the network of main inter-city
> long-distance motorways is completed, the pace of urban construction is
> likely to increase even further. Already, in 1963, work has begun on London's
> first urban motorway … The seeds of the American vicious circle are thus

---

84   Ibid.

85   Donald L. Foley, *Governing the London Region: Reorganization and Planning in the 1960s*,
      Berkeley/Los Angeles/London: University of California Press, 1972, page 118

already sown: constructing roads generates traffic, generates demand for
more construction, generates votes ... generates more construction.[86]

The boroughs also had to cope with the ministry's enthusiasm for gyratory
road systems, which often adversely affected roads like Gower Street that had
previously been quiet.[87] Boroughs such as Camden and Westminster, working
with TfL, are today removing many of these gyratories and restoring two-way
running in streets such as Pall Mall, Tottenham Court Road and Baker Street.

Policies for housing improvement and roadbuilding were part of wider,
partly planned changes to London in the mid-1960s. The inner core of the city
had witnessed declining population throughout the 1950s and early 1960s.
Overall, the number of residents was falling by about 50,000 per year in the
early 1960s, and was predicted to continue to do so during the 1970s. Outer
London's population was still rising slowly, as was the metropolitan ring. The
speed of decline in Greater London as a whole increased towards 100,000
per year by the mid-1970s.[88] Between the creation of the London boroughs in
1963–65 and the abolition of the GLC in 1986, the population fell by about a
million to 6.7 million. At one point during the 1970s, official projections suggested the number would drop to 5,700,000, largely because of out-migration.[89]

Unemployment was an issue in a number of the inner boroughs, particularly Westminster, Hammersmith, Islington, Lambeth, Tower Hamlets and
Hackney. Reasons for the relatively high level of unemployment included:
out-migration not keeping pace with the rundown in jobs; a lack of skills for
a changing labour market; and the impact of high levels of social housing on
mobility. Immigration was not seen as an explanation.[90]

Economic change was one of the key causes of declining employment

---

86   Peter Hall, *London 2000*, London: Faber & Faber, 1963 [updated 1969], page 142

87   Michael F. Collins and Timothy M. Pharoah, *Transport Organisation in a Great City – The Case of London*, London: George Allen & Unwin, 1974, page 542

88   John Salt, 'Population and Employment in London', in *Changing London*, Hugh Clout (ed.), Slough: University Tutorial Press, 1978, Chart 2.2, page 17

89   Ibid., page 25

90   Ibid., page 20

opportunities. From 1945, there had been restrictions on new industry and factories in London. Following a series of official reports, there was a broad political consensus that too large a share of the nation's population and industry was concentrated in and immediately around London. From 1965 onwards, there were restrictions on office development in central London, though only following apparently uncontrolled office-job growth in the late 1950s and early 1960s.[91]

Developers such as Joe Levy and Harry Hyams had mastered the postwar planning legislation to the point that they were, with architects such as Richard Seifert (of Centre Point fame), able to change the face of the capital.[92] New tower blocks were beginning to pepper the skyline in central London. George Brown, responsible for Harold Wilson's government's economic policy, imposed a requirement for developers to get a permit to build more offices. The policy proved badly flawed: shortages forced up rents and the City complained that invisible earnings would be reduced.[93] At the time the boroughs were created, industrial employment in much of London and office employment in the city centre were falling and, indeed, were expected to do so for some time to come. Some parts of outer London, most obviously Croydon, benefited from the office growth displaced from the central boroughs.

Another emerging challenge for some of the new boroughs and the GLC was the future of London Docks. In the mid-1960s, the Port of London was still the largest port in the UK and, in terms of tonnage handled, the third largest in Europe. About 30 per cent of the country's exports and imports passed through London's docks. The 'enclosed docks' handled about one-fifth of all trade, and Tilbury about 5 per cent. The remainder was dealt with by riverside wharves. By the 1960s, containerisation was already increasing and a number of docks had closed. Tilbury was to be developed as a container port. Proposals were drawn up by the new GLC to redevelop St Katharine Docks, while, in its first three years, the council worked with the City and

---

91   Peter Hall, *London 2001*, London: Unwin Hyman, 1989, page 33

92   For a detailed analysis of this phenomenon, see Oliver Marriott, *The Property Boom*, London: Abingdon Publishing, 1989

93   Ibid., page 13

Tower Hamlets to consider the future of the docks more widely.[94] What was not known in 1965 was that, by 1980, all the docks in London would be closed.

International in-migration was also becoming a public policy issue. The arrival of the *Empire Windrush* from the Caribbean in 1948 marked the beginning of a long period of adjustment for London. New Commonwealth immigrants boarded the ship in Kingston, Jamaica, and effectively started the move to London's contemporary status as a multicultural, global, city. Less recognised is the fact that a number of displaced women from Poland also arrived on the *Windrush* to settle in Britain.[95] Between the censuses of 1961 and 1971, the number of London residents born outside the United Kingdom rose from 847,000 to 1,113,000, an increase of 31 per cent.[96]

New Commonwealth migrants were, at this time, concentrated in inner London, particularly in Kensington & Chelsea, Westminster, Hammersmith, Wandsworth, Ealing, Haringey, Brent, Lambeth, Southwark and Lewisham. A number of wards in these boroughs had over 30 per cent of their population born in the new Commonwealth, with 63 per cent in the Northcote ward in Ealing. South of the river, there were concentrations in western Wandsworth, Lambeth, central Southwark and north Lewisham. Irish immigrants tended to group in Kilburn (Brent/Camden), Hammersmith and Ealing. Immigrants were beginning to move from inner to outer London.[97]

It was against this backdrop of economic, demographic, cultural and social change that the structural reforms of 1963–65 were to take place. The pressures for a major reconfiguration of the government system had long been building up, so it was only by coincidence that the moment of reform coincided with these contextual changes. In addition, a long period of Conservative government was drawing to a close. The mid-1960s were a remarkable period in Britain.

94   Greater London Council, *Greater London Development Plan Report of Studies*, London: GLC, undated, page 294

95   British Future, 'Who were the Windrush Poles?', 27 March 2015, http://www.britishfuture. org/articles/windrush-poles (accessed 12 May 2015)

96   John Salt, 'Population and Employment in London' in *Changing London*, Hugh Clout (ed.), Slough: University Tutorial Press, 1978, page 22

97   Ibid., page 25

CHAPTER 3

1963–65: CREATING THE BOROUGHS

Even before Royal Assent to the London Government Act 1963, it was evident that reform would take place. The LCC, Middlesex County Council and other opponents of change had to start the process of handing over their services to the London boroughs and the GLC. The thirty-two new councils faced the challenge of organising systems of schools, social services, planning, and housing departments. In inner London, the new boroughs had a significantly wider range of powers than their metropolitan borough predecessors. The new Inner London Education Authority (ILEA) started work in 1965, taking over the LCC's education responsibilities. The ILEA, like the GLC, was not destined for a long life and was abolished in 1990. Only at this later point, when local government control over education was dwindling, were the inner boroughs finally to take responsibility for schools.

In outer London, amalgamations of urban districts and municipal boroughs were to become far more powerful by taking over county provision, including education and social services. As in the inner boroughs, the step-up was significant, except in the ex-county boroughs of East Ham, West Ham and Croydon, where, if anything, the creation of a new 'Greater London' authority meant a slight reduction in power.

Bromley was the first of the new boroughs to set up a joint committee, in January 1962, to manage the transfer of powers from Kent and the former districts.[98] The final two committees were in Enfield (September 1963) and Newham (October 1963). Even before the legislation was passed, town clerks

---

98 Gerald Rhodes, *The Government of London: The Struggle for Reform*, London: Weidenfeld & Nicolson, 1970, page 200

of the existing councils started the process by meeting informally with their counterparts in the other authorities to initiate steps towards creating a joint mechanism. An example of how these early meetings occurred is considered in the section on Camden. However, because of opposition to reform in some councils, chief officers often had to meet secretly.[99]

Within two years of the creation of the boroughs, there were official, national reports on both local authority staffing and also on the quality of management. The second of these, the Maud report, wanted the majority of councillors to be more deliberative about policy while placing executive power with a management board of councillors and principal officers.[100] London boroughs prepared for their existence against a backdrop of increased interest in, and study of, management.

There was a surprising degree of continuity between the old and new authorities. Members of the new borough councils had, in many cases, been members of the previous ones. Of the 100 GLC councillors elected in 1964, seventy-two had been members of the LCC, Middlesex or another predecessor council. The position was similar in the boroughs: in Tower Hamlets and Westminster, forty-six of the sixty new councillors had been members of the constituent authorities. Taking councillors and aldermen together, it was rare to find less than two-thirds of the new members coming from the previous councils.[101] Members of the new borough councils provided a bridge from the old to the new authorities.

Issues to be determined included the number of councils and the creation of wards. The 1963 London Government Act allowed up to sixty councillors. Proposals for both warding and the number of councillors had to be submitted to the Home Secretary for inclusion in the charter or incorporation order for the new borough.[102] Borough names, as briefly considered earlier, were also a

---

99   Ibid.

100 'Editorial: Reflections on Maud and Mallaby', *Public Administration*, Vol. 45, No. 3, September 1967, pages 239–44

101 Gerald Rhodes, *The Government of London: The Struggle for Reform*, London: Weidenfeld & Nicolson, 1970, page 197

102 Ibid., page 201

challenge. Sir Keith Joseph proposed three principles: names should be short; should have local associations; and should not be hybrid or composite. Where there were disagreements, they were often bitter. Some of the names proposed, a number of which are considered in the borough-by-borough analysis that follows, were inventive to the point of eccentricity. When the minister proposed the name Kensington for the new borough that brought together the authority of that name with Chelsea, shoppers queued up in the King's Road to sign petitions under the headline 'Chelsea on the march: don't scrap the name'. Sir Keith gave way, and abandoned two of his principles, calling the new council the Royal Borough of Kensington & Chelsea.[103] In 1979, Hammersmith & Fulham (originally just Hammersmith) and, in 1980, Barking & Dagenham (originally just Barking) were allowed to re-attach their former other half's name.

The transfer of functions and staff was not simple. On 7 May 1964, 'shadow' councils were elected and, a little under a year later, on 1 April 1965, the new boroughs started their work. Labour won twenty of the new councils and the Conservatives nine. Three were in 'no overall control'. Labour had 1,112 councillors and the Conservatives 668. Turnout was 35.7 per cent.[104] The poll was held after twelve years of Conservative national government and, by 1964, the Tories were unpopular, damaged both by a long period in office, but also exhausted by scandal. Labour won control of the GLC, extending the party's many years of running London.

The new boroughs were initially organised along conventional lines, although the number of committees and departments created was rather lower than in the previous councils. But the impact of the Maud report on management in local government began to have effects. Some boroughs, like Camden in 1966, set up an advisory committee to co-ordinate major policy matters. By 1969, seventeen of the thirty-two boroughs had an equivalent committee.[105]

---

103 Ibid.

104 London County Council, *London Borough Council Elections 7 May 1964*, London: LCC, 1964

105 Gerald Rhodes (ed.), *The New Government of London: The First Five Years*, London: Weidenfeld & Nicolson, 1972, pages 436–7

Town clerks were rapidly re-designated as 'chief executives', though the City of London still uses the title 'town clerk and chief executive'. Wandsworth and Southwark appointed chief executives from outside local government, while Haringey employed two of its senior management team from private companies.[106] London government reform provided a stimulus to new forms of internal management.

Boroughs had to amalgamate predecessor authorities with different accounting, rate collection and housing rent policies. In Bromley, agreement was reached on all points, but few of the joint committees before April 1965 made such good progress. Standardising housing rent policies proved particularly difficult. In a number of cases, the joint committees simply referred matters on to the new council. But the committees generally consisted of those who were, after the 1964 elections, members of both the old and new councils – they provided a degree of continuity.[107]

There were three kinds of functional transfers. The simplest were those, such as environmental health, parks and libraries, where the services were common to the merging authorities. A second category, including planning, traffic and highways, were services where the novel division of powers between the GLC and the boroughs gave no guide as to the new administrative arrangements that might be required. The third type of service consisted of those functions, such as social services, public health and, in outer boroughs, education, that were to be transferred from counties and county boroughs to the new London borough councils. This third category was most challenging. It is rare in British local government reorganisations to break up existing services: more normally, amalgamations take place.

A particularly difficult problem was how to divide up children's homes. London and Middlesex had to arrange a complete transfer of all their homes, while the 'severed counties' (Essex, Kent and Surrey) had to balance the needs of the new boroughs with those of their remaining population. Problems

---

106 Ibid., page 437

107 Gerald Rhodes, *The Government of London: The Struggle for Reform*, London: Weidenfeld & Nicolson, 1970, page 203

of staffing loomed large in all three categories of service. Joint committees consisting of officials from the soon-to-die counties and the about-to-be merged districts met grudgingly between 1963 and 1965.[108]

The proposals that emerged from these meetings were complex. Within the LCC area:

> No borough's needs could be satisfied simply by the establishments … allocated to them, and all had a share in accommodation allocated to other boroughs. Furthermore, some of this shared accommodation was outside Greater London altogether. One large children's home with over 350 places situated in Surrey was allocated to one borough with four others sharing the accommodation provided. Only one borough (6) [Greenwich] had all the accommodation allocated to it within its own boundaries, and only one (11) [Hammersmith] had no accommodation allocated to it within its own boundaries. Between these two extremes there was a great variety of arrangements.[109]

In outer London, there was similar complexity. The new borough of Merton inherited only one home within its own boundaries and three in parts of Surrey outside Greater London with joint-user arrangements for two homes in other London boroughs formed from Surrey.[110] In addition to the challenge of allocating institutions, there was the issue of the children themselves: their social workers were, in some cases, linked to children's homes rather than local authority areas, old or new. Yet, from 1 April 1965, children in care became the responsibility of the borough where, in theory, they or their parents lived.

The process of determining what should go where and who would pay for the newly configured services generated 'an enormous quantity of minutes and memoranda'. At the same time, existing services had to be kept running. There is no doubt that the run-up to April 1965 placed a major burden on council

108 Ibid., pages 203–5

109 Ibid., page 205

110 Ibid., pages 206–7

officers and members, and there was a good deal of overtime.[111] Because of the breakup of former county services, the London reforms of 1963–65 were very complex. GLC abolition in 1985–86 was to create a smaller but similar challenge.

Sir Keith Joseph agreed to appoint a Staff Commission to oversee the process of recruitment to the new councils (including the GLC), and to protect the interests of existing local authority staff. One of a number of challenges facing the new boroughs was a shortage of staff at the time and the severed counties wanted to hold on to most of their existing officials.[112]

In appointments to the new authorities, the Staff Commission left the new boroughs with some freedom to determine their own policy about officers from constituent London councils. However, priority was to be given to staff from constituent authorities. Different regimes were put in place for medical officers of health, children's officers and other senior officers. The policy of giving priority to staff from predecessor authorities ensured redundancies were kept to a minimum.[113] The LSE's analysis of the 1965 reform wondered if the strong emphasis on staff protection might have reduced the potential management benefits of reform.[114]

Bromley, which had been first to set up a joint committee to manage transition, was also first to appoint its chief officers.[115] In Croydon, the former county borough officials, rather than those from smaller Purley and Coulsdon, took the top jobs. Kingston and Richmond appointed children's officers from outside London. Architects and planners were among the later posts filled. Under the London Government Act, boroughs had been given until 1 April 1968 to make the statutory appointment of an architect.

In many boroughs, there were complaints in the local press about the appointment of officers from one of the predecessor councils above those of the other constituent authorities. At Brent, it was alleged all the best jobs had

111 Ibid., page 219

112 Ibid., pages 210–11

113 Ibid., pages 212–14

114 Ibid., page 215

115 Ibid., page 216

gone to Willesden officers. There were similar allegations from Southgate that Enfield posts were being filled by Enfield and Edmonton candidates. In Richmond, it was argued Twickenham members were bulldozing decisions through the council against the wishes of Richmond and Barnes. A struggle over the appointment of the medical officer of health led to a letter of protest from the Richmond branch of the British Medical Association and a petition from a group of Richmond housewives.[116]

There was some evidence that costs rose as a result of the reform. Many boroughs had office accommodation that was on several sites. London weighting payments were extended to places that had not previously received them. The terms and conditions of transferred officials, particularly those from Middlesex County Council, were re-graded upwards. The government's requirement that all new staff and systems should be in place by April 1965 drove costs upwards.[117]

By 31 March 1965, the new boroughs and the GLC were ready to go. A change of government at Westminster in 1964 brought about one final proposal to amend the new arrangements. In December 1964, the incoming Labour government issued a circular letter outlining proposals for direct GLC involvement in borough children's services. The GLC would take over, at least for an initial period, the administration of specialised institutions and the LCC's larger homes. Borough representatives argued this proposal risked splitting the service between the two parts of London's new government. In February 1965, Richard Crossman, the new Minister for Housing & Local Government, accepted it was too late to make further changes.

Later in 1965, Anthony Crosland, the Secretary of State for Education & Science, announced that clauses in the London Government Act for a further statutory review of education in inner London, including the possibility of reforming the ILEA, would now be removed. The ILEA, a relic of the LCC, was safe, at least until 1990.

---

116 Ibid., page 217

117 Ibid., pages 220–22

PART II

HISTORY

CHAPTER 4

THE THIRTY-TWO BOROUGHS: A BRIEF HISTORY

What follows is a short analysis of each of the thirty-two boroughs that took office in April 1965. These stories differ significantly because each borough has been a separate, politically defined institution, with its own boundary, elected councillors, officers and town or city hall. Each one has also had an inheritance from one or more predecessor councils. Even in 2015, the Borough of St Pancras exists on street signs. The 1965 authorities often brought together very different political entities. Some of these differences were political: for example, Conservative and Labour councils were brought together in Camden.

Elsewhere, boroughs combined two authorities of the same party where there were radically differing political cultures, as was the case in Newham. Brent merged two previous councils that had fought hard to stay apart. Richmond, uniquely, lay on both sides of the Thames. Hounslow was remarkably wide with a spine of roads and railways. Others, notably Haringey, pushed together areas that were socially and demographically polarised. Harrow, uniquely, did not change its boundaries or its name. Seven or eight of the inner boroughs radiated out from the City, like the petals of a flower.

From 1965 onwards, each council has held its own elections, voted in councillors and been led by very different kinds of leaders. Some have never changed political control, while others do so regularly. People who live in a borough will very likely know its name and will have to deal with councillors and/or officers on a regular basis: paying council tax; seeking housing support; getting planning permission; using leisure facilities; and, inevitably, complaining about neighbourhood issues. Policies towards new development have varied within individual boroughs over time and, today, from borough to borough. Civic societies and neighbourhood associations in London are often very powerful and can lobby councils ferociously about particular issues.

To understand London, it is essential to understand the boroughs and the City of London. Together, these authorities control more than double the budget of the Mayor of London. Different boroughs' policies in relation, for example, to planning, roads, housing and the environment can be read on the streets and skyline of the city. In the early years of the outer boroughs, decisions were taken that have left grammar schools in some places but not others.

In their first fifty years, boroughs have had remarkably different policies about housing. At the time of their creation, and for the first five or so years, many inner boroughs built large new council housing estates to take the place of overcrowded slums. Leafier outer boroughs were often unenthusiastic about such estates, as they had relatively little poor-quality housing to begin with. There was resistance in outer boroughs even to transfers of poorer residents from the inner city.

Many boroughs did, however, react against the government and the GLC's road schemes. On this subject, there was near-unanimity as new boroughs attempted to thwart the development of a system of Ringways in all parts of the capital. Although not all these efforts were successful, the boroughs, anti-roads protesters and local MPs did halt many of the more egregious efforts to carve massive highways through the city centre.

Each London borough has developed a character of its own. They have been 'the council' for millions of Londoners for fifty years. To understand one borough does not provide an understanding of them all. Far from it. Some aspects of their behaviour are similar. Boroughs recognise each other as equals, though some of the central authorities self-evidently face a daily onslaught of commuting and economic activity that is vastly different from what goes on in most of the others.

Indeed, it is important to recognise the massive pressure put on Westminster, Camden, the City and the other boroughs that together constitute central

London. These councils are relatively small to be managing the centre of one of the world's most dynamic urban economies. In Paris, New York or Tokyo, the city-wide authority is responsible for the primary governance of the central business district (CBD). In London, the CBD is the responsibility of several boroughs, with the city-wide government providing only transport, police and fire services. London's main retail thoroughfare, Oxford Street, is Westminster City Council's responsibility, not the Mayor of London's.

The sections that follow briefly describe how the economies, demographics, politics and governments of each borough have evolved since 1965. Population figures for each borough can be found in Appendix 1. Given the wider scope of this book, these analyses inevitably concentrate on a number of key trends and events within the recent history of the council concerned. Taken individually and yet together, these borough stories make it possible to see why London has developed in the unique way it has in the fifty years since 1965.

Of course, many other institutions have had a role as parts of the London government machinery before and/or after 1965. This book is not about these bodies, though the story of the boroughs is inevitably intertwined with many of them. Appendix 2 includes a brief description and analysis of the key organisations that have played a role in London government and which have been important to the borough story.

INNER LONDON

CAMDEN

Camden brought together Holborn, St Pancras and Hampstead, linking the centre of London to the leafy heights of Hampstead and Highgate. During the years since 1965, Camden, along with Islington, has often been viewed internally and externally as a byword for progressive politics and political ideas.

The first step towards the amalgamation of the predecessor boroughs was taken in December 1961, when the Town Clerk of St Pancras wrote to his counterparts in the other boroughs to suggest a 'preliminary discussion'. During 1962, 'lunches ... began in a very cordial atmosphere as the three town clerks met to prepare reports, which would pave the way for the new London boroughs'.[118] There was enormous courtesy between officers and members during the creation of the new council, to the point that Labour St Pancras's representative proposed that Conservative Hampstead should first take the chair of the joint committee that had been set up to oversee the reform.[119]

As in other boroughs, a number of names were considered for the new authority. Because the River Fleet ran under all three of the predecessor authorities, Fleet and Fleethurst were considered, as was Heathfleet, which merged Hampstead Heath with the Fleet. Among others, the inventive St Bornham and Bornhamcras were suggested. St Pancras wanted Greater St Pancras.

---

118 Enid Wistrich, *Local Government Reorganisation: First Years of Camden,* London: London Borough of Camden, 1972, page 12

119 Ibid., page 15

Eventually, Camden was chosen as a compromise and the borough's head-quarters was located at St Pancras Town Hall on Euston Road.[120] Many senior officers were appointed from the predecessor councils and the LCC. As in other new boroughs, 1964–65 'was a year of preparation, stress and improvisation', as efforts were made to bring together the new authority.[121]

A competition took place during 1964 to choose a borough symbol. The design chosen was intended to show the links between the borough and the community by picturing four pairs of hands coming together. Variously described as 'the elephant's foot' or 'the abominable snowman', Camden's symbol became instantly recognisable and has been used ever since on official letterheads and street-name plates. Orange was chosen as the borough colour, making dustcarts and other municipal vehicles easy to spot.[122]

In March 1965, a minimalist advert was inserted in the local press to inform citizens about the new borough. It said: 'The first of April – birthday of the new borough. Its council sends good wishes to all citizens.' A list of services and offices followed. This notification was the limit of Camden's public relations to celebrate its beginning. Total expenditure on advertising in 1964–65 was £106.[123]

The new council, along with Westminster, the City of London and other boroughs, created the Central London Planning Conference. Camden fought to protect residents, sometimes bringing it into conflict with the GLC. In particular, the council fought County Hall over the development of Covent Garden, where the soon-to-depart wholesale fruit and vegetable market was up for redevelopment. Camden, supported by the Covent Garden Community Association, wanted additional housing in the area, while the GLC wished to build more hotels and offices.[124]

At King's Cross, Camden took the initiative when British Rail informed the council in 1966 that it was considering the merger of St Pancras and King's Cross

120 Ibid., pages 31–2, 53

121 Ibid., page 60

122 Ibid., pages 248–9

123 Ibid., page 56

124 Ibid., pages 171–3

stations, creating a massive opportunity to build new housing. Neighbouring Euston station and its Doric arch had been demolished five years earlier, triggering a campaign to protect high-quality architecture from developers. Camden, by this time, had proposals to redevelop nearby Tolmers Square, though this project, like the Euston Arch, developed into a cause célèbre with conservationists. The future of King's Cross became tangled in discussions about a third London airport. The area is still in the process of redevelopment half a century later, while London's airport capacity also remains work in progress.

There were plans in the late 1960s, which Camden opposed, to build a new national library in the residential area just south of the British Museum.[125] A former Holborn councillor said, in words that say much about the nature of central London communities at the time: 'We do not want one vast ghetto of science, learning and institutions. We have to have a properly balanced community there.'[126] Eventually, a much scaled-down British Library was built at St Pancras.

The borough was created at the highpoint of post-war planning policy, when comprehensive redevelopment, high-rise architecture and massive road schemes were considered desirable. Camden itself had large amounts of housing that was deemed obsolescent. Communities trapped in the middle of large policy experiments in many boroughs were barely consulted about comprehensive redevelopment. From its earliest years, Camden was willing to challenge this planning consensus, notably over housing policy and community development. The borough consulted residents extensively.[127]

Camden's first borough architect was Sydney Cook, who employed a number of graduates of the Architectural Association, the influential starting point for many British architects. According to David Kohn in *Building Design*:

> In only eight years, they managed to realise forty-seven social housing projects of a quality, scale and ambition that has arguably not

125 British Library, *History of the British Library*, London: British Library, http://www.bl.uk/aboutus/quickinfo/facts/history (accessed 12 October 2015)

126 Ibid., pages 174–5

127 Ibid., pages 181–3

been surpassed, despite subsequent spending booms. These include Alexandra Road, the Brunswick Centre, Highgate New Town and Branch Hill, designed by a roll call of talent including Neave Brown, Patrick Hodgkinson, Peter Tabori, Gordon Benson and Alan Forsyth.[128]

The new borough's politicians had a stated ambition to develop superior housing for low-income families. Cook gathered a team of ideologically driven young architecture graduates who wanted to have an input into the latter part of London's post-war reconstruction and improvement. According to Kohn: 'Cook purportedly handpicked a team able to get things done, and demonstrated great skill in spotting talent.'

Camden's efforts were generally admired, particularly as Cook's team refused to construct system-built high-rise towers. The borough was willing to put up the rates to fund high-quality architecture:

> The borough built some of London's most innovative social housing during the 1970s. The Alexandra Road estate near Swiss Cottage created high-density dwellings in a low-rise housing and is now listed as a building of historic and architectural importance. The Brunswick estate in Bloomsbury also combined high density and low rise and was much acclaimed for its unusual design.[129]

These estates are, unlike many unloved high-rises, still in use and generally popular. Their particular architectural style makes them attractive as locations for filmmakers.[130] It says much about Cook's legacy that New London Architecture, a development think tank, held an exhibition devoted to Camden's social housing in 2010.

---

128 David Kohn, 'Cook's Camden: London's Great Experiment with Social Housing', *Building Design*, 5 November 2010

129 The Twentieth Century Society, Exploring 20th Century London: Camden, http://www.20thcenturylondon.org.uk/place/camden (accessed 5 February 2015)

130 See, for example, *Breaking and Entering* (2006), directed by Anthony Minghella, which has much to say about contemporary Camden

Camden's political make-up has been profoundly influenced by the (generally Labour) leadership's views about social housing, but also about the need for an expanded state. Public sector tenants have continued to have a significant impact on debate and decision-making within the authority. Having said this, it was the Conservatives who, when in control between 1968 and 1971, were the first to take the then-radical step of introducing concessionary fares for older people.[131]

Apart from its housing policy, Camden has proved willing to spend at relatively high levels on care for children and older people. Few London boroughs have self-described themselves so clearly as 'progressive' and, apart from periods where the Conservatives and/or Liberal Democrats were in control, tied to traditional Labour views. Writing soon after Camden was created, Enid Wistrich commented:

> The ethos of the Camden Labour Group, inherited largely from St Pancras Labour Council, favoured increased spending, particularly on housing and the social services, and the improvement of services to the best possible standard. Overall control of the level of expenditure was of low priority.[132]

In 1972, Camden attempted the compulsory purchase of Centre Point, which stands at the boundary with the City of Westminster near Tottenham Court Road station. The building, developed by Harry Hyams and architect Richard Seifert, stood unoccupied from its completion in 1965. Camden's proposal led to a political storm in which Centre Point became the focus of criticism of developers. Lena Jeger, the MP for Holborn, stated: 'Centre Point is a symbol of a society in which those who make money are more blessed than those who earn money.'[133]

131 Michael F. Collins and Timothy M. Pharoah, *Transport Organisation in a Great City: The Case of London*, London: George Allen & Unwin, 1974, page 131

132 Enid Wistrich, *Local Government Reorganisation: The First Years of Camden*, London: London Borough of Camden, 1972, page 284

133 Peter Scott, *The Property Masters: A History of the British Commercial Property Sector*, Abingdon: Taylor & Francis, 1996, page 195

The borough's struggle with such a high-profile developer and its will-ingness to threaten the use of compulsory purchase are characteristic of the council and its political approach. Camden has, from time to time, been seen, both within and without, as attempting to deliver a form of radical municipal socialism. It was subject to rate capping because its expenditure and local taxes were higher than those of most neighbouring councils, though its politics stayed clear of the more radical excesses of the late 1970s and 1980s. That Camden had been self-consciously progressive and high-spending possibly made it less of a target for the new left, who took control of a number of other authorities.

During the 1978–79 'winter of discontent', Camden was one of a number of authorities that conceded the striking trade unions' full pay demand. This decision precipitated an investigation by the district auditor, who eventually ruled it a breach of fiduciary duty, though councillors were not surcharged because the High Court ruled the council had acted lawfully.[134]

The council has had critics. David Walker, local government correspondent of *The Times*, in his provocatively titled book *Municipal Empire*, saw the bor-ough as inefficient, and believed the settlement with the manual workers told a wider story about the growing power of union activists in the Labour Party, the coercion of councillors by party committees and 'the fact that Camden had been singled out by NUPE [a trade union] for specially harsh industrial action on the grounds that its political reputation made it a "soft touch".'[135]

Camden is, as in 1965, responsible for a wedge of inner London and for roughly a third of the city centre. There has always been a perception of a divide between north and south of the Euston Road. The predecessor boroughs of St Pancras and, particularly, Holborn were comfortable with substantial levels of office and other commercial development. During the years since 1965, a number of large projects have been undertaken within the borough, including British Land's Regent's Place development near Warren Street (by architect Terry Farrell), the British Museum Great Court (by Norman

---

134 David Walker, *Municipal Empire*, Hounslow: Maurice Temple Smith, 1983, page 64

135 Ibid.

Foster) and, spectacularly, the King's Cross regeneration scheme. With its location embracing a significant part of the West End, Camden has continued to develop business and employment, expanding central London towards Camden Town and Islington.

The area to the north and west of the three mainline stations, including Somers Town, Mornington Crescent and York Way, had long been blighted by trains, soot and noise. But electrification and deindustrialisation left a large and largely derelict zone. Camden encouraged community organisations to step in to create assets such as Camley Street Natural Park. Conservation groups sought to protect canals and gasholders on the site. When proposals came forward in the 1980s, there was fierce local opposition to redevelopment. It took many years and the involvement of Argent St George, a firm with expertise in the sensitive handling of communities, to deliver the King's Cross project, which includes fifty new buildings, 2,000 new homes, twenty new streets and ten public squares.[136] In 2014, Camden moved its own headquarters to the area.

Despite having one of London's most affluent populations, the borough has generally leaned leftwards politically. Labour has controlled it for forty-two out of the past fifty years, although there have always been safe Conservative wards in Hampstead. Sir Geoffrey Finsberg, who had led the council in 1968–70, was Conservative MP for Hampstead (later Hampstead & Highgate) from 1970 to 1992. The council's largely Labour political background has had a particular and visible impact on social policy and development within much of inner north London.

Frank Dobson, who went on to represent Holborn & St Pancras in Parliament, was the council's leader from 1973 to 1975. Dame Tessa Jowell was also a member of the council at this time and chaired its Social Services Committee. One of the council's longest-serving councillors in its first fifty years was Roy Shaw, who was born and lived in the borough all his life. He was first elected to Hampstead council in 1956, and, in 1962, became an

---

136 King's Cross Central Limited Partnership, King's Cross: An Extraordinary Piece of London
     is Taking Shape, http://www.kingscross.co.uk/the-development

alderman of the predecessor St Pancras council. He was leader of the council from 1975 to 1982, when Camden was described as the country's 'most progressive' local authority.[137] Recent leaders such as Jane Roberts, Richard Arthur and Sarah Hayward have overseen services which the Audit Commission ranked as among the best in local government.

Camden is still, despite its many years of 'progressive' politics and Labour control, similar in several ways to its Conservative neighbour Westminster. In particular, the two have most social and demographic characteristics in common. The boroughs are jointly responsible for the West End and are now working together on the future of this part of the centre of London through the West End Partnership, set up in 2014. As London's population grows, and if the high-speed rail line to Birmingham is built (profoundly affecting Euston and the surrounding area), the management of the balance between residents' neighbourhood concerns and the needs of a rapidly developing mega-city will be more and more challenging. Camden opposed HS2. Camden's policy is more generally to encourage both commercial and community development. This approach has been a characteristic of its fifty-year history.

GREENWICH

Greenwich was formed by the merger of the former metropolitan boroughs of Greenwich and Woolwich, except for North Woolwich, which became part of Newham. A free ferry still links North Woolwich and Woolwich. The predecessor authorities, particularly Woolwich, were relatively distant parts of the area covered by the LCC. In its early years, the authority was focused on service delivery and council house building. Housing was built by the council's own direct labour organisation.

Both Greenwich and Woolwich had been strongly associated with royalty and Britain's historic role as a sea power. Henry VIII and Elizabeth I were born at

---

137 Dan Carrier, 'Obituary for Roy Shaw', *The Guardian*, 19 March 2008

Greenwich. Eltham Palace was a royal residence for centuries, before it fell into disrepair. It was transformed into a high-society home in the 1930s and more recently restored and opened to the public.[138] Woolwich had served as a royal dock for 350 years, and was the world's largest centre of arms manufacture.[139] Employment had long been provided by arms-makers, the docks and the Royal Artillery Barracks. After the Second World War, these institutions declined, and Greenwich suffered a large rise in unemployment. Much effort has been made since the 1990s to rebuild the economy and economic base of one of London's most historic boroughs. Greenwich's history was recognised in 2012, the year of the Queen's Diamond Jubilee, by the granting of 'Royal Borough' status.

The 1960s and early 1970s saw Greenwich, like many other boroughs, building much new council housing. Major estates were constructed at Kidbrooke and a number in Woolwich: Connaught, Morris Walk and Maryon Road/ Grove. As elsewhere, much of this well-intentioned construction led to the creation of poor-quality, badly maintained and problematic neighbourhoods. But there were benefits as compared with earlier housing conditions: private renting, which often took place in poor quality housing, declined from 32 per cent to 8 per cent during the 1970s.[140] In this period, overcrowding fell and the standard of housing increased, before falling back again as the modern housing deteriorated.

The Connaught estate was designed by Greenwich council's architects, assisted by consultant engineers Jenkins and Potter. The project began in 1967 and construction was completed in 1970 by contractors Simms, Sons & Cooke. 'Five-storey blocks, open at ground level, form a north–south spine, off which range eight-storey blocks with basement garages, all punctuated by lift towers and stepping up the hill in a fish-skeleton layout (an echo, if unconscious, of a military hospital pavilion plan).'[141] The estate was demolished in 2012 and

---

138 English Heritage, Eltham Palace and Gardens, 2015, http://www.english-heritage.org.uk/ visit/places/eltham-palace-and-gardens/(accessed 10 September 2015)

139 Information provided by Royal Borough of Greenwich

140 Ibid.

141 English Heritage, *Survey of London*, Woolwich, Chapter 9, 2012

the area is being redeveloped in a way that moves away from a concentration of council tenants towards a mixture of social renting and owner occupation.

The Morris Walk estate consisted primarily of three-, four- and ten-storey point and linear slab blocks of flats, built in the 1960s using the Larson-Neilsen large panel construction system. It was the first to be 'system built' in London,[142] an inheritance from the LCC. The buildings are clad in large panels, covered in a form of smooth stone chippings. The housing follows the classic Corbusian ideal of point blocks surrounded by swathes of grass. There are also a large number of parking spaces. One road in the estate is called Tivoli Gardens, a reference to the Danish building techniques being used on the estate. Today, the name can be seen as a residual indicator of the idealism that accompanied the construction of such development. Although there were design faults, such as poor sound insulation and a lack of balconies, the estate has survived relatively well.

Maryon Road is another estate constructed in the 1970s. It comprised residential accommodation, arranged in sixteen four-storey blocks, that, along with Connaught and Morris Walk, has been the subject of comprehensive redevelopment plans and a move towards a more mixed population of social renting and owner occupation.

To the west of these Woolwich developments, the largest estate in Greenwich was the Ferrier at Kidbrooke, another inheritance from the LCC and constructed between 1968 and 1972. The architecture and layout were classic of their time: long grey slab blocks of five to twelve storeys, with elevated walkways and acres of car-parking space. Long blocks were laid out in rectangles, with gardens in the middle. In theory it was thought-through, idealised, social housing and a major improvement on inner-London slums. The development was award-winning. Families paid a rent premium to move in.[143]

The estate was initially popular with residents but started to deteriorate in

---

142 Greenwich Industrial History: Morris Walk, http://greenwichindustrialhistory.blogspot. co.uk/2009/08/morris-walk.html (accessed 7 March 2015)

143 Berkeley Group, Kidbrooke Village: A Regeneration Case Study, http://www.berkeleygroup. co.uk/media/pdf/i/b/berkeley-reports-and-opinions-case-studies-kidbrooke-village-large-scale-regeneration.pdf (accessed 7 March 2015)

the early '80s, and ranked in the bottom 3 per cent of estates for child deprivation. It became a byword for urban decay, though there was much competition
from other 1960s and 1970s developments for this accolade. Ferrier became one
of London's worst burglary black spots and was the setting for gritty (a gentle
euphemism) 1997 film *Nil by Mouth*.[144] Kidbrooke School, whose design was
inspired by the Festival of Britain (now Corelli College, a 'co-operative' academy), was Britain's first comprehensive school and, when run by the ILEA, one
of the largest secondary schools in Britain. From 2009 onwards, demolitions
took place and a massive regeneration project has initiated steps to improve
the area. The Ferrier estate has become Kidbrooke Village.

Thamesmead, which straddles the Greenwich/Bexley border, was another
major housing development by the GLC and eventually came to include both
social and market housing. Thamesmead Central, one of the area's four zones,
is partly in Greenwich (the other part being in Bexley) and was developed
in the early 1980s on land between the A2016 and A2041. Housing mostly
consists of a mixture of earlier concrete buildings and three-storey red-brick
town houses. The area has something of the feel of a new town and, once
completed, became home to people moving from Hackney and Southwark.[145]
Thamesmead West, which is in the Greenwich part of the development, was
built from the 1990s onwards. It is a significant distance from the original
development and consists mainly of medium-density residential development
with yellow-brick fascias, plus a number of taller buildings along the riverside.
Thamesmead is home to HM Prison Belmarsh, made famous in recent years
by its role in anti-terrorism cases.

In 1981, at its high point, council housing accounted for 47 per cent of
the borough's overall housing stock, providing Labour with a deep bedrock
of support. Apart from the creation of one arms-length company and tenant-
run organisations, Greenwich has kept its housing 'in house'.

---

144 Jonathan Prynn, 'Rising from the rubble, the £1 billion village replacing "hellhole"
     south-east London estate', *Evening Standard*, 3 July 2013

145 Interview with Len Duvall, former leader of Greenwich council, now London
     Assembly Member

Greenwich was one of the more radical boroughs during the 1980s, though not perhaps in the visible way Lambeth or Southwark were siding with the progressive urban Labour campaign against the Thatcher government. It was subjected to reduced budgets from 1980 onwards,[146] and later its rates were capped.[147] Greenwich followed the GLC and several other boroughs in creating a women's committee and having a race equality initiative,[148] and it was one of a tightly knit group of (mostly inner) boroughs that fully embraced the left's new equalities agenda. Greenwich is a borough outside central London which, in common with Richmond, is a tourist destination distinct from London as a whole.

Public service quality increased after the conflicts of the 1980s, with substantial improvements in school attainment during the 2000s and a sharp increase in young people progressing to higher education. Greenwich Leisure Ltd, a co-operative that started life as a borough-initiated social enterprise in 1993, has been a remarkable success, now managing leisure services for over 100 councils.[149]

The Thatcher government's London Docklands Development Corporation (LDDC) did not include any of Greenwich, but came close on both sides of the river to the borough's historic waterfront. The construction of a vast new office zone at Canary Wharf profoundly changed views from Greenwich Park, and had the effect of altering the nature of east London. Changes brought about by LDDC in Tower Hamlets, Newham and Southwark, such as the regeneration of Surrey Docks, the extension of the Jubilee line via North Greenwich, and the construction of the Docklands Light Railway (latterly extended to Greenwich and Lewisham), were to affect old Greenwich profoundly.

Greenwich Theatre opened in 1969, adding to the borough's long-term

---

146 David Walker, *Municipal Empire: The Town Halls and their Beneficiaries*, Hounslow: Maurice Temple Smith, 1983, page 135

147 Tony Travers, *The Politics of Local Government Finance*, London: Allen & Unwin, 1986, page 167

148 Martin Boddy and Colin Fudge (eds), *Local Socialism*, London: Macmillan, 1984, Chapters 5 and 6

149 Information provided by Royal Borough of Greenwich

association with the arts and culture. From 1981 onwards, Greenwich became the starting point for the London Marathon, the Thames Barrier opened in 1982, creating both flood protection and a new tourist attraction. In 1997, Maritime Greenwich was added to UNESCO's World Heritage Site list. Trinity College of Music joined with the Laban Dance Centre (in Deptford/Lewisham) to form the Trinity Laban Conservatoire of Dance and Music which opened in early 2005. The Cutty Sark and the Tall Ships Regatta have reinforced the continuing maritime heritage of the area. Parts of the Olympic and Paralympic Games were also hosted in Greenwich. 'New London' development has spread along the river from the South Bank and Bankside.

Although naval and military activities have declined in the years since 1965, Woolwich Barracks is still important to the borough. The Princess of Wales's Royal Regiment and the King's Troop Royal Horse Artillery have quarters there. Underlining its links to the armed forces, Greenwich has seen three major national terrorist attacks. IRA bombing incidents took place in the borough in 1974 and 1983. In 2013, Fusilier Lee Rigby was murdered by extremists in Woolwich.

Since the early 1990s, Greenwich has seen remarkable continuity in its government, with just two leaders between 1992 and 2014. First Len Duvall (1992–2000) and then Chris Roberts (2000–2014) adopted explicitly pragmatic approaches to the challenge of restoring the area's economy and physical environment. John Cartwright, Labour leader from 1971 to 1973, famously switched to the new Social Democratic Party and became its MP for Woolwich in 1974. Rosie Barnes was elected as SDP MP for Greenwich in 1987, meaning that, for three years, the borough had two SDP representatives. Nick Raynsford, who succeeded Barnes when Labour regained Greenwich in 1992, was the minister who piloted the Greater London Authority Act 1999 through Parliament, creating the Mayor and Assembly for London.

When, between 1990 and 1992, Michael Heseltine returned to be secretary of state with responsibility for local government and regeneration, Greenwich took him aloft in a helicopter over the borough's waterfront to show him what needed funding. Unlike a number of councils, Greenwich chose to accept central government regeneration grants from Heseltine and his successors which included conditions laid down by Whitehall about their use. Pragmatism became the rule.

The Greenwich peninsula and other parts of the waterfront have gradually been transformed since the 1990s. The council set up the Greenwich Waterfront Development Partnership in 1991, using resources won from a succession of new Whitehall funding pots, including City Challenge, the Single Regeneration Budget, and the Neighbourhood Renewal Fund. The University of Greenwich moved into the Old Royal Naval College in 1999. Subsequently, the Greenwich Partnership built on this regeneration by lobbying successfully for transport improvements, such as the Jubilee line and Docklands Light Railway extensions; North Greenwich station (on the Jubilee line) put the borough on the Tube map for the first time. Greenwich was also a contributor to the Labour government's Thames Gateway project, designed to redevelop land on both sides of the Thames Estuary. From late 2018, Crossrail will have stations in Greenwich at Abbey Wood and Woolwich.

The North Greenwich peninsula was selected to be the home of the Millennium Dome, the Lottery-funded exhibition built on the hitherto-isolated bend in the Thames. Despite the awkwardness of the Dome as a project, epitomised by images of the Queen holding hands with the Prime Minister while singing 'Auld Lang Syne' at midnight on New Year's Eve 1999, the Richard Rogers-designed structure became an instant icon for London. It is now, as The O2, one of Britain's leading concert and event venues. Subsequently, the fanciful Emirates Airline cable car opened, linking North Greenwich to the Royal Docks.

As London's economy has grown steadily from 1990 onwards, few boroughs have been as enthusiastic for development as Greenwich. In the years since 2003, planning permission has been given for 33,500 homes. Some 26,000 more are expected to be built between 2010 and 2020, with much former industrial land still available for re-use.[150] Master plans have been developed

---

150 Ibid.

for Woolwich, Charlton Riverside, Greenwich Peninsula and Eltham, some of which are designed to alleviate the problems created by the 1960s and 1970s' housing estates. Woolwich town centre has been singled out for improvement.

The North Greenwich peninsula is set to change in the years ahead. Large tracts of empty land are to be filled with towers and other new development, giving the area an increasingly high-rise look. TfL is consulting on the possibility of building a tunnel to link the peninsula to Silvertown (Newham), which would radically improve road-based connections to the other side of the river. Greenwich is today a property hotspot with pragmatic Labour leadership. It retains its maritime heritage and is likely to see radical social and demographic change in coming years.

HACKNEY

Few of the 1965 authorities have witnessed a rollercoaster ride as dramatic as Hackney. The borough was created from the former metropolitan councils of Hackney, Stoke Newington and Shoreditch. The last was, at one point during the long process of reform, proposed to be part of Tower Hamlets.[151] In the 1960s, inner east London was experiencing rapid industrial decline. Hackney and Shoreditch had long been part of the poor East End. As in Tower Hamlets, many new migrants had settled in Shoreditch, often fleeing persecution in Russia, Lithuania and Poland. Yet, by 2015, the borough has become one of the most fashionable parts of London, at least for young urban professionals. There had been a bleak period in the 1980s and 1990s when Hackney was a byword for failed government. Few boroughs have seen such a huge turnaround.

Furniture, clothing and printing were the main trades in Shoreditch and neighbouring Hoxton.[152] Canals and railways brought industry to Hackney

---

151   Gerald Rhodes, *The Government of London: The Struggle for Reform*, London: Weidenfeld & Nicolson, 1970, page 256

152   'Hackney: Economic History', in *A History of the County of Middlesex: Volume 10, Hackney*, T. F. T. Baker (ed.), London: British History, 1995, pages 92–101, http://www.british-history.ac.uk/vch/middx/vol10/pp92-101 (accessed 1 September 2015)

as to Shoreditch. Housing was often cramped and overcrowded. A significant proportion of the housing built came to be seen as sub-standard (though today it would be prized and conserved), and was eventually bombed in two world wars, before being comprehensively redeveloped.[153]

Hackney's population experienced great change during the mid-1960s. A traditional white working-class area witnessed new immigrants in the later 1960s and 1970s as a result of arrivals from the Caribbean, Turkey and Vietnam. An Orthodox Jewish community had settled in Stamford Hill at the end of the nineteenth century, and expanded dramatically before and after the Second World War, including survivors of the Holocaust.[154] It is now, with Gateshead, one of the largest such communities in the world.

In its early days the council opposed the North Cross Route, which was part of the GLC's 'Motorway Box' proposal. A complex interchange was to be provided at Dalston on the A10, with either a set of slip roads joining a gyratory system formed from existing streets or a Spaghetti Junction-style interchange connecting it to other upgraded roads in the vicinity. The area would have become little more than a massive traffic interchange. Opposition to the scheme stopped it, though 241 yards of the link between the North Cross Route and the East Cross Route were built at Hackney Wick.[155]

During the late 1960s and throughout the 1970s, Hackney's population fell sharply. Poverty increased as industry declined. The borough styled itself 'Britain's poorest borough'. Local elections in 1977 (GLC) and 1978 (borough) saw the far-right National Front winning about 15 per cent of the vote in some wards.[156] The council was proudly left-of-centre and found itself fighting racism and other discrimination. The Thatcher government was reviled,

153 Margaret Willes (ed.), *Hackney: An Uncommon History in Five Parts*, London: Hackney Society, 2012

154 Mick Brown, 'Inside the private world of London's ultra-Orthodox Jews', *Daily Telegraph*, 25 February 2011

155 'North Cross Route', cbrd.co.uk, http://www.cbrd.co.uk/articles/ringways/ringway1/north. shtml (accessed 3 March 2015)

156 Greater London Council, *London Borough Council Elections 4 May 1978*, London: GLC, 1978, pages 36–8

as Hackney joined some other boroughs in outright opposition to government policies of expenditure cuts and rate capping.

Hackney largely consisted of Victorian housing, some of it deemed slums. The LCC and the former boroughs had started a process of replacing the worst housing with council estates. The area was isolated from the Underground, meaning that, as recently as the late 1960s, it was less easily affected by the gentrification that had started to change neighbouring Islington. The east of the borough adjoined industrial Stratford (or the Queen Elizabeth Olympic Park, as it is now known) and was cut off from the rest of inner London.

In the early years of the new borough, a number of developments took place designed to replace poor-quality or derelict housing with new and improved estates. The council bought up the worst housing and attempted to use compulsory purchase orders to assemble wider tracts of land. The post-1965 borough inherited plans from the predecessor authority to purchase, demolish and replace De Beauvoir Town, a Victorian suburb. These proposals generated conservation and civic societies opposed to comprehensive redevelopment.

In his book, *A Journey Through Ruins*, Patrick Wright quotes Stuart Weir, then a *Times* journalist, capturing the spirit of the age:

> 'We're planning to keep the square,' said the man, who represented the ward but did not live there.
>
> 'Oh that's good,' replied Weir, brightening. 'They're in poor repair, but they're really attractive houses.'
>
> 'Oh no. We're knocking down the houses,' re-joined the councillor. 'We'll just keep the square.'[157]

Mapledene Road in Dalston similarly had to fight off council efforts to knock it down and replace it with modernist blocks. It survived to become highly desirable, and was, during the 1980s, the home of former Prime Minister Tony Blair.

Such stories could have been told of this time all over London and, indeed,

---

157 Patrick Wright, *A Journey Through Ruins: The Last Days of London*, London: Paladin, 1992, page 120

in Manchester or Glasgow. The New Deal for Communities programme was still operating in this way during the 2000s.[158] But Hackney's combination of new social housing and, in the 1980s and 1990s, poor management proved a damaging combination.

The Holly Street estate was built to the east of Kingsland Road on the site of Victorian terraced housing bombed during the Second World War. Because of their shape, the buildings were nicknamed 'The Snake'. Blocks were named after trees, such as Rosewood and Cedar. According to architectural critic Jonathan Glancey:

> At the foot of the towers are sixteen five-storey deck-access blocks; at the fourth-floor level these are connected by one continuous, quarter-mile-long 'street in the sky'. This has been a dream rat-run for the estates' many muggers and a nightmare for most residents. Those living on the fifth floor have been robbed by burglars who have punched their way through flat roofs.[159]

Glancey concluded: 'Holly Street estate is a textbook example of what went wrong with the system-built estates of the '60s and '70s. Although rooms are a generous size, standards of construction were questionable and the layout of the estate a disaster.'[160] The Holly Street estate came to embody problems found in estates in many London boroughs and, indeed, throughout the developed world.

Hackney was not alone in building such housing. What marked out Holly Street was the way it also fell victim to the council's failed administration during the 1980s and 1990s. The political struggle of the 1980s against Mrs Thatcher was lost, but damage had been done to the capacity of a number of boroughs. Hackney council's controlling Labour group degenerated into factionalism and, by 1996, was incapable of producing a functioning administration. Labour split.

---

158 David Blackman, 'Destroying the demons of demolition', *The Guardian*, 20 November 2001

159 Jonathan Glancey, 'Tower blocks fall victim to return of pre-war values', *The Independent*, 12 December 1992

160 Ibid.

One councillor at various times represented Labour (then Hackney New Labour), the Conservatives, independents, the Liberal Democrats and the Green Party.[161]

Stories about the dire quality of the council's services and, in particular, its housing were legion. The Town Hall in Mare Street was regularly picketed by disgruntled trade unions, complaints to the local government ombudsman grew in number, and staff absenteeism increased. Rubbish piled up and broken streetlights went unfixed. Housing maintenance failed. Cockroaches and rats prospered mightily. Tenants began to use the courts to pursue grievances against the authority. Head teachers passed a motion of no confidence in the council and eventually the government transferred control of schools to a not-for-profit trust for a ten-year period.[162] The borough did not know how many children it had in care. The district auditor issued a report revealing widespread financial mismanagement. An article in *The Guardian* quoted a resident saying Hackney was 'Britain's North Korea. It's the place modern politics forgot.'[163]

Labour councillors (led by Jules Pipe) and the Conservatives (led by Eric Ollerenshaw) for a time formed a joint administration between the 1998 and 2002 elections.[164] In 2000, Max Caller was appointed as chief executive to get a grip on the borough's chaotic government. These individuals faced remarkable levels of abuse and even threats of violence as they attempted to restore proper administration. In 2002, the borough chose to adopt a directly elected mayor model, and Pipe won the first and three subsequent contests. From this time onwards, Hackney's fortunes have changed beyond all recognition. The adoption of a directly elected mayor and the performance of Jules Pipe in office have together shown how skilful public administration can reverse the fortunes of a failed authority.

The turnaround in Hackney can be chronicled in the Audit Commission's

---

161 Jay Rayner, 'The worst-run place in Britain', *The Guardian*, 13 November 2000

162 Jules Pipe, 'Hackney's education story', London Councils, 2014, http://www.londoncouncils.gov.uk/our-key-themes/children-and-young-people/education-and-school-places/lessons-london/jules-pipe (accessed 1 September 2015)

163 Jay Rayner, 'The worst-run place in Britain', *The Guardian*, 13 November 2000

164 Information provided by London Borough of Hackney

'comprehensive performance assessment' results for the borough. In 2003, the council was adjudged 'poor'.[165] Within five years (the CPA's final year), the rating was 'good' and 'improving strongly'.[166] The commission added: 'The pace of improvement is higher than the national average, with three-quarters of performance indicators improving in 2007/08. Overall resident satisfaction has improved, with 60 percent of residents feeling their views are taken into account.' By 2015–16, council tax has been frozen for eleven years. More than any other borough, and faster, Hackney turned from being a governmental basket case to a model council.

The old, failing Hackney Downs School was replaced by the nationally renowned Mossbourne Community Academy. Every secondary school in the borough and most primaries are now rated 'good' or 'outstanding' by OFSTED.[167] The council has refurbished Stoke Newington Town Hall and restored Clissold Park. The London Fields Lido, left derelict during the 1980s, also re-opened.

Despite the turnaround, Channel 4's *Location, Location, Location* programme in 2006 judged Hackney to be 'Britain's worst place to live'.[168] This judgement was a lagging indicator, and changes to the borough since then have altered it further. TfL assumed responsibility for a number of former National Rail services in 2007 and has subsequently created the London Overground line, which has, in effect, put Hackney on the Tube. Services on the former, dreadful, North London line have been incorporated by TfL into a frequent inner-orbital service with new, bigger trains. The link to the former East London line, also now part of the Overground, has further improved connectivity.

---

165 Audit Commission, 'How is London Borough of Hackney Performing?', *Comprehensive Performance Assessment 2003*, http://archive.audit-commission.gov.uk/cpa/Scorecards2003/ScorecardPDFs2003/103591.pdf (accessed 11 June 2015)

166 Audit Commission, *Annual Audit and Inspection Letter 2007–08: London Borough of Hackney*, http://www.hackney.gov.uk/Assets/Documents/annual-audit-letter-07-08.pdf (accessed 1 September 2015)

167 See OFSTED, http://reports.ofsted.gov.uk/inspection-reports/find-inspection-report/results/1/any/any/any/any/Hackney/any/any/any/any/0/0 (accessed 11 June 2015)

168 'Hackney "worst place to live in UK"', *Evening Standard*, 22 January 2006

Dalston, Homerton and Hackney Wick have benefited enormously from the Overground. In addition, the 2012 Olympics gave a boost to infrastructure on the east side of the borough, which is no longer cut off from the West End.

The most remarkable physical change to Hackney has come to the south of the borough in Haggerston, Hoxton and Shoreditch. These formerly part-derelict semi-industrial areas have been engulfed by development and social change. The City of London worked with Hackney, Islington and Tower Hamlets on a 'City Fringe' initiative in the 1990s. The idea was to allow finance and related activities to spread into premises in the areas immediately to the east and north of the City.

Places in south Hackney such as Charlotte Road and Rivington Street, and then Old Street, have become London's most trendsetting districts. Nightlife and cutting-edge retail now cluster in south Hackney, while the Old Street roundabout is synonymous with Britain's burgeoning 'tech' industry.[169] Hackney has been heavily associated with the 'hipster' phenomenon, a contemporary fashion and lifestyle trend often associated with inner east London.[170]

Dalston is now one of the most multi-ethnic places in the country and is home not only to large Turkish and Kurdish populations, but also to a remarkable, culturally diverse market. Stoke Newington has remained a Tubeless settled community, but has nevertheless witnessed radical demographic change, including the accommodation of substantial Muslim and Jewish populations side by side. Stamford Hill has, since 1965, seen its Orthodox Jewish population grow to perhaps 20,000, generating complex neighbourhood planning issues over loft extensions.[171]

Contemporary Hackney has become a place of complex cultural and religious integration, with the modern young making its southern neighbourhoods among the most fashionable in Europe.

---

169   Max Nathan, Emma Vandore and Rob Whitehead, *A Tale of Tech City: The Future of Inner East London's Digital Economy*, London: Centre for London, 2012

170   Alex Rayner, 'Why do people hate hipsters?', *The Guardian*, 14 October 2010

171   Robert Booth, 'Hackney planning row exposes faultlines in Orthodox Jewish area', *The Guardian*, 8 March 2013

HAMMERSMITH & FULHAM

Formed from the former metropolitan boroughs of Hammersmith and Fulham, the new authority was one of several that stretched from the heart of the capital to more industrial areas on the northern edge of the former LCC area. Kensington & Chelsea and Westminster were similar: they had an affluent south part, including much high-end residential property, combined with a more deprived northern area that mixed small factories and much poor-standard housing.

The north of these new inner west boroughs was then subjected to a massive roadbuilding programme, as the Westway was constructed between 1964 and 1970. The new road relieved a serious traffic bottleneck around Shepherd's Bush Green by removing much of the through-traffic. A part of the West Cross Route, now the A3220, was built between an elevated gyratory at the Westway and a new roundabout at the western end of Holland Park Avenue. However, other parts of the Ringways were successfully resisted by the council.

Hammersmith was home to White City. The area's name was taken from the colour of the stucco cladding on the pavilions, which had been used for a number of international exhibitions held during the early part of the twentieth century.[172] The Olympic Games were held at White City in 1908. Greyhound racing was introduced in 1927, and the Amateur Athletics Championships were first held there in 1932, while Queen's Park Rangers adopted the ground as its home from 1931 to 1933. Nearby, the LCC and Hammersmith council built the Old Oak estate on garden suburb principles.[173] After the Second World War, the White City complex fell into disuse. The only surviving element today is Hammersmith Park.[174]

---

172 Ben Weinreb and Christopher Hibbert (eds), *The London Encyclopaedia*, London: Macmillan, 1983, page 953

173 Mayor of London, 'TA3 built and heritage context', *White City Opportunity Area Planning Framework*, London: Greater London Authority, 2013, page 216, https://www.lbhf.gov.uk/Images/TA3%20Built%20and%20heritage%20context_tcm21-159427.pdf (accessed 9 March 2015)

174 Ibid.

In the late 1930s, the LCC had built the White City estate on the western part of the White City exhibition grounds. More than 2,000 homes were constructed in five- and six-storey blocks in a grid plan, with tree-lined streets named after exhibition buildings, such as Australia Way and Commonwealth Avenue. At the time, the housing was of an exemplary standard, although the rigid grid was different from the 'garden suburb' approach taken to the west of the estate.[175] In 1960, the BBC opened Television Centre at Wood Lane. For many years, the corporation's television services, including national news, originated from this former site of the White City exhibition.

In preparation for the 1965 reform, the committee set up by Fulham and Hammersmith councils struggled to choose a name for the new borough. Fulham and Hammersmith considered twenty possibilities, but were unable to agree on one. The minister eventually proposed to call the new authority Hammersmith, which the predecessor councils accepted.[176] Following years of local pressure, '& Fulham' was added in 1979.

To the east of the West Cross Route, comprehensive redevelopment during the late 1960s produced the construction of the Edward Woods estate, consisting of approximately 800 homes, including four 22-storey tower blocks. The estate was promoted by the then mayor of Hammersmith, Ted Woods, who wanted to provide better quality housing for the inhabitants of the borough. The blocks and their residents suffered a number of problems, such as poor insulation from cold weather and against outside noise, poor communal facilities and inadequate building services. The blocks have subsequently been regenerated.[177]

In the 1970s, much of the south side of Shepherd's Bush Green and the streets behind it were demolished and replaced by a shopping precinct (now

---

175 Mayor of London, '03 Urban Design Strategy', *White City Opportunity Area Planning Framework*, 2013, page 46, http://www.lbhf.gov.uk/images/wcoapf_chp3-1_tcm21-181443. pdf (accessed 9 March 2015)

176 Gerald Rhodes, *The Government of London: The Struggle for Reform*, London: Weidenfeld & Nicolson, 1970, page 201

177 'Take Two for Edward Woods Estate', skyscrapernews.com, http://www.skyscrapernews. com/news.php?ref=2617 (accessed 9 March 2015)

the West 12 Centre), four tower blocks and a petrol station. The shopping centre was enclosed and refurbished and the pedestrian bridge across Uxbridge Road demolished in 2001. White City Close (1975–78), a residential estate to the north of BBC TV Centre, was designed by John Darbourne and Geoffrey Dark and is one of three local authority housing developments (the others being the failed Marquess estate in Islington and the successful Lillington Gardens in Westminster) by these architects. The development was part of a movement towards social housing on a more human scale, with greater emphasis on the creation of houses with front doors in streets using traditional materials, in comparison with the modernist blocks and slabs of the 1960s and early 1970s.[178]

The new borough of Hammersmith had a significant retail and office centre at Hammersmith Broadway. The completion of the Hammersmith Flyover in 1961 had carved a valley through the middle of this centre, taking a large section of St Paul's churchyard.[179] King Street and the Lyric Theatre were redeveloped as a consequence of the new road, though the theatre's original interior was saved. The flyover has adversely affected the town centre ever since, to the point that the contemporary council supports the Mayor of London's plan to bury the road in a tunnel.[180] The consequences of building the flyover included the creation of a gyratory around the town centre, which could be removed as a consequence of burying the flyover. A Hammersmith & Fulham study envisaged development on the land liberated by the disappearance of the road as a partial way of funding the project.[181]

Partly because of the impact of the road system, Hammersmith's importance as a London shopping centre declined between the 1960s and the mid-1980s,

178 Mayor of London, '03 Urban Design Strategy', *White City Opportunity Area Planning Framework*, 2013, page 220, http://www.lbhf.gov.uk/images/wcoapf_chp3-1_tcm21-181443.pdf (accessed 9 March 2015)

179 'St Paul's Churchyard and St Paul's Green', *London Gardens Online*, http://www.londongardensonline.org.uk/gardens-online-record.asp?ID=HAF055 (accessed 9 March 2015)

180 Hammersmith & Fulham Council, Hammersmith Flyunder Feasibility Study, March 2014, http://issuu.com/hammersmithandfulhamcouncil/docs/flyunder_feasibility_study_web_high (accessed 9 March 2015)

181 Ibid., pages 42–5

dropping from the twenty-third largest in the metropolitan region in 1961 to the forty-sixth in 1984.[182] On the other hand, the area around Hammersmith Broadway was, along with many other borough centres, designated one of the GLC's 'preferred locations for offices'.[183] In the early 1990s, London Transport redeveloped the District and Piccadilly line station and a bus garage into a bulky slab of postmodern architecture, including a shopping mall, and a new station with a bus interchange. The arrival of the bulky new development subsequently attracted other large additions to the area, notably the Ark, an office building that stands on the other side of the flyover. The borough's geographical position close to central London but only half an hour from Heathrow Airport has latterly made it an attractive location for a number of multinational businesses.[184]

In the early years of the new borough, there was a substantial employment loss, although from a relatively small base,[185] yet, by 2015, employment was higher than in 1965. The north of the borough, the Park Royal industrial estate and the riverside in Fulham, still contained a substantial number of small manufacturing companies and functioning riverside wharves. Park Royal was, and remains, an important site for the supply of London's industrial needs, though only the eastern end of the estate is in Hammersmith & Fulham. The remaining majority part is shared with Ealing and Brent. Because of its location at the edge of three boroughs, it has proved difficult to ensure Park Royal has moved with the times. A number of plans have been published by joint borough partnerships. Latterly, matters have become even more complex, following the decision to locate a Crossrail interchange at Old Oak Common.

As in most inner-London boroughs, an inflow of private capital has turned street after street from previously down-at-heel bedsits to some of the most

---

182   Barrie S. Morgan, 'The Emerging Retail Structure', in *London: A New Metropolitan Geography*, Keith Hoggart and David R. Green (eds), London: Edward Arnold, 1991, page 127

183   Michael Hebbert, 'The Borough Effect in London's Geography', ibid., page 201

184   Information provided by London Borough of Hammersmith & Fulham

185   Nick Buck, Ian Gordon and Ken Young with John Ermisch and Liz Mills, *The London Employment Problem*, Oxford: Clarendon Press, 1986, page 68

desirable homes in the capital. Areas such as Barons Court, West Kensington and, famously, Brackenbury Village (an area of terraced housing between Goldhawk Road, Ravenscourt Park and Hammersmith) have much improved. As Westminster and Kensington & Chelsea have become too expensive for many affluent middle-class Londoners, Hammersmith & Fulham has seen an increase in demand for its housing.

The northern border of the borough is home to Wormwood Scrubs nature reserve, the largest area of green space in Hammersmith & Fulham. Seven acres of 'the scrubs' were designated a Local Nature Reserve by the council in 2002. Much effort has been made by the council and 'friends of' groups to improve parks across the borough.[186]

As part of a major Hammersmith & Fulham plan to regenerate land between Shepherd's Bush and White City, Westfield London, a major new shopping and leisure complex, opened in 2008, close to the previous Franco-British exhibition site. As part of the development, the Underground's White City depot was relocated underground. Other elements of the redevelopment included an affordable housing development, a new Wood Lane station on the Hammersmith & City line, a new Shepherd's Bush station on the Overground, a modernised station at Shepherd's Bush on the Central line and a new bus station.[187]

Earlier transport improvements had taken place in 1994 when passenger rail services were re-introduced north of Kensington Olympia (which, despite its name, is in Hammersmith & Fulham) towards Willesden Junction. To the south, West Brompton platforms were reopened in 1999, and a refurbished Shepherd's Bush station opened on the northern section to coincide with Westfield's opening. This line from Willesden Junction now extends via Olympia to Clapham Junction and is part of the Overground. It has been a remarkable success and allows Hammersmith & Fulham residents and businesses to access north-west and south London without travelling into the city centre.

---

186 Information provided by London Borough of Hammersmith & Fulham

187 Mayor of London, '03 Urban Design Strategy', *White City Opportunity Area Planning Framework*, 2013, page 220, http://www.lbhf.gov.uk/images/wcoapf_chp3-1_tcm21-181443.pdf (accessed 9 March 2015)

The GLA has designated a Park Royal Opportunity Area (PROA), which covers 700 hectares, extending 5 kilometres west to east and 1–2 kilometres north to south. It includes Willesden Junction, Hanger Lane and Alperton in the west to the boundary of Kensal Green Cemetery in the east. Most of the northern boundary is formed by the railway line from Euston. In the main, the A40 Western Avenue acts as the southern boundary, although the PROA includes some industrial areas south of it.

The PROA is part of the Mayor of London's proposals to take advantage of development potential at Willesden Junction and potential links between the west coast and Great Western Railway lines. In Hammersmith & Fulham, there is the possibility of re-using ex-industrial and vacant land south of Old Oak Common.[188] If the London–Birmingham High Speed Two (HS2) is constructed, there will be a large interchange between HS2 and Crossrail at Old Oak Common in the north of the borough.

Charing Cross Hospital was relocated to Fulham Palace Road in 1973. With Hammersmith Hospital, Queen Charlotte's & Chelsea Hospital, and St Mary's Hospital, Paddington (in Westminster), it is now part of the Imperial College Healthcare NHS Trust. Plans during the 2010s to reduce services at Charing Cross Hospital proved controversial and played a part in the 2014 borough election, helping Labour to win the council from the Conservatives.

Also controversial have been plans to demolish Earl's Court, London's iconic 1930s-built exhibition centre, which straddles the Hammersmith & Fulham and Kensington & Chelsea border at West Brompton. In common with many underdeveloped 'border' areas of boroughs, it has latterly attracted the attention of developers. The exhibition centre is to be replaced with a large residential and retail development. The new Labour administration had opposed elements of the development, notably over inadequate provision of 'affordable' housing.[189]

---

188 Mayor of London, *Park Royal Opportunity Area Planning Framework*, London: Greater London Authority, 2011, page 13

189 Tim Clark, 'Labour council set for tough talks over £8bn Earls Court scheme', *Architects' Journal*, 17 June 2014, http://www.architectsjournal.co.uk/news/labour-council-set-for-tough-talks-over-8bn-earls-court-scheme/8664280.article# (accessed 31 August 2015)

Another consequence of the 2014 election was that the 'tri-borough' agreement, which had been put together by Hammersmith & Fulham, Kensington & Chelsea and Westminster councils, was thrown into doubt. The agreement to run some services and procurement jointly had been taken by the three authorities in 2011, when they were all Conservative-controlled. Labour's win in Hammersmith & Fulham in 2014 led to a review of the agreement, though it was decided to keep it with modifications such as having a separate chief executive for each council.[190]

The politics of the borough has seen control in the hands of Labour and the Conservatives and, briefly during the 1980s, a Conservative–Liberal administration. Despite the 2014 council election result, Hammersmith & Fulham's politics has shifted slightly away from Labour over the years, largely as a result of demographic change and lower rates of council tax, with efficient provision of services.

Hammersmith & Fulham has become a more affluent part of inner west London since 1965. It has benefited from being at the cusp of central London and the Heathrow economic area.

ISLINGTON

Islington was formed from the predecessor metropolitan boroughs of Islington and Finsbury. The latter had been associated with socialist radicalism. Along with its neighbour Camden, Islington has come to represent progressive values embodied in local policies in relation to housing, egalitarianism and liberal causes. Islington's reputation was reinforced by Tony Blair living in the borough when he became Labour Prime Minister in 1997 and because of a meeting that took place between Blair and Gordon Brown at Granita, a restaurant in Upper Street.[191]

---

190 Andrew Adonis (chair), Tri-Borough Review Critical Friends Board Report to the London Borough of Hammersmith & Fulham, London: LBHF, 27 October 2014, http://www.lbhf. gov.uk/Images/LBHF_Critical%20Friends%20Board_Tri-Borough%20Review_27Oct_ tcm21-191575.pdf (accessed 10 March 2015)

191 Brown promised not to run against Blair for the party's leadership in 1994 in exchange for Brown succeeding Blair at a later date

Although this book is concerned with London since 1965, it seeks to understand the underlying historical elements that have shaped individual boroughs. Finsbury had a radical political past, which has left an imprint on contemporary Islington, notably a large amount of social housing in the south of the borough. Lying just outside the City, Finsbury's open areas offered an opportunity for meetings and a chance to express religious and political dissent. During the nineteenth century, Finsbury returned radical MPs to Parliament. There were close links to Russian revolutionary thinkers. The communist *Daily Worker* and its successor the *Morning Star* were produced near Farringdon Road. *The Guardian*, 'the world's leading liberal voice', moved to Farringdon in 1976 and subsequently to Kings Place, also in Islington.[192] By the twentieth century, politics became more organised within parties and civic institutions, Finsbury Borough Council among them.[193]

Finsbury was the home of the Finsbury Health Centre, renowned as both a symbol of pre-Attlee welfare in Britain, but also the first modernist design ever commissioned in Britain by a public client with a political objective. Finsbury council was Labour-controlled and intent on socialist policies. The health centre was designed by Berthold Lubetkin, who had trained in Russia immediately after the 1917 revolution and was inspired by its socialist radicalism.[194] The building was created with the intention of improving public health through its construction, creating a sunny and airy atmosphere, and uplifting murals. When built, it 'stood as a shining white rebuke to the decayed area of Finsbury'.[195] Lubetkin designed a memorial, including a bust of Lenin, which was controversially displayed in Finsbury between 1942 and 1951. The bust is now in Islington Museum.[196]

192 'Our quest to become the world's leading liberal voice', *The Guardian*, 6 July 2010

193 David Green, 'Finsbury Past, Present and Future', One History: EC1 in the making, London Borough of Islington, 2009

194 Design Museum, 'Berthold Lubetkin', http://design.designmuseum.org/design/berthold-lubetkin (accessed 3 February 2015)

195 Edward Jones and Christopher Woodward, *A Guide to the Architecture of London*, London: Weidenfeld & Nicolson, 1983, page 123

196 BBC News, 'Bust of Vladimir Lenin', A History of the World, http://www.bbc.co.uk/ahistoryoftheworld/objects/MuiXkeJTSTC7oh60YfvfSQ (accessed 3 February 2015)

Islington was one of the most populous of the metropolitan boroughs, reaching a maximum population of 335,000 in the early twentieth century. Even though Islington (along with Kensington & Chelsea) is the most densely populated of the boroughs today, the density of predecessor Islington was twice the contemporary figure. The borough has important sub-centres at Angel and Holloway Road. Archway is being developed into a third. Angel has been the subject of a long-term regeneration project since the late 1970s, with the growth of a new office centre close to the Tube station. During the 2000s, a number of large residential towers were given planning permission along the City Road towards the City of London, and the vast King's Cross development has helped improve the previously seedy former industrial area in Islington near the main railway lands site across the border in Camden.

In its early days, the borough was seen as having developed good children's services, which reduced the number of children in care.[197] Islington's large social services department was recognised as one of the borough's achievements, although subsequent revelations by the *Evening Standard* about child abuse temporarily undermined its past reputation.[198] Subsequently, the situation recovered to the point OFSTED rated the borough's children's service as 'excellent'.[199]

The socialist history of the predecessor boroughs, particularly Finsbury, did not immediately lead to the same approach in the new borough of Islington. Senior figures on the new authority, such as Gerry Southgate, leader from 1971 to 1981, were generally moderate. Indeed, Southgate joined the SDP when he believed Labour had shifted too far to the left.[200] But even moderate council

---

197 Gerald Rhodes (ed.), *The New Government of London*, London: Weidenfeld & Nicolson, 1972, pages 131, 136

198 Paul Harris and Martin Bright, 'The Whistleblower's Story', *The Observer*, 6 July 2003

199 Care Quality Commission/OFSTED, Inspection of safeguarding and looked after children services. London Borough of Islington, CQC/OFSTED, 2012, http://reports.ofsted.gov. uk/sites/default/files/documents/local_authority_reports/islington/052_Safeguarding%20 and%20looked%20after%20children%20inspection%20as%20pdf.pdf (accessed 12 October 2015)

200 Tom Marshall, 'Tributes paid after death of 1970s leader of Islington council', *Islington Gazette*, 13 July 2011

---

leadership of that time sounds surprisingly radical today. Peter Redman, an officer of Islington council during the 1970s, outlined the borough's housing policy: 'When I started at Islington, we were buying up, at very low cost, streets at a time. The council moved from responsibility for managing mostly new or recently built estates to become a landlord of whole swathes of Victorian and Georgian terraces and squares.' Anne Power of the LSE noted that, as elsewhere, where the borough was clearing slums, tenants had few rights.[201]

Islington's policy during the 1970s of buying up row upon row of what today are gentrified Georgian and Victorian houses seems incredible today. At the time, London was losing population fast, and many of the streets concerned were decaying and occupied by poor tenants in overcrowded homes without bathrooms, toilets or central heating.[202] Such conditions were to be found in many other neighbourhoods in inner London, including North Kensington, Kennington and Stepney. Confidence in building high-rise, modernist estates had been undermined by evidence such edifices were already producing problems. The London Borough of Islington's willingness to buy up and improve street properties was seen as a safe way of avoiding new mistakes.

The council, in common with others in inner London, faced the occupation of empty properties by squatters, creating an ideological standoff between what were generally 'progressive' councillors and homeless people. Despite the rapidly falling population and the construction of over 500,000 homes in the thirty years after the Second World War,[203] housing was seen by many people as unaffordable. Areas of derelict dwellings proved tempting to squatters, providing the council, as well as owners, with a headache. Islington had a policy of not automatically re-housing families with children

---

201 Pete Redman and Anne Power, quoted at 'Breaking up communities? The social impact of housing demolition in the late twentieth century' conference, held at the University of York, 2 November 2012, authored by the participants, Becky Tunstall (ed.)

202 See John Shepherd, John Westaway and Trevor Lee, *A Social Atlas of London*, Oxford: Clarendon Press, 1974, Charts 3.5(a) and 3.5(b)

203 David Wilcox with David Richards, *London: The Heartless City*, London: Thames, 1977, page 79

who were evicted from squats. Councillors believed that squatting delayed the council's own housing programmes.[204]

The predecessor councils and Islington built large council housing estates in the borough, partly in response to war damage and partly to replace what was seen as time-expired housing. Priory Green estate at King's Cross was designed by Lubetkin for Finsbury council and, in its early years, was successful. By the 1990s, it was badly maintained and had become heavily used for drug sales and prostitution. The estate was part of a wider 'King's Cross problem', which affected the Camden side of the area as well. The issues often associated with major railway stations, including small hotels with transient populations and low-rent businesses, spread up Caledonian Road and Pentonville Road.

Priory Green was rescued by the Peabody Trust, which took it over in 1998 and subsequently nursed it back to life.[205] Some of the blocks have been changed from purely social housing to mixed tenure, and given a makeover by architects Avanti.[206] Spa Green, an estate built by Lubetkin for Finsbury, has survived, with some flats being bought by architectural enthusiasts as a result of the right-to-buy policy.[207]

At Islington's far southern tip on the City of London border lies the Whitecross Street estate, which is a mixture of classic Peabody tenement-type blocks, plus some built between the 1950s and 1970s. The north of the estate now finds itself on the edge of 'Silicon Roundabout' at Old Street and thus adjoining a rapidly changing neighbourhood. The original blocks were

---

204 Peter Somerville and Nigel Sprigings (eds), *Housing and Social Policy: Contemporary Themes and Critical Perspectives*, London: Routledge, 2005, page 205

205 lovelondoncouncilhousing, 'A lesson in love: Priory Green estate, King's Cross', 23 February 2013, http://www.lovelondoncouncilhousing.com/2013/02/a-lesson-in-love-priory-green-estate.html#more-41 (accessed 6 February 2015)

206 David Taylor, 'Avanti updates Lubetkin's Wynford House', *Architects' Journal*, 20 April 2000

207 'Spa Green to Skinner Street', in Survey of London: Volume 47, Northern Clerkenwell and Pentonville, ed. Philip Temple (London, 2008), pages 84–108, http://www.british-history.ac.uk/survey-london/vol47/pp84-108 (accessed 9 September 2015)

built in collaboration with the MBW[208] and therefore constitute a pre-LCC forerunner of council housing. The estate, including later modernist buildings, is still run by Peabody and, by the standards of much inner-London social housing, has been well-maintained. A 2010 report from consultancy company Publica prompted improvements to the estate's public spaces.

North and central Islington are home to much social housing, including the Andover, Barnsbury and Bemerton estates. The Andover estate in Finsbury Park, built by the council in the 1970s, was designed as a maze of courtyards and buildings with poor natural surveillance, which made it feel insecure and unwelcoming. Built in red brick and concrete, it followed the pattern of many such developments, with cul-de-sacs, elevated walkways and banks of garages for car parking. In 2007, it was the subject of an unflattering profile in a television programme presented by the former MP Ann Widdecombe, which led to accusations by Islington councillors and London councils that the programme had exaggerated the conditions faced by the estate's residents.[209] Local residents responded with a short film, 'Beyond the Hoodie'.[210]

In the light of the extraordinary history of Islington's gentrification and redevelopment since the 1960s, a new building within the Packington estate regeneration scheme acts as a summary of five decades of policy. The Hyde Group, a housing association, has constructed a remarkable pastiche Georgian terrace of housing association homes.[211] While this building is a block of social housing, it has been built to look like the traditional homes bought up by inward-moving owner-occupiers in the 1960s and 1970s.

The leadership of Islington council during the 1980s was seen nationally as part of the 'new left' takeover of parts of urban government. Margaret Hodge, who was leader between 1982 and 1992, had previously chaired the

---

208 Publica, *Whitecross Street Estate*, London: Publica, 2010, page 11

209 Amelia Hill, 'ITV under fire for attack on teens', *The Observer*, 23 September 2007

210 Michelle Golding (director), 'Beyond the Hoodie', https://www.youtube.com/watch?v=-gbX_wCHlzo (accessed 6 February 2015)

211 Patrick Butler, 'New London homes bridge the divide between rich and poor communities', *The Guardian*, 4 December 2012

housing committee at the time of a large house-building programme. Islington and its leader herself became closely associated with the Labour left's struggle against the Thatcher government, and the press rejoiced in stories about the 'loony' policies of the council.

Speaking in a parliamentary debate in 1984, Conservative MP Winston Churchill summed up the view of many Conservatives when he said: 'The squandermania of Islington and other Marxist-controlled boroughs knows no bounds.'[212] Local MP Jeremy Corbyn observed:

> There can seldom have been a local authority that has been more maligned and vilified by ministers and their friends in the press than Islington since the 1982 elections … Most weeks, *The Sun, the Daily Express*, the *Daily Mail* carry stories by journalists who are sent to look for dirt about Islington council and to follow councillors around. They even camp outside the council leader's house.[213]

Islington and the council were at the forefront of London's lesbian, gay and bisexual history. A number of key events in UK gay history took place in Islington, including the first public gay rights protest in Britain, in Highbury Fields in 1970, and the first London Pride marches along Upper Street in 1971 and 1972. Community organisations seeking equality for lesbian, gay and bisexual people have based themselves in the borough, including Stonewall. In the 1980s, Islington council had the first openly gay mayor in Britain. Chris Smith, MP for Islington South, was the first 'out' gay British Member of Parliament.[214]

Many charities and NGOs locate themselves in Islington. Its radical leanings and location near the City and West End have made it a favoured location

---

212 Hansard, HC Debates, Volume 52, London: TSO, 23 January 1984, Columns 637–724

213 Ibid.

214 London Borough of Islington, 'LGBT Islington', http://www.islington.gov.uk/ publicrecords/library/Community-and-living/Information/Guidance/2013-2014/ (2014-02-12)-Islington%27s-proud-LGBT-history.pdf (accessed 6 February 2015)

for not-for-profit organisations.[215] Latterly, the council has sought to protect its status as a location for charities among small businesses in the south of the borough.[216]

Islington is home to Arsenal, possibly London's most successful football team and certainly (along with Chelsea) its most high-profile. The writer Nick Hornby, in his book and film *Fever Pitch*, explained how a significant number of north London residents find their lives affected by the local team. In 2006, Arsenal moved into their new home, the Emirates Stadium, leaving the previous one nearby (occupied since 1913) to be redeveloped as flats. Arsenal, like the prisons Pentonville and Holloway, is an Islington place name with great resonance.

Radicalism affected the borough's schools from 1965 to 1990, when they were the responsibility of the ILEA. Two institutions, in particular, hit the headlines. One was Islington Green School, which became a byword for progressive education – a reputation reinforced by the fact that a group of its children got to sing ('We don't need no education') on Pink Floyd's anti-conformist anthem 'Another Brick in the Wall'.[217] The other was William Tyndale Primary School, which went on to affect schools' policy nationally. A radical head teacher took over the school when it was strife-torn because of disagreements between the teaching staff. The head and some of the staff went on strike when the ILEA sent in inspectors. An inquiry, undertaken by Robin Auld QC, was critical of the school and the authority. The scandal 'provided a ready stick with which to beat a large, Labour-controlled, urban education authority that was already a favourite target for the London-based popular media'.[218]

215 London Borough of Islington, 'Labour Market Analysis: Islington & London', http://
www.islington.gov.uk/publicrecords/library/Democracy/Quality-and-performance/
Statistics/2013-2014/%282013-06-03%29-Islington-Labour-Market-Briefing.pdf
(accessed 7 February 2015)

216 Rory Brigstock-Barron, 'Council reach deal to stop offices in Islington becoming flats',
Islington Gazette, 18 September 2014

217 BBC News, 'Just another brick in the wall', 2 October 2007, http://news.bbc.co.uk/1/hi/
magazine/7021797.stm (accessed 6 February 2015)

218 Stuart Maclure, *A History of Education in London, 1870–1990*, London: Allen Lane, 1990,
pages 202–5

The fallout from the William Tyndale affair informed Prime Minister James Callaghan's 'Ruskin speech', which started a process of reform that has, step by step, reduced local government control over schools.[219]

The changes affecting Barnsbury and Canonbury in the fifty years since 1965, like those in North Kensington, have come to symbolise a distinctively London form of property-led improvement. Young professionals identified the area as offering substantial and attractive older housing at low prices just outside the city centre. They acted as pioneers by buying dilapidated properties for, say, £5,000, moving in and paying for improvements.[220] Multi-occupied rented houses were turned into single-family owner-occupied ones.[221] Today, these homes are worth £1.5–2 million. London's vast supply of such houses means that a similar process is today underway in Leyton, Walthamstow and Plaistow.

The Islington Fairness Commission, appointed by the council, concluded: 'Rather perplexingly, despite being one of the most deprived local authorities in the country, Islington [also] ranks highly nationally on a prosperity index.'[222] Like Camden and Westminster, Islington is a borough of extreme contrasts, often across a street. The Caledonian Road exemplifies this divide: on the west side lies a large expanse of social housing, while on the east are some of the most desirable and expensive homes in London.

The name of Islington, probably more than any other borough, has become synonymous with progressive Labour politics and personalities. Jeremy Corbyn, MP for Islington North, became leader of the Labour Party in September 2015.

---

219 Ibid., page 205

220 A. P. Baggs, Diane K. Bolton and Patricia E. C. Croot, 'Islington: Growth, Barnsbury and King's Cross', in *A History of the County of Middlesex: Volume 8, Islington and Stoke Newington Parishes*, T. F. T. Baker and C. R. Elrington (eds), London: British History, 1985, pages 24–9, http://www.british-history.ac.uk/vch/middx/vol8/pp24-29 (accessed 15 September 2015)

221 Gerald Rhodes (ed.), *The New Government of London*, London: Weidenfeld & Nicolson, 1972, page 221

222 Islington Fairness Commission, 'Two Islingtons: Understanding The Problem', London Borough of Islington, 2011

KENSINGTON & CHELSEA

The Royal Borough of Kensington & Chelsea was the only post-1965 borough originally allowed to use both of its predecessors' names in the name of the new authority. Many other attempts to bolt together place names were ruled out by Sir Keith Joseph. Subsequently, Hammersmith & Fulham and Barking & Dagenham were allowed this privilege.

In 1965, Chelsea and Kensington were relatively less affluent than they are today in comparison with London as a whole. Chelsea was a more bohemian place, much loved by artists, while northern Kensington was an area of poor-quality housing, infamous for the activities of slum landlords such as Peter Rachman. Race riots had occurred in Notting Hill in 1958, and much of North Kensington consisted of unkempt terraces of badly maintained and multi-occupied housing. Near-contemporary films such as *Performance* and *10 Rillington Place* capture the shocking seediness of the area at the time.

In Kensington & Chelsea's early years, massive redevelopments took place in the north of the borough, some as the result of housing schemes promoted by the council, and others because of baleful effects of building the Westway, an elevated motorway promoted by the Ministry of Transport and the new GLC. Trellick Tower, located at the top of Golborne Road and designed by architect Ernő Goldfinger for the GLC, is a spectacular (and oddly fashionable) symbol of the development during the council's early years.[223] Instantly recognisable across the city because of its separate service tower, the building is widely considered a brutalist masterpiece.

In the central part of the borough, around Gloucester Road and South Kensington, there was substantial hotel and office development throughout the late 1960s and early 1970s. In late 1972, thirty-seven hotel schemes and 3 million sq. ft of new offices were underway, leading the borough to seek parliamentary powers to limit the scale of change in what was predominantly a residential area. Cromwell Road saw the construction of the

---

223 Katie Law, 'Trellick Tower's trendy takeover', *Evening Standard*, 7 October 2013

270-ft London Penta hotel, designed by Richard Seifert. The president of the London Tourist Board warned of the dangers of the area becoming the 'Costa Cromwellia'.[224] Seifert had already built the Royal Garden Hotel at the eastern end of Kensington High Street and the Park Tower Hotel on Knightsbridge near Sloane Street. Capital & Counties Properties, the developers, had proposals for a new 'gateway to London' at the junction of Knightsbridge, Brompton Road and Sloane Street, but these were eventually abandoned.[225]

Further south, in Chelsea, the council built the World's End estate, adding to the cluster of social housing built by the predecessor metropolitan borough at Cremorne Gardens. The project required the demolition of a number of streets of terraced housing, though, by the standards of much 1960s and 1970s social housing, the World's End estate has worn relatively well.

The borough planner, Charles Hudson, was seen as having reasonable control over the huge pressure for development that threatened the borough's beautiful terraces. Hudson came down heavily on developers who attempted to push through offices and hotels in place of residential accommodation.

It is impossible to underestimate the effect that building the Westway (a government project and not the responsibility of private developers) had on North Kensington and, indeed, on neighbouring North Westminster. The project was conceived as part of a pro-traffic policy designed to reduce congestion at Shepherd's Bush. The road was intended to link Paddington to Ringway 1, part of the London 'Motorway Box', which had its origins in the post-war planning of figures such as Sir Patrick Abercrombie.[226] Seven hundred homes were demolished and almost 1,600 residents had to be re-housed. Roads were truncated and people found their homes less than 20 feet from the new motorway. Properties received no government compensation if there was a gap of more than 15 feet between them and the road.[227]

---

224 Christopher Booker and Candida Lycett Green, *Goodbye London: An Illustrated Guide to Threatened Buildings*, London: HarperCollins, 1973, page 27

225 Ibid.

226 Patrick Abercrombie, *Greater London Plan*, HMSO: London, 1945

227 Information provided by Royal Borough of Kensington & Chelsea

Protests against the construction of the Westway attracted national media attention. The GLC eventually agreed to re-house over 100 families. Attitudes to roadbuilding were permanently affected by the struggle in North Kensington and in places such as Archway Road on the Islington/Haringey border. Apart from the largely rurally located M25, London has seen little substantive road-building since the Westway. It is a measure of the road's significance that it has featured heavily in popular culture.[228]

The birth of Kensington & Chelsea occurred at about the same time as that of the Notting Hill Carnival, a celebration of West Indian culture in London. Although there had been smaller events at St Pancras and elsewhere since 1959, it was in 1965 that the first carnival took place. Moving through the streets of North Kensington, the carnival had political and cultural purposes. It still does, despite disputes about the event's organisation, and a number of efforts, some initiated by the council, to divert it to different locations.[229] Kensington & Chelsea is carnival's home. It is also unusual, if not unique, among councils in its sponsorship, since 1996, of an opera company (Opera Holland Park) which offers several productions in summer months.[230]

The operation of Kensington & Chelsea council after 1965, including the handover from the predecessor authorities, is described in detail in a study by John Dearlove, an academic, published in 1973.[231] From 1968 to 1977, the council was led by Sir Malby Crofton, who pioneered the improvement of housing in North Kensington and who sat on the GLC and ILEA.

According to Dearlove, Crofton's election represented a deliberate effort to break with the old order in the predecessor councils. He brought in contractors to clear up the backlog of rubbish caused by a bin strike in 1970, provoking

---

228 For example, the cover for The Jam's album *This is the Modern World* included a picture of the Westway, but is by no means unique: the BBC World Service briefly ran a soap opera called *Westway* based on the lives of people living near the road

229 Gary Younge, 'The politics of partying', *The Guardian*, 17 August 2002

230 Information provided by Royal Borough of Kensington & Chelsea

231 John Dearlove, *The Politics of Policy in Local Government: The Making and Maintenance of Public Policy in the Royal Borough of Kensington & Chelsea*, Cambridge: Cambridge University Press, 1973

outrage from sections of the national press. Less controversially, he was instrumental in setting up the North Kensington Amenity Trust, which worked to
utilise the wasted space under the forbidding Westway, and he helped create
London's first community relations office to promote understanding between
the borough's different ethnic groups.[232] The policy approach of Kensington
& Chelsea in its early years included setting council house rents that were pro-
portionate to tenants' incomes, thus creating a cross-subsidy between more
affluent and poorer tenants.[233]

Early on, the borough commissioned Sir Basil Spence to design a new town
hall in Hornton Street. Work began in 1972, and the result can be seen today.
Along with Hillingdon Civic Centre and Colin St John Wilson's British Library
at St Pancras, Kensington & Chelsea Town Hall is a high-profile example of
1970s architecture, externally and internally.

Crofton's successor, Nicholas Freeman, also made the news. Infamously, in
1982, he ordered the demolition of the old Kensington Town Hall, which featured
an Italianate façade, hours before it was to be listed and thus protected.[234] Freeman
later became a strong opponent of the Thatcher's government's poll tax policy.

The Royal Borough was paradoxically home to one of London's best-known
comprehensive schools, Holland Park School. Close to the house of the radical Tony and Caroline Benn, whose four children attended it, the school was
seen as a bastion of progressive education. It was run by the ILEA, itself an
embodiment of the most modern of modern values. When the school building was replaced in 2012, the council produced a brochure, which stated that
the original institution 'had become a byword for all the ills of the education
system and the school of choice for few indeed'.[235]

The trendiness of Holland Park comprehensive was paralleled by the

232 Detail taken from council obituary provided by Royal Borough of Kensington & Chelsea

233 John Dearlove, *The Politics of Policy in Local Government: The Making and Maintenance
     of Public Policy in the Royal Borough of Kensington & Chelsea*, Cambridge University Press,
     1973, pages 36–7

234 Alec Forshaw, *1970s London: Discovering the Capital*, Stroud: The History Press, 2011

235 Esther Walker, 'Too cool for a school: "Socialist Eton" moves into new buildings with
     facilities to rival the real thing', *The Independent*, 14 November 2012

evolution of King's Road, Chelsea, as one of the coolest places in 'Swinging London'. Along with Carnaby Street, King's Road epitomised the emergence of London as a creative and relaxed city. Mary Quant opened her first shop there as far back as 1955, as, later, did Malcolm McLaren, and the former Derry & Toms building in Kensington High Street was briefly the home of Biba, Barbara Hulanicki's famous emporium. The Chelsea Drugstore (today a McDonald's) was used as a location in Stanley Kubrick's film *A Clockwork Orange*. Punk subsequently arrived in the area, too.

Kensington & Chelsea, a traditionally inclined council, played no instrumental role in the emergence of these leading indicators of contemporary London's youthful brand. The trends simply happened. Today, the area is established as an enclave of some of the capital's most attractive housing and shops.

During the 2000s, the borough pioneered improvements to the public realm, notably with schemes in Kensington High Street and Exhibition Road, led by Daniel Moylan. The latter scheme, also involving Westminster, has radically altered the use of roads and pavements, creating 'shared space' along the museum and college-lined boulevard that runs from Cromwell Road to Kensington Road.[236] The area outside South Kensington station has been turned into a piazza. But a scheme to improve Sloane Square was halted by local celebrity opposition.[237]

Kensington & Chelsea has, since October 2011, worked with Westminster and also Hammersmith & Fulham (all Conservative-controlled at the time) on a 'tri-borough' arrangement to deliver better and more efficient public services across the three authorities. Faced with substantial reductions in council spending after 2010, the three authorities brought together their services for children, adult social care, youth offending and libraries.[238] Other provision

---

236 Simon Jenkins, 'Rip out the traffic lights and railings; our streets are better without them', *The Guardian*, 29 February 2008

237 RV, 'Council shelves Stanton Williams' Sloane Square scheme', *Architects' Journal*, 25 April 2007

238 Royal Borough of Kensington and Chelsea, Westminster City Council and the London Borough of Hammersmith and Fulham, *Tri-Borough One Year On: Delivering our promise to improve lives and make public funds go further*, http://www.rbkc.gov.uk/pdf/one_year_on_ tri_borough_2012.pdf (accessed 10 May 2015)

was arranged across two of the three boroughs. For a time in 2013–14, Nicholas Holgate was chief executive of both the Royal Borough and Hammersmith & Fulham. The 'tri-borough' agreement has been seen beyond west London as offering an example of how councils co-operate to cut costs and preserve services. Despite a change in political control in Hammersmith & Fulham at the 2014 local elections, the 'tri-borough' project survived.

Following the banking crisis of 2008 and subsequent global economic challenges, London became the object of much international property investment. The exquisite housing in Kensington & Chelsea and neighbouring Westminster made the boroughs locations of choice for international 'hot money' seeking a safe bolthole. Foreign buyers have seen the borough as a good place to find a house and, at the same time, hold capital safely. An increasing number of these buyers are rarely present in their trophy homes. Simon Jenkins, writing in the *Evening Standard*, commented: 'Whole blocks in Kensington are dark at night, with underground car parks and residents' bays empty and corner shops closing. The Phillimore neighbourhood off Kensington High Street resembles a ghost town.'[239]

It is hard to assess the full impact on inner and central London of the inflow of overseas property buyers. Some observe that parts of the borough are being changed by globalised capital. There is little the council alone can do about such an inflow of investment, though there is a risk that central government will make changes to tax policy that will have an impact on the prices of high-end London property.

High property prices have also, in part, prompted a spate of basement developments under houses as owners create more space or seek a windfall. The disruption to neighbours in this densely populated borough has led to the council challenging residents' right to dig deep and wide.[240]

The borough council has remained more formal than most other London councils. When council business is being transacted publicly, councillors refer

---

239 Simon Jenkins, 'London cannot prosper as a city only for the rich', *Evening Standard*, 28 January 2014

240 Information provided by Royal Borough of Kensington & Chelsea

to officers as 'Mr' or 'Ms', while elected members are always called 'Councillor'. The style of the council's Conservative group is moderate, and has perhaps more in common with shire Tories than urban ones.

Leaders of Kensington & Chelsea have generally served for ten years or longer, which is longevity by the standards of many London councils. Two leaders, Joan Hanham and Merrick Cockell, between them held office for twenty-four years from 1989 to 2013. Long service by councillors has been a feature, largely because of the political stability of the council. It has been held by the Conservatives continuously since 1965. Periods of twenty, thirty or forty years as a councillor are not uncommon, with one current councillor, David Campion, having been first elected in the Conservatives' massive London election victory in 1968.

Kensington & Chelsea is a remarkable place. No authority in Britain is quite like it. It is traditional, has areas of great affluence and also moderate politics. North Kensington is still, however, relatively deprived.

LAMBETH

Lambeth was largely created from the predecessor metropolitan borough of the same name, which, in turn, had been a vestry and parish since even before the early nineteenth century. Like its neighbour Southwark, Lambeth occupied the south bank of the Thames, opposite the developed and powerful City and Westminster. This southern extension of London was often used for entertainment and other activities that the north bank preferred to keep at a slight distance.[241] Before the river was hemmed in by the embankment in the nineteenth century, both sides included deep shorelines and were, from time to time, linked, when the shallower Thames froze over during cold winters.

The new Lambeth appointed its own chief architect, Ted Hollamby, who brought together an idealistic team of young (often socialist) colleagues,

---

241 Peter Ackroyd, *London: The Biography*, London: Random House, 2001, page 690

committed to high standards of housing and design.[242] George Finch, who was one of these architects and who had worked under Leslie Martin at the LCC architects' department, designed Lambeth Towers, Cotton Gardens and Brixton Rec. These projects contributed to the slum-clearance policies that were being pursued in most parts of inner London during the late 1950s and throughout the 1960s.

Lambeth Gardens, started by the LCC near the Imperial War Museum, remains a highly recognisable feature of the south London skyline. It provided high-standard housing, a doctor's surgery and a lunch club for older people. The homes were stacked maisonettes, providing balconies and views in two directions. The architecture is different from much of the mass-produced tower blocks of the time and is still relatively popular. Cotton Gardens at Kennington, though more like standard towers, used a similar craggy style, which still marks them out from many other modern developments. Brixton Rec, an iconic part of Brixton, originally part of a massive (and otherwise abandoned) scheme to create a new town centre over a motorway, has long had problems and proved expensive to maintain. However, Lambeth leader Lib Peck said in 2013 that 'the Rec is a treasured, landmark building and is part of what makes Brixton so special and unique',[243] and promised it would be retained by the council.

Brixton, at the heart of Lambeth, became the home of many Caribbean immigrants during the 1950s and 1960s. The first wave of immigrants, encouraged to come to Britain to take jobs in London transport and the NHS, were temporarily housed in Clapham. The nearest labour exchange was in Coldharbour Lane, which, in turn, meant many of the new arrivals sought homes nearby.[244] This new population has had a profound and lasting effect on the area and, indeed, the word Brixton is today synonymous with black London in the way

---

242 Utopia London, 'George Finch', http://www.utopialondon.com/george_finch (accessed 4 February 2015)

243 Better the feel good place, 'Brixton Rec: The Future – New Council Leader Pledges to Improve Brixton Rec' http://www.better.org.uk/leisure/brixton-recreation-centre/news/796 (accessed 4 February 2015)

244 Richard Cavendish, 'Arrival of SS *Empire Windrush*', *History Today*, Vol. 48, No. 6, 1998

Harlem is for African Americans. In recognition of this heritage, the council has created Windrush Square. Nelson Mandela visited Brixton in 1996.[245]

The politics of Lambeth was initially characterised by Labour majorities, though, in the Conservative landslide borough election victory of 1968, the Tories won control. One of their new councillors was John Major, the future Conservative Prime Minister. Ken Livingstone has remarked of Major's defeat in the Labour landslide of 1971: 'Poor old John Major didn't deserve to lose the night I won in Lambeth in 1971. That Tory council was the best for thirty years – highly imaginative and I agreed with almost everything it did.'[246]

In Livingstone's remark is implied evidence of the new Labour left's take on the kind of Labour administration that held office in Lambeth and elsewhere in the 1960s and 1970s. The new left saw traditional Labour councils as old fashioned and locked into policies that were unwilling to challenge social and political orthodoxy. In Lambeth, the council was to become, during the late 1970s and 1980s, a byword for political extremism and, eventually, administrative collapse.

Council elections in 1974 and 1978 saw a number of self-proclaimed left-wingers elected into office. They defined themselves against the moderate Labour figures who had run the borough and GLC. In particular, they disliked the administration of GLC leader Sir Reg Goodwin, which, in the left's view, sold out to successive governments during the economic crises of the 1970s. When Mrs Thatcher became Prime Minister in 1979, the stage was set for a struggle with the government at Westminster.

Ted Knight had become leader of Lambeth in 1978. Knight had been expelled from the Labour Party in the 1950s, but re-joined the Norwood branch in 1970. Ken Livingstone was also a party member in Norwood. Knight had been able to ensure that a majority of his supporters, generally well to the left of the Labour Party, were placed in winnable Lambeth seats. Knight was widely described as a 'Trotskyite', a label he made no effort to reject.

---

245 Symeon Brown, 'Remembering Why Mandela Chose To Visit Brixton', *The Voice*, 6 December 2013

246 'In conversation with … Ken Livingstone', *Total Politics*, http://www.totalpolitics.com/print/1613/in-conversation-with-ken-livingstone.thtml (accessed 2 February 2015)

Lambeth adopted policies that were seen at the time as beyond the Labour mainstream. They were not alone: a number of other councils and, later, the GLC pursued a similar line. Their detractors called them the 'loony left'. Many of the policies adopted were not particularly costly, but had the effect of polarising opinion. Declaring the borough a 'nuclear-free zone', coupled with support for ethnic and other minorities, provoked a rabid response from sections of the media.

Cyril Townsend, the Conservative MP for Bexleyheath from 1974 to 1997, speaking in 1981 said:

> We are faced with a different London Labour Party. We are talking not about the London Labour Party of Herbert Morrison or Reg Goodwin of only a few years ago, but about the party of Ted Knight and Ken Livingstone. In the Labour Party's manifesto for the GLC election, it is implicit that Labour intends to use the GLC's financial resources to redistribute wealth.[247]

In 1981, a series of riots affected inner urban parts of British cities. Brixton suffered serious physical damage to shops and housing. This unrest led the government to appoint Lord Scarman, a senior judge, to inquire into community relations and policing The Scarman Report was critical of policing and other aspects of governance.[248] The early 1980s was a bad time for Lambeth.

The operation of council business was often poisonously bitter, with long meetings and fractious debates. The quality of Lambeth's administration worsened and, eventually, the authority's oppositional policies led to a decision by the majority group not to set a lawful local tax. The Thatcher government had introduced 'rate capping' in 1984–85, which had required councils to set their expenditure at or below a specified figure. Lambeth's delay in setting a lawful rate led the district auditor to rule that the council had incurred a financial

---

247 Hansard, HC Debates, Volume 3, London: HMSO, 28 April 1981, Columns 697–761

248 Scarman, Lord J, *The Brixton Disorders, April 10–12 1981: Report of an Inquiry by the Rt. Hon. The Lord Scarman, OBE (Cmnd 8427)*, London: HMSO, 1981

loss. A number of councillors, including Ted Knight, were surcharged and disqualified from office.

Knight was succeeded in 1986 by Linda Bellos, another radical left-winger, although she led a council that set lawful rates. But the new administration was not willing to move the council back towards the political mainstream. According to a newspaper article written during the mid-1990s: 'Inquiries and investigations became a way of life amid the chaos and growing corruption of Lambeth. The construction services directorate and the housing maintenance programme were heavily criticised.'[249] In 1988, Bellos was succeeded by Dick Sorabji, the beginning of a move towards more moderate leaders who started to get a grip on the borough's administrative capacity.

Sorabji was succeeded by Joan Twelves, who, in 1990, was suspended by the Labour Party 'for advocating non-payment of the poll tax and holding a council meeting opposing the Gulf War'.[250] But, thereafter, the process of re-establishing moderation was renewed, with leaders such as Jim Dickson, Tom Franklin, Peter Truesdale and Steve Reed running the council in such a way as to empower senior executives to get a grip of the administration and thus make it work in a more effective way.

The impact of the political turmoil began to have an impact on Labour voting in Lambeth. The Labour vote in 1978 had been 49 per cent. In 1982, it slumped to 33 per cent, a fall of sixteen percentage points. The London-wide result for Labour in 1982 saw a fall in vote share from 39.6 per cent to 30.4 per cent, down just nine percentage points. The Lambeth result was relatively and absolutely worse. Labour in Lambeth had been outpolling their London vote share by 9 to 10 per cent in 1974 and 1978, but this number fell to just 2.8 per cent in 1982, at the height of the ideological struggle with central government.[251] The party's vote share then began to increase again from 1986 onwards, as relative peace was restored.

---

249 Will Bennett, 'The rise and fall of Red Ted's Loony Lefties', *The Independent*, 29 July 1995

250 Ibid.

251 Derived from Greater London Authority, *London Borough Council Elections 22 May 2014*, London: GLA, 2014, pages xv, 117

From the late 1980s, efforts were made to restore good government in the borough. In 1995, Heather Rabbatts was appointed chief executive by the new leadership, with the explicit objective of doing whatever was required to rescue the administration. Over five years, she won national recognition for the hard work necessary to turn the borough around.[252] But to do this, she required the support of the new political leadership, as well. It was Lambeth's political leaders who determined the borough had to change. Rabbatts was the officer who, more than any other, regained control, though from 2006 to 2014, Derrick Anderson (as chief executive) oversaw the further modernisation of the borough.

Under a succession of leaders and effective chief executives, Lambeth gradually restored its reputation. Parts of the borough that had been a byword for urban decline and disorder improved rapidly. Commerce and street life returned to Brixton, which evolved into a fusion of traditional Caribbean London and a contemporary 'cool' location for the young. The process of improvement went so far that, by 2015, there were disturbances in protest against the extent of Brixton's 'gentrification'.[253] The South Bank Centre, which had first become a cultural centre for the 1951 Festival of Britain, developed into one of the country's leading arts districts.

Since the early 2000s, Lambeth and its neighbours Wandsworth and Southwark have widened the redevelopment of inner south London. The full stretch of Lambeth's riverfront from Vauxhall to Blackfriars Bridge, including the area down towards Elephant & Castle, is in the process of radical redevelopment.

In particular, a number of tall residential buildings have been given the go-ahead by the council. Vauxhall has seen the development of low- and high-rise blocks of flats, which are part of an emerging 'cluster' of tall buildings at Vauxhall Nine Elms. The borough, working with the GLA, has negotiated

---

252 'Heather Rabbatts: The terminator in see-through heels' (interview), *The Guardian*, 13 December 1999

253 Tom Marshall, 'Brixton march: Protesters smash up Foxtons shop front and storm Town Hall during Reclaim Brixton event', *Evening Standard*, 25 April 2015

an extension of the Northern line from Kennington to Battersea. Lambeth has a target for 40 per cent of the homes at Vauxhall to be 'affordable'. The Shell Centre, the centrepiece of the South Bank, is being redeveloped into a further cluster of towers. The area of 1960s offices around Waterloo is also to be regenerated.

Few of the boroughs have experienced such a rollercoaster ride within their fifty-year existence. From initially being a somewhat old-fashioned Labour council, Lambeth became synonymous with radical political extremism before returning to stability and rapid economic transformation. These changes probably tell us something about the wider socio-political development of London since 1965. Certainly, the 'gesture politics' of the 1980s has been left far behind in Lambeth, which today is pro-development and politically moderate.

LEWISHAM

Lewisham was formed from the former metropolitan boroughs of Lewisham and (most of) Deptford, creating a new authority that, in the north, just touched the Thames, and also stretched inland to the edge of the former Kent. This merger linked a classic inner-city borough to a largely suburban one. Deptford has one of the richest maritime histories in Britain: Henry VIII established a major dockyard there; Peter the Great briefly studied naval architecture in Deptford in 1698.[254] John Evelyn, gardener and diarist (he was a contemporary of Samuel Pepys), lived at Sayes Court in Deptford.[255] Today, a street and a ward in the northernmost part of borough are named after him. The coming of the North Kent Railway during the mid-nineteenth century encouraged Blackheath, Forest Hill and Sydenham to expand as a residential area for rapidly growing London. There is a rich but under-appreciated

---

254 Edward Walford, 'Deptford', in *Old and New London: Volume 6*, London: British History, 1878, pages 143–64, http://www.british-history.ac.uk/old-new-london/vol6/pp143-164 (accessed 8 September 2015)

255 See John Eve, *The Diary of John Evelyn*, London: Everyman, 2006

architectural history in Lewisham, including homes influenced by the Dutch renaissance, Queen Anne revival and Arts & Crafts style.[256]

In 1968, Lewisham was badly affected by floods following torrential rain across the south-east of England. The River Quaggy, normally 6 inches deep, rose in some places to 15 feet. Flooding stretched from Catford to New Cross. The *Daily Mirror* ran a front-page lead with the headline 'THE LAKE IN LEWISHAM HIGH-ST' and a photograph of the flooded shopping area.

The LCC had been active between the wars in building 'model' housing in Lewisham, notably the Bellingham and Downham estates to the south of the predecessor borough of Lewisham, on the Bromley border. The LCC generally built large estates, while the borough tended to construct smaller ones.[257] Extensive bombing during the Second World War led to a need to rebuild the area around the docks and a Lewisham town centre. The borough's first tower blocks and slabs date from this period. The City of London Corporation built the Lammas Green development in Sydenham, as a 'conscious return to the Kentish vernacular, with colour-washed walls, pantile roofs and stout brick chimneys – out of step perhaps with the prevailing trends in architecture'. This remarkable understatement is taken from a document published by the council in 2010.[258]

When the borough came into existence, the LCC (then the GLC) was building the Pepys estate in Deptford. Long blocks linked by high-level walkways were a feature of the scheme. At the time the estate was built, the view along the south bank of the river and across to the Isle of Dogs was of rapidly declining and derelict docklands.[259] Post 1965, Lewisham council developed Milton

256 London Borough of Lewisham, *Lewisham Character Study Final Report*, September 2010, pages 33–6, https://www.lewisham.gov.uk/myservices/planning/policy/Documents/LewishamBoroughWideCharacterStudyP2.pdf (accessed 5 November 2014)

257 Michael E. Stone, *Social Housing in the UK and US: Evolution, Issues and Prospects*, 2003, page 40, https://www.gold.ac.uk/media/Stonefinal.pdf (accessed 5 November 2014)

258 London Borough of Lewisham, *Lewisham Character Study Final Report*, September 2010, page 40, https://www.lewisham.gov.uk/myservices/planning/policy/Documents/LewishamBoroughWideCharacterStudyP2.pdf (accessed 5 November 2014)

259 Michael E. Stone, *Social Housing in the UK and US: Evolution, Issues and Prospects*, 2003, page 42, https://www.gold.ac.uk/media/Stonefinal.pdf (accessed 5 November 2014)

Court, which was a mixture of slab blocks and houses. The borough's let-tings policy was reportedly more open to immigrants than the GLC's estates. Lewisham's population, particularly in Deptford, changed from largely white working class to one with a substantial minority ethnic component. Milton Court became a focal point for tensions between the police and black youth; although, during the 1980s, more sensitive policing reduced this problem.[260] The area was substantially redeveloped during the decade that followed.

Partly as a reaction to the social and design failings of many system-built estates, Lewisham is home to Walter's Way (at Honor Oak) – self-build hous-ing by pioneering Swiss-born architect Walter Segal. The houses, which can be built quickly, are of lightweight timber-framed construction, flat roofs and limited foundations.[261] Over fifty such homes have been constructed in the borough since 1979. They have a look that combines elements of Swiss cha-lets, post-war prefabs and Tudor cottages.

Between 1965 and the mid-1980s, the stock of council housing in Lewisham doubled. In 1986, Lewisham was responsible for at least 43,000 council homes.[262] There were stock transfers before and after the GLC was abolished. Subsequently, the right-to-buy policy and stock transfers to housing associa-tions have radically reduced the number of homes run by the borough. Deptford City Challenge, launched in 1991, focused on the regeneration of the Pepys, Milton Court and Evelyn estates in Deptford. Hyde Housing Association, set up in Lewisham in 1968, was one of the key agents of improvement.[263] The regeneration of Aragon Tower by Berkeley Homes in 2006 won awards, though the BBC series *The Tower*, shown in the summer of 2007, revealed just how stark the differences were between Deptford's newest and former residents.[264]

260 Ibid., page 43

261 'Walter Segal', *The Modern House*, http://www.themodernhouse.net/directory-of-architects-and-designers//walter-segal/ (accessed 6 November 2014)

262 Michael E. Stone, *Social Housing in the UK and US: Evolution, Issues and Prospects*, 2003, page 44, https://www.gold.ac.uk/media/Stonefinal.pdf (accessed 5 November 2014)

263 Ibid., page 46

264 Gareth Potts, 'Regeneration in Deptford', London, 2008, http://www.ucl.ac.uk/urbanbuzz/downloads/projects_09/Regeneration_in_Deptford.pdf (accessed 5 November 2014)

The economy of Lewisham suffered along with more general industrial decline in London during the 1970s and 1980s. Deptford is still an
area of workshops, office buildings and warehouses dating mainly from the
mid-nineteenth to the mid-twentieth century, illustrating the last phase of
a predominantly river-related industry before its decline in the late twentieth century.[265] Lewisham was a location for some moderately sized industry,
including Robertson's jam factory in Catford, where Golden Shred marma-
lade was produced. It closed in 1970.

Lewisham's economy today is relatively small compared with other boroughs. Its position on the edge of central London and without any major
employment locations of the kind developed at Canary Wharf or Vauxhall
makes its dependency on jobs in other boroughs inevitable. The geographical shape of the borough, with its small river frontage, has affected
its development.[266]

Deptford and its surrounds have been the object of every kind of UK regeneration programme, including City Challenge, four Estate Action Programme
projects, six Single Regeneration Budget programmes, and a New Deal for
Communities programme in New Cross Gate.[267]

There were problems in Lewisham between the 1970s and the 1990s as neo-
Nazi and other extremists embedded themselves in and around Deptford and
New Cross. Similar problems emerged briefly in Tower Hamlets and later in
Barking & Dagenham. In July 1976, the National Front and the National Party
polled 975 votes between them in a by-election in Deptford ward, together
outpolling the victorious Labour candidate.[268]

In response, the All Lewisham Campaign Against Racism and Fascism
(ALCARAF) was launched, with the support of trade unions and anti-fascist

265 London Borough of Lewisham, 'Deptford Creekside Conservation Area Appraisal', 2012,
       page 10

266 Information provided by Barry Quirk, chief executive, London Borough of Lewisham

267 Gareth Potts, 'Regeneration in Deptford, London', 2008, http://www.ucl.ac.uk/urbanbuzz/
       downloads/projects_09/Regeneration_in_Deptford.pdf (accessed 5 November 2014)

268 Greater London Council, *London Borough Council Elections 4 May 1978*, London: GLC,
       1978, page 11

organisations. In May 1977, the National Front planned a march from New Cross to Lewisham town centre in support of police action against a gang of muggers in the area. The police were asked by Lewisham council, church leaders and others to ban the march, but the Metropolitan Police refused to do so. ALCARAF and other organisations arranged a counter-march. The Socialist Workers Party broke away from a peaceful protest and, in frustration at having failed to prevent the National Front march, a number of anti-fascist supporters vented their anger on the police.[269] The resulting mêlée, which led to riot shields being used for the first time in the UK outside Northern Ireland, was called the Battle of Lewisham.

Four years later, in 1981, a fire killed thirteen young black people in a house in New Cross. Given the degree of racial tension and the activism of extremist groups in the area at the time, accusations were made that the fire had been started deliberately. In the aftermath of the fire, there was a march from Fordham Park in New Cross to Hyde Park. The inquest returned an open verdict, suggesting the cause was accidental. The fire has continued to generate controversy and African-Caribbean political activism.[270] Lewisham council erected a commemorative stained-glass window at St Andrew's Church in Brockley, where a number of those killed attended a youth club.

The British National Party (BNP), the National Front's successor, subsequently sought to exploit resentment among the remaining white voters in areas where unemployment was high. Silwood estate on the Southwark/ Lewisham border, where the BNP put up a candidate in the May 1994 local elections, was considered one of the most problematic areas, with significant harassment of minority residents.[271]

The challenges outlined above were not unique to Lewisham. During the

---

269 '1977: Violent clashes at NF march', On This Day: 13 August, BBC, http://news.bbc.co.uk/
onthisday/hi/dates/stories/august/13/newsid_2534000/2534035.stm (accessed 5 November
2014)

270 'Did the New Cross fire create a black British identity?', BBC Caribbean.com, 18 January
2011, http://www.bbc.co.uk/caribbean/news/story/2011/01/110118_birth_black_britain.
shtml (accessed 5 November 2014)

271 Hansard, HC Debates, Volume 240, London: HMSO, 28 March 1994, Columns 756–68

period of economic decline which took place between the late 1960s and the late 1990s, the politics of inner south-east London was seriously affected by a reaction to immigrants arriving in the area. Southwark and Bexley faced a similar challenge. Over the years since the 1990s, Lewisham has become a more relaxed place. Professor Les Back of Goldsmiths, University of London, says that 'popular racism at street level has become muted because the geography and cultural demography of London has changed' to create a 'mundane, everyday multiculturalism'.[272]

Lewisham was controlled by Labour from the 1964 'shadow' election until 1968, when the Conservatives swept to power. Labour regained control in 1971. There has only been one period since 1964 when there has not been a majority for Labour or the Tories. From 2006 to 2010, the council had 'no overall control'. Andy Hawkins led the council from 1971 to 1984, while Steve Bullock has been leader from 1993 to 1998 and then mayor. The pragmatism of Labour in Lewisham can be traced back to the involvement of Herbert Morrison in the borough's politics.[273] Under Hawkins's progressive leadership, Lewisham was among the first councils to allow the public to attend planning meetings, and the first to allow them to speak. The council rejected high-rise flats in favour of terraced houses with gardens, and led the field in protecting Victorian houses, by placing them in conservation areas. Lewisham was the first council in the country to set up a committee on women's issues.[274]

Lewisham has enjoyed long periods of political stability, although it was one of the local authorities set itself against the Thatcher government during the 1980s. The borough was subject to rate capping from 1985–86 onwards, and was seen as a high-spending, moderately radical, Labour council with few

272 'Did the New Cross fire create a black British identity?', BBC Caribbean.com, 18 January 2011, http://www.bbc.co.uk/caribbean/news/story/2011/01/110118_birth_black_britain. shtml (accessed 5 November 2014)

273 Information provided by Barry Quirk, chief executive, London Borough of Lewisham

274 Nicholas Taylor, 'Other lives: Andy Hawkins', *The Guardian*, 23 October 2007

extremist politicians.[275] Lewisham was one of a number of councils that signed up to a policy of refusing to set a rate. But at a chaotic meeting in April 1985, Conservative councillors voted through a lawful budget while Labour councillors were at a private meeting following a disturbance in the council chamber.[276] Steve Bullock became the first directly elected mayor of Lewisham, and has been re-elected three times. Lewisham under Bullock's four terms has seen economic recovery and the redevelopment of the town centre. He had, as a GLC officer, worked on the Marshall inquiry discussed later in this book. Barry Quirk, a leading local government thinker, has been chief executive since 1993.

One of the council's biggest campaigning efforts in recent years, as part of the Save Lewisham Hospital campaign, was against the downgrading of services at Lewisham Hospital. The South London Healthcare Trust, which ran the hospital, had been burdened by a huge private finance initiative (PFI) scheme during the Blair–Brown government, and was put into administration in 2012. As the costs of servicing the PFI deal grew, the trust sought to cut costs by closing Lewisham Hospital's maternity and A&E services, even though the PFI deal itself had been used at the Queen Elizabeth Hospital in Woolwich, not at Lewisham.[277] The High Court and the Appeal Court overturned the government's efforts to reduce services at Lewisham.[278]

The borough lobbied successfully to bring the Docklands Light Railway to Lewisham. More recently, the creation of the London Overground line has, as in Hackney, been a significant boost to the borough. Major developments are now taking place in Lewisham on the riverside at Convoys Wharf and in Lewisham town centre. Rising demand for homes, as London's population increases, has made Lewisham attractive to investors. Large residential towers are proposed for the former Deptford dockyard site, not far from the

---

275 Information provided by Barry Quirk, chief executive, London Borough of Lewisham

276 Graham Taylor, 'Red faces as Tories pull off rates coup', *South London Press*, 10 April 1985

277 Nicholas Watt and James Meikle, 'NHS trust and £150m debt situation "indefensible", says senior Tory', *The Guardian*, 26 June 2012

278 James Meikle, 'Jeremy Hunt loses appeal as Lewisham hospital cuts ruled illegal', *The Guardian*, 29 October 2013

Pepys estate and the stretch of riverside that is Lewisham's. The proposals caused much controversy.

As London's skyline reaches upwards, boroughs such as Lewisham, which were almost entirely 'suburban' in character, are seeing the development of metropolitan-scale architecture: providing a remarkable sign of change for Deptford and for the borough.

SOUTHWARK

The former metropolitan borough of Southwark, with a population of about 85,000, was one of the smaller of the pre-1965 London authorities. Camberwell, its neighbouring borough, with a population of 176,000, was big, and so the Herbert Commission originally suggested it should become one of the fifty-one proposed boroughs, and that Southwark should join with Bermondsey. But the government wanted fewer authorities, and proposed a different configuration that put together Southwark and Lambeth. The challenge of creating the new Wandsworth (which involved splitting the former borough of that name) was such that proposals came forward that would have added Lambeth to part of Wandsworth, thus leaving Southwark orphaned. Eventually, the former boroughs of Southwark, Camberwell and Bermondsey were brought together into today's Southwark.[279]

The new authority covered a large section of inner south-east London, and included a big part of London Docks. The Pool of London, immediately east of Tower Bridge, and Surrey Commercial Docks were still active in 1965. Southwark had, before the creation of the LCC, been in Kent. Surrey Docks were so-called because they were to be linked to Epsom and Portsmouth by the Grand Surrey Canal.[280] In its early years, Southwark council made efforts

---

279 Gerald Rhodes, *The Government of London: The Struggle for Reform*, London: Weidenfeld & Nicolson, 1970, pages 146–9

280 Philip Daniell, *Retracing Canals to Croydon and Camberwell*, Bromley: Living History Publications, 1986.

to protect the remaining sections of the canal for recreational uses, but the Port of London Authority, which owned the canal, wanted to fill it in and sell off the land thus created.[281]

The early politics of Southwark was 'traditional Labour'. The area had suffered extensive bomb damage during the war and had substantial areas of dilapidated and sub-standard housing. The Milner Holland report on housing in London showed that, in the former borough of Southwark, 59 per cent of households did not have access to a bath, while in Bermondsey the figure was 49 per cent. Sixty-eight per cent of homes in the former Southwark lacked hot water, a bath or a WC. Southwark's housing was not the worst in the city, but it was not good.[282]

The new council, like many in inner London, set about demolition and renewal. The Aylesbury and Heygate estates were constructed between Elephant & Castle and the New Kent Road, in an area that had been devastated by wartime bombing. Elephant & Castle was remodelled, and a shopping centre built in the middle of a large new gyratory. The scale and ambition of redevelopment in this area by the LCC and, later, Southwark have had dire consequences there ever since.

Southwark council was responsible for the Aylesbury and Heygate developments. The borough's architects designed modernist, system-built blocks with elevated walkways and open land between the buildings. The new homes were built to Parker Morris (official minimum space) standards and, for most of their initial residents, offered a vastly better standard of housing than the slum dwellings many people still occupied. All the new flats had central heating, bathrooms and their own front door.

Yet, both the Aylesbury and Heygate estates declined in status from the beginning. Budgets had been cut back during construction, and the scale of the estates made them hard to maintain properly. The district heating system on the Aylesbury estate failed intermittently and there was much vandalism.

---

281 'The canal that lives, and the one that's dying', link [but no newspaper title] from 'The Grand Surrey Canal', London Canals, http://www.londoncanals.co.uk/grsurrey/gsc01.html

282 *Report of the Committee on Housing in Greater London (Cmnd 2605)*, chairman Sir Milner Holland, London: HMSO, 1965, page 89

A number of elevated walkways were also removed to cut off criminals' escape routes. By the 1990s, the estate was a synonym for urban decay.[283] Tony Blair visited Aylesbury to make his first speech as Prime Minister in 1997, declaring that his government would improve the lives of the poorest in society.[284]

Heygate, like Aylesbury, became representative of the failure of council housing. It was used as the location for *Harry Brown*, a 2009 dystopian vigilante film starring Michael Caine. The architectural critics Edward Jones and Christopher Woodward observed of Aylesbury and Heygate: 'The unremittingly regimented and public nature of this heavily vandalised estate was used by the American critic Oscar Neuman to support his thesis that private or "defensible" space is necessary in housing design, a theory [that] has since been extended and endorsed by many other critics.'[285]

However, the motives of Southwark council's architect, Tim Tinker, are relevant to many of the grand housing projects the boroughs delivered in their early years:

> Utopian is a dangerous word … but if you're working in local authority housing you're bound to have a utopian view. What's the point of doing it otherwise? You look back now and ask why people were enamoured with modern architecture, and I would suggest it was to do with light, sunlight. At that time, these inner-city areas were extremely nasty, smoky, dirty places. The Elephant was still pretty bad, with tanneries and God knows what else. The flats built at Heygate and Aylesbury were light and airy, built in such a way as to minimise noise from main roads, while the abandoned walkways were created to keep pedestrians away from cars.[286]

---

283 'Put it on the Map SE17', http://www.putitonthemap.org/history1-2 (accessed 3 May 2015)

284 Paul Vallely, 'He visited in glory days of '97, but has Blair kept his vow to Aylesbury estate?', *The Independent*, 12 April 2005

285 Edward Jones and Christopher Woodward, *A Guide to the Architecture of London*, London: Weidenfeld & Nicolson, 1983, page 326

286 Stephen Moss, 'The death of a housing ideal', *The Guardian*, 4 March 2011

Nearby, the large road junction at Elephant & Castle houses a shopping centre constructed just before Aylesbury and Heygate in the late 1960s. The LCC held an architectural competition to redevelop what Sir Isaac Hayward, leader of the LCC, called 'the Piccadilly Circus of south London'.[287] The project was developed at great scale, involving 'two huge roundabouts, connected by an eight-lane dual-carriageway, in order to cope with the traffic from six main roads'. By mid-1966, traffic levels at the Elephant were so high the GLC was considering a bypass around the roundabouts.[288] In the middle of the round-abouts was to be a covered American-style shopping mall with new buildings surrounding the intersection. The LCC's planning committee described the winning proposal as 'being quite outstanding in its original conception of an arcaded multi-level shopping centre'.[289]

The developers had previously been house builders, and the Elephant was an experiment for them. The chosen architects had come second in the competition for the Sydney Opera House, but had never designed a shop-ping centre. When the centre opened in early 1965, only half the shops were let, and it was spoken of in the property industry as the 'White Elephant'.[290] Access required crossing the motorway-scale roads by long subterranean pas-sages which had been narrowed to save money. The developer was saved from the poor returns from this venture at the Elephant by letting a large office block at Victoria as a new headquarters for the Metropolitan Police.[291]

In common with a number of boroughs, the politics of Southwark changed during the late 1970s and early 1980s. Political life in the borough had been dominated by traditional Labour politicians, notably Bob Mellish MP, a for-mer dock worker, and John O'Grady, council leader from 1968 to 1982. As the new left gained control of Southwark, the old right became embittered.

---

287 Oliver Marriott, *The Property Boom*, London: Abingdon Publishing Company, 1989, page 215

288 Ibid., page 216

289 Ibid., page 217

290 Ibid., page 219

291 Ibid., page 222

Mellish resigned his seat in 1982 in protest at the leftward drift of the Labour Party. The ensuing by-election was poisonous. Peter Tatchell was selected as Labour candidate and faced homophobic campaigning from both his main opponent and from Labour traditionalists. O'Grady stood as a 'real Bermondsey Labour' candidate.

The atmosphere was febrile: Labour was in desperate political trouble and faced the Thatcher government soon after its triumph in the Falklands. As if to reinforce the strangeness of the political environment in Southwark at the time, other candidates at the by-election included at least three Labour splinter groups, Screaming Lord Sutch, the National Front, a Communist, a Revolutionary Communist and the Dowager Lady Birdwood, a Holocaust denier. Tatchell lost to Simon Hughes, a Liberal, suffering a massive 44 per cent vote swing. Hughes has subsequently apologised to Tatchell for some of the campaigning, notably the Liberals' use of the term a 'straight choice' (a reference to Tatchell's homosexuality) in Liberal Alliance campaign literature.[292]

Many Southwark councillors, as elsewhere in inner London, had jobs on other councils or in other parts of the public sector,[293] a practice that was eventually challenged by the report of the Widdicombe Committee.[294] Southwark embraced the full range of new left causes: the council was one of the first to set up a women's committee; there were race equality, jobs & industry and community affairs committees.[295] As Southwark was still seen as lacking the kind of feminist networks of Camden and Islington, the Women's Committee wrote to playgroups, mothers' and toddlers' groups, old people's clubs, tenants' associations and other women's organisations inviting them to Women's Committee meetings. Such meetings were open to all, with all having speaking

292   Peter Tatchell, Simon Hughes, 'Bermondsey by-election 1983: homophobia, hatred, smears and xenophobia', *The Independent*, 24 February 2013

293   David Walker, *Municipal Empire*, Hounslow: Maurice Temple Smith Ltd, 1983, pages 94–5

294   *Committee of Inquiry into the Conduct of Local Authority Business Report (Cmnd 9800)*, chairman David Widdicombe QC, London: HMSO, 1986

295   Herman Ouseley, 'Local Authority Race Initiatives', in *Local Socialism*, Martin Boddy and Colin Fudge (eds), London: Macmillan, 1984, page 154

rights.[296] However, meetings took many hours, and factionalism and differences of opinion were significant problems, as was the difference between 'feminists' and 'ordinary women'.[297] Unlike many new left councils, Southwark was unenthusiastic about decentralisation to neighbourhoods.[298]

Southwark, led by Tony Ritchie, was one of the first councils to be designated for rate capping.[299] The borough, in common with seven other London councils (Camden, Greenwich, Hackney, Haringey, Islington, Lambeth and Lewisham), delayed setting a rate for 1985–86. After a series of chaotic and noisy meetings during April and May 1985, Southwark finally set its rate, thus avoiding the threat of surcharge.[300] The Labour group split led, as elsewhere in London where the same moderate versus hard left divide occurred, to bitter political recriminations. During this period, and in the run-up to the introduction of poll tax in 1990, Southwark saw rent and rate arrears grow substantially.[301] The quality of the borough's administration suffered as ideological struggles dominated local politics. For the first time in its history, Southwark fell out of Labour control in 2002, with a Liberal Democrat administration (either as a minority or with Conservative support) taking over until 2010. Labour has once more controlled the council since then.

By the early 1990s, the Conservative government had defeated and/or abolished virtually all of the new left insurgency that had affected London councils. Southwark was no exception. Susan Fainstein, writing in 2001, cites borough officers explaining the change that had occurred during the 1990s:

> According to the development director in Southwark, 'The [Labour-dominated] council was totally committed to [commercial] development.

---

296 Sue Goss, 'Women's Initiatives in Local Government', ibid., pages 114–15

297 Ibid., pages 127, 129

298 Colin Fudge, 'Decentralisation: socialism goes local?', ibid., page 193

299 Tony Travers, *The Politics of Local Government Finance*, London: Allen & Unwin, 1986, page 165

300 Ibid., pages 170–71

301 Hansard, HC Debates, Volume 145, London: HMSO, 19 January 1989, Columns 497–579

> Previously, it had been totally opposed ... If nothing happens, there
> is no money for housing improvement.' Bob Colenutt, now a local
> authority official, observed in 2000 that 'the action groups of the '70s
> and '80s demanding affordable housing etc. are much quieter ... There
> is controversy over environmental issues but not equity. Has anything
> really changed? Regeneration is [still] primarily property-led. There
> is no public sector alternative program to private sector leadership ...
> Social goals depend on private market initiatives.[302]

By the end of the 1990s, Southwark was 'to Blairism what Wandsworth was
to Thatcherism: a local test bed for new ideas. It's engaged on [sic] a major
project of social engineering.' The borough's director of regeneration, Fred
Manson, and chief executive Bob Coomber worked with John Sienkiewicz, a
free-thinking civil servant, to deliver the contemporary version of Southwark.[303]
From having a remarkably high proportion of social housing, it was decided
to move to a more mixed economy of council housing and owner occupiers.

Bankside, a stretch of the river from east of the South Bank Centre to
Bermondsey, was to become a seething concentration of loft apartments and
Conran restaurants, also housing the Design Museum, the Millennium (briefly
'wobbly') Bridge and Tate Modern. Shakespeare's Globe theatre was recon-
structed nearby.[304] Because it had fortuitously been left behind by industrial
change, this section of the Thames was available for massive regeneration.
Unlike the City of London and Westminster across the river, Bankside still
had a large number of beautiful former factories and flat-iron-shaped buildings, which were becoming essential elements of the postmodern, revived

---

302 Susan S. Fainstein, *The City Builders: Property Development in New York and London,*
     1980–2000, Oxford: Blackwell, 2001, page 91

303 Paul Barker, 'The *New Statesman* Profile – Southwark borough', *New Statesman*,
     13 December 1999

304 The reconstruction of the Globe Theatre was the result of fundraising and other efforts
     by the American actor and director Sam Wanamaker; Wanamaker had been blacklisted
     during the McCarthyite 'Red Scare' period in the United States (see Karl E. Meyer, 'Sam
     Wanamaker's Great Obsession', *New York Times*, 29 December 1996)

inner city. Britain's tallest building, the Shard, was completed at London Bridge in 2012.

The regeneration boom that started in inner-south London in the 1990s has continued ever since. Southwark has implemented redevelopment plans for Elephant & Castle and for the Heygate and Aylesbury estates. New residential towers have appeared both at the Elephant (to be called 'Elephant Park') and along the Thames. To the south, Peckham has been improved by regeneration and the arrival of the Overground. Peckham Library, designed by Will Alsop, received the Stirling Prize for architectural innovation in 2000. Its fourth floor offers views of St Paul's Cathedral and central London.[305]

The question of how to manage community expectations and desires looms large in the redevelopment of north and central Southwark. The scale of redevelopment often appears alien to local people,[306] yet the council has few options but to capture the benefits of major regeneration projects.[307] Southwark, in common with many other London councils, can raise substantial resources for housing and community facilities, but only by allowing major developments. Local residents often find it hard to understand the complex balance between development, particularly of tall and bulky buildings, and the need for improved services.[308] Leader Peter John has defended Southwark's approach against accusations that it fails to deliver sufficient social benefit. The council has been defended for its policy.[309] This conundrum continues to affect London borough politics throughout the city.

Southwark, like its neighbour Lambeth, has emerged from a complex political past into being one of the most progressive, pro-development of all the boroughs. The transformation was a miracle of modern local government.

305 Tom Ravenscroft, 'Stirling Prize revisited: Alsop looks back at Peckham Library', *Architects' Journal*, 26 September 2013

306 Matthew Ponsford, 'Could "co-design" help Peckham where community consultation failed?', *The Guardian*, 21 July 2014

307 David Hill, 'Love to hate luxury property in London: this is why you're wrong', *The Guardian*, 27 July 2015

308 'Campaigners warn against record number of London skyscraper plans', *Financial Times*, 27 January 2014

309 Dave Hill, 'Elephant & Castle regeneration: what are the rights and wrongs', *The Guardian*, 13 February 2013

TOWER HAMLETS

The name Tower Hamlets sounds as if it is a modern construct, chosen to bind together a number of former councils into a new one in 1965. In fact, the name had been used since 1605 to describe an area within which the Lieutenant of the Tower of London could muster a militia. It continued to be used for administration of justice, and was the name given to the 1832 parliamentary borough.[310] The name ceased to be used from 1918, until it was revived for the new local authority created from the former metropolitan boroughs of Bethnal Green, Stepney and Poplar.

The area had been developing since the late sixteenth century and became a centre of docking, weaving and other industry. It was long associated with international immigration: Huguenots arrived from France during the eighteenth century, while Jews escaping persecution in eastern Europe also settled in the area. Some immigrants moved on from the East End to the United States. A notable example was Abe Beame, who was born in Whitechapel, moved to Brooklyn and went on to become Mayor of New York City.[311]

Tower Hamlets's importance as a first home for immigrants is, like Manhattan's Lower East Side, legendary. It has attracted migrant groups for over 300 years. The best-known example of this historic influence is the Brick Lane Mosque, which was previously a synagogue and before that a Huguenot meeting house.[312] Political radicalism has played a role in local history: Poplarism is a term still used to refer to the radical socialism of George Lansbury when he was leader of Poplar borough council in the 1920s.[313] The borough's political, social and industrial histories have intertwined to provide a path to today's remarkable Tower Hamlets.

---

310 Ben Weinreb and Christopher Hibbert (eds), *The London Encyclopaedia*, London: Papermac, 1983, pages 869–70

311 Godfrey Hodgson, 'Obituary: Abe Beame', *The Guardian*, 13 February 2001

312 Richard Tames, *London: A Cultural History*, Oxford: Oxford University Press, page 267

313 George Lansbury, as leader of Poplar Borough Council, went to prison in 1921 for refusing to pay over a precept to the LCC on the grounds the council needed the money to support the local unemployed

A measure of the area's particular history is that, in the 1964 borough election, three Communists were elected in St Mary's ward (Whitechapel), while in two Bethnal Green wards, six Labour councillors were elected unopposed. Levels of political engagement were low, with an average turnout of 15.3 per cent.[314] Because of the East End's history as a place where poor immigrants congregated, Tower Hamlets was a relatively deprived borough which at this time had few non-white residents.[315]

Big changes took place in the composition of the Tower Hamlets population from the 1970s onwards. The borough became home to a new Bangladeshi neighbourhood in and around Brick Lane. During the 1990s, the council erected lamp posts around 'Banglatown' made in a south Asian style and painted in green and red, the colours of the Bangladeshi flag. (In the Bangladeshi city of Sylhet, there are businesses with names that refer to London: a shopping centre called London Mansions and shops named London's Fashions and London's Shoes.)[316] The City/Tower Hamlets fringe has become as symbolic of British Bangladeshis as Canary Wharf has of bankers, an importance reinforced by Monica Ali's novel, *Brick Lane*, about the complexities of immigrant life in a new country.

When the borough was created in 1965, the old industries of the area still predominated, though the docks were in free-fall decline. East India Docks closed in 1967, followed by the St Katharine and London Docks in 1968. Tower Hamlets worked with the City of London and, separately, Newham to examine the potential for large housing developments in these former docking areas.[317] During the late 1960s, it was hoped by some policymakers to consolidate within Newham all of London's remaining docks.

314 London County Council, *London Borough Council Elections 7 May 1964*, 1964, https://
      londondatastore-upload.s3.amazonaws.com/docs/LBCE_1964-5-7.pdf (accessed 4 May
      2015)

315 Tony Travers, 'The impact of migrants on London Politics', in *Migration and London's
      Growth*, Ben Kochan (ed.), LSE London, 2014, page 186

316 Audrey Gillan, 'From Bangladesh to Brick Lane', *The Guardian*, 21 June 2001

317 Greater London Council, *Greater London Development Plan Report of Studies*, undated
      (probably 1969), page 294

By the end of the 1970s, all docks in Tower Hamlets had closed; the Royal Docks in Newham were the last to go, closing in 1981.[318] A number of related sectors, in particular railways and the gas industry, were badly affected as a result.[319]

The dockland boroughs lost 150,000 jobs between 1966 and 1976, representing 20 per cent of all jobs in the area.[320] The former docks area in Tower Hamlets and the other boroughs fell into dreadful decline. The Conservative Environment Secretary in the early 1970s, Peter Walker, commissioned Travers Morgan, a consultancy, to consider the future of the area. The consultants suggested five possible scenarios for the development of the docks, though their report met with opposition from local residents.[321] Indeed, the report galvanised tenant and community organisation opposition to gentrification in the area.[322]

There were some signs of progress. The St Katharine Docks, close to Tower Bridge, were redeveloped as a hotel, offices and a marina. Billingsgate Fish Market moved from the City of London to the Isle of Dogs. Some other office development spilled from the City into Aldgate. But, compared with the scale of the economic change engulfing Tower Hamlets and its neighbours, these improvements were tiny.

Speaking in a parliamentary debate in 1976, Labour's Environment Secretary Peter Shore (coincidentally a local MP) accepted that the docklands area 'presents a sorry spectacle of abandonment, inactivity and decay. Everyone recognises the need to bring new life to the area.'[323] A debate was held at around the time the Docklands Joint Committee (DJC) had approved a strategic plan for the future of the area. The committee had been created by

---

318 James Bentley, *East of the City*, London: Pavilion Books, 1997, page 38

319 Roy Porter, *London: A Social History*, London: Penguin, 2000, page 425

320 James Simmie, *The Changing City: Population, Employment and Land Use Change Since the 1943 County of London Plan*, London: Corporation of London, 2002, page 34

321 Janet Foster, *Docklands: Urban Change Cultures in Conflict Worlds in Collision*, London: Routledge, 2005, page 41

322 Richard Batley, 'London Docklands: An Analysis of Power Relations Between UDCs and Local Government', *Public Administration*, Vol. 67, No. 2, June 1989, page 170

323 Hansard, HC Debates, Volume 916, London: HMSO, 5 August 1976, Columns 2133–43

Tower Hamlets, Newham, Southwark, Lewisham, Greenwich and the GLC. Its strategy was to acquire and assemble land essential for redevelopment. Housing and new employment for local people were the main objectives.

The DJC, which was formed in 1974 by the government, proved an underpowered and cumbersome mechanism. It can now be seen as the product both of the decline of the docks and also of longer-standing social problems in the area. The GLC, five boroughs, the Port of London Authority, trade unions and community representatives together constituted the committee, and attempted to come to terms with the massive structural economic change affecting east London.[324] Land was owned by the Port of London Authority, nationalised industries and private companies. There was little public money for land purchase or improvements. The DJC was weighed down by policies that had as their objective the provision of thousands of new industrial jobs and large quantities of social housing.[325] Tower Hamlets and Southwark wanted 70–80 per cent of the new homes to be council housing.[326]

The election of Mrs Thatcher's government in 1979 signalled the end of the DJC approach.[327] In 1981, the government-appointed London Docklands Development Corporation (LDDC) took over responsibility for much of the former docks area on both sides of the river. An 'enterprise zone' was designated around the former docks on the Isle of Dogs, offering tax breaks to investors and developers.[328] The effect on Tower Hamlets was profound. The LDDC became the planning authority for its area and was given resources to improve transport links. Most importantly, the corporation was tasked with attracting substantial private investment in the area. The boroughs, including

---

324 Richard Batley, 'London Docklands: An Analysis of Power Relations Between UDCs and Local Government', *Public Administration*, Vol. 67, No. 2, June 1989, page 170

325 Janet Foster, *Docklands: Cultures in Conflict, Worlds in Collision*, London: Routledge, 2005, page 51

326 London Docklands Development Corporation, *Initiating Urban Change: London Docklands before LDDC*, London: LDDC Monograph, http://www.lddc-history.org.uk/beforelddc/ (accessed 6 May 2015)

327 Richard Batley, 'London Docklands: An Analysis of Power Relations Between UDCs and Local Government', *Public Administration*, Vol. 67, No. 2, June 1989, page 171

328 James Bentley, *East of the City*, London: Pavilion Books, 1997, page 62

Tower Hamlets, were bitterly opposed to the imposition of the LDDC and to its pro-private development policy.[329]

Over time, borough opposition softened and the LDDC evolved into an institution that could deliver benefits for local residents. The LDDC may have been turning the traditional Isle of Dogs and Poplar neighbourhoods into a radically different kind of area but, in doing so, they were able to spend public resources to improve colleges, schools, housing and other sub-standard local provision. In particular, the LDDC helped fund the regeneration of the Barkatine estate, which had been started by the LCC but was completed after 1965. The Docklands Light Railway was opened in 1987 linking central London to the southern end of the Isle of Dogs, providing much-improved connectivity for local residents, as well as new businesses.[330]

Noting that the City of London was, at the time, resistant to major office expansion, an American developer, G. Ware Travelstead, proposed a major new office centre at West India Docks. When his scheme proved impossible to finance, the Canadian company Olympia and York (O&Y) took over plans for a cluster of towers.[331] O&Y, which had been successful with huge office schemes in Toronto and New York, brought a sensitive approach to development which further aided community relations.[332] O&Y and its owners the Reichman brothers lobbied successfully for the Docklands Light Railway to be enhanced, and also for the extension of the Jubilee line to Canary Wharf. The Limehouse Link tunnel was built to carry road traffic onto the Isle of Dogs. Crossrail will also have a stop there.

One Canada Square was built between 1988 and 1991, creating the focal point for London's most important transformation since 1945. The building is a 770-ft skyscraper designed by star architect Cesar Pelli and topped by a blinking beacon. This silvery obelisk and its burgeoning cluster of towers are

329 Ibid., page 79

330 Helen Pidd, 'Manchester Metrolink line opens more than a year ahead of schedule',
      The Guardian, 2 November 2014

331 James Bentley, *East of the City*, London: Pavilion Books, 1997, page 65

332 Jay Rayner, 'A tale of two cities', *The Observer*, 20 April 2000

now heavily used as visual identifiers of London's modernity. Canary Wharf, where the biggest development took place, was previously the arrival point for sugar, rum and even elephants.[333]

The LDDC has now been abolished and its powers have reverted to Tower Hamlets and other boroughs. The borough itself has given planning permission for potentially dozens of new towers at Wood Wharf and South Quay. The Isle of Dogs, Limehouse and Wapping have become a heavily developed district of office towers, reconditioned warehouses and waterside apartment blocks. Mile upon mile of dereliction has been turned into a massive redevelopment zone.

Despite the spectacular economic turnaround, life chances for the local population in this part of Tower Hamlets changed far less than might have been expected. Community lobbyists in the late 1970s and 1980s argued that Canary Wharf would not produce jobs and prosperity for those left behind by the closure of the docks, and they had a point. Wards in the area still show concentrations of extreme poverty.[334] There have been significant improvements to the quality of social housing and the public realm on the Isle of Dogs, but the people who live there have only partly benefited from the gleaming towers nearby.

The development of Docklands by LDDC initiated major changes to the economy and demography of Tower Hamlets. But not everyone agreed with the form of urban regeneration. Moreover, the ethnic make-up of the borough continued to change, bringing about political stress. Evidence of the resentment felt by some local people surfaced when in 1993 Derek Beackon was elected to represent the BNP in the Millwall ward in a by-election in which Labour accused the local Liberal Democrats (who controlled the council) of distributing literature that appeared to accuse Labour of distributing resources in a way that favoured Asian communities – a point the Liberal Democrat national leadership agreed to investigate.[335]

---

333 'Remarkable photographs of Canary Wharf show how busy financial centre was once a thriving port taking in sugar, rum and elephants', *Daily Mail*, 18 May 2013

334 London Borough of Tower Hamlets, *Child Poverty in Tower Hamlets*, July 2013

335 BBC, '1993: Shock as racist wins council seat', http://news.bbc.co.uk/onthisday/hi/dates/stories/september/17/newsid_2520000/2520085.stm (accessed 6 May 2015)

The politics of Tower Hamlets has changed in a number of ways since 1965. In the first election, Labour won all the seats apart from three Communist ones and two independents. In some wards, Labour won over 90 per cent of the vote. There were few Conservatives or Liberals, and where they did stand, they lost badly. Yet, after years of gaining strength, the Liberal Democrats won Tower Hamlets in 1986, going on to implement a radical decentralisation policy between 1986 and 1994, with seven neighbourhood councils, though Labour abandoned the policy on winning back control in 1994, under leader John Biggs.[336] The Conservatives have moved from virtual non-existence in Tower Hamlets to winning 20.4 per cent of the vote and eight councillors in 2010.[337]

Labour then rebuilt its strength in Tower Hamlets. In 2010, a referendum was held about whether or not to introduce a directly elected mayor. The borough voted in favour by 60 to 40.[338] After the local elections (held on the same day as the referendum), the Labour leader, Lutfur Rahman, was replaced by Helal Uddin Abbas. In September 2010, the Labour Party in Tower Hamlets selected Rahman as its candidate for mayor. Following a number of allegations concerning both the eligibility of participating voters and his conduct, Labour removed him and replaced him with Abbas.[339]

In the mayoral election, Rahman stood against Labour as an independent and won. He did so again in 2014, against John Biggs, winning a second term. For the 2014 election, some of Rahman's supporters stood on a Tower Hamlets First ticket, splitting the Labour vote and pushing the council to 'no overall control'. Politics in Tower Hamlets became subject to ethnic factionalism and also to a number of allegations of improper electoral practice.[340] Subsequently,

336 John Torode, 'Bad neighbours in Bow', *The Independent*, 12 December 1994

337 Greater London Authority, *London Borough Council Elections 22 May 2014*, London: GLA, page 169

338 London Borough of Tower Hamlets, 'Referendum Results for Tower Hamlets, 2010, http://moderngov.towerhamlets.gov.uk/mgElectionAreaResults.aspx?ID=102&RPID=5541854 (accessed 15 July 2015)

339 Dave Hill, 'Tower Hamlets: Lutfur Rahman removed as Labour mayoral candidate, *The Guardian*, 21 September 2010

340 Andrew Gilligan, 'Judge to see forensics that point to Tower Hamlets vote fraud', *Daily Telegraph*, 1 February 2015

Conservative Communities Secretary Eric Pickles sent in commissioners to take over a number of the borough's responsibilities.[341] Despite all the change and improvement to Tower Hamlets in the period since 1965, local politics had continued to be at risk of tumultuous and unsettling change.

In April 2015, an Election Court case brought against Rahman led to him being removed from office for corrupt and illegal practices.[342] The judge ordered the mayoral election be re-run. In June 2015, Labour's John Biggs was elected mayor of Tower Hamlets. Complex politics is the hallmark of contemporary Tower Hamlets, though development continues at probably the fastest rate in Britain.

WANDSWORTH

Wandsworth was formed from the former borough of Battersea plus a large proportion of the predecessor borough of Wandsworth. A long sliver, consisting of Clapham and Streatham (which had been part of predecessor Wandsworth), became the western side of the new London Borough of Lambeth. The post-1965 borough was smaller in population and geography (with different boundaries) than the predecessor metropolitan borough of Wandsworth. The previous authority had a population of 340,000 within 14.2 sq. miles in 1961, whereas the new one was to have 322,000 residents within 13.4 sq. miles.[343]

Of all the boroughs created in 1965, few neighbours have travelled on such different paths as Wandsworth and Lambeth. The former came to be seen as the leading model of Thatcherite local government, while the latter endured a long period as an exemplar of a chaotic left-wing council. Latterly, they have

341 BBC, 'Eric Pickles sends in commissioners to Tower Hamlets', 17 December 2014, http://www.bbc.co.uk/news/uk-england-london-30518821

342 Paul Chesson and Joseph Watts, 'Lutfur Rahman corruption verdict: Tower Hamlets mayor guilty of corruption and election result is declared void', *Evening Standard*, 23 April 2015

343 (i) *Royal Commission on Local Government in Greater London 1957–60 Report (Cmnd 1164)*, London: HMSO, 1960, pages 261, 308; (ii) Gerald Rhodes, *The Government of London: The Struggle for Reform*, London: Weidenfeld & Nicolson, 1970, page 256

converged again to work jointly on the massive Battersea/Nine Elms development, where their approaches are similar despite different political control.

Housing and development have been features of the borough throughout
its first fifty years. Wandsworth inherited the large, modernist Roehampton
estate, which had been inspired by the architectural theory of Le Corbusier
and built by the LCC on the edge of Richmond Park. This development
included maisonettes and tower blocks set in an area of mature parkland. An
Open University analysis of the development observes: 'The absence of friv-
olous detailing and the angular simplicity of the concrete frames signalled a
return to basic modernist principles.'[344]

Further east, Battersea had suffered significant wartime bombing, leading
to the construction of a series of high-rise towers during the 1960s and lower-
rise properties during the 1970s. English Heritage described the area to the
south of Battersea Park Road:

> [H]ousing estates dominate the district. They range from the Edwardian
> Latchmere estate, one of Britain's foremost early essays in municipal
> housing, to the calamitous Doddington estate of 1967–71. Incoherent
> in the mass, they add up to a 'museum' of public housing, reflecting the
> changefulness and pressures attending the construction of this building
> type, especially in the post-war years. These later estates destroyed
> swathes of banal artisan streets of the 1860s and '70s, worn out by the
> time of their replacement.[345]

The Doddington estate was seen by Wandsworth's Housing Committee
in June 1966 as 'the largest industrialised building project yet undertaken

---

344 Open University, OpenLearn (2001), http://www.open.edu/openlearn/history-the-arts/
history/heritage/roehampton-alton-east-alton-west-estates

345 English Heritage, 'Battersea Park Road to Latchmere Road', *Survey of London*, 2013, page 1,
http://www.english-heritage.org.uk/content/imported-docs/a-e/battersea-vol-50-chap-6.pdf,
(accessed 9 November 2014)

in the London area'.[346] The Housing Committee chairman, Sid Sporle, pushed through a massive slum clearance programme but ended up being imprisoned after becoming involved in a corrupt network of politicians and builders, including Newcastle City Council leader T. Dan Smith and architect John Poulson.[347] Some of this corruption involved the blocks built on the Doddington estate.

The Doddington estate remains a familiar sight to anyone travelling by rail between central London and Clapham Junction station. Although providing a large number of new and improved housing units, the homes were blighted by a poor district heating system, vandalism and crime.[348] Other smaller developments at locations such as Latchmere Road and St James's Grove proved more successful.

The early years of post-1965 Wandsworth saw Douglas Jay, MP for Battersea and a senior figure in the Labour Party nationally, work successfully with the council to lead opposition to the GLC-supported London 'Motorway Box', which would have created a series of massive new roads in the borough. The authority passed a resolution stating 'that the council recognis[ed] that Wandsworth's opposition to the GLC's destructive motorway programme can only be effective if linked to general opposition to Ringways 1 and 2, as they affect London in general, as well as Wandsworth in particular'. Labour had won twenty-two boroughs in the 1971 elections, having broken ranks with the Conservatives over the future of the Ringways project.[349]

Vestiges of the planned system of inner-city motorways can be seen today, notably the so-called West Cross Route between Shepherd's Bush and the A40. The Wandsworth gyratory and roundabout were constructed by the council

---

346   English Heritage, 'Battersea Park Road to Latchmere Road', *Survey of London*, 2013, page 23, http://www.english-heritage.org.uk/content/imported-docs/a-e/battersea-vol-50-chap-6.pdf (accessed 9 November 2014)

347   Michael Gillard, *Nothing to Declare: The Political Corruptions of John Poulson*, London: John Calder, 1980

348   English Heritage, 'Battersea Park Road to Latchmere Road', *Survey of London*, 2013, page 24, http://www.english-heritage.org.uk/content/imported-docs/a-e/battersea-vol-50-chap-6.pdf (accessed 9 November 2014)

349   Michael F. Collins and Timothy M. Pharoah, *Transport Organisation in a Great City: The Case of London*, London: George Allen & Unwin, 1974, page 126

itself and were, remarkably, not part of the Ringway system.[350] An underpass beneath the Wandsworth gyratory was used as the location for an infamous scene where a tramp is attacked in Stanley Kubrick's film *A Clockwork Orange*.[351]

As in a number of other inner boroughs, the government reforms of the mid-1960s coincided with sharp industrial decline. By the early 1970s, an arc of unemployment had begun to emerge from Wandsworth to Greenwich.[352] The Wandle Valley, running to the Thames from Croydon, housed much industry, including well-known names such as Morgan Crucible, manufacturers of crucibles and other heat-resistant materials. Battersea was home to one of London's biggest power stations: half of it closed in 1975 and the remaining half in 1983. From the early 1980s onwards, major political and social changes affected Wandsworth in ways that have had long-term effects. Battersea became an 'overspill' area for fashionable Chelsea.

The Conservative victory in the 1978 borough elections was suggestive of things to come. Labour had won the council easily in 1964, 1971 and 1974, but, in 1978, the Tories won it for the second time, having taken it in the Conservative landslide year of 1968. The Conservatives had won the GLC in 1977, led by populist right-winger Horace Cutler. In 1979, Christopher Chope became leader of the council, heralding a move to the low-tax, privatising, 'small state' local government for which the borough has become recognised. The GLC and Wandsworth victories were leading indicators of a period of dominance by Tories, who wanted a smaller, more efficient state.

There was no ideological commitment to changing the government of Wandsworth. Past leaders insist they simply decided a common-sense approach to government was required.[353] In a pamphlet published during 1987, former leader Paul Beresford explained the thinking behind the Wandsworth experiment:

---

350   'Western Link', cbrd.co.uk, http://www.cbrd.co.uk/articles/ringways/ringway2/west.shtml

351   Simon R. H. James, *London Film Location Guide*, London: Batsford, 2007, page 141

352   George Gardiner, *The Changing Life of London*, London: Tom Stacey, 1973, page 78

353   Based on discussion between author and past/present Conservative leaders: Christopher Chope MP, Sir Paul Beresford MP, Sir Edward Lister and Ravi Govindia, 4 September 2014

Conservative Wandsworth council has proved that it is possible, by using ordinary common sense, to produce high-quality services at relatively low cost. This contrasts and repudiates the Labour Party approach of high borrowing, high central funding and high rates. The effect of this approach may be measured by the Conservative success, first in attaining power in 1978, then in being re-elected in 1982 and 1986.[354]

Beresford quoted the *Sunday Times*, which had reported: 'On almost every count, Wandsworth provides a better service than Lambeth – yet it still charges its residents half the rates collected in Lambeth.'[355] The three key strategies adopted had been: the efficient management of services; a policy of selling assets; and capital investment using the receipts from assets sold. A table showed how Wandsworth operated with half the staff of Lambeth.[356] Another showed that the council had sold 21 per cent of its social housing compared with less than 3 per cent in Labour-controlled Lambeth, Southwark and Islington. Beresford explained that 'trade union intransigence on street cleansing and refuse collection left Wandsworth council with no alternative but to embark on competitive tendering. Street cleansing was not only over-manned, but many "beats" were left unswept for weeks, if not months, due to unions' refusal to adopt flexible working practices.'[357] The outsourcing of street cleaning was soon followed by refuse collection.[358] In 1990, when the community charge was introduced, the council set the lowest rate in the country.[359] During the 1980s and early 1990s, Cabinet members were fond of using streets on the Wandsworth/Lambeth border in political broadcasts to contrast the difference between Conservative and Labour councils.

---

354 Paul Beresford, *Good Council Guide Wandsworth – 1978–1987 (Policy Study No. 84)*, London: Centre for Policy Studies, 1987, page 5

355 Ibid., page 6

356 Ibid., page 8

357 Ibid., page 20

358 Ibid., page 21

359 David Butler, Andrew Adonis and Tony Travers, *Failure in British Government: The Politics of the Poll Tax*, Oxford: Oxford University Press, 1994, page 150

There is truth in Beresford's observation about 'common sense'. Many Labour politicians in 2015 would accept that a number of councils controlled by the party in the 1980s concentrated on issues other than delivering decent, efficient services. Tony Belton, the Labour leader of Wandsworth for almost thirty years, commented:

> Wandsworth's Tories were bold to take on the unions, who in their turn were crass in their failure to recognise the limits both of their power and of their support. The unions still flush with their 'success' in the 1970s did not understand that the public were prepared not to have their bins collected for a week or so if the council was able to tough things out and to win the conflict.[360]

But Belton was critical of some of the policies of the Conservatives, in particular the impact of development: 'Wandsworth is now one of the most harshly divided of all boroughs, with levels of deprivation in a few areas alongside some of the richest parts of the country.'[361]

The Wandsworth model of government is remarkable, partly because it proved so successful for the local Conservatives and partly because it did not spread directly to other boroughs. John Davis observed that 'full-blooded municipal Thatcherism hardly spread beyond Wandsworth and Westminster'.[362] Westminster, which is indeed often bracketed with Wandsworth, was rather different in that its radicalism was driven by a single, dominant figure (Shirley Porter). Wandsworth, under successive leaders, chose, for most of the years of its 'commonsense revolution', to keep relatively isolated from other boroughs. It was not, for example, particularly active in lobbying for the abolition of the GLC.

---

360 Tony Belton, 'Thatcher and her Jewel in the Crown', Newsletters, reviews and political thoughts [blog], 10 April 2013, https://tonybelton.wordpress.com/category/wandsworth-tory-howlers/

361 Ibid., later in blog

362 John Davis, 'From GLC to GLA: London Politics from Then to Now', in *London From Punk to Blair*, Joe Kerr and Andrew Gibson (eds), London: Reaktion Books Ltd, 2003, page 113

The approach adopted by Wandsworth between 1978 and 1987 has continued. Services are routinely contracted out, with much-reduced town hall staffing. Efficiency and good management are now the hallmark of most London boroughs, and, because other councils have adopted something like its model, Wandsworth now appears more mainstream.

Battersea, which was a poor district in 1965, is today one of London's most fashionable neighbourhoods. The film *Up the Junction*, made in 1968 (based on a book of short stories by Nell Dunn, published in 1963), involves a privileged young woman leaving rich Chelsea to go and live in the industrial poverty of Clapham Junction. Today, Latchmere Road, St John's Road and Northcote Road are affluent, successful streets within an area that has been characterised as 'South Chelsea'.

Over much of the life of the post-1965 borough, developers have sought to re-use the Battersea Power Station site. Several ambitious masterplans have come and gone, with developers beaten by the complexities of the scale of the site, its poor transport links and the need to preserve the power station.[363] Successive development companies have faced the challenges required by central and local government to restore the Grade II-listed power station, and find a way of paying to improve the area's inadequate public transport. The site is now finally being developed because of investment by a Malaysian consortium that has been able to put up sufficient capital to initiate a massive redevelopment at a good time in the property investment cycle.

The long delay in regenerating Battersea Power Station has fortuitously meant that a much wider development is now possible on a long stretch of the Thames from Vauxhall station to the derelict power station site. New Covent Garden Market is being redeveloped, as is a chunk of land between Vauxhall and Battersea. The new American embassy is to be located there. Lambeth and Wandsworth councils have worked together on this massive scheme, which, once completed, will leave Vauxhall with a large cluster of towers, and Battersea Power Station surrounded by dense development. The planning permissions

363　Julia Kollewe, 'Battersea Power Station pushes another developer into administration', *The Guardian*, 12 December 2011

given have allowed this scale of building because the developers will be paying for the rehabilitation of the power station, a spur off the Underground at Kennington, and a variety of other community benefits.

The scale of change has been criticised by community groups and architectural critics, on the grounds it is overdeveloped and includes too many tall buildings.[364] The way the development has been driven by the councils, the Mayor of London and Whitehall makes certain it will consist of big buildings at a scale not normally seen in London. If the government does not pay for such amenities as Tube lines and social housing, then large, densely packed buildings, homes and commercial properties will be required to pay for new facilities.

Wandsworth styles itself the 'Brighter Borough' on signs at its boundaries. It has changed substantially from the relatively industrial place it was in the 1960s; its social and demographic make-up is different now from in 1965. It was one of the areas that first welcomed immigrants, and today it has a non-white British population of approaching 50 per cent. The politics of the council has moved sharply from a position where Labour won control in three out of the first four elections to one where the Conservatives have won every election since 1978. Rapid changes in the social structure of the north of the borough and increasing owner occupation have affected voting patterns. The future is likely to see a radical urbanisation of the north of Wandsworth, linking it more strongly to central London.

WESTMINSTER

Today's City of Westminster brought together three metropolitan boroughs: St Marylebone, Paddington and the predecessor (smaller) City of Westminster. During the passage of the London Government Bill in 1963, two MPs (Eric Lubbock and John Parker) put forward an amendment[365] to create

---

364 Julia Kollewe, 'Battersea is part of a huge building project – but not for Londoners', *The Guardian*, 14 February 2015

365 Hansard, HC Debates, Volume 670, London: HMSO, 24 January 1963, Columns 423–38

a central London borough that would embrace the whole of old Westminster, Holborn and Finsbury, plus parts of Shoreditch, Stepney, Bermondsey, Southwark, Lambeth, Chelsea, Kensington, Paddington, St Marylebone and St Pancras. Crucially, it would have absorbed the City of London. Sir Keith Joseph rejected the proposal. Had he not done so, the post-1965 City of Westminster would not have become, as it has, the key West End authority, responsible for many of the best-known parts of central London.

Westminster had a long history even before the late-Victorian reorganisation created the metropolitan boroughs. For centuries, there had been a separation between the different forms of power exercised at the far ends of the Strand: the mercantile strength of the City in the east, and the Church and the Crown established in the west at Westminster.

This separation of economic and state power has affected London and its development ever since. Westminster is home to the UK capital city's activities, many of its company headquarters, national museums, theatres and the country's leading retail centre. The West End, an aspirational and glamorous term, is substantially within Westminster. Camden, which is responsible for the West End at Covent Garden and Fitzrovia, has a number of the same characteristics, but on a smaller scale.

One of the City of Westminster's early actions was to commission contemporary street signs for the new borough. They were designed using a unique typeface by Misha Black, a Russian-born architect and an academic at the Royal College of Art. Black was the designer of the 1967 Victoria line trains, the famous orange, yellow, brown and black 'moquette' fabric for the Tube and bus seats, the decorative panels at Baker Street station, and a number of iconic British Rail locomotives.[366] The Westminster street signs have become as recognisable as red buses, black taxis and the Underground roundel as signifiers of London, suggesting they are a true design classic. Other boroughs, notably Hackney and Southwark, have subsequently developed street signs that echo Westminster's.

---

366 *Anthony Powell Society Newsletter*, Issue 49, winter 2012, http://www.anthonypowell.org.uk/
    reflib/nl49.pdf, (accessed 14 September 2015)

The year 1965 saw the flowering of 'Swinging London'. Carnaby Street in west Soho had seen boutiques emerge since John Stephen moved there in the late 1950s. Other fashion retailers, including Warren Gold (who ran the Lord John boutique) and Irvine Sellar (who developed the unisex shop Mates), added to the lustre of the area. Sellar later became a property developer, responsible for the Shard in Southwark. By the mid-1960s, Carnaby Street was a byword for dazzling and trendy gear, and 1965 was probably the final year of the ascent of the original version of the street before it became more of the tourist attraction it is today.[367]

In 1967, the Beatles' Apple Boutique (not to be confused with today's Apple stores) was opened at 94 Baker Street. The boutique had a huge psychedelic mural painted across the front, for which Westminster council had refused planning permission. It subsequently required the building to be repainted in its original colour. The store was a commercial failure and closed in 1968.[368] Both Paul McCartney and Ringo Starr were married at Marylebone Town Hall, a location of celebrity weddings over many years.[369]

Economic change in London meant the new council inherited a number of major central London planning issues. Piccadilly Circus had been the subject of Ministry of Transport and LCC efforts to redevelop it with tower blocks and elevated walkways, though the project had been halted by public protest.[370] Westminster's subsequent modest remodelling of the area, involving the Shaftesbury Memorial Fountain (Eros) being moved slightly south from an island to a new peninsular, was widely seen as superior to the LCC's proposals.

Covent Garden Market was also under threat. Operating a wholesale fruit and vegetable market in heavily congested central London was increasingly

367 Shawn Levy, *Ready, Steady, Go!*, London: Fourth Estate, 2003, pages 224–5

368 Ibid., pages 304–8

369 'The Beatles, Oasis and Hollywood A-listers – welcome to the UK's coolest register office', *Daily Mirror*, 6 September 2006

370 Simon Jenkins, *Landlords to London: The Story of a Capital and its Growth*, London: Constable, 1975, page 223

impractical, so it was officially proposed to move the market to Nine Elms in Vauxhall. During the late 1960s, the GLC planned a comprehensive redevelopment of Covent Garden, but the publication of such plans kindled the opposition of the Covent Garden Community Association. In response, Environment Secretary Geoffrey Rippon listed over 100 properties in the area, effectively sabotaging any major change.[371] As at Piccadilly Circus, London was spared a bleak, modernist solution to an historic piece of city. Westminster's City Hall at Victoria Street was a speculative sub-Manhattan office building, acquired by the post-1965 council. During the 2010s, the Victoria area near City Hall has been redeveloped and remodelled by developers Land Securities.[372]

The 1965 council inherited large social housing estates in Pimlico and Paddington, while setting out to develop new ones in Lisson Green, Queen's Park and on Vauxhall Bridge Road. The modernist Churchill Gardens estate in south Pimlico was already completed by 1965, but another large development was undertaken at Lillington Gardens by the predecessor and new City of Westminster councils between 1961 and 1971. It avoided high-rise buildings and made extensive use of brick rather than concrete, in a style dubbed the 'new vernacular'.[373] Lillington Gardens was a signal that the slabs-and-concrete era was coming to an end and that more accessible architecture was making a comeback. The estate and its surrounds are now part of a conservation area, further evidence of its success.[374]

The Lisson Green estate, north of Marylebone station, was designed in the 1960s and built between 1970 and 1975. Lisson Green consisted of 1,500 flats in twenty-three medium-rise blocks, all of which were originally linked by elevated walkways of the kind loved by architects inspired by Le Corbusier. The walkways were described as 'an almost uninterrupted run of three-quarters of a

---

371 Ibid., page 257

372 'Land Securities in £655m central London development', *Evening Standard*, 19 January 2010

373 Edward Jones and Christopher Woodward, *A Guide to the Architecture of London*, London: Weidenfeld & Nicolson, 1983, page 323

374 City of Westminster, *49 Conservation Area Audit*, Lillington and Longmoor Gardens, 2012

mile from one end of the estate to the other'.[375] Crime and graffiti led the estate to become associated with poor management and antisocial behaviour,[376] but the removal of the walkways and the introduction of entry phones and guard patrols produced a substantive reduction in these problems. Lisson Green was regenerated in the decade ending 2007, including the demolition and replacement of some of the original blocks.

Lisson Green is close to the Church Street ward, which has long been one of the most deprived in London. Despite Westminster's reputation as a rich borough, wards to the north of the Westway are among the most deprived and socially complex in the city. Like North Kensington, the pre-1965 borough of Paddington was poor: when the new boroughs were created in 1965, the north of Westminster still included tenements and suffered from Rachmanism. Peter Rachman had an office at the corner of Westbourne Park and Monmouth Street and probably acquired his first property to let at 32 St Stephen's Gardens in a street that is today gentrified.[377]

Near Westbourne Park the new city council located the Brunel estate, which consisted of six-storey blocks, lower-rise houses and plenty of open green space. The development was built in such a way as to 'turn its back' to surrounding streets, a model also seen at Holcroft Court in Fitzrovia. Internally, the development was of reasonable quality, but it did not link effectively to its neighbourhood.

In Queen's Park, the Mozart estate was constructed. It consisted of forty buildings of two to six storeys, faced with red brick, whose design won an award in 1973. The nearby Lydford estate, consisting of three-storey buildings, received a similar award in 1977. East of these estates was the Elgin estate, which included the 21-storey Hermes and Chantry tower blocks, built

---

375 Barry Poyner, *Lessons from Lisson Green: An Evaluation of Walkway Demolition on a British Housing Estate*, London: Poyner Research Consultancy, 1986

376 Ibid.

377 T. F. T. Baker, Diane K. Bolton and Patricia E. C. Croot, 'Paddington: Westbourne Green', in *A History of the County of Middlesex: Volume 9, Hampstead, Paddington*, C. R. Elrington (eds), London: British History, 1989, pages 198–204, http://www.british-history.ac.uk/vch/middx/vol9/pp198-204 (accessed 9 September 2015)

of storey-high, lightweight glass-reinforced plastic panels, with distinctive round-cornered windows.[378] None of these estates wore well, and all have required substantial regeneration since their construction.

The latter blocks took centre stage in the 'homes for votes' scandal that engulfed Westminster during the 1990s. A separate scandal emerged from the sale of three municipal cemeteries. Shirley Porter, the Westminster leader at the time, was a high-profile figure who wanted to bring business principles to local government. She was leader of the council at the same time Margaret Thatcher was Prime Minister, and the two women were seen as strong-willed and decisive bringers of change. 'She was to local government what Mrs Thatcher was to national government ... She displayed a mixture of right-of-centre radicalism with metropolitan populism.'[379] Porter launched the Westminster initiative, which was designed to improve the quality and cleanliness of the streets. She created the first 'one-stop shop', where members of the public could access all council services in a single place. This latter innovation has been widely copied by other councils.

In 1987, Westminster sold three cemeteries, in Hanwell, Mill Hill and East Finchley, which had been used by the former metropolitan boroughs of Westminster, Paddington and Marylebone respectively. They were disposed of for a nominal sum to transfer the cost of annual maintenance to private owners who were required to maintain them. But the contract was written in such a way as to allow the land to be re-sold to other owners, who would not be contractually required to keep up the maintenance.[380] The cemeteries were re-sold by the new owners at a substantial profit.

Relatives found that the cemeteries became overgrown and that graves were vandalised. There was a public outcry that led to the case being referred to the local government ombudsman, which ordered the council to buy back

---

378 Ibid., pages 217–21, http://www.british-history.ac.uk/vch/middx/vol9/pp217-221 (accessed 14 September 2015)

379 Ian Mackinnon, 'The Westminster Scandal: council became flagship for Thatcherism – where wealth and poverty formed a volatile and high-profile arena for some radical and sometimes disastrous policies; the borough', *The Independent*, 14 January 1994

380 Andrew Hosken, *Nothing Like a Dame*, London: Granta Books, 2006, page 100

the graveyards.[381] The district auditor ruled that the sales had been unlawful, and the graveyards were re-purchased by the council for £4.5 million.[382]

In 1989, the 'homes for votes' scandal erupted. It was to prove even more damaging to the council than the cemeteries debacle. Following the 1986 borough elections, when the Conservatives' majority on Westminster was cut to four, a policy of 'building stable communities' was instituted in an attempt to ensure the erosion of Conservative support would be reversed. The policy involved selling off council housing as it became vacant. But the sell-offs were concentrated in particular wards and, as a consequence, homeless families were increasingly housed in poor areas, notably in the Chantry and Hermes tower blocks in the Harrow Road ward, which Labour held with a large majority.

Labour councillors and other campaigners referred the policy to the district auditor, John Magill, in 1989. After a long investigation, Magill concluded that both the decision to increase the number of designated sales and the selection of the properties designated for sale were influenced by 'irrelevant considerations', namely the electoral advantage of the majority party. The auditor determined the 'building stable communities' policy to have been unlawful. Dame Shirley Porter and other councillors and officers were then surcharged for the resources deemed to have been lost. After a further set of legal cases in the High Court, Court of Appeal and the House of Lords, the council agreed to accept £12.3 million from Porter as the maximum of the surcharge amount that was likely to be paid.[383]

It took Westminster years to escape the fallout from the cemeteries and 'homes for votes' scandals. Two of the leaders who came after Shirley Porter

---

381 Paul Dimoldenberg, *The Westminster Whistleblowers: Shirley Porter, Homes for Votes and Scandal in Britain's Rottenest Borough*, London: Politico's, page 27

382 Ian Mackinnon, 'The Westminster Scandal: council became flagship for Thatcherism – where wealth and poverty formed a volatile and high-profile arena for some radical and sometimes disastrous policies; the borough', *The Independent*, 14 January 1994

383 BBC, 'Porter pays £12m to Westminster', 5 July 2004, http://news.bbc.co.uk/1/hi/uk_politics/3867387.stm (accessed 15 September 2015)

– Simon Milton and Colin Barrow – apologised for what happened.[384] Labour, led for many years by Paul Dimoldenberg and throughout this period of scandal, used the Conservatives' past housing policies as part of its weaponry ever since. As the years have passed and council membership has changed, normality has been restored. Simon Milton, who substantially re-cast Westminster's approach while leader, went on to be chief of staff and deputy to Greater London Mayor Boris Johnson. Planning chair Robert Davis has, since 2001, been important in shaping the council's built environment.

In 2012, leader Philippa Roe initiated the West End Commission to review and make proposals to improve the quality of the traditional West End of London. The commission was chaired by Sir Howard Bernstein, chief executive of Manchester City Council. It made a number of proposals about the operation and governance of the area, including a suggestion that a 'new leadership and governance model is required … It is also about winning the argument for greater devolution for London as a whole.'[385] Following the commission's report, Westminster set up the West End Partnership, which, recognising the West End is partly in Camden, included one of its neighbour's senior councillors among its members.

For the whole of the council's fifty years, Westminster has managed Soho, London's historic nightlife zone. What has been variously seen as a cosmopolitan or bohemian area has required substantial management by Westminster. Conflicts between residents and nightlife are inevitable in crowded city centres. The council has prioritised keeping Soho clean and safe, leading to accusations of 'social cleansing'.[386] The reality is that the growth of '24-hour London' has made life in the city centre more noisy. Moreover, restrictions on development have driven up property costs, changing Soho in ways that reduce the space available for classic nightlife activities.

---

384 Mira Bar Hillel, 'Westminster chief: we're sorry for Dame Shirley and "homes for votes"', *Evening Standard*, 27 November 2009

385 West End Commission, *West End Commission Final Report*, April 2013, page 4

386 Chris Michael, 'Rupert Everett: We've lost our London – and Soho is the last victim', *The Guardian*, 28 April 2014

Public pressure has demanded police and council action against some forms of behaviour. A leading commentator on Soho and London's counter-culture, Barry Miles, believes that 'now, more than a location, the [counter-cultural] underground is a state of mind', an observation which may point to a 'virtual' (and less visceral) future for Soho.[387]

At the other end of the borough, the government of Westminster, at least in Queen's Park, changed in 2014, with the election of London's first contemporary parish council. Eric Pickles, the then Communities Secretary, described parishes as 'localism's magic wand'.[388]

Westminster has been a starting point for a number of national politicians. MPs such as Greg Clark, Nick Boles, Karen Buck and Diane Abbott were all councillors at Westminster before being elected to Parliament. The council has, for many years, held local taxation down, and, with Wandsworth, it has often been seen as a 'flagship' council for the Conservatives. From 2011, Westminster became part of the 'tri-borough' initiative (with Kensington & Chelsea and Hammersmith & Fulham) to provide a number of local services jointly.

Westminster is today a more politically relaxed place than in the past. It remains central London's primary guardian and protector against a massive daily onslaught of development, noise and people. It manages services for residents, commuters and tourists. To a significant extent, London will always be judged by what people see in the streets of the City of Westminster and those of its neighbours Camden and the City of London.

---

387 Barry Miles, *London Calling: A Counter-cultural History of London since 1945*, London: Atlantic Books, 2010, page 416

388 James Derounian, 'Queen's Park: home of London's first parish council', *The Guardian*, 2 February 2014

OUTER LONDON

BARKING & DAGENHAM

Barking & Dagenham has a modern history closely shaped by a particular industrial planning decision. In this sense, it has much in common with Croydon (1960s office policy), Hillingdon (the location of London's main airport) and Tower Hamlets (docklands/Canary Wharf), in that a one-off policy decision has profoundly affected the area ever since. It is impossible to understand the borough without reference to the LCC's decision in 1919 to create a large planned settlement at Dagenham, which was supplemented by a major industrial plant. Ford's at Dagenham is a concept still powerfully suggestive of Britain's industrial past, both good and bad. There is even a film and stage musical, *Made in Dagenham*, about it, which rekindled memories of the borough's manufacturing heritage and also of the poor industrial relations which latterly plagued Ford's in Britain.

Made in Dagenham told the story of women who fought for equal pay at Ford, which led to the Equal Pay Act, 1970. Mary Wollstonecraft, author of *A Vindication of the Rights of Women*, had lived in the borough,[389] as did the last surviving Suffragette, Annie Clara Huggett.[390]

The borough was an amalgamation of the former municipal borough of Barking and the municipal borough of Dagenham, both in Essex. As a result of the government's insistence on simple, non-compound, names it was called

---

389 'Mother of feminism who had a Barking childhood', *Barking & Dagenham Post*, 26 May 2009

390 Information provided by London Borough of Barking & Dagenham

simply Barking, though it was extended to Barking & Dagenham in 1980. Barking had been an Essex town for hundreds of years, while Dagenham was chiefly a product of the LCC's contribution to the government's 'homes for heroes' policy after the First World War. Fishing and then industry were the staple economic activities in Barking. The Becontree estate, built, in part, to accommodate Ford's workers, was the largest council housing estate in Britain, with 27,000 homes and a population of 100,000.

Much of the land was compulsorily purchased, requiring the clearing of ancient manor houses, farms and cottages. Eastbury Manor House, a William & Mary structure, is today surrounded by the Becontree estate. Becontree was designed as a cottage garden estate, with homes fitted to high standards. Street layouts included cul-de-sacs known locally as 'banjos' because of their shape. The scale and ambition of the Becontree estate are still impressive. As an early commentator on the project observed:

> If the Becontree estate were situated in the United States, articles and news reels would have been circulated containing references to the speed at which a new town of 120,000 people had been built. The work of the firm of contractors would have been shown as an excellent example of the American business ideal of service to the community. If it had happened in Vienna, the Labour and left Liberal press would have boosted it as an example of what municipal socialism could accomplish ... If it had been built in Russia, Soviet propaganda would have emphasised the planning aspect.[391]

Given the subsequent failure of utopian solutions (particularly in the 1960s and 1970s) to London's housing needs, Becontree and other similar estates, such as the Bellingham and Downham estates in Lewisham, were remarkably successful. Their scale was more human and, in the sense that they used a recognisable housing type, they were less experimental.

---

391 Terence Young, *Becontree and Dagenham: A Report Made for the Pilgrim Trust,* London: The Pilgrim Trust, 1934, page 23

Ford's plant opened in 1931 and largely closed in 2002, though a diesel engine plant remains. In 1920, it was suggested that Dagenham, then a parish of Romford Rural District Council, should be divided between the urban districts of Ilford and Barking, but the proposal was rejected by Essex County Council.[392] If this change had occurred, part of the Becontree estate might today be in Redbridge.

The borough has been profoundly affected by its industrial development and subsequent economic decline. Many of its residents moved downriver from the East End, or from West Ham or East Ham, and were, in many cases, families previously involved with London Docks. There was a strong tradition of leaving school early and going directly into semi-skilled or unskilled employment. There were powerful community ties, inherited from the old East End: the borough probably had the strongest white working-class culture of any in the London area.[393] Before the 1990s, the minority ethnic population of the borough was among the smallest in London.

Another agent of change was the Thatcher government's 'right to buy' policy, which allowed the residents of the Becontree estate and other council-owned housing to purchase their homes from the council. The make-up of the population has changed, particularly as it has become possible for people from elsewhere in London to buy homes. Many minority ethnic residents have moved in because of the reform of housing tenure. Thus, as the result of a housing policy change, the borough has seen a radical change in its population make-up.[394] From having 97 per cent of the borough's population born in the UK in 1971, the figure had dropped to 64 per cent in the 2011 census and, in the Abbey ward, the white British population was just 15.8 per cent.[395] The impact in schools has been even more marked.

---

392 'The borough of Barking', in *A History of the County of Essex: Volume 5*, W. R. Powell (ed.), London: British History, 1966, pages 235–48, http://www.british-history.ac.uk/vch/essex/vol5/pp235-248 (accessed 17 August 2015)

393 Information provided by London Borough of Barking & Dagenham

394 John Harris, 'Safe as Houses', *The Guardian*, 30 September 2008

395 London Borough of Barking & Dagenham, 'Census 2011 Second Release Key Statistics for Wards London Borough of Barking and Dagenham', February 2013, pages 20, 24

This rapid change has had political consequences. The borough has always been won by Labour, even resisting the 1968 wipe-out for the party in London. The council was solid, traditional, and never susceptible to the siren calls of the new left. Indeed, when Labour councils split from Conservative and Liberal Democrat ones during the 1980s to form the Association of London Authorities (ALA), Barking & Dagenham alone remained as a Labour member of the LBA. (It also joined the ALA.) The Conservatives regularly won 15 to 30 per cent of votes, but few seats.[396]

However, the arrival of a rapidly growing minority population during the 1990s and early 2000s led to the emergence of a challenge to Labour and other mainstream parties from the BNP. The party won a seat in a 2004 by-election, and then, in 2006, it won twelve seats on the council, gaining in the Alibon, Goresbrook, Mayesbrook, Eastbury, Parsloes, Valence and Village wards.[397] A seat was also won in neighbouring Redbridge. The BNP claimed, falsely, that Barking & Dagenham's housing stock was being given to people from outside its boundaries, mainly asylum seekers and refugees. The BNP leafleted the electorate suggesting grants of up to £50,000 were being given by nearby boroughs to encourage people to move into Barking & Dagenham, thus helping them to buy the cheapest housing stock.[398]

This advance for the BNP, which had seen the party win councillors in Epping Forest, Stoke-on-Trent and Sandwell, had the effect of galvanising the Labour Party, particularly Barking MP Margaret Hodge, into a massive counter-offensive. The 2010 borough elections coincided with the general election, which provided the BNP leader Nick Griffin with an opportunity to challenge Mrs Hodge for her seat. After what was termed by a Channel 4 documentary 'The Battle for Barking', Hodge easily defeated Griffin. The BNP subsequently lost all its council seats. But the rise of the BNP in Barking & Dagenham and

396 Greater London Authority, *London Borough Council Elections 22 May 2014*, London: GLA, page 1

397 Greater London Authority, *London Borough Council Elections 4 May 2006*, London: GLA, 2006, pages 2–3

398 Steve Boggan, 'Lies, myths and falsehoods: a day in the life of the BNP's stronghold', *The Guardian*, 8 July 2006

elsewhere produced a bout of soul-searching within British politics about the failure of the mainstream political parties any longer to offer much to the remaining white working class.[399] The subsequent success of UKIP, though it did not occur in Barking & Dagenham, has been seen in a similar way.[400]

For most of the life of the borough, the council has had to cope with the consequences of de-industrialisation. The need to re-train the workforce and to generate new employment has been a continuous challenge for Barking & Dagenham. Traditionally, as in many inner-London boroughs, many young people left school early and went straight into work. In the years from the mid-1990s to the mid-2010s, educational attainment has moved from being among the lowest in the country to above the national average. The borough is now at or above the national average on most education indicators, including attendance.[401] The council introduced a school improvement service to strengthen the teaching of maths. OFSTED has recognised the improvement in Barking & Dagenham schools.[402]

The borough is located within the Thames Gateway, which the 1997–2010 Labour government promoted as the largest 'brownfield' area within the southeast of England, stretching downriver through Havering into Essex. Much of the planned development will involve the conversion of former industrial sites to housing land. Key regeneration locations include Barking Riverside, a 200-hectare site that is the largest brownfield site in western Europe and was once occupied by three power stations and a refuse tip. Development is also planned for Dagenham Dock, a 133-hectare site identified by Barking & Dagenham for employment, and promoted as a location for green industries. Smaller developments are to take place in South Dagenham, an 80-hectare site identified for a mix of commercial and residential development, and in

---

399 See, for example, Michael Brown, 'Margaret Hodge is right about the BNP, *The Independent*, 18 April 2006

400 See Robert Ford and Matthew Goodwin, *Revolt on the Right: Explaining Support for the Radical Right in Britain*, London: Routledge, 2014

401 Information provided by London Borough of Barking & Dagenham

402 OFSTED, *Twenty outstanding primary schools: excelling against the odds*, London: OFSTED, 2009, page 78

Barking town centre, seen by the council as offering potential to accommodate a significant number of new homes.[403] The Mayor of London's 'London Plan' envisages Barking Riverside and South Dagenham delivering 15,000 new homes in the coming years.

The council inherited a number of poor modern housing schemes, which have been refurbished or replaced. Tanner Street, Axe Street and the Foyer in Barking were redeveloped in the mid-2000s. Thames View East, constructed more recently, is an award-winning project consisting of 'affordable' homes on the site of the former Thames View estate. The latter consisted of four bleak 1950s slab blocks developed by the former Barking council in the 1950s and early 1960s. The Gascoigne estate, the borough's largest, is being regenerated. Four towers and four smaller blocks have been demolished as part of a development to provide 1,500 new homes. Goresbrook estate, close to the A13, is also being redeveloped. Goresbrook achieved fame during 2010, when it was one of the estates featured in the reality documentary *Tower Block of Commons*. MP Mark Oaten was filmed living there.[404]

In Barking town centre, the William Street Quarter is being built. The council has created its own housing company, Barking & Dagenham Reside, to manage a number of the new developments, such as Thames View East and William Street Quarter. Many of the properties are privately funded and available only to tenants who are in work.[405]

The council has lobbied successive administrations at City Hall for better public transport to and within the large Barking Riverside development zone. Although the area is capable of providing a considerable amount of new housing, it has long suffered from poor transport links. Plans for an extension of the Docklands Light Railway were scrapped by Boris Johnson, although subsequently TfL has consulted on the possibility of connecting the area to

---

403 London Borough of Barking & Dagenham, *Planning for the future of Barking & Dagenham: Core Strategy*, 2010, pages 11–12

404 Michael Atkins, 'Tower blocks demolition and new homes agreed for Dagenham', *Barking & Dagenham Post*, 13 February 2013

405 Mike Brooke, 'First tenants move into Barking council's Thames View East – only if they have jobs', *Barking & Dagenham Post*, 20 December 2013

the Gospel-Oak-to-Barking section of the Overground.[406] Barking Riverside is still relatively isolated within London.[407]

Despite Barking & Dagenham's image as a traditional industrial and residential borough, it is home to two remarkable country houses. Eastbury Manor House was opened to the public in the 1990s with support for restoration from the Heritage Lottery Fund (HLF). Valence House, which served as the former Dagenham council's town hall until 1937, was refurbished with help from the HLF, and houses a remarkable collection of Sir Peter Lely's paintings. The borough provided a home for a number of 2012 Olympic training facilities and was the opening ceremony's rehearsal space.

Barking & Dagenham, like Newham, Tower Hamlets, Southwark, Lewisham, Greenwich and Bexley, and, indeed, riverside authorities in Essex and Kent, has spent a significant amount of time during its first fifty years dealing with the long-term consequences of London's industrial past. Starting with only a relatively small middle class, and with much housing built within a short period, the council has faced continuous pressure to manage change, often with limited resources. Only latterly has major privately funded development become a possibility.

The challenge facing the council has been made the greater by the remarkable increase in the borough's immigrant population since 1965. The UK government's approach to immigration and asylum will inevitably have radically different consequences from place to place. Barking & Dagenham, now under a more modern leader, Darren Rodwell, has been one of a number of London councils that have had to manage the consequences of major changes to immigration policy that central government did not announce or plan for.

The Queen visited Barking & Dagenham during the summer of 2015, at the invitation of the leader, to celebrate the fiftieth anniversary of the boroughs. Today, the borough has positioned itself as a growth area of London rather than as two outward-facing Essex towns. The cottage garden estate borough is embracing the metropolis.

---

406   Dave Hill, 'The Osbornomics of Barking Riverside', *The Guardian*, 23 March 2014

407   Tim Burrows, 'No café, no pub, no doctor in London's most isolated suburb', *The Guardian*, 17 August 2015

BARNET

B arnet was formed by the amalgamation of three Middlesex councils, Hendon, Finchley and Friern Barnet, and two urban districts, East Barnet and Barnet, from Hertfordshire. Unusually, it combined five predecessor authorities from two counties. Suggested names included Northgate or Northern Heights, though Sir Keith Joseph (the minister) chose the more down-to-earth Barnet.

Like Croydon and Bromley, Barnet covers a large area compared with inner-London authorities, stretching from the north of Hampstead Heath to the edge of the green belt, 7 miles away. It today has the largest population of the thirty-two boroughs and is likely to be the first to exceed 400,000.

At its inception in 1965, Barnet had a significant number of industrial jobs. Manufacturing has declined from 16.4 per cent of employment in 1981 to barely 3 per cent by 2011. The numbers of residents working in small companies and in the finance industry have significantly increased. Hendon Aerodrome was functioning in 1965, but later became the site of the RAF Museum, the Graham Park estate and the Peel Centre, a police training college. Latterly, the area has seen the regeneration of Beaufort Park.

Graham Park was jointly developed by the council and the GLC. It consisted of 1,777 homes, a relatively big housing development for an outer borough. Although the low-rise, block-style buildings were not of the type built in many other parts of the city in the 1960s and early 1970s, the development was badly cut off from surrounding areas. A significant concentration of disadvantaged residents was established there over time. More recently, the borough and a housing association have worked to regenerate the estate and build more owner-occupied homes.

Barnet council strongly supported the development by Hammerson of Brent Cross shopping centre, which opened in 1976 and was expanded in 1995.[408] For many years, Brent Cross was the acme of malls, a precedent for

---

408 Peter Jackson, Michael Rowlands and Daniel Miller, *Shopping, Place and Identity*, London: Routledge, 1998, Chapter 2

the Bluewaters and Westfields that opened four decades later. Brent Cross was unusual in that it was built on a previously undeveloped site away from a traditional town centre, though not in a completely new town.[409] The council held onto the freehold, from which it derived a substantial income.[410] The new centre was intended to take the pressure off the West End and not expected to damage local centres. Nevertheless, it was bitterly opposed by traders in Hendon.[411] Although it had a 'concrete island' location, surrounded by graffitied flyovers and traffic jams on the North Circular road, it included 'an impossibly glamorous indoor fountain that drew day-trippers from all over London' and was the first standalone shopping centre in Britain.[412]

It remains successful. But like many shopping malls, it inspired distaste among the intelligentsia. Authors who studied the development of Brent Cross and other retail centres in Britain cited the following tangled assessment from the magazine *New Society* in 1978:

> The massive and featureless rectangles of the Brent Cross Shopping Centre … come as no surprise. They are just as hideous as everything else. But step through the doors and here is prettiness and femininity – just as soulless and just as commercialised as the filth outside, but a veritable perfumed nirvana.[413]

The area around Brent Cross is still being developed. In 2010 and 2014, planning permission was given by the council for a £4 billion regeneration project embracing Brent Cross and Cricklewood railway lands, to include 7,500 homes, 27,000 jobs, a riverside park, a bridge across the North Circular

---

409 Ibid., page 32

410 Ibid., page 34

411 Ibid., page 35

412 Zoe Wood, 'Why developers have stopped building shopping centres', *The Guardian*, 4 May 2012

413 Peter Jackson, Michael Rowlands and Daniel Miller, 'Nirvana with shops', *New Society*, 2 February 1978, cited in *Shopping, Place and Identity*, London: Routledge, 1998, page 48

and a new Thameslink station.[414] The 151-hectare site is defined to the west by the Edgware Road (A5) and the Midland mainline railway line, and to the east by the A41, and it is bisected east to west by the A406 North Circular Road.[415] As a result of having such a large tract of railway land, Barnet has been able to contemplate a far larger scale of development than would be possible in most other boroughs.

The urban environment at the intersection of the North Circular road, the M1 motorway, the A41, the national railway and the Underground near Staples Corner (which was named after a mattress factory) with the Brent Cross Interchange is a classic of the kind used by novelist J. G. Ballard to evoke urban alienation. Originally, it was proposed to build the M1 south to Hyde Park Corner.[416] Indeed, this area gives a sense of how the government's 1960s Ringways policy would have affected London if it had been completed. The Staples Corner interchange was bombed by the Provisional IRA in 1992.[417]

In addition to the mass of road spaghetti, the Barnet/Brent boundary runs down the middle of the A5. At one point, Hendon Way (A41) has crash barriers along the middle of the road, presumably to protect fast-driving vehicles from each other, while on the inside lane there is nothing apart from the pavement, gardens and residents' sitting rooms. Suburban houses often have front gardens a few feet from three-lane (sometimes four-lane) motorway-style roads. Pedestrians are given the option of occasional forbidding metal bridges or enforced separation. Most of this infrastructure overload was not of Barnet's own making, but the council is left with the challenge of delivering improvements to counter noise, pollution and other aspects of the lives of local residents. Barnet has another major intersection at Henlys Corner in East Finchley.

---

414 Myron Jobson, 'Mayor of London approves as £4bn Brent Cross Cricklewood development is given green light', *Brent & Kilburn Times*, 24 July 2014

415 Greater London Authority, *Brent Cross Cricklewood*, planning report PDU/1483/01, 11 February 2009, http://www.london.gov.uk/olc/docs/brent-cross-report.pdf

416 Peter Baldwin, John Porter and Robert Baldwin, *The Motorway Achievement: Visualisation of the British Motorway System: Policy and Administration*, London: Thomas Telford, 2004, page 155

417 Terry Kirby, 'IRA City bombers identified by police', *The Independent*, 15 July 1992

Elsewhere in the borough, road-widening was controversial in the early years. Ernest Marples, transport minister from 1959 to 1964, wanted to create a 'lorry route' from the new M1 to London Docks along the A1 through Hampstead Garden Suburb. Although this original scheme was dropped, a separate one to widen the A1 on Falloden Way did go ahead. A public inquiry was held in 1969. The objectors' case was strengthened by the fact that Barnet had designated the whole of the Garden Suburb a conservation area, though the council itself had no particular objection to the scheme.

The inspector ruled in favour of the widened road. However, Peter Walker, the secretary of state at the new Department of the Environment, rejected the inspector's findings. A further study was ordered. Shortly after, the government decided to appoint Barnet council as agents to carry out short-term improvements to the road, including some widening. The possibility of a tunnel to carry the A1 under the Garden Suburb was considered.[418]

The Bishops Avenue, one of London's most expensive roads, brings a touch of Hollywood to Barnet. Other parts, such as Burnt Oak, are more restrained. High Barnet and Edgware are well known to many Londoners as endpoints of the Northern line. Given its massive passenger numbers and the long intervals that can occur on the line, these place names would have a good claim to be among the most observed (and wished-for) in London.

In 1965, Friern Barnet Hospital was still in use. It had long been the area's leading psychiatric institution, whose forbidding reputation was known across London. It closed, as part of the government's 'care in the community' policy, in 1993, and has subsequently been turned into flats. Indeed, the northern reaches of Barnet have continued to offer some of London's most desired and expensive properties, as at Totteridge. These areas have seen far less change since 1965 than the Cricklewood/Brent Cross area in the south of the borough.

Golders Green is the heart of London's large Jewish population. In the 2011 census, Barnet was home to 54,000 Jews, about a fifth of the UK total.

---

418 Michael F. Collins and Timothy M. Pharoah, *Transport Organisation in a Great City: The Case of London*, London: George Allen & Unwin, 1974, pages 355–66

The number had increased by 6,000 since 2001.[419] Britain's first 'eruv', a
designated zone within which Jewish residents can carry certain objects outside their own homes on the Sabbath, was set up there in 2003. Other eruvs
have followed. London's Jews have, since the late nineteenth century, moved
from poverty in Tower Hamlets to relatively well-off outer boroughs such as
Redbridge and then Barnet. The borough is also home to London's largest
Chinese population,[420] which started life in the East End at Limehouse. Barnet
today is an affluent cosmopolitan area.

The council has been Conservative-controlled for all but eight of its fifty
years. Towards the end of the eighteen years of Tory government after 1979,
a minority Labour administration ran the council, though the political divi-
sions in Barnet have been small by comparison with many other boroughs.
As in Croydon, the differences between the major parties have been limited
by a broadly common approach to development and government, even during the politically charged 1980s.

In 2009, Barnet launched what became known as the 'budget airline'
approach to public services, and was, from time to time, referred to as the
'EasyCouncil' model. The authority was quoted as intending to make sav-
ings of up to £15 million a year by outsourcing services and reducing the
size of its directly employed workforce. Private sector organisations and
charities were to be contracted to deliver services such as streets, parking,
planning, environmental provision, residential care, housing, refuse and
recycling. It was suggested people might pay extra for a premium service,
as with budget airlines.[421] The council outsourced services to Capita in a
£320 million contract. A legal challenge launched to stop the policy failed
and it was implemented.[422]

---

419 Simon Rocker, 'Census 2011: The Jewish breakdown', *Jewish Chronicle*, 13 December 2012

420 'Welcome to Barnet: A Place of Contrasts', Barnet Clinical Commissioning Group, 2012

421 Robert Booth, 'Tory-controlled borough of Barnet adopts budget airline model',
     The Guardian, 27 August 2009

422 Sarah Marsh, 'Barnet outsourcing scheme to go ahead – local government news round-up',
     The Guardian, 10 August 2013

The council became well known as a result of the Barnet 'graph of doom', created by Andrew Travers, finance director at the borough in 2011. A PowerPoint slide showed how, within a decade or so, social services spending would consume 100 per cent of the council's budget. Chief executive Nick Walkley explained to *The Guardian*:

> In five to seven years, we get to the point where it starts to restrict our ability to do anything very much else. Over a twenty-year period, unless there was really radical corrective action, adult social care and children's services would need to take up the totality of our existing budget.[423]

Other local authorities and services subsequently adopted similar ways to describe their financial future.

Reginald Maudling, a Conservative grandee of the Macmillan/Heath era, was MP for Chipping Barnet from 1959 to 1979. His political career ended unfortunately because of his business links to John Poulson, against whom allegations of corruption had been made. There was no evidence of wrongdoing by Maudling, but he was Home Secretary at the time, with responsibility for the Metropolitan Police.[424]

The architect of the politics of the 1980s, Margaret Thatcher, was MP for Finchley from 1959 to 1992. She may have been a controversial figure nationally, but she was seen as a good constituency representative, with a remarkable memory for people and a willingness to engage opponents in debate. While she was Prime Minister, she was identified, fairly or otherwise, with 'suburban values' which Finchley, in some ways, came to embody. Other London boroughs, notably Lambeth under Ted Knight, saw Thatcher (said venomously) as the enemy in the struggle-to-the-death between left and right that

---

423 David Brindle, 'Graph of Doom: a bleak future for social care services', *The Guardian*, 15 May 2012

424 Samuel Berlinski, Torun Dewan, Keith Dowding, *Accounting for Ministers: Scandal and Survival in British Government 1945–2007*, Cambridge: Cambridge University Press, 2012, page 142

were often fought out in London town halls. Barnet itself was immune from this ideological war.

Mrs Thatcher was often seen as antipathetic to local government in general, not just left-wing, Labour-controlled councils. Interviewed by the *Finchley Times* in 1988, she discussed the system of local government that existed before the 1965 reforms:

> The whole organisation of local government was different because we had our Finchley council and our Friern Barnet council, and we were very proud of both. Friern Barnet especially was a very proud place, full of local spirit. They were smaller areas than today, so we knew all the councillors and aldermen very well. It was much more intimate. If we had a housing problem we knew the housing manager and we'd ring him up. If we had an education problem, we knew the education chief officer so we'd speak to him. These people were leaders of the community in a much more pre-eminent way than they are today. Those memories are very vivid.[425]

There is a clear implication here: smaller is best. Such opinions help explain her view that local government was inefficient and required reform.[426] Against this backdrop, it is ironic that Barnet has not only become the biggest borough in population, but also one that has pioneered radical outsourcing to drive down costs.

Despite the roadbuilding in parts of Barnet, the borough is remarkably green, and borders on open countryside. Like many outer boroughs, Barnet has developed from being a traditional suburb to being one of the most multinational places in Britain. It has some of London's best schools and remains an attractive destination for families.

---

425 Robin Stacey, citing 'My Finchley past and present ... by PM Margaret Thatcher, first lady of Barnet', in *Finchley Times*, 19 February 1988, *Financial Times*, 25 February 1988, accessed from Margaret Thatcher Foundation, http://www.margaretthatcher.org/document/107176

426 For an exposition of her views and influence see Simon Jenkins, *Thatcher and Sons*, London: Penguin Books, 2006

BEXLEY

Bexley was formed from the former municipal boroughs of Bexley and Erith, the urban district of Crayford, and part of Chislehurst & Sidcup.[427] All had been in Kent. The borough brought together councils that bordered the Thames to the north, inner London to the west and rural Kent to the east. It took its name from Bexley village, also known as 'Old Bexley', in the south of the borough.

The area had rapidly developed during the inter-war years, and much of its housing consists of semi-detached homes of the kind built extensively in outer London between 1918 and 1939. Bexleyheath had been a small market gardening community and was turned into the retail heart of the new borough. Blackfen in Sidcup includes a crescent of shops with Tudor-style gables and a municipal garden. Northumberland Heath in Erith was an area with large numbers of smaller retail outlets, which, as in many parts of London, suffered competition from the larger shops and centres that were gaining strength at the time the boroughs were being created.[428]

A significant proportion of Bexley's population had moved outwards from overcrowded inner south-east London and brought with them the traditional working-class Londoner's aspiration for improvement. The authority and its people still have cultural links to the core of the city, as well as good links to the Medway towns.

The council, in common with the other thirty-one boroughs created in 1965, was born in the middle of a political and social revolution. Faced with a new Labour government's requirement that secondary schools be reorganised along comprehensive lines, Bexley's Labour-controlled council was one of a small number that pressed ahead urgently with comprehensive reorganisation.[429]

---

427 Gerald Rhodes, *The Government of London: The Struggle for Reform*, London: Weidenfeld & Nicolson, 1970, page 257

428 For a wider analysis see London Borough of Bexley, *Bexley's Local Distinctiveness: A Characterisation Study of the London Borough of Bexley*, May 2011

429 Gerald Rhodes (ed.), *The New Government of London*, London: Weidenfeld & Nicolson, 1972, page 176

However, when the Conservatives won in 1968, they withdrew Labour's proposals to reorganise.[430] The selective education system still exists today and continues both to draw young families to the borough and to act as a magnet for children from the surrounding areas. Prime Minister Tony Blair opened the country's first academy school at Thamesmead in the borough in 2002.[431]

Social change was embraced more cautiously. In Bexley's pamphlet 'Your Council', published in 1967, it was announced:

> The council has given permission for the Corinthian Restaurant to be used on Friday nights by a discotheque club. There will be entertainment with a difference for teenagers and a feature is the psychedelic lighting, which changes colour on a musical impulse.[432]

Urban design was changing. Immediately before the borough's creation, in 1964, the former council decided to improve Erith. The Erith Redevelopment Plan involved the demolition of almost the whole of the traditional shopping area and its replacement by a modern centre, incorporating both retail and residential development. The architect of the new development and the nearby Riverside Swimming Centre was Richard Seifert, who was responsible for Centre Point and Space House in central London. Demolition started in 1966, with Mitchell's, the area's oldest department store, being the first to be knocked down. The project was dogged by problems, public opposition and, when completed, high rents. Many shops remained vacant. In 1996, the council published an Erith Town Centre Strategy to sort out the problems left by the previous development, and to begin to use the riverfront for new development.

The town has retained some of its most important amenities, including its Carnegie Library, the Erith Playhouse and riverside swimming facilities. Recent

---

430 Ibid., page 178

431 Information provided by London Borough of Bexley

432 Ibid.

years have seen a concerted effort to regenerate the area. Aided by a popular new town centre superstore (Morrisons' first southern store), it was followed by a new health, leisure, shopping and housing facilities.

Bexleyheath has prospered since it was decided to make it the borough's key centre. Its shopping area has expanded and a new mall opened. The old Broadway was pedestrianised and new Civic Offices opened in the former headquarters of the Woolwich Building Society.[433] Nearby Crayford has a rich industrial heritage, which included the historic David Evans silk factory and a vast Vickers factory. Today the Vickers site is home to the Tower Retail Park and the new Town Hall development. In the south of the borough, Sidcup has become home to an increasingly successful arts hub. Rose Bruford College and nearby Bird College train professionals for the theatre, and for careers in singing and dancing.[434]

The borough has over 100 parks and green spaces. Danson House, a Grade I-listed Georgian mansion in Bexleyheath, has been restored, while its park has won prizes.[435] Since 1999, retail areas in Bexley have had to compete with the vast Bluewater mall in neighbouring Dartford though, given the rising population of London, the impact of malls on existing town centres in eastern boroughs has probably been less challenging than originally feared.

Employment in Bexley has depended heavily on jobs in inner and central London. The railways that allowed the borough to develop in the first place have made it possible for a significant proportion to commute into the City and West End. Local industry has been centred on light manufacturing, back-office services and food, together with services. Recent years have seen the opening of a major new Tesco distribution centre and the start of construction of another by Ocado, set to be among the largest in the UK.[436]

One of the most radical changes to affect Bexley (and its neighbour

---

433 Ibid.

434 Ibid.

435 See London Borough of Bexley, *Bexley's Local Distinctiveness: A Characterisation Study of the London Borough of Bexley*, May 2011

436 Information provided by London Borough of Bexley

Greenwich) since 1965 was the development of Thamesmead by the GLC.[437]
The release by the Ministry of Defence of 1,000 acres of marshland, previously occupied by the Royal Arsenal, allowed a massive urban redevelopment
project. Originally called the Woolwich/Erith project, it envisaged a series of
villages on concrete platforms linked by bridges to keep residents safe from the
threat of flooding. Eventually, the council decided to build a pumping station,
canals and channels to provide a drainage system. Three miles of riverbanks
were raised and strengthened to prevent future flooding.

A competition was held to find a name for the new district. Suggestions
put forward included Waterville, Blumguston and, exotically, New
Wooabbeleri. The pastoral Thamesmead, put forward by Barnehurst resident Anthony Walton, won. Construction started at Abbey Wood in 1967.[438]
The first two stages were built using concrete slabs that were fitted together.
Walkways connected different buildings. It was intended that Thamesmead
would be a self-contained, balanced community, with housing, schools
and shops.

For a time, Thamesmead, in common with a number of British social housing experiments, became infamous for its social problems and deprivation. Its
reputation was not enhanced by Stanley Kubrick's decision to use Thamesmead
as the home of antihero Alex in his film *A Clockwork Orange*.

The architectural critic Jonathan Glancey has written about Thamesmead in
a way that accurately describes many such developments from the early years
of the boroughs:

> One could not say that Thamesmead was in any way cynical, a form
> of middle-class or local-government manipulation of the lives of those
> way down the pecking order. It wasn't. Nor was it cheap. A fortune was
> spent in the first five years (1965–70). Local government was a costly
> business in the '60s because there was a consensus that new housing,

---

437 See Greater London Council, *Thamesmead: A Riverside Development*, London; GLC, 1967

438 Information provided by London Borough of Bexley

schools, hospitals, parks and other amenities were needed and that these could not, should not, be left in the hands of the private sector. Certainly, the private sector would never attempt to build a housing development as complex and costly as Thamesmead. It was true, though, that the concrete flats leaked and were prone to condensation, and the smell of the sewage works on summer days was 'strong enough to peel paint at fifty paces', according to one local.[439]

Thamesmead is today a better place. When the GLC was abolished in 1986, the neighbourhood voted to pass responsibility for the estate to a company controlled by residents. It is today owned and run by Peabody, the social landlord.[440] Peabody is responsible not only for housing, but also for commercial areas, open spaces, recreation and industrial estates. The population of Thamesmead Town is now 45,000. Crossrail, which, from 2018, has a station at Abbey Wood, will allow passengers to travel to Tottenham Court Road in just twenty-three minutes. Off the back of Crossrail, 20,000 new homes are planned for north Bexley.[441]

Race relations were poor in parts of south-east London (though not particularly in Bexley) from the 1970s onwards.[442] The decision of the BNP to locate its headquarters in Welling in 1990 came about, in part, because of historic links between this part of the borough and inner south-east London. In April 1993, Stephen Lawrence, a black teenager, was killed in a racially motivated attack while he waited for a bus in Well Hall Road in neighbouring Eltham (within Greenwich). Later that year, there was a major demonstration outside the BNP's office.[443] Bexley council managed, after a

439 Jonathan Glancey, 'Welcome to *Clockwork Orange* country', *The Guardian*, 13 March 2000

440 Peabody, *About Thamesmead*, London: Peabody, 2015, http://www.peabody.org.uk/ thamesmead/about-thamesmead (accessed 15 September 2015)

441 Information provided by London Borough of Bexley

442 Clive Bloom, *Violent London: 2000 Years of Riots, Rebels and Revolts*, London: Palgrave, 2010, pages 371–6

443 BBC News, 'Shut down the BNP demo', 2012, https://www.youtube.com/ watch?v=KxWrK22WNik (accessed 14 May 2015)

struggle, to close the BNP headquarters in 1995, on the basis of a breach of planning law.[444]

The BNP did not stand in any wards in the 1994 local elections in Bexley, so it is hard to see the location of the party's headquarters as having encouraged people to support it locally. A few candidates stood in 1998, but won derisory votes.[445] In 2002, the party managed to come second in all three seats in the North End ward, but, overall, the results were again poor.[446] Little further progress was made in 2006, though in 2009 the BNP came within eight votes of winning a by-election in East Wickham.[447] In 2010, the BNP made a stronger showing in a number of wards, before falling back in 2014. Latterly, UKIP has emerged as a more mainstream alternative for voters previously tempted by the BNP: in 2014, UKIP won 23.4 per cent of the vote and three council seats. Indeed, in the parallel European elections, UKIP had the highest vote share of any party.[448]

The council has been won by both the Conservatives and Labour since 1964. The first elections put Labour in power, followed by an all-Conservative council in 1968. Subsequently, the borough has been more Conservative than Labour-controlled. Over fifty years, the politics of the borough has seen a swing from Labour to the Conservatives. Notwithstanding the BNP, UKIP and others, Bexley has broadly remained a traditional Conservative–Labour battleground. Under leader Theresa O'Neill, Conservative dominance has grown and the borough has, over time, shifted towards the Tories.

For many years, the parliamentary constituency of Edward Heath was in Bexley. He was Conservative Party leader from 1965 to 1975, Prime Minister from 1970 to 1974, and took Britain into the common market (now the

---

444 'Inquiry controversy as Bexley tries to shut BNP premises', *Local Government Chronicle*, 18 April 1995

445 London Research Centre, *London Borough Council Elections 7 May 1998*, London: LRC, 1998, page 12

446 Greater London Authority, *London Borough Council Elections 2 May 2002*, London: GLA, 2002, page 13

447 Greater London Authority, *London Borough Council Elections 6 May 2010*, London: GLA, 2010, page 19

448 Greater London Authority, *London Borough Council Elections 22 May 2014*, London: GLA, 2014, page ii

European Union). Sir Edward, as he became, represented a constituency in the borough from 1950 to 2001.

Bexley has one of the highest rates of home ownership in London, 82 per cent in 2011. It has built relatively few homes since 2000.[449] This situation is likely to change as London's economic growth reaches the traditional riverside industrial areas to the east of London. For now, the borough has generally low levels of personal income and wealth compared with the rest of the capital. These income and wealth levels are reflected in house prices, which are among the lowest in London. But there are also areas of high quality homes in the southern part of the borough. Much of Bexley's housing was built between the two world wars and reflects the building styles of the period, with mostly detached and semi-detached two-storey homes. Densities are generally low, with large plots.[450]

Bexley contains a significant proportion of south-east London's industrial and warehousing floor-space stock. The amount of industrial land has been declining, although warehousing space has increased by around 50 per cent since 2000. Office accommodation has been increasing, although the overall quantity is low compared with other boroughs. Less than half of Bexley's working residents are employed in the borough.[451]

The borough is located in the heart of the Thames Gateway regeneration area, and includes two designated London Plan 'opportunity areas' that cover large parts of the north of the borough at Bexley Riverside and Thamesmead. These areas are planned by the council to be the main locations for much future housing and employment growth.[452] A new river crossing at Belvedere is intended to be a further spur to growth.

---

449 Greater London Authority, *Housing in London 2014: the evidence base for the Mayor's Housing Strategy*, London: GLA, 2014, page 15, https://www.london.gov.uk/sites/default/files/Housing%20in%20London%202014%20-%20Final_1_0.pdf (accessed 20 May 2015)

450 London Borough of Bexley, *Bexley's Local Distinctiveness: A Characterisation Study of the London Borough of Bexley*, 2011, page 18, http://www.bexley.gov.uk/CHttpHandler.ashx?id=8889&p=0 (accessed 21 May 2015)

451 Ibid., page 16

452 Ibid., page 14

Bexley has become more ethnically diverse since 1965. In 2011, 23 per cent of the population was non-white British, higher than the national average. Wards in the north of the borough are the most diverse. Nevertheless, 77 per cent of the population was white British at the time of the 2011 census, compared with a London average of 45 per cent.

Growth prospects for Bexley are now substantial, with two road and possibly one rail river crossings possible. Bexley has come full circle since its inter-war expansion, providing homes for the aspirant masses, though now in a denser and more intensified form.

BRENT

Brent, though an outer borough, reaches into central London. The tip of the former borough of Willesden, which touches Shirland Road W9, is less than 2 miles from Marble Arch. Like its cousins Haringey and Newham, Brent has been synonymous with the dramatic social and demographic change that has affected London in the fifty years since the boroughs were created.

The original fusion of Conservative, low-rated Wembley with Labour-controlled and high-rated Willesden caused difficulties, including in choosing a name. Brent was selected based on the fact it was the river that *divided* the two predecessor boroughs.[453] Indeed, in the early 1980s (at a time of polarised national politics) some of the Conservatives in Wembley called for their part of the borough to secede from Brent.

The borough's position in the hinterland between inner and outer London has created major housing pressures and a need to build (and then rebuild) improved housing. Prefabricated houses for residents who had been made homeless by wartime bombing remained on Harlesden Road until the late

---

453 Grange Museum of Community History and Brent Archive, *Places in Brent – Church End and the Parish of Willesden*, http://www.brent.gov.uk/media/387240/ChurchEnd.pdf (accessed 2 February 2015)

1960s, and redevelopment, including the construction of new flats, did not occur in some areas until the 1970s.[454]

In the years immediately after 1965, Brent witnessed the development of one of London's most intrusive urban road schemes since the construction of the Westway and the Hammersmith Flyover. The North Circular Road at Neasden had been a notorious bottleneck and, despite residents' opposition, the Ministry of Transport enlarged the North Circular and diverted traffic on Neasden Lane into an underpass. This project, which involved the demolition of a substantial number of homes, was finished in 1973. The project reduced traffic problems at the North Circular/Neasden Lane junction, but Neasden Shopping Centre, which had already been chopped in half by the North Circular, was then also separated from its southern hinterland. The opening of a major shopping mall at Brent Cross further undermined Neasden's position.

Immigration is today recognised as a major element in Brent's demography and politics. After the Second World War, many Irish nationals moved to Cricklewood, partly as people left overcrowded Kilburn and partly because of high unemployment in Ireland: Labour shortages in England, which had attracted Caribbean and Asian immigrants, also encouraged people to come to London from rural parts of the Republic of Ireland. Many Irish women became nurses, domestic staff, worked for London Transport, or took jobs in the many light industrial companies that flourished in north-west London after 1945. Irish men often worked in construction, rebuilding war-damaged properties and constructing the many modern housing estates built in the 1950s, 1960s and 1970s.

However, Britain's industrial decline hit areas such as Brent, Ealing and Harrow hard. The shrinkage of south Brent's manufacturing industries, and the growth of out-of-town shopping centres such as Brent Cross (confusingly, across the border in Barnet), led to a significant rise in long-term unemployment. Dollis Hill was the scene of one of the best-known industrial struggles of the late 1970s, when a dispute involving workers at the Grunwick photographic

---

454 Ibid.

processing company became the focus of a national campaign, initiated by
Brent Trade Union Council, which regularly brought a large picket to the
area, and involvement by mounted police and a number of national politicians. The government set up a judicial inquiry, but, in the end, the workers
did not achieve the union recognition they had sought.[455]

According to Brent Archives, at its peak in the 1960s, Park Royal (a massive industrial park) was employing 45,430 people. But, from the 1960s
onwards, the effects of the UK's de-industrialisation began to be felt in north-
west London, and Park Royal was vulnerable:

> The comparatively narrow roads were unsuitable for large lorries; there
> were few car parks despite growing car ownership and the estate had
> no shops, few pubs and minimal social facilities, encouraging skilled
> workers to find work elsewhere. Thousands of jobs were lost between
> 1977 and 1983 as firms went bust, moved away or 'downsized'. The
> Wall's factory on Atlas Road closed. Park Royal Vehicles, which had
> been at Park Royal since 1919 and was famous for making London
> bus bodies, shifted production to Cumbria in 1980. In 1984, following
> an industrial dispute, the *Radio Times* stopped being printed at Park
> Royal. The Heinz factory survived, but at a cost. In 1964, it employed
> 3,500 people. Thirty years later, it employed only 500. By 1987, Park
> Royal was described as 'depressed'.[456]

A number of attempts were made to reverse this decline by national government, the Greater London authorities and (because Park Royal straddled
borough boundaries) the boroughs of Brent, Ealing and Hammersmith &
Fulham. Park Royal remains an important industrial zone in west London.

---

455 BBC News, '1977: Home Secretary jeered on picket line: On This Day', 27 June 2005,
      http://news.bbc.co.uk/onthisday/hi/dates/stories/june/27/newsid_2520000/2520097.stm
      (accessed 4 February 2015)

456 Grange Museum of Community History and Brent Archive, *Places in Brent – Twyford
      and Park Royal*, http://www.brent.gov.uk/media/387388/Twyford%20Park%20Royal.pdf
      (accessed 4 February 2015)

Today, there are plans, evolved jointly by the boroughs and the Mayor of London, to develop the wider Old Oak Common area. This issue is also discussed in the Hammersmith & Fulham section. Park Royal potentially stands to benefit from these changes and the arrival of Crossrail and HS2 in the area.

Brent was the first authority in the UK to have a non-white majority population. By the time of the 2011 census, 64 per cent of Brent residents were from black and minority ethnic communities.[457] Immigration has had many effects on the borough and its neighbourhoods. For example, in the 1960s and 1970s, a number of Asian people who had fled east Africa came to Kingsbury. Some of the new arrivals almost immediately bought local shops that would otherwise have closed.[458]

Further south in the borough, other Asian immigrants have influenced the development of neighbourhoods:

> In the 1970s, Ealing Road was an unimportant 'secondary parade' facing possible demolition. Then east African Asians, mainly Gujaratis, opened shops along Ealing Road. Some sold sarees, tropical vegetables or sweets, but many set up jewellery shops and began crafting 22-carat gold, sometimes in their own homes. The area became an Asian Hatton Garden. Not only have these changes kept the shopping parade alive, but the presence of open-fronted food shops means that Ealing Road feels more like a pre-war shopping street than do many suburban parades.[459]

Most aspects of the economy and political life of Brent have been changed by immigration, and not only from south Asia. Many other ethnic and religious groups have settled in the borough since 1965. Brent is now home, in Neasden, to what was, for a time, the biggest Hindu temple outside India.

457 London Borough of Brent, *Brent Diversity Profile*, July 2014, https://intelligence.brent.gov. uk/BrentDocuments/Brent%20Diversity%20Profile.pdf (accessed 5 February 2015)

458 Grange Museum of Community History and Brent Archive, *Places in Brent – Kingsbury*, http://www.brent.gov.uk/media/387296/Kingsbury.pdf pdf (accessed 5 February 2015)

459 Grange Museum of Community History and Brent Archive, *Places in Brent – Alperton*, http://www.brent.gov.uk/media/387236/Alperton.pdf pdf (accessed 5 February 2015)

Early on in Brent's life, there was a bitter dispute over the development of Chalkhill in Wembley.[460] A plan had been developed by one of the former councils to build a high-density council estate at Chalkhill to house people moved out of Willesden. Chalkhill House, a seventeenth-century building in Forty Lane, had been demolished in 1963. The suburban houses of the Chalkhill estate were demolished, in some cases following compulsory purchase. The scheme was unpopular with Conservative Wembley councillors and the new Borough of Brent came into existence amid significant political bitterness.

Brent used compulsory purchase powers to buy homes that were barely forty years old.[461] The new estate mostly consisted of a series of eight-storey, white concrete slabs, set at odd angles and linked by elevated and tarmac walkways. There was some more traditional housing at the eastern end of the estate, but the slab blocks resembled the infamous Park Hill estate in Sheffield. People were moved from Stonebridge, prior to a major housing development there, too. The homes were let at relatively high rents and proved hard to fill; as a consequence, the council turned to new immigrants from the West Indies to ensure the flats were fully occupied and, for a time, the estate was a mixed community with better homes than those that had existed previously.[462] Nevertheless, by the 1980s, Chalkhill had gained a bad reputation for crime and drug problems. From 1987 onwards, the walkways between the blocks were closed and door entry systems installed to improve tenants' security.[463] Brent underestimated the maintenance that the high-tech estate needed, a problem made worse by central government cuts.[464]

Like many in London, the estate went from construction to demolition within a remarkably short time:

---

460 Diane K. Bolton, H. P. F. King, Gillian Wyld and D. C. Yaxley, 'A History of the County of Middlesex: Volume 4', *British History Online*, T. F. T. Baker, J. S. Cockburn and R. B. Pugh (eds), http://www.british-history.ac.uk/vch/middx/vol4 (accessed 6 February 2015)

461 London Borough of Brent, 'Chalkhill – 1,000 years of history', page 4, https://brent.gov.uk/media/1717937/Chalkhill_1000%20years%20of%20history.pdf (accessed 6 February 2015)

462 Ibid., pages 5–6

463 Ibid., page 6

464 John Cunningham, 'Estate of flux', *The Guardian*, 5 July 2000

In 1971, Senator Edward Kennedy was impressed on his visit to what was billed as one of Britain's finest housing projects. But, by 1992, local MP Ken Livingstone was commiserating with a harassed resident with these words: "Nobody in their right mind wants to live [there]. It's a riot just waiting to explode."[465] In a tenants' referendum, 88 per cent voted for a change of control from the council to a housing association.[466]

Willesden council had planned the redevelopment of Stonebridge from the late 1950s. More than 2,000 housing units were eventually built, mostly in high-rise buildings. The first of these opened in 1967. Many streets were erased, as were a number of shops. At its inception, Stonebridge was seen as a modern and vastly improved form of housing. Yet, by 1977, the estate was notorious for broken lifts and, even before it was finished, some residents threatened a rent strike. Stonebridge gained a reputation for crack dealing and violent crime. The lifts never worked properly, leaving residents to climb up to seventeen storeys, while walkways provided escape routes from the police.[467] By the 1990s, efforts were being made to improve the estate. In 1994, the estate was taken over by Stonebridge Housing Action Trust,[468] which started the improvement of the area with resources from the Harlesden City Challenge and, later, a Housing Action Trust. However, troubles continued in the early 2000s, with serious gang-related gun and knife crime.[469] Latterly, the area has much improved, with replacement low-rise housing.[470]

---

465 Ibid.

466 Ibid.

467 Helen Pidd and Sandra Laville, 'Gang wars made estate no-go zone for police – until they found a supergrass', *The Guardian*, 15 December 2009

468 Grange Museum of Community History and Brent Archive, *Places in Brent – Stonebridge*, http://www.brent.gov.uk/media/387380/Stonebridge.pdf (accessed 6 February 2015)

469 Helen Pidd and Sandra Laville, 'Gang wars made estate no-go zone for police – until they found a supergrass', *The Guardian*, 15 December 2009

470 'Gun crime: notorious north London housing estate is reborn – exclusive', *Daily Mirror*, 24 July 2009

From its inception, Brent had been divided along Wembley/Willesden lines. Industrial and social change from the 1960s onwards emphasised some of these differences. The population of the borough became increasingly divided between a relatively affluent north/east and a more deprived south. This geographical divide continued to be reflected in political control of Brent, where there was often heated debate and a balance of power that, in part, reflected historical geographies. In 1983, Labour lost control of the council as the result of a single defection. It regained power in 1986, but lost again in 1990 because of a tiny splinter group. Five years later, a single by-election defeat denied control to the Conservatives.

Such historical differences were reinforced during the 1970s and 1980s by changes in national politics, though this impact was by no means limited to Brent. The recession of the early 1980s led to a major increase in unemployment in the borough. Brent's highly marginal political control, combined with the post-1986 Labour administration's emphatic support for radical equal opportunities policies, led to acrimony in the council chamber and highly critical coverage in the national press. In common with boroughs such as Lambeth, Southwark and Haringey, Brent was seen by sections of the press and by Mrs Thatcher's government as being 'loony left'. A number of 'creative accountancy' manoeuvres gained the council notoriety for its financial management. Brent also challenged the government's local authority grant system in the courts.[471]

Brent became a combatant in a brutal culture war between new left radicals and the right-of-centre media. The story of Maureen McGoldrick provides a glimpse into the struggles of the time, and not only as they affected Brent. Ms McGoldrick was head teacher of Sudbury Infants School and was suspended by Brent council in July 1986 for making an allegedly racist remark. The school's governors rejected the allegation, but the council refused to reinstate her. School teachers went on strike in her support, backed by the National Union of Teachers (NUT) and others. Indeed, the NUT won an interim injunction to stop a disciplinary hearing. The High Court ruled in favour of the NUT,

---

471 Martin Loughlin, *Legality and Locality: The Role of Law in Central–Local Relations*, Oxford: Oxford University Press, page 274

but Brent appealed. McGoldrick remained suspended. Kenneth Baker, the Secretary of State for Education, wrote to Brent to ask for their reasons for continuing the suspension. He then sent in inspectors to Brent schools.[472]

This escalation of the case continued through the autumn of 1986, moving further up the court system. In the end, Baker used government powers to direct the council not to proceed with any further action against McGoldrick. Brent complied. This involvement by Baker in Brent was part of a wider move to strengthen Whitehall control over councils, which has continued across England ever since.

A 2005 analysis of Brent and Maureen McGoldrick, by academics broadly sympathetic to the council, accepts she never made the remark that started the conflict.[473] They place the case in the context of Brent's efforts to improve opportunities for black and Asian children and to fight racism. Having said this, to have lined up the school's governors, the NUT, the Conservative minister and even *The Guardian* on the same side against the council suggests Brent had become involved in a totemic fight rather than a rational one.

The McGoldrick affair provides an insight into Brent's troubles at the time. 'Barmy Brent does it again!' was a typical newspaper headline from early 1987.[474] Hackney, Lambeth, Islington and others were in much the same position, but Brent certainly faced some of the most aggressive coverage. Throughout the later 1980s, the council faced a hostile press, with many of its race, gender and women's initiatives attacked by the media. The Conservatives prospered in the local elections in 1990 and 1994 as a result of Labour's problems.

During the 1990s and 2000s Brent, like several other left-wing authorities, moved back towards the political centre. Housing estates, including Chalkhill and Stonebridge, were regenerated. Under recent leaders such as Ann John, Paul Lorber and Muhammed Butt, the regeneration of the borough became a

---

472 For a full description of this controversy, see James Curran, Ivor Gaber and Julian Petley, *Culture Wars: The Media & The British Left*, Edinburgh: Edinburgh University Press, 2005, pages 122–4

473 Ibid., page 123

474 Ibid., page 93

major purpose of the council. Wembley Stadium was demolished and a new one built. The council moved its headquarters alongside the stadium as part of a wider scheme for redevelopment in the area. The wider Wembley area, including the High Road at Wembley Central, is being developed with new shopping, hotels and homes. A French lycée is now located at the old Brent Town Hall.[475] Ealing Road, which is an important centre of specialist south Asian food and fashion, is also being improved.[476]

Ken Livingstone, who led the GLC from 1981 until its abolition in 1986, and was then Mayor of London from 2000 to 2008, has long lived in the borough. He was also MP for Brent East from 1987 to 2000, and has always identified his relatively modest lifestyle with residence in Dollis Hill.

By the mid-2000s, the Audit Commission's comprehensive performance assessment was showing the council 'improving well' and gave it a 'three star' rating.[477] An objective measure of this sort was evidence that the problems of the 1980s had been left far behind. With Wembley developing into one of London's new hubs outside the city centre, today's Brent bears no relation to the strife-torn place of the 1980s.

BROMLEY

The new authority was created from the predecessor municipal boroughs of Beckenham and Bromley, plus the urban district councils of Orpington, Penge and Chislehurst & Sidcup. Before 1965, these authorities were all in Kent, though Penge had been in Surrey before 1889, and in the county

---

475 Lorraine King, 'Independent French school in Wembley to be named after Winston Churchill', *Brent & Kilburn Times*, 24 January 2015

476 London Borough of Brent, *Wembley Calling: A 10 Year Vision for Regeneration in Wembley*, 2015, https://brent.gov.uk/media/13023448/Wembley%20Calling%20vision%20document. pdf (accessed 6 February 2015)

477 Audit Commission, 'Brent London Borough Council Comprehensive Performance Assessment (CPA) scorecard 2007', London: Audit Commission, 2007, http://democracy. brent.gov.uk/Data/Performance%20and%20Finance%20Select%20Committee/20080311/ Agenda/Brent%20CPA%20Scorecard%202007.pdf (accessed 6 February 2015)

of London between 1889 and 1900. In 1969, Knockholt transferred from the London Borough of Bromley back into Kent.[478]

Bromley covers a large area compared with the inner boroughs. It is 59 square miles, and thus bigger than the total (52 square miles) of the seven inner boroughs north of the Thames and the City. The eastern part of the borough includes large amounts of farmland and most of its inhabitants see themselves as living in Bromley, Kent, rather than in London. Only a tiny part of the borough is within the London postal districts.

This sense of detachment has led Bromley to adopt policies that have, from time to time, put it at odds with the prevailing orthodoxy, particularly that emanating from County Hall or City Hall. In the early days of Greater London, Bromley was opposed to inner-London residents being re-housed in outer London.

Soon after the new authority was formed, a new shopping development, The Mall, was given the go-ahead in the main Bromley shopping area near Bromley South station, starting a longer-term process of redesigning and redeveloping this part of the borough. In the 1970s, a major investment was made nearby with the opening in 1977 of the new Bromley Central Library and the Churchill Theatre. The latter, built on a hill, has become successful at both putting on its own productions and receiving touring shows.[479]

In 1982, the council moved into the old Bromley Palace and created a modern civic centre (which opened in 1985) to the east of Kentish Way, a new main road bypassing the town centre. This development complemented the growing town centre that housed the library, theatre and shopping centre. This cluster of activities was further strengthened by the opening, in 1991, of The Glades shopping centre, which was substantially larger than The Mall, and of a leisure centre. Between 1965 and the mid-1990s, Bromley oversaw the creation of a modern and planned town centre for the borough.[480]

---

478 London Borough of Bromley, 'History of the Bromley Area', http://www.bromley.gov.uk/
     info/200064/local_history_and_heritage/379/history_of_the_bromley_area/2 (accessed
     17 December 2014)

479 Information provided by London Borough of Bromley

480 Ibid.

Bromley has been Conservative-controlled for all but three years (1998–2001) since it was created, with the form of politics owing more to traditional than to David Cameron-style Conservatism. The Labour-controlled GLC, in office from 1973 to 1977, pursued a policy of transferring families from inner London to outer boroughs and beyond. The GLC's housing committee, chaired by Gladys Dimson, pursued both transfer policies and the construction of new council housing estates in outer London. A number of Conservative-controlled outer boroughs, among them Bromley, strongly opposed this policy. Such opposition was founded on the belief that Bromley was a different kind of place from inner London, though people moving from inner to outer London were more likely to be Labour than Conservative voters.

Bromley subsequently supported Sir Horace Cutler's Conservative administration at County Hall (1977–81) in its policy of transferring control of the GLC's housing stock to the boroughs. This move had been encouraged by the Marshall inquiry,[481] and had the effect of reducing the risk that people would be moved from inner to outer London.

The Labour-controlled GLC's policies in the mid-1970s sowed seeds that were to take root in the early 1980s. The GLC, now back under Labour control and led by Ken Livingstone, introduced a 'fares fair' policy in October 1981. This initiative cut fares on London's Underground and buses with a corresponding increase in local taxation to pay for the revenue loss. Bromley, led by Dennis Barkway, challenged the policy in the courts on the grounds that the borough's ratepayers would have to fund the tax increase even though the Tube did not run there. Having lost in the High Court, the borough won on appeal.[482] However, aspects of the 'fares fair' policy, such as zonal fares and Travelcards, continued, while a more modest fares reduction was subsequently ruled legal. Nevertheless, Bromley had scored a major victory over the GLC.[483]

---

481 Sir Frank Marshall, *The Marshall Inquiry on Greater London: Report to the Greater London Council*, London: GLC, 1978

482 John Carvel, *Citizen Ken*, London: Chatto & Windus, 1984, pages 117–18

483 Hansard, HC Debates, Volume 69, London: TSO, 12 December 1984, Columns 1078–1184

The 1980s was a highly charged time in London politics. Ken Livingstone and his Labour group at County Hall believed they and a number of other Labour councils (including several London boroughs) were locked in an ideological war with Margaret Thatcher's Conservative government. Bromley councillors, emboldened by their success against 'fares fair', subsequently created a lobby to abolish the GLC altogether.

Bromley was not alone in believing the GLC was too big, radical and inefficient. But it was Simon Randall, leader after Barkway (1976–81), who started the campaign to abolish the GLC when he was elected to it in 1981.[484] Working with other Conservative boroughs, the council began to make the case for abolition of the GLC. Bromley, Kensington & Chelsea, Wandsworth and Westminster published a report that estimated they would be £35 million better off if the GLC were abolished.[485] Neighbouring Croydon also supported Bromley.

The 1983 Conservative manifesto included a commitment to scrap the GLC. Now that it had been turned into an apparent victim by the threat of abolition, Livingstone mounted a clever and widely based campaign to save the GLC. However, Mrs Thatcher, with her large majority, was convinced it should go, and, in March 1986, it was abolished.

Bromley was unenthusiastic about the creation of the GLA when Labour took office in 1997. Simon Randall mounted a 'no' campaign to encourage London voters to reject the offer of a mayor and assembly.[486] The title Randall chose for his group – Oh No, Not The New GLC – unashamedly played on fears of the former council's alleged extremism.[487] In the end, all thirty-three London authorities voted in favour of creating the GLA, though Bromley voted 'yes' by the smallest margin (57 per cent to 43 per cent).

The GLA's first year coincided with Croydon Tramlink arriving at

---

484 Ben Pimlott and Nirmala Rao, *Governing London*, Oxford: Oxford University Press, 2002, page 70

485 Hansard, HC Debates, Volume 69, London: TSO, 12 December 1984, Columns 1078–184

486 Ben Pimlott and Nirmala Rao, *Governing London*, Oxford: Oxford University Press, 2002, page 70

487 Ibid.

Beckenham Junction and Elmer's End, thus creating a south London link from Bromley via Croydon to Merton. Subsequently, the London Overground reached Bromley, serving the north-west of the borough, notably Crystal Palace.

Crystal Palace Park, home to the Eiffel Tower-like television transmitters visible across London, and once housing Sir Joseph Paxton's Crystal Palace, has been a long-term challenge for Bromley council. The Crystal Palace moved to the area after the Great Exhibition in Hyde Park, but burned down in 1936. The park is home to the National Sports Centre, includes one of London's premier 50-metre swimming pools, an international-standard athletics track, a modern gym and an outdoor beach sports facility. The sports centre sees itself as the spiritual home of British athletics, though the development of Stratford for the 2012 Olympics has made it less important than before.

Efforts to redevelop Crystal Palace are made more complex by its location at the edge of five boroughs. Although the park is fully in Bromley, it is bordered by Croydon, Lambeth, Southwark and Lewisham. In 2013, it was announced by Bromley and the Mayor of London that the ZhongRong Group, a Chinese investor, was seeking to reconstruct the Crystal Palace, though these negotiations eventually ceased. The council had been less than enthusiastic about the developers' plans.[488]

While Bromley is self-evidently keen to reconstruct and improve Crystal Palace, the council is more generally in favour of avoiding the scale and type of development now common in inner London or, indeed, in neighbouring Croydon. The authority's policy is summarised in this extract from its response to the revision of the Mayor's London Plan. Bromley supports development at relatively low densities by London standards:

> [Bromley] OPPOSE Policy 3.3 [concerning the density of new hous-
> ing developments] on the grounds that 641 dwellings per annum is an

488 BBC News, 'Ultimatum issued to ZhongRong Group over Crystal Palace rebuild plans',
        9 February 2015, http://www.bbc.co.uk/news/uk-england-london-31320833 (accessed
        17 December 2014)

unsustainable target over the plan period that will put green belt, MOL [metropolitan open land] and local character at risk in the future. The council maintains that 470 homes per annum is the sustainable figure for the period of the plan. There is already substantial pressure for additional infrastructure particularly in school places ... If housing completions do not come forward at the rate assumed in the target, there is a risk that developments at densities out of character with local context or on sites in the green belt or MOL will be promoted by developers as a means of meeting the target.[489]

Bromley's policy as expressed by its most recent leader, Steven Carr, is for control over its own development, at a scale it believes is appropriate for the borough. In a document entitled Building a Better Bromley, published in 2009, the local strategic partnership stated: 'Housing policy will reflect the changing needs of our residents, but we must ensure that the very special nature of the borough is preserved.'[490] The challenge, both for the council and the London Mayor, is that London as a whole is facing rapid population growth, with a need for significantly more housing. Bromley's desire to sustain its particular scale, type of development and density has proved a continuing point of disagreement with City Hall for a number of years and is likely to remain so. But the residents of Bromley support this policy of containment.

Of all the boroughs taking office in 1965, it is hard to believe any has viewed the Greater London project with less enthusiasm than Bromley. The council has often been uncomfortable with the efforts of the GLC and GLA to deliver metropolitan policies in localities that often feel they are distant from London. It continues to assert its independence.

---

489 London Borough of Bromley, *Response to Draft Further Alterations to the London Plan (2014) Consultation*, http://www.london.gov.uk/sites/default/files/018LBBromleyResponse.pdf

490 Bromley Local Strategic Partnership, *Building a Better Bromley – 2020 Vision*, March 2009, page 22, file:///H:/BTCAAP019BuildingaBetterBromleySustainableCommunityStrategy.pdf

CROYDON

Croydon was formed from two predecessor councils: the county borough of Croydon and the Coulsdon & Purley urban district. The former had been incorporated as a municipal borough in 1883 and then as a county borough in 1889. It had thus existed as a neighbour to the LCC throughout its life. As a county borough, it could have had its own police force, but agreed to remain part of the Metropolitan Police district, though with a commander based in Croydon. The policies of the LCC were to have a profound effect on Croydon, as will be seen below. Coulsdon & Purley was a more rural area, created during the early twentieth century, and had been within Surrey County Council's jurisdiction, though also part of the Metropolitan Police district.

Like East Ham and West Ham, Croydon had been an all-purpose county borough long before the London government reforms of the 1960s. Croydon's long-used name, pre-existing self-government and, until the 1920s, its separation from London have given it a powerful and historic civic identity. The authority's distinct identity stemmed in part from a connection with the Archbishop of Canterbury: Croydon Palace and later Addington Palace were the summer home of the archbishop.

Croydon was the home of London's aerodrome (though it was partly in Sutton) for many years until Heathrow was designated London Airport in 1946. The final flight from Croydon took place in 1959. But the airport was important in the economic development of the borough, and created the basis for significant expansion in the post-war period.

The Croydon Corporation Act had been passed in 1956, allowing the former council to build new offices in the late 1950s at a time when the Macmillan government was beginning to encourage businesses to move out of central London.[491] The Location of Offices Bureau, set up in 1963, was part of a policy to disperse employment from the city centre. Croydon, which was only

---

491 For a brief description of how offices were dispersed from central London to the suburbs, see David Wilcox with David Richards, *London: The Heartless City*, London: Thames, 1977, pages 39–44

fifteen or twenty minutes from Victoria, Waterloo and London Bridge, proved an ideal site for corporate relocation. The town boomed as an important business centre in the 1960s, with an increasing number of office blocks being built, notably in the area between Wellesley Road and East Croydon station.

The Fairfield Halls, a major arts and cultural institution, opened in 1962. Taberner House, a brutalist tower completed in 1967, became the administrative headquarters of the post-1965 London Borough of Croydon. As part of these 1960s developments, a new underpass, flyover and several multi-storey car parks were built. Croydon town centre also developed as south London's largest retail area, with the Whitgift Centre opening in 1969.[492]

Croydon became the largest office and retail centre in south-east England outside central London. Less encouragingly, the borough's 1960s 'Manhattan skyline' often came to be seen as the archetype of a grey and soulless office centre. Indeed, the borough's success in accommodating many of the offices pushed out of central London by government policy had a long-term consequence. Brutalism, which was popular among architects in the 1960s, produced local buildings such as the Nestlé Tower (1964) and the NLA Tower (1970).

The fact that Croydon had been so successful in developing during the 1960s meant that, by the 1980s and 1990s, its office stock was all becoming obsolete at the same time. Croydon's towers had been built to a standard well below the new offices being constructed in the Thatcherite post-'Big Bang' boom in places such as Canary Wharf and, subsequently, the City of London. According to the council itself: 'Much of the building stock in Croydon town centre is out of date, and the balance between retail, leisure, offices and residential does not fit 21st-century choices made by individuals and companies.'[493]

From the 1990s onwards, some of the unfashionable 1960s office blocks have been demolished. North End was pedestrianised in 1989, while the Clocktower, a new culture and arts centre, opened. East Croydon station,

492 Croydon Online, *The Town of Croydon*, http://www.croydononline.org/history/origins/
     croydon.asp (accessed 10 November 2014)

493 London Borough of Croydon, *Croydon Economic Development Plan, 2013–2018*, 2013,
     page 11

which is one of the most heavily used in London, was revamped in 1992. The Centrale Shopping Centre was developed. TfL's new urban light rail system, Croydon Tramlink, started to operate in May 2000, and is a good example of bipartisan working in the borough: both the Conservatives and Labour supported the scheme. London Overground has been developed from two points in inner London, notably the East London line of the Underground, to West Croydon. West Croydon is now just thirty-seven minutes from Shoreditch High Street by Overground.

Unlike many boroughs, Croydon has lobbied hard to have improved roads in the borough. The A23 runs north–south through the area and, as Purley Way, was originally intended to be a bypass for Croydon. The aerodrome was located here as were industry, housing estates and a power station. As industry declined in the 1970s and 1980s, superstores opened, including a Chinese one with a pagoda-style entrance. Leisure and recreation facilities began to locate here, too.

The development of big stores (notably the development of Valley Park) has led to a growing problem of traffic congestion, especially at weekends, on what is still an important trunk road.[494] The council was broadly supportive of extending the M23 north towards the inner-London part of the government and GLC's system of Ringways. But as the GLC became concerned at public opposition to roadbuilding during the late 1960s and early 1970s, the Ringways policy was dropped. The A23 remained un-widened and the M23 stopped at Hooley.[495]

Croydon, both in its pre- and post-1965 forms, has been more pro-development than many of its neighbours, largely because the borough sees itself as a freestanding town, albeit one within the London conurbation. Evidence of this civic self-belief can be seen by both the current Croydon council and its predecessor Croydon Corporation applying for city status on three occasions: in 1954, 2000 and 2002, though none of these efforts proved successful.

---

494 Croydon Online, *Purley Way and Valley Park*, http://www.croydononline.org/history/places/purleyway.asp (accessed 12 November 2014)

495 Hansard, HC Debates, Volume 793, London: HMSO, 9 December 1969, Columns 62–3

The council has been governed by Conservatives for most of its existence, though Labour has, over time, made headway. After an initial period
of 'no overall control' from 1964 to 1967, the Conservatives ran the council from 1967 to 1994, then again from 2006 to 2014. Labour was in
control from 1994 to 2006 and won in May 2014. But the politics of the borough have remained overwhelmingly moderate, with policy little changed by
differences in party control. The strength of Croydon's civic identity is such
that there has been less room for ideology than in many London boroughs.
Post 2014, Labour council leader Tony Newman was as pro-development
as his Conservative predecessors.

The south of the borough, where London gradually gives way to the green
fields of Surrey, has been far less changed than central Croydon. Coulsdon &
Purley, characterised by larger inter-war semi-detached houses and many free-
standing homes with large gardens, has changed far less than the north of the
borough. The population make-up of areas such as Norwood, Norbury and
Thornton Heath has changed substantially in the fifty years since 1965. The
occupants of the terraced housing common in north Croydon how have similar demographic characteristics to those in neighbouring inner-city Lambeth.
Croydon North is today a safe Labour parliamentary seat, while Croydon
South is rock-solid Conservative. Croydon Central, including the borough's
commercial heart, is highly marginal.

The council is planning a full-scale revamp of the borough's central business district around Park Lane and Wellesley Street, to make it a 'third centre'
for the capital. The Mayor of London has designated a Croydon Opportunity
Area within the London Plan. As a result of these initiatives Croydon town
centre is now the subject of a substantial and comprehensive programme of
redevelopment, with the council shaping the process from offices next door
to Taberner House where a new complex houses the council and other public
services. It represents a further stage in the development of an improved civic
quarter, including the old town hall. Taberner House has been demolished.[496]

---

496 Information provided by London Borough of Croydon

A number of other 1960s office slabs are going. A third Westfield shopping centre, following major developments at Shepherd's Bush and Stratford, is to be built to replace the existing Whitgift and Centrale centres. There are 'masterplans' for East Croydon, West Croydon, Mid-Croydon and the Fairfield Halls area. In addition, there are proposals to regenerate the Wellesley Road and Park Lane corridors substantially, improving access for pedestrians and making them less hostile.

The regeneration plans are expected to bring 17,000 new residents to the centre of Croydon and 230,000 sq. ft of new office space, as well as modernising the standard of existing stock quality. Central Croydon has seen a boom in the construction of high-rise apartments, such as IYLO and Altitude 25. There are wider developments under way, which will deliver new homes and offices, for a refurbishment of Fairfield Halls and for a new extension to Croydon College.

Consistent with the recent traditions of central areas within the borough a number of developers are proposing to build additional large residential towers alongside East Croydon station and at Saffron Square near West Croydon. West and south of the town centre, Purley Way, which has long been a distribution and 'out-of-town' facilities zone, is seen by the council as offering opportunities to strengthen manufacturing prospects.

As evidence of Croydon's long-term status as a separate town within the London boroughs' constellation, it has operated within two Local Enterprise Partnerships, which is unusual. It is both part of the London Enterprise Panel area and of the Coast to Capital LEP. The latter, which covers Gatwick Airport, is important to Croydon, whose economy depends on its own self-generated activity, central London's dynamism and the Gatwick/Brighton corridor's success. Perhaps Croydon, rather than Balham, is the 'gateway to the south'.[497]

Croydon has tended to stand out from other boroughs in its self-awareness as a freestanding town on the edge of the capital. In some ways it resembles, say, Reading or Woking as much as a traditional London authority. In other

---

497 Comedian Peter Sellers famously produced a spoof radio documentary about 'Balham, Gateway to the South', originally written by Frank Muir and Denis Norden

ways, in particular its willingness to build and knock down offices, it has much in common with the City of London. Its 'Manhattan skyline' is unusual for outer London. But as inner London's population mix has moved south, the borough now has more in common with, say, Lambeth and Southwark than in the 1960s. Like boroughs such as Enfield, Redbridge and Barnet, it is far less suburban than in 1965.

Croydon has a powerful sense of civic identity, derived from having been a county borough for so long. Arrival by train at East Croydon has the feel of arriving in a major centre such as Leeds or Birmingham. In many ways, it is a city within a city.

EALING

The authority was formed by the merger of three former municipal boroughs: Ealing, Southall and Acton, all of which were within the county of Middlesex. The area had been built up towards the end of the nineteenth century, as trams, buses and railways expanded outwards from London. Ealing, created in 1901, had been the first borough in Middlesex. Greenford and Perivale (both within the former Ealing local authority area) saw massive industrial expansion between the world wars, becoming home to well-known companies such as Hovis and J. Lyons.

The Great Depression (1929–39), which led to unemployment and decline in many regions of Britain, was a time of industrial expansion in west London. Park Royal (partly in Ealing, Brent and Hammersmith & Fulham) saw the development of munitions factories during the First World War, but then, subsequently, the expansion of factories making foodstuffs, electrical equipment, motors, paper products and other machinery.[498] The rapidly growing western

---

498 Diane K. Bolton, Patricia E. C. Croot and M. A. Hicks, 'A History of the County of Middlesex: Volume 7, Acton, Chiswick, Ealing and Brentford, West Twyford, Willesden', T. F. T. Baker and C. R. Elrington (eds), *British History Online*, http://www.british-history.ac.uk/vch/middx/vol7 (accessed 13 September 2015)

suburbs of London became home to a series of new, modern consumer industries, which, in turn, created a magnet for people from other, economically depressed parts of the UK. Park Royal became the biggest industrial estate in Europe.

Ealing was the home to Britain's most famous and influential film company. From 1931, a series of important films were produced in the borough, although the best-known Ealing films were made before the London Borough of Ealing came into existence. The cultural views and approach of the filmmakers of Ealing Studios embodied many of the attributes that help to inform our understanding of London's inter-war suburban development. More broadly, these films tell us much about Britain and British values of the time.

Charles Barr, the film historian, sees Ealing films as having an 'allegiance to the ideal community defined in *Passport to Pimlico* and *The Blue Lamp*: stable, gentle, innocent, already consciously backward-looking, and based on … [an]elaborate set of loyalties and renunciations'.[499] Barr quotes Ealing's head of publicity, who described the studios as having 'the air of a family business, set on the village green of the queen of the London suburbs … The administrative block, which faced the green, looked like a country cottage and was separated from the studios by a neat little rose garden.'[500]

Ealing was (and is) by no means a purely residential borough. But its leafy streets epitomise early suburban London's growth, embracing villages and towns into the growing metropolis. Like many of the post-1965 boroughs, it inherited or started large housing developments very different from the terraces of Victorian and Edwardian homes that were, until 1939, typical. Many large nineteenth-century houses were demolished to make way for new public and private homes. Partly as a reaction to the loss of older housing, conservation areas have evolved in areas such as Ealing Green and Hanger Hill Garden estate.[501]

---

499   Charles Barr, *Ealing Studios*, London: Cameron & Hollis, Moffat, 1998, page 177

500   Ibid., page 6

501   See Jonathan Oates and Peter Hounsell, *Ealing: A Concise History*, Amberley Publishing: Stroud, 2014

The Grange estate was built by Wates Limited in two phases between 1963 and 1966, in a style strongly influenced by the contemporary SPAN developments in Ham Common, New Ash Green (a modernist village in Kent) and elsewhere. SPAN housing was pioneered by the architect Eric Lyons, in partnership with developer Geoffrey Townshend and the builder Leslie Bilsby. An early SPAN publication summarised the origin of the name: 'It spans the gap between the suburban monotony of the typical "spec building" and the architecturally designed individually built residence.'[502] Lyons, who had worked with Walter Gropius, was also the architect of the World's End estate in Chelsea.

The South Acton estate was started after the Second World War, but the bulk of it was built during the 1960s and 1970s. It comprises a series of street-long six- to eight-storey blocks, with some point towers. Many of these buildings, as in other boroughs, are now tired-looking. Some are being replaced. A number of the 1970s buildings use friendlier red bricks. In traditional Corbusian style, the buildings are surrounded by open space and garages. Residents of South Acton often worked in local companies such as Wilkinson Sword and Lucas Aerospace. The estate is close to Acton Town Tube station, and thus to employment at Heathrow Airport.

Another notable (and still visible) 1960s development was the Holy Family Church in Hanger Hill, which now has the appearance of a classic example of 'concrete box' architecture. It is described by architectural critic Nikolaus Pevsner as 'an irregular pentagon of irregular profile', though its inside is more pleasing.[503]

In West Ealing, the Green Man Lane estate was built by Ealing Council in the 1970s, following slum clearance of small terraced houses in what had been called Stevens Town. The new estate consisted of seven- or eight-storey buildings, a number of four-storey maisonette blocks and a small number of

---

502 London Borough of Ealing, *Grange and White Ledges Conservation Area Character Appraisal*, April 2009, page 8

503 Bridget Cherry and Nikolaus Pevsner, *The Buildings of England, London 3: North West*, Yale University Press, Newhaven and London, 2002, page 157

three-storey town houses. By the 2010s, Ealing council was of the view that the Green Man Lane estate 'needs a lot of work to address the improvements needed to bring it up to the government's decent homes standard', and suffers from a number of problems, such as having insufficient family homes.[504]

Copley Close in Hanwell is an estate of largely brick construction built by the GLC and opened in 1979. It contains 626 homes comprising mostly one- and two-bed flats, twenty-four houses and a sheltered housing scheme. The estate is characterised by its linear layout, stretching across a narrow piece of land that follows the Greenford rail line into Paddington. The most dense part of the estate sits on an 'over bridge' above a rail tunnel. The architecture is rather better than that found in many earlier estates, and uses large quantities of red brick. However, it has classic design failures common in social housing built during the 1970s, such as connecting walkways, underground parking and little amenity space.[505] There is a major regeneration plan for the estate, including replacing some housing, and building a mixture of new owner-occupied and social homes.

Ealing's *Official Guide 1973–74* proudly claimed: 'With good schools, several excellent shopping centres and a wealth of open spaces and sporting amenities, Ealing seems set fair to continue as one of London's most attractive and progressive residential boroughs.' A housing guide at the same time observed the borough 'isn't really trendy ['Ealing nightlife is dead'], but is certainly better than average suburbia ... [A] Gathering ground for young executives ... Transport facilities are good ... Plus plenty of open space, good schools and shops.'[506] Ealing Hospital, a major district general facility, was opened in Southall in 1978, replacing a number of smaller health hospitals.

The borough has devoted much time and effort to the development of Ealing Broadway and Uxbridge Road in West Ealing. During the 1970s, it was

504 Ealing Council, Green Man Lane, 2015 http://www.ealing.gov.uk/info/200200/housing_regeneration/373/green_man_lane (accessed 17 September 2015)

505 Ealing Council, *Copley Close Vision*, Appendix 1 of Item No. 10, Cabinet Papers of 21 February 2012

506 See Jonathan Oates and Peter Hounsell, *Ealing: A Concise History*, Stroud: Amberley Publishing, 2014

proposed to link the two town centres with a new four-lane highway, though this plan was subsequently dropped. Ealing Broadway Centre, a covered mall, was developed on the south side of Ealing Broadway. Other shopping centre developments have followed and, most recently, a series of metropolitan-scale housing blocks have been built north of Ealing Broadway, at Dickens Yard, close to the station.

The borough is on many major transport routes in and out of London. Western Avenue (A40) carves a path through Acton in a challenging way, carrying large traffic volumes that often run close to residential properties. During the 1980s, over 150 houses and office blocks were demolished to allow a central government road-widening scheme, which, in the event, was never undertaken.[507] Even today, the sites of the destroyed buildings remain a bramble-covered wilderness. The Hanger Lane gyratory system, a starring feature of London traffic reports, is where Western Avenue meets the North Circular Road. The huge gyratory roundabout is topped by an Underground station in an urban transport engineering fantasy worthy of the novels of J. G. Ballard.

Ealing, both at the borough and parliamentary level, has been a classic Conservative/Labour marginal. Both the major parties have run the council: indeed, until recently, Ealing's periodic changes in political control at borough level proved a good predictor of the result of the following general election. Latterly, the Labour Party has seen its vote share grow in the borough, making it relatively more likely the party will win control. But Ealing remains marginal and will still be winnable by the Conservatives if Labour is in power (and unpopular) nationally. Labour, under Julian Bell, won in 2014. Former Labour leader Neil Kinnock and his wife Glenys Kinnock MEP at one time lived in Ealing.

In 2002, an attempt was made to introduce a directly elected mayor to replace the current, more traditional, leader-and-cabinet model of local government. Virtually all local politicians and MPs were opposed to the idea and, on a low turnout, the proposition was rejected by 55 per cent to 45 per cent.[508]

---

507 Mira Bar-Hillel and David Williams, 'Scandal of the A40', *Evening Standard*, 29 July 2004

508 See Jonathan Oates and Peter Hounsell, *Ealing: A Concise History*, Stroud: Amberley Publishing, 2014

In common with most boroughs, Ealing has witnessed substantial economic change in the years since 1965. The new industries that had prospered at Park Royal and elsewhere in the inter-war period declined as Britain's economy de-industrialised during the 1970s and 1980s. Organisations with significant employment today include AMT Coffee, Bestway, Carphone Warehouse, Diageo, Ealing Studios, Ealing Hospital NHS Trust, Glaxosmithkline (GSK), Initial Security Ltd, JRS Asian Foods, Katsouris Fresh Foods, MW Kellogg Ltd, Noon Products Ltd, Sunrise Radio, The Tetley Group, TNS, Ultra Electronics, United Biscuits, Walkers and West London Mental Health Trust.[509] Healthcare, pharmaceuticals, food and drink processing, and warehousing are important local employers.

The borough has a relatively highly skilled workforce, with professional employment being significantly above the national average.[510] Proximity to Heathrow is of obvious importance to Ealing, both for businesses and as a place to live. Few places in Britain can more perfectly balance the advantages and disadvantages of being close to a major international airport.

Ealing's population was 301,000 in 1961, then fell to 275,000 by 1991 before growing to 350,000 in 2015. Official projections show the population rising towards 400,000 by the early 2030s.[511] The borough has seen substantial international in-migration since 1965, notably from the Indian sub-continent and from Poland. There was a substantial Polish population in the borough well before contemporary European Union immigration. The south Asian population has become most apparent within Ealing, most particularly in Southall and Hanwell. About 20 per cent of the population describe their ethnic origin as being Indian, Pakistani or Bangladeshi. The 2011 census showed that over 20,000 Ealing residents were born in India and over 5,000 in Pakistan.[512]

---

509 Ealing Council, *State of Ealing Economy and Enterprise*, 2012, file:///H:/State_of_
    Ealing_2012_ECONOMY_AND_ENTERPRISE%20(1).pdf (accessed 13 September
    2015)

510 Ibid.

511 Ibid.

512 Ibid

The borough and its neighbourhoods have been among the more stable and unchanged within London since 1965. While the demographics of the area have altered substantially, its character and political nature have remained broadly recognisable as compared with the period when they were created.

ENFIELD

Enfield brought together the three former municipal boroughs of Edmonton, Enfield and Southgate, which had been in Middlesex. A 'characterisation study', undertaken in 2009, considered the way different parts of the post-1965 borough had evolved. This study provided a subtle and informed understanding of the way many outer boroughs developed:

> While all modern London boroughs are composed of older administrative units, Enfield holds within itself very strong contrasts between east and west, north and south, which are reflected in its formal boundaries partly as cause and partly as effect. Edmonton is associated with the large-scale industry and transport infrastructure of road and rail in the south-east corner closer to London, Southgate represents suburban enterprise, and Enfield early rural industry, agricultural outlooks and a market town character.[513]

The study went on to explain how the development of churches, schools, libraries, parks, swimming baths, electricity sub-stations, water works and postal sorting offices in the predecessor authorities had long-term effects that can still be seen:

> These 'civic markers' identify local centres in what is now a continuous suburban spread, and are usually notable for their size, their quality

---

513 London Borough of Enfield, *Characterisation Study*, Consultation Draft, London Borough of Enfield, 2009, page 9

of detailing and their confident design ... Examples of high-quality
survivors include elementary schools by the first independent and local
authority school boards, and secondary schools by Middlesex County
Council ... Carnegie libraries at Enfield and Edmonton, the postal
sorting offices at Grove Park and New Southgate, and the electricity
station at Ladysmith Road.[514]

In discussing the housing built in the predecessor authorities during the inter-
war period (as the road system and Underground expanded), the authors note:
'Few of the developers active in outer London in the 1930s employed architects.
This was partly due to the client-led market, whose priorities and preferred
domestic environment differed from those of architectural theorists.'[515]

Such an observation, although made in 2009 and presumably with an
understanding of the architect-led housing experiments in the late 1950s,
1960s and early 1970s, is of great significance. The authors were, in fact,
writing about a reaction to the 'garden city movement', which had created
social housing that was too communal for many tastes. But the remark could
easily have been applied to much of the large-scale modern housing built by
councils after 1965.

In the first years of the new borough, there were acrimonious protests against
Enfield's proposals to move to a system of comprehensive education. Labour
had a small majority in the 1964 elections, but was nonetheless determined
to press ahead with comprehensive reorganisation. The existence of a number of well-known grammar schools in the borough, notably Enfield Grammar
School, provided a focus for the opponents of the council's scheme. As in other
Labour-controlled boroughs, objecting parents were viewed by the majority
party as a front organisation for the political opposition.

Fearful of losing control at the next borough elections, Labour Enfield was
keen to press ahead with reform. Similarly, opponents thought they could save

---

514 Ibid., page 13

515 Ibid., page 18

the grammar schools if they could hold out for a Conservative victory in 1968. Opponents challenged the legal validity of the council's proposals and were successful in delaying the incorporation of the schools concerned until early 1968. Despite this delay, the Conservatives, who did indeed win in the elections later that year, did not reverse reform.[516]

Enfield civic centre became the administrative hub of the council in 1971. In 1972, work began on an eleven-storey tower to house Enfield offices. Edmonton Town Hall, an imposing Victorian Gothic edifice, was demolished in 1989. Southgate Town Hall is today being converted into housing and an improved library.[517]

Growth after the end of the Second World War was constrained by new planning restrictions. Enfield and its predecessors faced a problem also seen in all the boroughs that bordered the green belt. They were now hemmed in and could not build cheap new homes on farmland as they had in the 1920s and 1930s. Semi-detached 1930s housing marches northwards in Enfield and then stops, dead, at roads such as Clay Hill and Forty Hill. Where continuous residential and industrial development preceded the imposition of the green belt, Enfield merges into urban Broxbourne. This long finger of city, hugging the River Lee, extends for several miles to Hoddesden and almost to Harlow and Hertford. The rail line through this area, from Liverpool Street to Cheshunt, was taken over by London Overground during 2015, offering hope it will improve.[518]

Tower blocks were built by Enfield Borough Council in the 1960s. These new homes either replaced older terraces, as happened near Ponders End station and at Bush Hill Park, or were built on open land belonging to the council, as at Lavender Hill.[519] In 1965, a comprehensive mixed-use rebuilding scheme was agreed for Edmonton Green. It was completed in 1974. Enfield's

---

516 Gerald Rhodes (ed.), *The New Government of London: The First Five Years*, London: Weidenfeld & Nicolson, 1972, page 179

517 Information provided by London Borough of Enfield

518 Gwyn Topham, 'Clean, reliable and integrated: all change for neglected rail services in London', *The Guardian*, 29 May 2015

519 London Borough of Enfield, *Characterisation Study*, Consultation Draft, London Borough of Enfield, 2009, page 19

predecessor, Southgate council, built some 500 flats and houses at about the same period, the majority as semi-detached houses or three-storey blocks rather than in tower blocks. Large parts of New Southgate were redeveloped between the 1950s and 1974 by Southgate council and then Enfield.[520]

A regeneration scheme called 'Shaping New Southgate' was initiated by the council to make improvements to municipally built estates, shops, open spaces, community facilities, parking and transport. The most significant element of the project is the redevelopment of the Ladderswood Way estate and the adjoining New Southgate industrial estate, which is due for completion in 2017.[521] The project was developed as a joint venture between Mulalley and housing association One Housing Group, appointed by the council.

Ladderswood was a classic mix of a medium-rise block and four-floor concrete buildings interspersed with car parks. The estate has looked bleak from the start. The redevelopment will link residential and industrial estates with the network of surrounding Victorian streets. There will also be a hotel.[522]

The Alma estate project at Ponders End, costing £150 million, is Enfield's largest housing estate renewal scheme. Plans for the original estate were approved over two phases in 1966 and 1967. Phase 1 included the construction of two 23-storey tower blocks, and Phase 2 added a further two. All the blocks are of identical design and were built in 1968.[523] The redevelopment is intended to act as a catalyst for the wider regeneration of Ponders End. The Alma estate was prioritised for renewal because it has been costly to maintain, suffered from structural defects and proved unpopular with residents.

At Highmead estate in Edmonton, Enfield has, as elsewhere, worked with a developer and a housing association to make good a previous generation's

520 Ibid., page 19

521 Hidden London, *New Southgate, Enfield/Barnet*, 2015, http://hidden-london.com/gazetteer/ new-southgate/ (accessed 12 September 2015)

522 'Ladderswood', Pollard Thomas Edwards, http://pollardthomasedwards.co.uk/project/ ladderswood/ (accessed 12 September 2015)

523 Laura Mark, 'PTEa scoops contest to regenerate huge north London estate', *Architects' Journal*, 31 October 2013

house-building failures.[524] The regeneration at Highmead replaces a poor-standard eleven-storey 1960s tower block and out-of-date shops with 120 mixed-tenure homes, retail space, a community centre and new mews housing with a garden.[525] Edmonton Green, a scheme dating from 1965, is also being regenerated.

Enfield was part of the Lee Valley industrial expansion of the late nineteenth and early twentieth century. The manufacturing heritage of Enfield – and its neighbours Waltham Forest and Haringey – is easy to forget. It was in Enfield that the Lee rifle and the Bren gun were invented. Belling created the first infra-red fire bar, which increased temperatures in British homes in the years before central heating. Other local inventions included the halogen cooker, digital telephone equipment enabling the earliest transatlantic calls, colour television distribution systems, manmade fibres, and the diode valve.[526]

The decline of manufacturing industry during the second half of the twentieth century has affected all British cities. Service industries, warehousing, retail parks and superstores have replaced factories. The effect of this global change has been particularly evident in Enfield, because the borough's east/west divide concentrated industry in the east. The Great Cambridge Road, for many years, had factories along its length.[527] More affluent areas such as Cockfosters, Hadley Wood and Crews Hill have continued to prosper, while the east has seen decline. Commenting about the difference between the east and west parts of the borough caused by industrial decline, journalist Aditya Chakrabortty, who was brought up in Enfield, observed: 'On one side of a dual carriageway, you're in Surrey; on the other, Sunderland.'[528]

---

524 Charlie Peat, 'New housing estate in Edmonton nears completion', *Enfield Independent*, 17 June 2014

525 'Green light for Highmead estate', *World Architecture News*, 24 February 2011, http://www.worldarchitecturenews.com/project/2011/15934/hawkinsbrown/highmead-estate-in-edmonton-north-london.html?i=26 (accessed 12 September 2015)

526 Aditya Chakrabortty, 'The Enfield Experiment: London's fortunes distilled into a single borough', *The Guardian*, 3 February 2014

527 London Borough of Enfield, *Characterisation Study*, Consultation Draft, London Borough of Enfield, 2009, page 19

528 Aditya Chakrabortty, 'The Enfield Experiment: London's fortunes distilled into a single borough', *The Guardian*, 3 February 2014

In the early twentieth century, the North Circular Road, new arterial roads such as the Great Cambridge Road and the extension of the Piccadilly line formed an infrastructure that, at the time, increased the development of Enfield. The M25 now defines the north edge of the borough.[529] Enfield is home to some of London Underground's most important station architecture. Built in the early 1930s as part of the London Passenger Transport Board's expansion programme, Arnos Grove, Southgate, Oakwood (originally to be called Enfield West) and Cockfosters were all designed by Charles Holden, who was also responsible for London Transport's headquarters at 55 Broadway, and for Senate House in Bloomsbury.

Arnos Grove, Southgate and Oakwood are of great interest to architectural historians. Indeed, Arnos Grove 'was used at the time as proof of the moral fitness of the style for a modern transport system and, by extension, for modern life'.[530] These stations, in an austere and undecorated style, have circular or rectangular 'lanterns' atop them, so that light can shine up through their windows. Cockfosters does not have such an architectural topping, though it does have an impressive concrete canopy of a kind also found at the opposite end of the line in Uxbridge.

The borough's characterisation study describes Enfield Town, Edmonton Green and Southgate as 'major centres; Enfield Town, as the largest centre and the retail focus of the borough, has suffered severe damage to its earlier infrastructure through redevelopment and its fortunately brief flirtations with 1960s fashions in ring roads and high-rise building'.[531] The pre-1965 Enfield council had proposed to build a three-lane ring road around the town centre, with a traffic-free shopping precinct. The project was abandoned after a ministerial decision in 1967.[532]

In addition, new immigrants are far more likely to settle in outer boroughs than in the 1960s and 1970s. There are established migrant populations from countries such as Cyprus, Turkey and Greece, and new growing communities

---

529 London Borough of Enfield, *Characterisation Study*, Consultation Draft, 2009, page 8

530 Edward Jones and Christopher Woodward, *A Guide to the Architecture of London*, London: Weidenfeld & Nicolson, 1983, page 343

531 London Borough of Enfield, *Characterisation Study*, Consultation Draft, 2009, page 19

532 Ibid.

include Somalis, Nigerians, Ghanaians, Congolese and eastern Europeans, notably Kosovans and Albanians.[533] Many people move from Haringey into Enfield. The Trust for London believes: 'Enfield is ... becoming more deprived, relative to the rest of London.'[534]

The political make-up of Enfield has seen a Labour–Conservative contest ever since 1964. Although Labour won that year, the Conservatives were then in control continuously from 1968 until 1994. Labour has done better in recent years, as the population make-up has changed. The Conservatives still won twenty-two seats out of sixty-three in 2014, but it is becoming harder for them to control the council.[535] Ted (now Lord) Graham was the first leader of the council and subsequently became a local (Labour) MP, before sitting for many years in the House of Lords. Former Conservative Cabinet minister Michael Portillo was MP for Enfield Southgate, before unexpectedly losing his seat in the 1997 general election.

Enfield has changed socially and demographically since 1965. In common with Croydon, Redbridge and Barking & Dagenham, the borough has witnessed the impact of inner-London characteristics moving outwards. Changes in the local economy and elsewhere in London have affected the make-up of the area. Poorer residents have moved to Enfield because of rising house prices and rentals in inner London. Changes to the benefit system, designed to move people away from expensive boroughs, will inevitably have moved some of them to cheaper locations such as Edmonton and New Southgate, though it is hard to measure this phenomenon.

The borough today faces the challenge of handling significant numbers of relatively deprived in-comers at a time of much-reduced resources where central government support mechanisms no longer take account of increasing expenditure needs. Having said this, much of the northern part of Enfield remains affluent and green.

---

533 'Enfield', London's Poverty Profile, 2015, http://www.londonspovertyprofile.org.uk/indicators/boroughs/enfield/ (accessed 12 September 2015)

534 Ibid.

535 Greater London Authority, *London Borough Council Elections 22 May 2014*, London: GLA, 2014, page 49

HARINGEY

Haringey was formed of the former municipal boroughs of Hornsey, Tottenham and Wood Green, which had been in the county of Middlesex. It is thus part of outer London, though, for a number of statistical definitions, it and Newham are classified as within inner London. It merged two significantly different kinds of area: Hornsey and Wood Green were largely affluent and often Conservative-voting, whereas Tottenham was industrial and generally Labour-supporting. This east/west division is still visible today, though the political boundary has become less obvious since the elections of 2014 and 2015.

Haringey had a relatively large Caribbean population in 1965. Between 1961 and 1971, the number of West Indian immigrants increased in Haringey, Newham and Brent. By contrast, there was an absolute decline in the proportion of the population born in the Caribbean who lived in Camden, Westminster, Kensington & Chelsea and Tower Hamlets, to the point that, in the latter grouping, the proportion was below the London average. In the early years of Haringey, it became, along with Lambeth and Brent, one of the most significant concentrations of black Londoners.[536]

There were disputes early in the life of the new borough about policies such as 'banding'. A system of comprehensive schools was being introduced by the new authority, and efforts were made to ensure all schools had a range of abilities within them. In an attempt to deliver this range, observations were made about the performance of Caribbean children which were heavily criticised by campaign groups.[537] These issues were not only prevalent in Haringey; the ILEA, widely seen as progressive, was similarly criticised. There were also early calls for a curriculum to include black culture and history in Haringey.[538]

---

536 John Shepherd, John Westaway and Trevor Lee, *A Social Atlas of London*, Oxford: Clarendon Press, 1974, page 55

537 Paul Warmington, *Black British Intellectuals and Education: Multiculturalism's Hidden History*, London: Routledge, 2014, pages 46–9

538 Ibid., page 49

The borough was in these early years the site of one of the biggest struggles against the government and GLC's roads programme, with the council
initially acting as the GLC's agent. Conservative Transport Minister Ernest
Marples wanted to improve the A1 so as to take traffic from London Docks to
the new M1. A section of the road ran through the new borough of Haringey
and then on to Falloden Way in Barnet. Traffic would have run northbound
up Highgate Hill and then through Highgate Village. Southbound traffic was
to use Archway Road. Some local residents supported this option because it
avoided the need to widen Archway Road. The council approved, in princi-
ple, the widening of Archway Road in 1967, though opposition was increasing
by this time. The Highgate Society, a civic group, fought the widening, and
proposed local side-road closures to stop rat-running.[539]

Haringey's policy began to change. Andrew McIntosh, vice-chairman
of the Planning Committee, attempted to mount a campaign of opposition
from within the authority. In March 1968, the Archway Road Campaign was
launched. In May that year, the Conservatives took control of Haringey but,
by now, opposition was bipartisan. The council and campaigners called for a
public inquiry.[540] In the event, the government commissioned consultants to
review the project. New protesters, representing Shepherds Hill on the east
side of Archway, appeared. Their chairman, George Stern, argued against any
widening of Archway Road. Piecemeal widening of Archway Road occurred.
There were disagreements between different anti-roads groups. The ministry
attempted to play off opponents in Haringey with those opposing the widening of Falloden Way nearby in Barnet.[541]

After further years of debate and struggle, the plan was eventually abandoned in 1990 and the road became a pilot for 'red routes' (major urban roads
with parking restrictions). Years of debate about possible schemes resulted in
the area becoming blighted and run-down, because many of the properties

539 Michael F. Collins and Timothy M. Pharoah, *Transport Organisation in a Great City:
      The Case of London*, London: George Allen & Unwin, 1974, pages 366–8

540 Ibid., pages 368–9

541 Ibid., pages 370–72

that had been scheduled to be demolished were let out by the owners on short leases and were not well maintained.[542]

Haringey, with the GLC's support, promoted Wood Green Shopping City, a large in-town shopping mall built during the 1970s. It was unusual in having a road (the A105) running through the middle of it. The top floors of the development included three floors of housing, which is also uncommon for such centres.[543] Wood Green (now called 'The Mall Wood Green') has survived for almost forty years as a large shopping centre, and has worked relatively well because of Haringey's population which is, generally, relatively affluent. Crouch End, which is another key shopping district in the borough, has remained a successful local high street.

Within two years of Haringey's creation and at the time of the struggle over roads, work was started on the Broadwater Farm estate in Tottenham, on land previously used for allotments. It is built in the Moselle Valley and, so as to avoid the risk of flooding, there was only car parking at ground level. The design was inspired by Le Corbusier and consisted of twelve interconnected buildings each named after a Second World War aerodrome.[544] There were two large towers, Northolt and Kenley, and a ziggurat-shaped one, Tangmere. Designed by the borough's own architect, Broadwater Farm was to become one of the most notorious housing estates in Britain.

As early as the mid-1970s, there were problems with the estate, in particular with its elevated walkways. There were robberies, the housing was poorly maintained, roofs leaked, there were pest infestations and

542 London Borough of Haringey, *Revised Archway Road Neighbourhood Plan*, July 2002, page 6, http://www.haringey.gov.uk/sites/haringeygovuk/files/revised_archway_road_neighbourhood_plan_with_map.pdf (accessed 15 July 2015)

543 Twentieth Century Society, 'Building of the Month', October 2013, http://www.c20society.org.uk/botm/wood-green-shopping-city-london (accessed 15 July 2015)

544 Peter Antwi, *Broadwater Farm Estate (BWFE) The Active Community*, http://web.archive.org/web/20080228054558/http://www.regenerate-uk.org/downloads/7_london.pdf (accessed 16 July 2015)

wiring problems.[545] By 1976, the Department of the Environment decided the estate was of such degraded quality that it should be demolished.[546] Subsequently, efforts have been made on a number of occasions to refurbish the estate. The piecemeal renewal of Broadwater Farm over many years today provides layered evidence of several governments' initiatives to deliver improvements.

In 1985, there were serious disturbances at Broadwater Farm as a result of the death of Cynthia Jarrett while police were at her home, following the arrest of her son. The next day, there was a demonstration outside Tottenham police station, during which police officers and journalists were attacked. Later that evening, a large riot occurred, and police were attacked with knives and machetes. PC Keith Blakelock was killed and another officer badly injured.[547]

The riot and the killing of PC Blakelock were among the most shocking events to occur in London during the first fifty years of the London boroughs. The event directed attention at the problem of the existing relationship between the police and young black men in many parts of the city, in much the same way that the Brixton riots had in 1981. Lord Scarman's report on those earlier disturbances had concluded that police methods and recruitment should be improved. It also stressed the importance of tackling racial discrimination.[548]

In the wake of the disturbances, Broadwater Farm was the focus of national and local efforts to regenerate the estate. Overhead walkways were demolished, shops were developed in some of the ground-floor space and CCTV installed. Haringey set up a local management team. Space between the blocks was landscaped, and concierges were put in place to protect entrances. Crime

545 Ibid.

546 'Broadwater Farm Housing Estate', Haringey Community Centres Network, http://ourtottenham.org.uk (accessed 16 July 2015)

547 Olga Craig, 'They butchered Keith Blakelock and they wanted to butcher me', *Daily Telegraph*, 3 October 2004

548 *The Brixton Disorders, April 10–12, 1981: Inquiry Report*, Report of an inquiry by the Rt Hon. Lord Scarman, OBE *(Cmnd 8427)*, London: HMSO

rates fell. Despite its complex and brutal past, Broadwater Farm became an example of how regeneration could, in fact, change an estate.[549]

As had happened in several boroughs during the 1970s, the left had taken control of Haringey. In 1985, Bernie Grant was elected leader and became a national figure in respect of his particular brand of politics. In an obituary, Grant was described by Mike Phillips as: 'A red rag to the bulls of right-wing politics. A black man with a left-wing trade union background, he was also an anti-apartheid campaigner, a supporter of revolutionary governments, feminist causes, black studies and a multiracial school curriculum.'[550] In the context of the late 1970s and early 1980s, Bernie Grant made perfect sense. He was a radical who attacked racism full-on, to the point that it discomforted the political establishment. The things he said and the way he approached politics were intended to be provocative. As Phillips made clear, Grant's survival in politics owed much to the strength of his base in Tottenham, where he became MP in 1987.

The culture war stirred up by the left's involvement in Haringey and elsewhere could be seen in the national and local press, which ran countless stories about supposed extremist or 'loony' policies being pursued by councils. For example, in the autumn of 1986 there was a major tabloid controversy about Haringey council's requirement that the rhyme 'Baa, Baa, Black Sheep' be rewritten to refer to 'green sheep', on the grounds that the original title was racist. This story was picked up in the national press, but also in local papers across the country. A similar one later re-surfaced in Islington.[551] Haringey was also attacked (among many other things) for banning 'racist' bin-liners, anti-heterosexism and for promoting homosexuality.[552] Tabloid newspapers regularly referred to Grant as Barmy Bernie.

---

549 Peter Antwi, *Broadwater Farm Estate (BWFE) The Active Community*, London, http://web.archive.org/web/20080228054558/http://www.regenerate-uk.org/downloads/7_london.pdf (accessed 16 July 2015)

550 Mike Phillips, 'Bernie Grant: Passionate left-wing MP and tireless anti-racism campaigner', *The Guardian*, 10 April 2000

551 James Curran, Ivor Gaber and Julian Petley, *Culture Wars: The Media & The British Left*, Edinburgh: Edinburgh University Press, 2005, pages 100–105

552 Ibid., pages 87, 159–61

Even after the political struggles of the 1980s had come to an end, another issue was to surface that would also affect the borough's reputation for years to come. In February 2000, an eight-year old girl, Victoria Climbié, was beaten to death by her great-aunt and the latter's boyfriend. Victoria died of malnutrition and hypothermia. Her body was covered in bruises and burns. She had, in effect, been tortured to death. In the aftermath of the trial, the government set up an inquiry, under Lord Laming. The inquiry report was highly critical of Haringey council and other public agencies in London:

> It is deeply disturbing that during the days and months following her initial contact with Ealing Housing Department's Homeless Persons' Unit, Victoria was known to no less than two further housing authorities, four social services departments, two child protection teams of the Metropolitan Police Service (MPS), a specialist centre managed by the NSPCC, and she was admitted to two different hospitals because of suspected deliberate harm. The dreadful reality was that these services knew little or nothing more about Victoria at the end of the process than they did when she was first referred to Ealing social services by the Homeless Persons' Unit in April 1999. The final irony was that Haringey social services formally closed Victoria's case on the very day she died.[553]

The report added:

> [T]he manner in which a number of senior managers and elected councillors within Haringey discharged their statutory responsibilities to safeguard and promote the welfare of children living in the borough was an important contributory factor in the mishandling of Victoria's case.[554]

---

553 *The Victoria Climbié Inquiry Chairman: Lord Laming Report*, Cm 5730, London: TSO, 2003

554 Ibid., page 197

Haringey was not the only public institution criticised by Laming, but, more than any other, its social workers were responsible for Victoria Climbié at the point when her problems became apparent.

Seven years later, a child abuse story in Haringey again made national news. Seventeen-month-old 'Baby P', Peter Connolly, died from horrific abuse at the hands of his mother and a friend of hers. After they had been found guilty of neglect and abuse, Children's Secretary Ed Balls announced an inquiry into the role of the council, the health authority and the police. Following an OFSTED report into Haringey Children's Services, its leader George Meehan and Cabinet member for children and young people Liz Santry resigned.[555]

Sharon Shoesmith was removed as the local authority's director of children's services. Balls said 'deep-rooted and fundamental failures' had been identified in the Baby P case, and more widely in Haringey. He ordered a new serious case review, with an executive summary to be published by the end of March, and described an earlier review, which was chaired by Shoesmith, as 'inadequate'.[556] Lord Laming was asked to undertake a review of progress in the improvement of child care.

In 2011, Shoesmith won a court case having claimed she had been unfairly dismissed,[557] and was subsequently given a payoff. Three years later, BBC London political editor Tim Donovan made a documentary showing that responsibility for the Baby P failures went far wider than Haringey social services and that, in effect, the council and its staff had been unfairly selected to take all the blame.[558] A book by Professor Ray Jones also attempted to paint a wider picture.[559] The impact of the Baby P case on children's social care has

555 Haroon Siddique, 'Baby P council officials resign as minister receives inquiry findings',
     The Guardian, 1 December 2008

556 Haroon Siddique, 'Baby P report: Balls removes council child protection chief',
     The Guardian, 1 December 2008

557 Patrick Butler, 'Sharon Shoesmith wins appeal against sacking over Baby P', *The Guardian*,
     27 May 2011

558 Patrick Butler, 'Baby P: the untold story is the anatomy of an establishment cover-up',
     The Guardian, 27 October 2014

559 Ray Jones, *The Story of Baby P: Setting the Record Straight*, Bristol: Policy Press, 2014

been profound across the country: more children are now referred to social services and more removed from their families.[560]

Haringey also found itself the location of further civil disorder during August 2011. The shooting, by the police, of Mark Duggan became the starting point for urban riots in Tottenham, other parts of London (such as Croydon, Hackney, Clapham and Woolwich) and in some cities outside the capital.[561] As after the 1985 disturbances, additional public resources were promised. The Mayor of London appointed Sir Stuart Lipton to act as 'champion' for Tottenham. Lipton chaired a panel of experts who produced a report, tellingly titled *It Took Another Riot*, which proposed: an improved multi-agency governance arrangement; high-quality design and a better physical environment; substantial regeneration of housing estates; enhanced co-ordination of charities; improved relations between the police and the community; and, using Lipton's own word, more 'fun'.[562] Lipton and his panel contributed to the council's own Tottenham Task Force, chaired by local councillor Alan Strickland.

But, by 2011, Haringey council was politically different than it had been in the 1980s, though the years of radical politics and the childcare scandals were still taking their toll on service quality. The Audit Commission had reported in its 2007 Annual Audit and Inspection Letter that Haringey was 'improving well' and that, overall, it received a 'three-star' rating, including three stars for the borough's 'children and young people' service.[563] By the March 2009 letter, considering 2007–08 and published after Peter Connolly's death, the borough was 'not improving adequately', and received just one star for its 'children and young people' service.[564]

---

560   Shona Macleod, Ruth Hart, Jennifer Jeffes and Anne Wilkin, *The Impact of the Baby Peter Case on Applications for Care Orders*, LGA Research Report, Slough: NFER, 2010

561   Greg Morgan, 'Mark Duggan: a single death that sparked the riots', *Daily Telegraph*, 8 January 2014

562   Sir Stuart Lipton (chair) *It Took Another Riot: The concluding report of the Mayor of London's Independent Panel on Tottenham*, Don Levett (ed.), December 2012

563   *Annual Audit and Inspection Letter*, Haringey London Borough Council, London: Audit Commission, March 2007, page 5

564   Ibid.

Alexandra Palace has proved a complex burden for Haringey. The original home of BBC Television, the council took over the hilltop venue from the GLC (for £1) in 1980. Shortly after, there was a major fire that caused massive damage. Subsequently, the council has operated 'Ally Pally' through a charitable trust, though the pace of regeneration has been slow and often controversial because of resource constraints.[565]

New leadership provided by Claire Kober, who took over after the Baby P case, has driven service improvement and a pragmatic approach to redevelopment. The area around Tottenham Hale has been substantially regenerated, with a large amount of new, owner-occupied housing. Tottenham Hotspur Football Club is in the process of redeveloping its ground at White Hart Lane, providing development benefit at the north of Tottenham. Moreover, as inner London has become more expensive, affluent buyers who previously targeted Crouch End and Hornsey (in the west of the borough) now started to move into the east, from Seven Sisters northwards.

Another of Haringey's earlier, moderate leaders was Toby (now Lord) Harris, who played a prominent role in the Association of London Government, forerunner of London Councils. Harris was an important figure in London-wide governance after the abolition of the GLC, particularly in working with London First and the Major government to develop and promote London. Of the two Haringey MPs today, one, David Lammy, was a contender for the Labour mayoral nomination in 2016, while the other, Catherine West, was formerly leader of Islington. The borough's politics started as a Labour–Conservative marginal, but moved to being a Labour–Liberal Democrat contest, split east–west within the borough. In 2014, Labour won council control easily.

Today, Haringey is one of the most ethnically diverse places in Britain. It has a substantial Turkish and Cypriot population, but also a rich mosaic of other different nationalities and religions. Green Lanes, with its miles of restaurants and shops, is evidence of the strong Turkish influence on the area. Its

---

565 See, for example, 'The restoration of Alexandra Palace after the fire', A Hornsey Historical Society lecture by Richard Loren, Save Ally Pally, http://www.saveallypally.com/history.html (accessed 2 September 2015)

past now defines it less because of better government and the pace of social and economic change.

HARROW

H arrow was the only London borough to be created in 1965 that was unaffected by boundary changes. The predecessor Harrow municipal borough, created in 1934 from former councils in Harrow-on-the-Hill, Hendon and Wealdstone, was a district council within the county of Middlesex. It was incorporated by the Queen in 1954.[566] Reform in 1965 meant, therefore, that the authority was not subject to boundary upheaval, while it gained powers over services such as education and social care. However, changes were made to the number of councillors per ward.[567] The council built a civic centre for itself at Wealdstone in 1972, designed by Eric Broughton, in association with the borough architect. The building is a straightforward modern box of which, according to the borough, the 'dominant structural theme is seen in bold profiles of pre-cast concrete'.[568]

Harrow has long-developed town centres at Harrow-on-the-Hill and Pinner, plus 'Metroland' (the name given to suburban areas of north-west London served by the Underground's Metropolitan line) suburbs at Rayners Lane and South Harrow. The inter-relationship between Harrow and the Underground's Metropolitan line is an important feature of its character. Harrow-on-the-Hill is just seventeen minutes from Baker Street by Tube. Uniquely for an outer borough, Harrow is served by four Underground lines, giving it excellent access to central London and to Heathrow. Housing includes several inter-war types, including gabled 'Tudorbethan' semis, and also a number of Art Deco properties. This heritage includes the Grade II-listed Elm Park Court, an Art Deco masterpiece on Elm Park Lane. Pinner is one of London's

---

566 Information provided by London Borough of Harrow

567 Ibid.

568 Ibid.

beautiful villages, with a view up the High Street that is among the best in the capital.

In the 1960s, there were still two RAF bases in Harrow: Bentley Priory (the nerve centre for the Battle of Britain) and Stanmore Park. Both have subsequently been decommissioned and used for housing developments. The tallest structure in the borough was a gas holder on Northolt Road, which was eventually demolished in the 1980s. Painted on one side of the gas holder was a large white 'NO' (for Northolt, or possibly 'No') to deter Heathrow-bound aircraft from mistaking Northolt for Heathrow.

Five cinemas survived in Harrow in 1965. Before television, there had been many more. The progress of the buildings that housed the borough's cinemas is instructive, and not unique to Harrow. The Dominion on Station Road, today called the Safari, shows Asian films and is also a bingo hall. The Granada on Sheepcote Road in Harrow is now a gym, while the Odeon in South Harrow was demolished and replaced by flats. An Odeon on Rayners Lane is a Zoroastrian centre, and the ABC/Langham in Pinner is now a supermarket. Instead of this variety of cinemas, there is a multiplex in the St Georges Shopping Centre.

The borough, along with its neighbours Wembley and Alperton (in Brent), flourished as part of the inter-war suburban growth of London, with a number of factories specialising in (what were then) new industrial sectors. Harrow contributed to the growing photographic industry in Britain:

> The first large industrial premises at Wealdstone were erected in 1890 for the Kodak organisation on a site north of Headstone Drive ... by 1965, they comprised over 100 buildings on a 55-acre site. About 5,500 people were then employed in research and producing film, chemicals, and other photographic accessories.[569]

---

569 Diane K. Bolton, H. P. F. King, Gillian Wyld and D. C. Yaxley, 'Harrow, including Pinner: Local government and public services', in *A History of the County of Middlesex: Volume 4, Harmondsworth, Hayes, Norwood With Southall, Hillingdon With Uxbridge, Ickenham, Northolt, Perivale, Ruislip, Edgware, Harrow With Pinner*, T. F. T. Baker (ed.), J. S. Cockburn and R. B. Pugh, London: British History, 1971, pages 237–49, http://www.british-history.ac.uk/vch/middx/vol4/pp237-249 (accessed 17 September 2015)

Kodak's factory was Eastman Kodak's first manufacturing base outside America.[570] Other major employers included Her Majesty's Stationery Office (HMSO), which had over 1,000 staff, and companies in sectors such as glassware, electrical, mechanical and household goods. Kodak was an important source of employment and wealth for the citizens of Harrow. But radical changes in photography meant Kodak's manufacturing declined and the company sold off most of its Harrow estate. Industrial change and its consequences also affected other local companies. For example, a protracted inter-union disagreement about the use of new technology at the Harrow press of HMSO left Parliament without its daily printed Hansard in 1974. Phonebooks also went unprinted.[571]

The industrial sectors that had flourished as London grew in the early part of the twentieth century have declined continuously in the fifty years since the London Borough of Harrow was created. Manufacturing peaked in around 1970, when about 30 per cent of employment was in the sector. Today, less than 4 per cent of the population work in manufacturing.[572]

Industrial history and change in the borough can be seen to influence current council policy. The Harrow and Wealdstone Area Action Plan has identified the former industrial areas between Harrow and Wealdstone as a location for substantive development in the coming years. This area was described in the mid-1950s as the 'capital city of Metroland', covers 177 hectares and is located towards the centre of the borough:

> This area [the two town centres of Harrow and Wealdstone, the Station Road corridor linking the two centres, and the industrial land and open spaces surrounding Wealdstone, including the Kodak site, Headstone Manor and the Harrow Leisure Centre] has been identified by the Council and the Mayor for London as priority area for regeneration … The area will be the subject

---

570 Bruce Thain, 'Kodak: 123 years of history in Harrow', *Harrow Times*, 16 December 2013

571 Hansard, HC Debates, Volume 878, London: HMSO, 31 July 1974, Columns 874–81

572 Information provided by London Borough of Harrow

of significant growth and change over the next fifteen years and beyond.[573]

Unlike a number of inner boroughs, Harrow did not build large housing developments in the 1960s and 1970s. But it did undertake medium-scale schemes such as the Rayners Lane council estate, built in the 1960s and now one of the most deprived parts of the borough. Some 500 homes there have been demolished and replaced by 800 new ones. The original housing suffered from damp, condensation, poor energy efficiency and ineffective sound insulation. The new development includes homes to rent, low-cost home ownership and family homes for sale.[574] Grange Farm Close estate in South Harrow, with 260 flats and bungalows, was constructed in the 1970s and is today also seen as in need of full regeneration and possibly redevelopment. The estate includes a number of buildings constructed using non-traditional materials, which are now prone to damp.

The proportion of households living in different housing tenures has remained remarkably constant over fifty years. The 1961 census showed 68 per cent of households in owner-occupied homes, which fell marginally to 66 per cent in 2011. Social renting was 10.2 per cent in 1961 and 10.6 per cent in 2011. This latter proportion, although low by the standards of inner boroughs, is the more remarkable, given the impact of right-to-buy policies pursued by central government over many years.[575]

The 1960s also saw the start of a period of growth in office construction, particularly in Harrow town centre. A number of public sector organisations moved to Harrow, including the National Coal Board, the Land Registry and part of the Inland Revenue. Residential homes made way for the new offices. By the 2010s, many of the buildings constructed in the 1960s and early 1970s

573 London Borough of Harrow, *Harrow and Wealdstone Area Action Plan Final*, 2013, https://www.harrow.gov.uk/www2/documents/s108616/HarrowandWealdstoneAreaActionPlan.pdf (accessed 4 June 2015)

574 Information provided by London Borough of Harrow

575 Ibid.

have been granted planning permission for redevelopment or conversion into housing.[576]

The council has promoted a major retail centre at Harrow-on-the-Hill. The original development took place in 1987, followed by a further stage in the 1990s. St Anns Shopping Centre was opened in 1987, involving the demolition of much of St Anns Road and College Road. The St Georges Shopping Centre opened in 1996 and has attracted more upscale outlets than St Anns. The council has pedestrianised part of the area to add to its appeal. Along with Brent Cross, Harrow-on-the-Hill is now one of the largest shopping destinations in north London.

Harrow's demographics have changed enormously over the fifty years since 1965, when the largest non-British-born population was from Ireland. The overseas-born population has risen from 5 per cent (actually quite high for the time) to 40 per cent. The borough has gone from having a population that was mostly of white British origin to one that is among the most diverse in the country. The minority ethnic population was under 5 per cent in 1965, while today it is about 70 per cent.[577] The biggest group within this substantial increase has been south Asians, in particular those from India.

The start of the process of change came with the arrival of Ugandan Asians in 1974. Expelled from Africa, this motivated and creative population settled in Kenton and South Harrow. They and their children have profoundly affected the borough, helping to drive up aspiration in schools and setting up new businesses. Like Redbridge, Harrow has become one of the most ethnically and religiously diverse places in the UK. Today, 26.4 per cent of Harrow's residents are of Indian origin, the largest minority ethnic group. Over eighty different languages are spoken in schools, with migrant groups from India, Ireland, Kenya, Romania and Sri Lanka. With this population has come a renewal of religion. The borough houses Buddhist,

---

576 Information provided by London Borough of Harrow

577 London Borough of Harrow, 2011 Census – Key Results for Harrow, http://www.harrow.gov.uk/info/200088/statistics_and_census_information/495/2011_census/2 (accessed 5 June 2015)

Christian, Hindu, Muslim, Jain, Jewish, Sikh and Zoroastrian places of worship.[578]

Harrow was controlled by the Conservatives continuously from 1964 to 1994, except for a period of 'no overall control' between 1971 and 1974. In 1968, Labour's worst ever year, the Tories won all the seats except one held by a Labour alderman. 1994 saw a Liberal Democrat surge, with the party becoming the largest on the council. Labour were then in control from 1998 to 2006, before the Conservatives regained control. Labour won in 2010 and 2014, though the Conservatives remain close behind.[579] In 2002, the Liberal Democrats found almost all their candidates barred from standing because their nomination papers were delivered late.[580]

Sir Horace Cutler, who was leader of Middlesex County Council and, from 1977 to 1981, leader of the GLC, represented Harrow. Cutler was heavily involved in the setting-up of the GLC in 1964 and 1965. Navin Shah was the first leader of Harrow (2004–06) of Indian origin. The borough's first Labour MP, Gareth Thomas, was elected in 1997. Two former Harrow chief executives have left to take up national office. Sir Tony Redmond chaired the Local Commissioner for Administration (the 'local ombudsman') while Christine Gilbert became head of OFSTED.

Harrow is an outer borough that has sustained a mixture of village and suburban style while accommodating immigrants from many countries. It is a settled and often traditional place within one of the world's most complex cities.

HAVERING

Havering was created from the municipal borough of Romford and Hornchurch urban district council in Essex. Its name was derived from

578 Information provided by London Borough of Harrow

579 Greater London Authority, *London Borough Council Elections 22 May 2014*, London: GLA, page 77

580 Kevin McGuire, 'Sixty Lib Dems barred from poll in mix-up', *The Guardian*, 9 April 2002

the manor of Havering-atte-Bower, a Royal Liberty formerly in the possession of the Crown. The amalgamation was described as an 'unhappy marriage' by the *Romford Recorder*. Nevertheless, the newspaper produced a commemorative souvenir edition with a picture showing local scenes within an ornate wedding-style frame: 'Commemorating the Union of Romford and Hornchurch – New Greater London Borough'.[581]

The Herbert Commission had proposed fifty-two London authorities, which would have left Romford and Hornchurch as separate boroughs. The old border between the two districts is still marked by a white boundary marker at Roneo Corner. Professor Ged Martin observed: 'Romford felt it was a self-contained community whose identity was tied to being the first town in Essex, not the last town in London.'[582]

Martin recalled one Hornchurch official's comments: 'If you've got to choose between two ugly sisters, pick the one with the bigger dowry.' Romford Town Hall became Havering Town Hall. Langtons House, used as Hornchurch's council offices from 1929, became a register office. 'It meant that it looked like a Romford takeover. And that did cause some noses to be put out of joint in Hornchurch,' added Martin. More optimistically, the editor of the *Romford Recorder* wrote: 'In years to come, when the towns of Romford and Hornchurch are vague memories revived in history textbooks, we can tell our grandchildren proudly: "We were there when Havering was born."'

From the start, few issues split the new Havering community more than the question of whether they live in London or Essex. None of the new borough was in the London postal area. 'Many people had moved to Hornchurch and Romford from inner London. They had "made it" out to Essex and did not want to feel dragged back again.'[583] Even after fifty years, television and radio reports often refer to 'Romford, in Essex'.

Labour won the 1964 election, a minority Labour administration gained the

---

581 Sebastian Mann, 'Havering's awkward birth: Ugly sisters and a Romford takeover recalled as borough turns 50', *Romford Recorder*, 2 January 2015

582 Ibid., quoting Professor Ged Martin

583 Ibid.

borough an early reputation for political instability, Professor Martin recalls, and the phrase 'wavering in Havering' came into use.[584] The borough has been in 'no overall control' for twenty-nine out of the fifty-one years since the 1964 election, an unparalleled record for any London borough.[585] There has been a strong Residents' Association presence on the council in most years. In 2014, councillors were elected from the Conservatives, Labour, a Residents' Association, the Rainham & Wennington Independent Residents and UKIP. In the past, there have been Liberal Democrats, too.

Architectural critic Nikolaus Pevsner observed of Havering:

> The character of its buildings is shared equally between the suburbia of its western neighbours and the rural vernacular of the Essex countryside. This mix is unique in East London, comprising still remote medieval parish churches along the Thames marshlands, tiny rural villages, farmhouses set in open fields, a scattering of mansions, leafy Edwardian suburbia, and at its heart the brash commercialism of Romford.[586]

Havering today has the second-highest number of semi-detached homes in London as a proportion of total stock (42 per cent) and the lowest proportion of flats of any London borough.[587]

Romford had been a major agricultural market town. Its cattle market survived until 1958,[588] making it almost the last example of such an activity within the area of the post-1965 boroughs. The extent and local importance

---

584 Ibid.

585 Greater London Authority, *London Borough Council Elections 22 May 2014*, London: GLA, 2014, page 83

586 *Romford Conservation Area Character Appraisal and Management Proposals*, The John Drury Partnership, London Borough of Havering, undated, page 4

587 London Borough of Havering, *Core Strategy and Development Control Policies Development Plan Document Adopted 2008*, 2008, page 34

588 'Romford: Economic history', in A *History of the County of Essex: Volume 7*, W. R. Powell (ed.), London: British History, 1978, pages 72–6, http://www.british-history.ac.uk/vch/essex/vol7/pp72-76

of a contemporary street market continuing the market tradition mean that Romford's character changes radically on market days, becoming more active and animated. Romford was for many years home to the Star Brewery, which was a major employer until it closed in 1993. The railway station was surrounded by goods areas, partly to deal with brewery traffic, and sidings to the east, including cattle facilities. The brewery site is now covered by a supermarket, cinema and shops.

The town centre plan of 1965–70 led to the construction of a ring road and began a significant redevelopment of the centre of Romford, as a loose association of shopping precincts.[589] Market Place is the dominant space, set in a conservation area. Its width and openness on non-market days (and its intense activity on market days) dwarf the neighbouring streets.

From the 1960s, Romford has been developed as a major London retail location, consisting of the Rumford Shopping Hall (early twentieth century), the Quadrant Arcade (1935), plus an earlier version of the Liberty Shopping Centre in the 1970s, The Brewery (2001), The Liberty and The Mall (2004). Efforts to improve the shopping environment led to the closure of Market Place to through traffic in 1969.[590] The town centre, now the fourth largest in London, has had to compete with massive shopping mall developments at Lakeside in Thurrock and Bluewater in Kent. Romford has a developed nighttime economy with one of the highest concentrations of bars and nightclubs anywhere in London outside the West End.

The Romford Ring Road is a 2-mile-long dual carriageway that encircles the historic town centre. Plans for the ring road were approved in 1966, and a phased construction followed, incorporating stretches of existing highways and new roads. The entire circuit of the route was completed in the 1980s. Few town centres in London are encircled by their own ring road: Romford's has been identified as a physical and (it has been argued) psychological barrier to

---

589 Ibid., page 13

590 Ibid., page 15

people.[591] A policy of improvement has been put in place, including efforts to use green spaces near the road and to plant trees.[592]

In Hornchurch, the borough built the Queen's Theatre in 1975, designed by the borough architect. The theatre replaced an earlier one built by Hornchurch council.[593] The council bought Risebridge manor lands in 1969 and opened an eighteen-hole golf course in 1972.[594] The course is currently leased to Risebridge Golf Ltd.

Within the Thames Gateway area, which was developed by the 1997–2010 Labour government, there were fourteen 'zones of change', six of which were within London. London Riverside, which covered the riverside areas of Havering and Barking & Dagenham, was identified as a zone of change. In April 2004, the Mayor of London endorsed a London Riverside Urban Strategy, which set out plans for the regeneration of the area, including the creation of compact mixed urban communities and a centre for innovation and high-tech manufacturing. The Rainham Marshes were highlighted as a potentially important environmental and leisure asset for east London. Rainham Village is recognised by English Heritage as the key historic centre within the Thames Gateway.[595] Since 2010, Thames Gateway policy has declined in importance in Whitehall.

Havering inherited a larger former GLC (formerly LCC) estate at Harold Hill, which had been proposed in the Greater London Plan (1944) as part of a wider policy to alleviate housing conditions within the LCC area. The estate is low-rise and made up of a mixture of brick-built houses and occasional small

---

591 London Borough of Havering, *Greening Romford Ring Road*, What if: projects Ltd, September 2012, page 21

592 Lee-Ann Richards, '100 new trees for Romford Ring Road', *Romford Recorder*, 19 February 2013

593 'Hornchurch: Introduction', in *A History of the County of Essex: Volume 7*, W. R. Powell (ed.), London: British History, 1978, pages 25–31, http://www.british-history.ac.uk/vch/essex/vol7/pp25-31 (accessed 15 September 2015)

594 'Romford: Manors and other estates', in *A History of the County of Essex: Volume 7*, W. R. Powell (ed.), London: British History, 1978, pages 64–72, http://www.british-history.ac.uk/vch/essex/vol7/pp64-72 (accessed 15 September 2015)

595 London Borough of Havering, *Core Strategy and Development Control Policies Development Plan Document Adopted 2008*, 2008, page 32

blocks. The first GLC tenant to exercise the 'right to buy' lived at Harold Hill, and the occasion was marked by a visit from the then leader of the GLC, Desmond Plummer. Years later, 39 Amersham Road, Harold Hill, was visited by Prime Minister Margaret Thatcher to celebrate the sale of council housing.[596]

Havering council has latterly pursued a Harold Hill Ambitions programme designed to tackle problems associated with a large estate that is now sixty years old. People who live in Harold Hill are more likely to have a long-term illness and less likely to have qualifications or a full-time job than residents in other parts of Havering. Perceptions of Harold Hill are worse than for other areas of the borough.[597]

Elsewhere, the Mardyke estate at Rainham was built by Hornchurch urban district council in the 1960s to house workers from Ford's Dagenham plant. It included six high-rise blocks and became 'notorious for crime and dilapidation as the decades progressed and jobs were axed'. The homes proved difficult to let.[598] The council balloted residents in 2007 to find out whether they wished to be transferred from council control, which they did.[599] A six-year redevelopment will be completed in 2015, providing 555 new homes. It has been renamed Orchard Village. Havering has a significant estate of high- and medium-rise homes at Waterloo Road in Romford.

There will be three Crossrail stations in Havering. Romford, Gidea Park and Harold Wood stations are all being improved as part of the run-up to the opening of the line in 2018. The south of the borough has long been associated with the District line. Upminster is the easternmost terminus of the line and is unusual in that Underground users can glimpse the Upminster

596 Melanie Hall, Andrew Hough and Martin Evans, 'What happened to Margaret Thatcher's first right-to-buy council house?', *Daily Telegraph*, 14 April 2015

597 London Borough of Havering, 'Harold Hill Ambitions', https://www.havering.gov.uk/Pages/Services/Harold-Hill-Ambitions.aspx#Areasofregeneration (accessed 10 June 2015)

598 Greater London Authority, 'The Mardyke Estate Rainham', Planning Report PDU/2196/02, 1 July 2009, http://static.london.gov.uk/mayor/planning_decisions/strategic_dev/2009/20090701/the_mardyke_estate_report.pdf (accessed 17 September 2015)

599 Ramzy Alwakeel, 'Orchard Village five years on – we look back at Rainham's Mardyke estate as regeneration hits halfway mark', *Romford Recorder*, 19 June 2013

Windmill from the train. The council is restoring the structure with help from the Heritage Lottery Fund.[600]

Havering is the second-largest London authority, with half of its land area within the green belt. In Upminster, Cranham and around Dagnam Park on the far east of the borough, London's built-up area simply stops at the point the green belt was imposed. The final streets provide a physical reminder of when the metropolis stopped growing outwards. Brentwood is protected from London's embrace by the M25 and a short tract of open land.

When UKIP won seven seats in the 2014 borough elections it provided evidence about the politics of Havering. In a number of ways, the borough still looks to Essex, where the party has prospered. Andrew Rosindell has been Conservative MP for Romford since 2001 and has won more than 50 per cent of the votes in each election. Even in the 2015 election, with a UKIP surge, Rosindell still achieved a remarkable 51 per cent of the poll. As MP, he has placed great emphasis on marking St George's Day, is an enthusiast for Margaret Thatcher and for traditional Essex. He has campaigned with a dog that wore a Union Jack waistcoat, and has trodden 'a narrow path between patriotism and nationalism'.[601] In doing so, Rosindell has been successful in preventing UKIP success.

Havering's 'London/Essex' location is important. Like Redbridge and Barking & Dagenham, the borough and its people look two ways: both in towards Liverpool Street and the City, but also out to leafy Essex. Its politics today has more in common with Essex than London.

HILLINGDON

Hillingdon was formed from three urban districts (Hayes & Harlington, Ruislip-Northwood and Yiewsley & West Drayton) and Uxbridge municipal borough, all of which had been in Middlesex.

600 Heritage Lottery Fund, 'Upminster windmill to be saved', press release, 10 July 2014

601 Alan Mace, *City Suburbs: Placing suburbia in a post-suburban world*, Abingdon: Routledge, 2013, page 142

Unlike many boroughs, Hillingdon does not have a legacy of 1960s and 1970s social housing estates that have subsequently required massive corrective action. The authority's social housing is not located in large estates. There are a few four-storey housing blocks in Harmondsworth and Hayes, though they are generally well-maintained. Most social housing was built of brick in small terraces or as semi-detached houses. Hillingdon did not inherit grandiose housing projects intended to replace slums and reduce overcrowding. The predecessor authorities handed across a relatively large number of council homes, 16,273, compared with many other new boroughs. In common with Croydon, Ealing and Enfield, Hillingdon agreed a deal with the GLC that the borough would provide some homes for GLC-nominated households in exchange for the GLC not building any estates in the borough.[602]

Hillingdon, under Conservative control, explicitly argued against GLC development in outer London:

> The Council has never accepted that fact that the ultimate solution of the overall London problem will be found in this way [i.e., by the GLC having the power to build social housing or nominate social tenants]; or if it is, the effect on the outer London areas will be disastrous. Fortunately, the population of inner London is falling far quicker than was estimated.[603]

When the GLC was won by the Conservatives in 1967 and again in 1970, policy changed: whereas Labour at County Hall had, from 1965 to 1967, continued the LCC's activist policies to transfer families from inner to outer London and beyond, the Tories were content to allow the boroughs to have greater influence.

Hillingdon saw a change in political control in 1971 when Labour took the council. Rates went up by over 100 per cent in two years. The new administration and its leader John Bartlett proposed to build more council housing and were prepared to use compulsory purchase powers to buy private land

---

602 Gerald Rhodes (ed.), *The New Government of London: The First Five Years*, London: Weidenfeld & Nicolson, 1972, page 232

603 Ibid., pages 237–8

and homes to be used for the development of additional and more densely settled mixed-tenure areas.

Bernard Levin, writing in *The Times*, likened this process of winkling out owner-occupiers to 1950s Rachmanism.[604] Bartlett retaliated in a letter to the paper, explaining:

> The local authority … can only look for land in the area it covers. At the present moment, there is virtually no undeveloped land in this area, other than 14,000 acres of green belt and open spaces, and therefore the only way of increasing the number of council houses for letting is by redevelopment of land occupied by low-density housing to a higher density, so that housing gain can be achieved.

Bartlett was accused by Conservatives of wanting to build council houses in people's gardens.[605]

Like Kensington & Chelsea, Hillingdon commissioned a remarkable new municipal building early in its life. New boroughs had to make judgements about how to rationalise their civic buildings,[606] and, in Hillingdon, a grand gesture was made. The council decided to construct a major new civic centre in Uxbridge and, as it turned out, the controversy surrounding the new building proved emblematic of a struggle between different interests in the area. Labour wanted to urbanise the borough while the Conservatives preferred to preserve Hillingdon's suburban tranquillity.

The cost and splendour of the brick-clad chateau-style civic centre ('the apotheosis of brick')[607] built in Uxbridge became national news.[608] As a

---

604 Hansard, HC Debates, Volume 910, London: HMSO, 28 April 1976, Columns 396–522

605 Cyril Taylor, *Sir Cyril: My Life as a Social Entrepreneur*, Stroud: Amberley, 2013

606 For a consideration of this issue see Michael Hebbert, 'Defining the Borough Effect', in *London: A New Metropolitan Geography*, Keith Hoggart and David R. Green (eds), London: Edward Arnold, 1991

607 Andrew Rosen, *The Transformation of British Life, 1950–2000: A Social History*, Manchester: Manchester University Press, page 136

608 Philip Sherwood, *Around Uxbridge Past & Present*, Stroud: Sutton Publishing, 2007

civic-office development, the scale of the project was unparalleled in post-1965 borough history. Designed by architects Robert Matthew, Johnson-Marshall & Partners, and constructed between 1973 and 1977, the civic centre is analysed by architectural critics Edward Jones and Christopher Woodward as follows:

> That the imagery of vernacular housing should be applied to a large bureaucratic institution ... is a sad comment on the times and evidence of an architectural loss of nerve. The adoption of 'friendly' forms is intended to make unwieldy local government less inaccessible. Architecturally, the opposite proves to be the case, for, in a secular age, civic centres are one of the last institutions that can legitimately be distinguished from housing or commercial building. But the building is very popular and a relief from the banal office blocks normally associated with local authorities.[609]

Hillingdon civic centre is probably the most important municipal building constructed in London since 1965. Only Kensington & Chelsea's (also brick-clad) headquarters is similarly recognised as both 'of its time' and architecturally striking. Both buildings cost significantly more than originally planned. The controversy about the civic centre's construction is now forgotten, and the quality of the building is admired. Moreover, the building has prospered in a way that much social housing built across London at the time has not.

The Bartlett administration was well known for its decision to build a ski slope at Park Road in Uxbridge. Like the civic centre and housing policy, the slope became emblematic of Hillingdon's particular brand of municipal socialism in the 1970s. John Bartlett was seen by sections of the press as the embodiment of high-spending municipal enterprise. Camden was seen similarly because of its willingness to build expensive council housing and to set high rates.

Hillingdon is a borough of powerful and sometimes dramatic transport infrastructure. In addition to two airports, Brunel's Great Western Railway

609 Edward Jones and Christopher Woodward, *A Guide to the Architecture of London*, London: Weidenfeld & Nicolson, 1983, page 363

runs across the south of the area. The Grand Union Canal runs north–south through Uxbridge, Hayes and onto the Thames at Brentford (in Hounslow). The Western Avenue (A40) and the M4 are massive road conduits running east–west. The M25 borders Hillingdon to the west. For many years, vehicles attempting to move north–south between the A40 and the M4 caused serious traffic jams in Hayes Town. A long campaign was waged to build a bypass, which was originally to be part of Ringway 3 of the London Motorway Box.[610]

The GLC under both the Conservatives and Labour (including the anti-road Livingstone administration) was prepared to build the new highway, though competition for resources delayed construction for many years.[611] John McDonnell, now MP for Hayes & Harlington and previously its GLC member, took part in a sit-in on a zebra crossing in Pump Lane, Hayes, in 1984, to protest against delays in building the bypass.[612] What is now known as the Hayes By-Pass was eventually competed in 1992. Recently, Hillingdon council has started a process of improving Hayes town centre.

In the years since 1965, Hillingdon has been the home to the airports of Heathrow and RAF Northolt. The latter is the base of No. 32 (The Royal) Squadron, the Queen's Colour Squadron and the Central Band of the Royal Air Force, and has an important role as an airport for military, governmental and VIP flights. Heathrow has grown to be the biggest international airport in the world, handling almost 75 million passengers a year.

It is rare for a council the size of Hillingdon to be home to two such significant airports. The scale and growth of Heathrow has presented the borough and neighbouring authorities with a complex challenge. Civil aviation has generated tens of thousands of jobs and is the guarantor of prosperity for local residents. Heathrow alone employs almost 70,000 people, though not all of them live in the borough. On the other hand, noise, pollution and the threat of

---

610 cbrd, *Western Section*, http://www.cbrd.co.uk/articles/ringways/ringway3/west.shtml (accessed 12 September 2015)

611 Hansard, HC Debates, Volume 976, London: HMSO, 17 January 1980, Columns 2058-68

612 *Hayes People's History*, March 2007, http://ourhistory-hayes.blogspot.co.uk/2007/03/hayes-bypass-was-fought-for-by-local.html (accessed 1 June 2015)

expansion have proved serious challenges to the quality of life for many in the south of the borough. The council leadership has supported Boris Johnson in his attempts to move London's main airport to the Thames Estuary.

Much of the borough's employment lies between the A40 and the M4. Stockley Park, one of Europe's largest business parks, is in this part of the borough. It was the work of the doyen of London developers, Sir Stuart Lipton, and includes buildings designed by Eric Parry, Foster & Partners and Skidmore Owings & Merrill. It has been described as bringing high-quality US-style landscaped office development to the UK and has variously been referred to as 'a place that is "not really suburban, urban or rural", "a wolf in sheep's clothing", and – rather more positively – "the Portmeirion of the business world"'.[613] But Stockley Park and Heathrow have together made Hillingdon one of the most prosperous places in the UK.

Large concentrations of traditional manufacturing can be found in the borough on the Uxbridge industrial estate and along parts of the Hayes/ West Drayton corridor. Employment in Hillingdon increased by over 70 per cent, faster than in any other borough, between the years 1961 (just before the new boroughs were created) and 2012.[614] Brunel University is located in Uxbridge. The University of West London, Bucks New University and Uxbridge College and are all within a short distance of the town centre. Film production is another local industry. Pinewood Studios has been given permission to expand within the green belt on the edge of the authority.[615] In addition to Pinewood, Hillingdon is close to a number of major studios at Elstree, Shepperton and Ealing. The A40 links Pinewood to post-production facilities in the West End.

Politically, the borough has swung between the Conservatives and Labour since the first election in 1964, though there were 'no overall control' periods

---

613 Ken Powell, 'Taking Stock at Stockley Park', *Building Design*, December 2008

614 Sir Stuart Lipton (chair), *It Took Another Riot: The concluding report of the Mayor of London's Independent Panel on Tottenham*, Don Levett (ed.), December 2012, Appendix 3, Table 1

615 Michael Donnelly, 'Pickles backs Pinewood green belt expansion', *Planning Resource*, 19 June 2014

from the late 1980s until the early 2000s. Latterly, the Tories have been securely in power. As in a number of boroughs, there have been periods with a single leader for many years. Ray Puddifoot, who became leader in 2000, was still in office fifteen years later. In the 2015 general election, Boris Johnson, the Mayor of London, became MP for the safe Conservative seat of Uxbridge & South Ruislip.

Hillingdon is the only London borough to include a lake with a functioning beach. Ruislip Lido, which doubled for the Atlantic Ocean in the British *Titanic* film *A Night to Remember*, has a big area of sand at its south end. The borough, because of Heathrow's presence, is the UK's gateway to the Atlantic, North America and indeed the rest of the world. This position brings significant employment benefits but also environmental problems and public service costs.[616]

HOUNSLOW

Hounslow brought together two former municipal boroughs – Brentford & Chiswick and Heston & Isleworth, with Feltham urban district – all of which were in Middlesex. It was at Heston (near Hounslow town) that Neville Chamberlain landed with his piece of paper declaring 'peace for our time' on his return from seeing Adolf Hitler in Munich in 1938. The aerodrome, which closed in 1947, is recalled in a number of street names, such as the pleasantly laid-out area around Bleriot Road, Sopwith Road and Brabazon Road in Heston. During the 1960s, the Heston service area on the M4 was built over the northern part of the aerodrome.

Much of today's Hounslow was market gardens and orchards before 1918. During the eighteenth and nineteenth centuries, Isleworth had seen the construction of a number of imposing villas and houses, most famously Syon

---

616 Health and Social Care Overview Scrutiny Committee, *The Impact of Heathrow Airport on the Hillingdon Health & Social Care Economy Final Report*, London Borough of Hillingdon, 2006, file:///H:/heathrow_impact%20(1).pdf (accessed 13 October 2015)

House.[617] Today, Isleworth consists of houses built in a number of styles from the 1850s to the 1950s. The industrialisation and suburbanisation of west London between the wars profoundly changed the Isleworth and Brentford area.[618] Old Isleworth was comprehensively redeveloped by Speyhawk in the early 1980s.

The Great West Road, the first part of which opened in 1925, was built to relieve congestion through Chiswick, Brentford and Hounslow. It allowed the development of a 'Golden Mile' of manufacturing firms which were household names, such as Firestone and Gillette, making tyres and razors respectively.[619] These modern factories, with their lawns in front and Art Deco styling, have come to be seen as an important part of London's architectural history. The Firestone Building, with a pillared classical colonnade, Egyptian-style and coloured ceramic tiles, was demolished in 1980 before a notice could be served to protect it.[620] Like the Euston Arch, this demolition has become a symbol of the damage that can happen to unprotected London architecture.

The creation of Hounslow was heavily influenced by the Great West Road and its links to central London and, later, Heathrow. The elevated section of the M4 from Chiswick roundabout to Brentford, which links to the A30 at Hounslow West, was opened by film star Jayne Mansfield in 1959.[621] It has become an iconic part of the country's motoring heritage.[622] The borough was

---

617 For an appreciation of Syon's remarkable location within contemporary Isleworth, see Simon Jenkins, *The Companion Guide to Outer London,* London: Collins, 1981, pages 109–16

618 See, for example, London Borough of Hounslow, *Osterley and Spring Grove* and *Great West Road,* http://www.hounslow.gov.uk/lbhc_c_3_3_osterley_and_spring_grove-2.pdf, and http://www.hounslow.gov.uk/lbhc_c_3_11_great_west_road-2.pdf (accessed 4 May 2015)

619 Ben Weinreb and Christopher Hibbert (eds), *The London Encyclopaedia,* London: Macmillan, 1983, page 331

620 Simon Jenkins, '100 Buildings, 100 Years review –"A battle between modernism and tradition"', *The Guardian,* 12 November 2014

621 Nick Curtis, 'The sweet little Chiswick flyover hits 50', *Evening Standard,* 1 October 2009

622 Jack Watkins, 'Road to redemption: How the architectural influence of the motor car transformed England', *The Independent,* 1 December 2012

given responsibility for running a 12-mile section of the M4 and was the first council in the country to be put in charge of a stretch of motorway.[623]

The road has been a mixed blessing for Hounslow, and the borough was opposed to the GLC's motorway plans.[624] On the one hand, it brings employment and business opportunities, while, on the other, it causes pollution and creates a barrier between communities to its north and south. In 2009, the mayor of Hounslow, Paul Lynch, speaking at a fifty-year anniversary event for the flyover, neatly summed up the earlier fascination with large-scale 1960s redevelopments by saying: 'It [the flyover] symbolises a rush to modernity, a belief that things would get bigger and better. The flyover raised the curtain on the motoring age, and we're now dealing with that legacy: we let a lot of genies out of bottles back then.'[625] As if to signal how different things are today, a Russian Orthodox cathedral opened in 1999 just off the A4 in Chiswick, allowing drivers to glimpse the building's blue onion dome from the road.

In its early days, Hounslow, along with many other new boroughs, wished to create family health centres with GPs working in groups, a policy still advocated in official reports.[626] Hounslow planned to spend over £700,000 on health centres,[627] with Heston Health Centre designed by the borough's architect. The new council made a film in 1965 to explain what it was doing for the public: Hounslow was handling 60,000 tons of rubbish per year, maintaining 250 miles of roads, managing 1,800 acres of parkland, 20,000 street lights (each adopted by a local resident) and eighty-four schools.[628]

623 London Borough of Hounslow, *The First Stage – Hounslow A New Borough*, a film made by the council, 1969, http://www.theguardian.com/uk-news/davehillblog/2015/aug/09/fifty-years-of-hounslow (accessed 16 September 2015)

624 Michael F. Collins and Timothy M. Pharoah, *Transport Organisation in a Great City: The Case of London*, London: George Allen & Unwin, 1974, page 574

625 Nick Curtis, 'The sweet little Chiswick flyover hits 50', *Evening Standard*, 1 October 2009

626 Greater London Authority, *London Health Commission*, London: GLA, 2014, page 57

627 Gerald Rhodes (ed.), *The New Government of London: The First Five Years*, London: Weidenfeld & Nicolson, 1972, page 121

628 London Borough of Hounslow, *The First Stage – Hounslow A New Borough*, a film made by the council, 1969 (see link above)

The film is remarkable, because it shows the council as a mini welfare state with a wide range of directly provided services for children, the disabled and older people. The elderly were offered 'luncheon clubs' and were able to take holidays for a nominal payment at a large house in Sussex owned by Hounslow. Buses in the council's livery were shown taking people on holiday.

'The borough treasurer's department now has a computer,' enthused the narrator, while the film showed workmen using a large crane as they struggled to manoeuvre a piece of equipment the size of a small car through what appears to be a specially drilled hole in the wall of the council's offices.

Some parts of Hounslow were seen as in need of conservation, while others required regeneration and renewal. Of Strand-on-the-Green, the Hounslow film said: 'What could be lovelier? There's no room for modern progress here.' But Brentford riverside is described as 'a sad place … where everything's grown old and derelict'.

Like many other new London boroughs, though less true of the outer ones, Hounslow was involved in a major scheme to replace obsolescent housing with a series of modernist towers. Efforts had been made since 1959 to redevelop the former waterworks site by the Thames at Brentford, but the new authority compulsorily purchased the site in 1966, and the GLC then developed a large new estate there.[629]

Instead of old terraced housing, the GLC built six identical 23-storey tower blocks, which created a consistent architectural image with a distinct sense of place. They remain, like the M4, strategic landmarks for Brentford. More recently, a strip of two- and three-storey terraces has been built to the north of the towers.

The building of this new social housing did not fully revive this part of Brentford. At the end of the 1970s, the area was still seen as 'depressed and

629 Diane K. Bolton, Patricia E. C. Croot and M. A. Hicks, 'Ealing and Brentford: Growth of Brentford', in *A History of the County of Middlesex: Volume 7, Acton, Chiswick, Ealing and Brentford, West Twyford, Willesden*, T. F. T. Baker and C. R. Elrington (eds), London: British History, 1982, pages 113–20, http://www.british-history.ac.uk/vch/middx/vol7/pp113-120 (accessed 15 September 2015)

depressing', with decaying slums and empty sites. Deindustrialisation around the Golden Mile was further blighting the area.[630]

The redevelopment of Brentford has been ongoing from 1965 to the present. The council launched the Brentford Initiative in 1993, with the aim of revitalising the area. A short distance to the north of the Brent/Thames junction is Brentford Lock, where major redevelopment has occurred since the 1990s, transforming the area into a classic modern mixture of canal-side greenery and contemporary flats. The River Brent at this point is the last stretch of the Grand Union Canal: the two divide just south of Ealing Hospital.

Even today, Hounslow council concedes that 'Brentford ... struggles to perform its function to provide local goods and services with regards to both the quantity and quality of floor space provided. The town centre also has an incoherent and run-down appearance and suffers from a constant stream of traffic travelling along the High Street.'[631]

Town centre managers have been appointed to support Brentford, Hounslow, Chiswick and Feltham town centres. The council is delivering regeneration projects in Hounslow and Brentford town centres, with resources from the Mayor of London's Outer London Fund. Feltham town centre has been subject to a master-planning exercise with a view to regenerating it.[632]

There have been significant developments in other parts of the borough. In 1988, Hounslow gave planning permission for developers to create a business zone and a country park in an area of dereliction that had been formed by gravel excavations in the west of the borough at Bedfont. Improvements led to the construction of small hills and the Bedfont Lakes.[633] The business

630 Ibid.

631 London Borough of Ealing, *Brentford*, http://www.ealing.gov.uk/download/downloads/id/6689/ed59-annex_2_hounslow_councils_draft_character_and_context_study_for_brentford (accessed 4 May 2015)

632 London Borough of Hounslow, *Consultation on Feltham Town Centre Masterplan*, 2015, http://www.hounslow.gov.uk/news_mod_home/news_mod_year/news_mod_month/news_mod_show?year1=2015&month1=2&NewsId=65983 (accessed 4 May 2015)

633 London Borough of Hounslow, 'About the Lakes', http://www.hounslow.info/parks-open-spaces/find-your-park/bedfont-lakes/about-the-lakes/ (accessed 4 May 2015)

park, close to Heathrow Airport, is home to a number of major companies, such as BP and Birds Eye.

The North Feltham trading estate, along with the Golden Mile and Transport Avenue in Brentford and Chiswick Park, has been regenerated in response to the expansion of Heathrow. Chiswick Park has been developed by Stanhope since the late 1990s on the site where the former London Transport Chiswick Bus Works built and serviced buses. Routemasters were designed and built here.[634] Like Stockley Park in Hillingdon and nearby Bedfont Lakes, Chiswick Park is a place of low-rise high-quality commercial buildings set in manicured lawns, lakes and a nature reserve.

Hounslow has had its share of problems with previously constructed social housing that, over time, fell below acceptable standards. The Beavers estate in Hounslow was built in 1967, with the architects attempting to avoid the mistakes made in previous GLC estates. The development was to be low-rise, spacious and green, and laid out and managed as if a private estate. There were 5 acres of open space, and hundreds of mature trees and saplings. The names chosen for roads, including Chinchilla Drive, Sable Close and Opossum Way, are among the most animal-themed in London. But the construction method used meant many of the homes were full of asbestos and suffered from damp.[635] It took many years for market conditions to move to the point at which a mixture of demolition, new homes and sales allowed the regeneration of the area.[636]

The Page Road estate in Bedfont consisted of run-down and unloved 1950s blocks of flats. Catalyst Housing developed an attractive red-brick replacement for the former estate, producing 320 new homes, of which 137 were for social rent, fifty for sale and 120 for shared ownership.[637] Catalyst delivered a

634 Information provided by James Marshall, Local Studies Librarian, Hounslow Borough Library Service

635 Hansard, HC Debates, Volume 177, London: HMSO, 19 October 1990, Columns 1543–50

636 Hounslow Homes, *Beavers Estate*, 2013, http://www.hounslowhomes.org.uk/index/about_us/new_build_and_regeneration/beavers_estate_regeneration.htm (accessed 4 May 2015)

637 Catalyst Housing, 'Page Road, Hounslow', http://www.chg.org.uk/development-regeneration/regeneration/regeneration-schemes/page-road-hounslow/ (accessed 5 May 2015)

smaller housing project at The Greenway on Staines Road, turning a former petrol station into eighteen environmentally sustainable homes. Hounslow works with Brent, Hillingdon, Ealing, Harrow and a number of housing associations through Locata, a vehicle to allow tenants and those seeking social housing to find and/or exchange properties.[638]

Compared with many outer boroughs Hounslow was more willing to house GLC tenants and to develop social housing. As a result, the borough's housing legacy has more in common with inner boroughs than its neighbours.

Immigration has been a significant factor affecting Hounslow since 1965. In the early years, the borough's population was over 90 per cent born in Britain and/or white, though even at that point, Hounslow already had one of the larger minority ethnic populations of any authority in Britain. The 2011 census showed Hounslow as 62 per cent non-white British, with 34 per cent being Asian. 19 per cent of Hounslow's population described themselves as Indian in 2011.[639]

The politics of Hounslow has seen Labour in power for forty-two out of fifty years, with the Conservatives winning, as in virtually all London authorities, in 1968–71, and falling to 'no overall control' between 2006 and 2010. Labour, under Steve Curran, won in 2014. Unlike in a number of inner boroughs, there was no radical change in ideology during the 1970s and 1980s. The industrial and economic decline that affected both employment and the politics of inner and east London had far less impact on west London boroughs, like Hounslow, whose politics remained mainstream.

Hounslow has benefited enormously from being on major roads and railways linking Heathrow Airport to central London. It is still a modern industrial location as well as a classic suburb.

638 Locata Home, http://www.locata.org.uk/ (accessed 5 May 2015)

639 London Borough of Hounslow, 'How has Hounslow's demographic profile changed?', 2013, http://www.hounslow.gov.uk/demographic_profile_analysis_jsna.pdf (accessed 5 May 2015)

KINGSTON-UPON-THAMES

The Royal Borough of Kingston-upon-Thames combined two municipal boroughs in Surrey: Kingston and Malden & Coombe. As a result of the removal of parts of the county from Greater London during the process of moving from the Herbert Commission's report to Royal Assent, Kingston is a peninsula, sticking out from south-west London. The town had long been the county town of Surrey and it remains so. Surrey County Council has kept its headquarters in its pre-1965 County Hall. The borough was granted a Royal Charter in 1964 by the Queen and is, with Greenwich and Kensington & Chelsea, one of three royal boroughs in the capital.

Contemporary Kingston expanded rapidly during the nineteenth century after the construction of a new bridge across the Thames in 1828 and the growth of the railway. Surbiton was still farmland at this time. Kingston rejected the railway in the 1830s and, consequently, the first railway in the area went through Surbiton in 1838 (on its way from London to Portsmouth) leading to expansion around the new station.[640]

The railway did not open in Kingston till 1863, encouraging a housing boom there, too. Much of the remaining open land around Kingston was developed by the 1890s. Norbiton subsequently became linked to Kingston by ribbon development along the London Road.[641] New Malden grew quickly following the opening of a railway station, whereas, as late as the 1920s, Tolworth consisted of little more than isolated farms, though it became a substantial suburban housing area following the construction of the Kingston bypass.[642]

According to a character study produced for the borough:

---

640 'Kingston-upon-Thames: Introduction and borough', in *A History of the County of Surrey: Volume 3*, H. E. Malden (ed.), London: British History, 1911, pages 487–501, http://www. british-history.ac.uk/vch/surrey/vol3/pp487-501 (accessed 16 September 2015).

641 Ibid.

642 Royal Borough of Kingston-upon-Thames, *Kingston: Towards a Sense of Place, A Borough Character Study to support the Kingston Local Development Framework*, January 2011, page 6

Beyond the heartland of Coombe and to the north lies the 1930s housing estate built on Robin Hood Farm, to a high standard of layout, benefiting from the woodland backdrop and the hillside topography. As Kingston Hill falls towards the town and Victorian Canbury, there is a cluster of tall buildings set back from the road and in a wooded area, together with flats and houses of varying character, described below. Kingston hospital and some crude blocks of flats define the western limit of this area. An enclave of offshoot cul-de-sacs on Coombe Lane West marks the southern edge of the area, with houses of varying character in the slither of land between Kingston Hill and Richmond Park wall.[643]

This description of part of outer London is revealing, mostly in a good way. It describes part of the borough that is a mixture of town and countryside, *rus in urbe*, but includes hills, wooded areas, but also 'crude blocks of flats' and tall buildings. It is a useful reminder that Kingston, Sutton and Richmond are places where rural Surrey and Greater London meet, with the urban equivalent of continent-shaping tectonic impacts.

Although usually seen as part of deeply suburban 'Surrey in London', Kingston had a manufacturing past, with Hawker Siddeley, Sopwith and Hurricane building planes in the borough.[644] The Thames was used as a landing strip for float planes.[645] According to Pathé News, parking meters were manufactured in the borough at the point the 1965 London government reorganisation was taking place.[646] Meters made in Kingston were sent to central London for use.

The borough today has a higher proportion of small enterprises than the regional and national averages, with relatively few large firms.[647] Kingston

---

643 Ibid., page 2

644 Information provided by Royal Borough of Kingston-upon-Thames

645 Kingston Aviation, 'Sopwith Aviation and Hawker Aircraft Canbury Park Road, Kingston', http://www.kingstonaviation.org/js/plugins/filemanager/files/Brief_History_Banner__15B_Layout_1.pdf (accessed 17 September 2015)

646 British Pathé, 'Parking Meters 1965', http://www.britishpathe.com/video/parking-meters/query/Kingston (accessed 16 September 2015)

647 Ibid., page 7

is characterised by generally low levels of deprivation, and is ranked as the 252nd most deprived local authority area out of 326 in England.[648] However, this borough-wide analysis hides significant variations within. There are still pockets of long-term unemployment and worklessness in parts of Norbiton, Chessington and Hook.[649] Kingston has recorded job growth in line with the national average in recent years, but has fallen below the fast-growing London trend. Kingston has to compete with Wimbledon and Richmond, which have excellent transport links to the West End.[650]

Kingston is a major shopping destination for south-west London and Surrey. Today, the borough's retail system consists of Kingston (a metropolitan centre), plus local retailing at New Malden, Surbiton and Tolworth. There are many smaller parades and shopping areas.[651] The construction of Eden Walk in the 1960s and 1970s provided the basis for today's major retail centre in Kingston.[652] A shopping area at the site was first proposed in 1936 by the predecessor Kingston council to provide, among other things, a multi-storey car park. There has been continued redevelopment on the site for the past fifty years as Kingston has further developed as an important shopping destination for London and Surrey.

After the war, Eden Street was identified as a good location for a car park and shopping area because the council already owned land in Eden Street. Eden Walk Phase One began in 1964 and was completed in 1968. The council then planned a second phase, which was built between 1977 and 1979. The development was enlarged between 1983 and 1985. Kingston is currently seeking to improve the attractiveness of the town centre.[653] The Bentall Centre

---

648 Nathaniel Lichfield & Partners, Royal Borough of Kingston upon Thames Economic Analysis Study Final Report, 2014, pages 17–18

649 Ibid., page 17

650 Ibid., page 38

651 Ibid., page 4

652 British Land, 'British Land Acquires 50% Stake in Eden Walk Shopping Centre, Kingston-upon-Thames, South West London', 31 July 2012, http://www.britishland.com/news-and-views/news/archive/2012/31-07-2012.aspx

653 See Royal Borough of Kingston-upon-Thames, Kingston Town Centre Area Action Plan, 2008, file:///H:/Kingston_town_centre_DPD%20(1).pdf (accessed 13 September 2015)

was built in 1987 and 1992. This further development was to include a five-storey department store and a four-level adjoining shopping mall. Today, it is a cathedral-like space that allows Kingston to include a mall-scale shopping centre inside a large, traditional town centre. Retail analysts have summarised the local retail potential in the following, revealing, way:

> The catchment population of Kingston is extremely affluent. Over 50 per cent of the resident catchment population is classified as 'symbols of success' and 'urban intelligence', compared to 17 per cent nationally. 74 per cent of all shoppers are in the ABC1 profile and household income is … [well] above the national average.[654]

However, the local authority believes there needs to be more investment to enhance and update the retail offer within Kingston town centre. There is, according to the council, 'a lack of available retail units that adequately meet modern retailer requirements, subsequently hindering the town's offer'.[655]

Areas around the town centre have witnessed significant new residential development in recent years, including the Kingston Heights development on the site of a former power station on Skerne Road, and the Royal Quarter close to the station. Former factory sites on Seven Kings Road have also been used for housing, with other developments at The Boatyard, Waters Lane, and The Royal Gallery on Skerne Road. The majority of these new developments have been flats.[656] Many of these new blocks are at a 'metropolitan' scale, with large blocks of five, six or eight storeys. Their construction has parallels in a number of other outer boroughs, where ex-industrial land near town centres is rapidly being re-used for high-density housing.

---

654 Completely Retail, 'The Bentall Centre', 2015, http://completelyretail.co.uk/portfolio/Aviva/scheme/The-Bentall-Centre-Kingston-Upon-Thames/index (accessed 16 September 2015)

655 GVA (for RBKT), *Kingston Eden Quarter Market Report*, February 2015, pages 16–17

656 GVA/Allies & Morrison/The Urban Engineering Studio (for RBKT), *Eden Quarter Development Brief SPD*, March 2015, page 78

The borough has a number of social housing estates, dating back to before the 1965 borough came into existence. There is an estate regeneration programme to improve three housing estates – Cambridge Road, Kingsnympton Park and Sheephouse Way – with the possibility that the School Lane and Alpha Road estates may be included.[657]

The development of Kingsnympton began in 1950. Leigh, Milton and Newdigate were the first three blocks to be built and, at the time, were considered of high quality. The Cambridge Road estate is the largest concentration of council housing in the borough. It has over 900 homes, which include four fifteen-storey blocks, plus sixteen low-rise, deck-access blocks of four or five storeys in height. The estate was built in the 1970s, near Norbiton town centre.[658] Alpha Road estate was built in the mid-1970s in southern Kingston and consists of over 500 properties in mainly four-storey blocks of flats. There are also some terraced houses, mostly sold under the right-to-buy policy.

Kingston has the advantages and disadvantages of having a number of major roads, including the (A3) Kingston bypass, which serves as an important east–west corridor across the borough. The borough relies on suburban rail services, which link Surbiton, Kingston, New Malden and Norbiton with Waterloo, though no part of the borough is on the Tube.[659] London's last trolleybus service ran in Kingston in 1962, while in 1989, a gyratory road system was introduced to Kingston in an attempt to ease congestion and direct traffic away from the town centre. In 2001, Kingston Bridge was widened and strengthened.[660]

Indeed, in its submission to the Mayor's Outer London Commission, Kingston concluded:

---

657   Royal Borough of Kingston-upon-Thames, Residents, Health and Care Services Committee, Housing Estate Regeneration Programme, Report by the Director of Place, 17 June 2015, http://moderngov.kingston.gov.uk/documents/s58163/Appendix%20E.pdf (accessed 16 September 2015)

658   Kingston Federation of Residents, 'Member Residents' Associations', 2015, http://kingstonfed.org/member-residents-associations/ (accessed 17 September 2015)

659   Nathaniel Lichfield & Partners, Royal Borough of Kingston upon Thames Economic Analysis Study Final Report, 2014, page 3

660   London Transport Museum, *Kingston: The growth of London through transport*, 2007, http://www.ltmuseum.co.uk/assets/downloads/Kingston.pdf (accessed 11 September 2015)

[T]he borough has no underground services or orbital rail routes. Regional transport provision to Kingston town centre in particular is relatively poor considering its important regional role as a metropolitan town centre. Kingston is therefore heavily reliant on its comprehensive network of frequent and reliable bus services for public transport provision.[661]

It is planned that Crossrail 2 will cross London from Alexandra Palace via Tottenham Court Road to Chessington, which would radically improve links to central London. But the project was only just starting in the mid-2010s, so is unlikely to be completed before 2030.[662]

As local government spending constraints affected London boroughs and other councils in the years since 2010, Kingston put forward an innovative bid to central government to gain freedom from Whitehall funding. According to the press, Kingston wants 'to sever all links from central government and become a flagship independent authority'. The leader, Kevin Davis, said his ambition was for the borough to be 'independent from grant completely', and should move away from a system where central government hands out monies to us and we have to spend it in the most reasonable way we can find. I want to see whether we can give [it] back to government, in return for which they need to give us some freedoms – in particular, give us a bit of an uplift in business rates.[663]

Kingston's radicalism was rewarded: in his speech to the Conservative party conference at Manchester in October 2015, Chancellor George Osborne announced that such a reform would be introduced by 2020.[664]

---

661   Royal Borough of Kingston-upon-Thames, *Submission by the Royal Borough of Kingston upon Thames to the Outer London Commission Round 3*, RBKT, 2013, http://www.london. gov.uk/olc/docs/Outer%20London%20Commission%20Submission%20-%20RBK.%20 FINAL.pdf (accessed 17 September 2015)

662   Nazia Dewji, 'Mayor Boris Johnson backs Crossrail 2 route including five Kingston borough stations', Surrey Comet, 29 October 2014

663   Jane Merrick, 'Tory-controlled Kingston upon Thames council could be the first to become flagship independent authority', *The Independent*, 18 January 2015

664   Nicholas Watt, 'Osborne to allow local councils to keep £26bn raised from business rates', *The Guardian*, 5 October 2015

The council has been politically balanced between the Conservatives and Liberal Democrats in recent years, though the Tories won in 2014. There have been several periods of 'no overall control' between 1986 and 2002. As in Richmond and Sutton, Labour has significantly declined since the 1960s. The Conservatives and Liberal Democrats, when in control, have been moderate in their leadership of the council.

Kingston is a London borough largely surrounded by Surrey, whose county town it remains. It has a royal past and retains its 'royal borough' status. It is a prime example of how London's outer areas can be both within the city, but also part of a lush rural hinterland.

MERTON

Merton was created from two former municipal boroughs, Mitcham and Wimbledon, plus Merton & Morden urban district council. In parts of these former Surrey districts, uncontested elections were still common before 1965, though after the creation of the new borough, this phenomenon disappeared.[665] As in a number of other 1965 boroughs, efforts were made to create a single identity from its constituent parts. The nature of Merton as a unified authority was

> reflected in the borough coat of arms, which features emblems linked
> to the heritage of its predecessor authorities. They include lavender
> sprigs associated with the famous Mitcham crop; a fret taken from the
> crest of Merton Priory; the black lion emblem used by the Garth fam-
> ily, lords of the manor of Morden and the Cornish chough, once the
> heraldic symbol of Thomas Cromwell, who was awarded the manor
> of Wimbledon by Henry VIII.[666]

---

665 Gerald Rhodes, *The New Government of London: The First Five Years*, London: Weidenfeld & Nicolson, 1972, page 72

666 London Borough of Merton, 'Merton Heritage Strategy 2015–2020', pages 4, 5, www.merton.gov.uk/merton_heritage_strategy_2ah_amend__2_.docx (accessed 30 August 2015)

Post 1965, Merton was an area that had prospered mightily as the Underground expanded. The Northern line reached Morden in 1926, bringing the area within half an hour of central London. Frank Pick, then joint assistant managing director of the Underground (and its chief executive from 1933 to 1940), described Charles Holden's modernist design for the station in these excited terms: '[A] new style of architectural decoration will arise', appropriate to the city of the future 'modern London – modern not garbled classic or Renaissance'. Holden's revolutionary station entrance kiosks were the main focus of attention at Morden, with 'striking white Portland stone structures dotted along a drab south London high street'.[667] Seen today, the station and its surrounds, including the borough's offices, have a mild flavour of pre-1989 East Berlin.

As in virtually all the new boroughs, there was a challenge in bringing together different constituent parts: former councils had existed for many years and local institutions had been used to dealing with smaller units of local government. In the first year or two, Merton's chief executive showed an awareness of this problem by having lunch in a different school each week.[668]

The council inherited only a single children's home within its own boundaries and three in parts of Surrey outside Greater London, with joint-user arrangements for two other boroughs formed from within Surrey.[669] Unlike many Conservative-controlled councils, Merton undertook a full reorganisation of its secondary schools along comprehensive lines 'because of the moderating leadership of Sir Cyril Black and Alderman Talbot'.[670] Cyril Black was MP for Wimbledon from 1950 to 1970, and, during this time, mayor of Merton. A street is named after him in Wimbledon.

---

667 Oliver Green, *Frank Pick's London Art, Design and the Modern City*, London: V&A Publishing, 2013, page 81

668 Ibid., page 169

669 Gerald Rhodes, *The Government of London: The Struggle for Reform*, London: Weidenfeld & Nicolson, 1970, pages 206–7

670 Gerald Rhodes, *The New Government of London: The First Five Years*, London: Weidenfeld & Nicolson, 1972, page 177

The borough is primarily residential, with town centres in Wimbledon, Mitcham, Morden and Colliers Wood. It inherited control of part of the St Helier estate (part is in Sutton), which was built by the LCC in Morden between 1928 and 1936 as an out-of-town cottage development and was the second largest of its kind after the Becontree estate (Barking & Dagenham). It was named after Lady St Helier, an LCC alderman. The risk of monotony was avoided by the use of a range of different materials, including bricks, slate and different-coloured roof tiles. The architectural detailing includes gables, porches and door canopies.[671]

Boris Johnson observed of the estate and its history: 'There are many hidden cultural stories throughout our city, which tell us as much about our identity and history as the grand displays of institutions like the Tate Modern and the National Gallery.'[672] In common with other major housing estates built both before and after 1965, St Helier has faced a need to adjust to the complexities of being part of a modern metropolis. Like Becontree or the Bellingham estate (Lewisham), the garden city ideal can still be understood in St Helier. Terraces of small cottages look out over grass verges and trees.

Although the LCC had moved inner-London residents out to Merton's predecessor authorities, the borough did not have much sub-standard property to clear. It undertook its own large housing development along All Saints Road in Colliers Wood. Built in the 1980s, the All Saints estate consists of low terraces of two- and three-storey homes. It resembles the St Helier estate more than the modernist ones built in many inner boroughs.

Two- and three-storey terraces form the perimeter of the estate with lower two-storey horseshoe and curvilinear terraces at the centre. The terraces are a mixture of houses and flats. The architecture includes red brick with slate tiles on mansard roofs. Some homes have recessed balconies. The blocks were arranged around pockets of open space that provide pedestrian routes within

---

671 Merton Historical Society, 'St Helier Estate', 2006, http://www.mertonhistoricalsociety.org.
     uk/topics/St+Helier+Estate (accessed 31 August 2015)

672 London Borough of Merton, 'Life in St Helier', a film made by Medium Rare, 2009, http://
     www.merton.gov.uk/leisure/arts/life-in-st-helier.htm (accessed 31 August 2015)

the estate. Plenty of car-parking spaces were provided, made more attractive by wooden pergolas and raised planters. Much of the estate is enclosed from the surrounding street network, though some blocks face onto All Saints and East Roads, while three-storey blocks face onto Haydons Road and North Road.[673]

The All Saints estate marks a break with the social housing experimentation attempted in many inner boroughs during the 1960s and 1970s. Everything about it is different, with smaller brick-built terraces of houses, pitched roofs, grass verges and easy-to-maintain flowerbeds.

Merton has been one of London's most important centres of retail warehousing.[674] Unlike inner-London boroughs, Merton was early to capitalise on the trend towards out-of-town retail development. As deindustrialisation affected the capital in the 1970s and 1980s, Merton was well placed to benefit from the land made available. Colliers Wood was historically the heart of Merton's industrial heritage, including calico bleaching, paper production, precision engineering, paint and varnish manufacture.[675]

Wimbledon was identified in the Strategic Planning Guidance for London in 1996 as a 'major centre' and is the largest retail district in the borough. It is a strategic location that provides arts, cultural, entertainment and leisure facilities. The former Wimbledon Town Hall, now a Tesco Metro, was developed to be part of the Centre Court Shopping Centre in the early 1990s. A former fire station was embraced by this development.

Wimbledon has continued to evolve as Merton's most important shopping and business centre, largely because of its excellent railway and Underground provision. Land development that attracts a high density of activity has been encouraged. Morden and Mitcham town centres are smaller and have traditionally provided for neighbourhood retailing. Mitcham has suffered relative

---

673 London Borough of Merton, 'Borough Character Study 3. Haydons Road Neighbourhood', 2015 https://www.merton.gov.uk/cabinet_borough_character_study_part_1_haydons_road.pdf (accessed 12 August 2015)

674 Keith Hoggart and David R. Green (eds), *London A New Metropolitan Geography*, London: Edward Arnold, 1991, page 134

675 London Borough of Merton, 'Merton Heritage Strategy 2015–2020', pages 4, 5, www.merton.gov.uk/merton_heritage_strategy_2ah_amend__2_.docx (accessed 30 August 2015)

decline and has latterly been designated an 'urban village' by the council, as part of a regeneration effort.[676]

A new railway station opened at Mitcham Eastfields in 2008, after almost eighty years of discussion. The town centre was badly served by public transport (the nearest station at Mitcham Junction was a mile away) and the council had lobbied Network Rail and its predecessors to open a station.[677]

Merton was connected to the Tramlink when it opened in 2000. Although often referred to as 'Croydon Tramlink', the capital's only tram service runs from Wimbledon, Merton Park, Morden Road, Phipps Bridge, Belgrave Walk and Mitcham within Merton through to Croydon. The council and its neighbour Sutton have been encouraging TfL to extend the Tramlink via Morden to Sutton, and possibly to South Wimbledon. TfL requested the two boroughs carry out a consultation to test opinion. A loop on the extension was supported to improve the accessibility of St Helier Hospital.[678]

Wimbledon is home to two theatres. The New Wimbledon Theatre, one of the largest in London, has been the starting point for a number of productions that have transferred to the West End. The architecture, which dates from 1908, is a major local landmark. Its 'well-decorated three-balconied auditorium with iron-balustraded fronts is of a type most unusual in Britain (comparable in London only to the Playhouse) but common in Spain and Portugal'.[679] Since 1994, the main theatre has been supported by an eighty-seat studio space, now used by the Attic Theatre Company. The Polka Theatre for

---

676   London Borough of Merton, 'Chapter 1. Local Socio-Economic and Demographic Context', Borough Context, https://www.google.co.uk/webhp?sourceid=chrome-instant&rlz=1C1SKPL_enGB409&ion=1&espv=2&ie=UTF-8#q=merton+borough+devel opment+1960s+1970s

677   London Borough of Merton press notice, 'Dream rail connection nears reality', 9 January 2008, http://news.merton.gov.uk/2008/01/09/pressrelease-1745 (accessed 30 August 2015)

678   London Borough of Merton, *Extending Tramlink from Wimbledon to Sutton via Morden Public Consultation*, Report to the London Boroughs of Sutton and Merton, Report by OPM Group, September 2014, https://www.merton.gov.uk/morden-sutton_tramlink_consultation_report_final_sept14.pdf (accessed 30 August 2015)

679   Theatres Trust Theatre Database, 'New Wimbledon Theatre', http://www.theatrestrust.org.uk/resources/theatres/show/2036-new-wimbledon-theatre (accessed 30 August 2015)

children was opened in the former Holy Trinity Church hall in 1979.[680] The Art Deco Mitcham Majestic Cinema (which for a time became a bingo hall) was demolished in 1978. A Sainsbury's supermarket was built on the site – it has now been succeeded by a further development.[681]

Wimbledon Windmill was opened as a museum in 1975, and a grant from the Heritage Lottery Fund in 1999 enabled the sails to be restored to working order and the museum to be extended.[682] Mitcham Abbey Mills was restored in 1989, creating London's only riverside village. The council continues to support cultural initiatives, including the proposed transfer of Wandle Industrial Museum to Ravensbury Mill and the development of Merton Priory Chapter house as a visitor attraction.[683]

Merton has seen the construction of two major places of worship. The Buddhapadipa Temple opened in Calonne Road 1980 and was the first Thai Buddhist temple to be built in the UK. It houses a series of murals that attract worshippers and tourists from far afield.[684] There is a house and a pond, as well as several bridges within the temple grounds. Merton is home to the largest mosque in western Europe. The Baitul Futuh Mosque opened in Morden in 2003. It has a 15-metre-diameter dome and minarets 36 metres and 23 metres high, accommodating thousands of worshippers in each of its two prayer halls. The building is a blend of Islamic and modern British architecture and incorporates much of the structure of an old dairy site.[685]

680 London Borough of Merton, '50 Merton Moments: A History of the Borough', Acava (Association of Cultural Advancement Through Visual Art) for London Borough of Merton, *Londonist*, http://londonist.com/2015/04/50-merton-moments-to-celebrate-50-years-of-merton (accessed 30 August 2015)

681 Cinema treasures, 'Majestic Theatre', http://cinematreasures.org/theaters/13742 (accessed 30 August 2015)

682 Wimbledon Windmill, 'Wimbledon Windmill History', http://www.wimbledonwindmill.org.uk/history (accessed 30 August 2015)

683 London Borough of Merton, 'Merton Heritage Strategy 2015–2020', page 8, www.merton.gov.uk/merton_heritage_strategy_2ah_amend__2_.docx (accessed 30 August 2015)

684 For a full description, see Sandra Cate, *Making Merit, Making Art, A Thai Temple in Wimbledon*, Honolulu: University of Hawaii Press, 2002

685 Open City, 'Baitul Futuh Mosque', Open House London 2015, http://events.londonopenhouse.org/building/15924 (accessed 30 August 2015)

Like the contemporary Hindu temple at Neasden (Brent), the Sikh temple in Southall (Ealing) and the Russian Orthodox church in Hounslow, the temple and mosque in Merton have been built in the decades since the boroughs were created. These buildings are a physical manifestation of the 'multicultural' city London has become since 1965. Not since the Gothic Revival during the nineteenth century can so many grand religious buildings have been constructed in the city. Immigrants from Africa and eastern Europe are now reviving Christian churches. Merton, like Brent, Ealing and Hounslow, has been the cultural beneficiary of this fortuitous regeneration.

The borough has seen relatively slow housing growth in recent years with an increase of only 1 per cent in the stock of dwellings between 2001 and 2012. Merton's population density is relatively high by outer-borough standards.[686]

Merton has been a classic Conservative–Labour marginal borough. There was no overall control 1964–68, then the Conservatives won 1968–71, with Labour gaining control 1971–74. The Tories won the council back in 1974 and held it until 1990 when Labour won again. Labour then kept control until 2006, before the Conservatives re-took power. Finally, in 2014, Labour regained the council. Like Haringey, Merton is a borough of two political halves: Wimbledon and the west is broadly Conservative, while Mitcham, Morden and the south are generally won by Labour. Although the Liberal Democrats managed to win over 20 per cent of the vote in 1982 and 1986, the party has never won more than three seats.[687]

There has been political controversy in recent years about the future of the St Helier Hospital, a large Art Deco institution in Morden of great significance to local residents. There have been plans to close St Helier and rebuild it and/or to re-configure hospital services for the wider south-west London area, including Merton, Sutton and Epsom (in Surrey).[688] A major

---

686 Greater London Authority, *Housing in London 2014: The Evidence Base for the Mayor's Housing Strategy*, 2014, pages 47, 123

687 Greater London Authority, *London Borough Council Elections 22 May 2014*, London: GLA, 2014, page 131

688 BBC News, 'Epson and St Helier could be replaced under new hospital plan', 14 April 2015, http://www.bbc.co.uk/news/uk-england-32297664 (accessed 31 August 2015)

redevelopment of St Helier was cancelled in 2014 on cost grounds, though further proposals were subsequently made.[689]

During 2015, the leader of the council, Stephen Alambritis, chaired the efforts of the South London Partnership (consisting of Merton, Croydon, Richmond, Sutton and Kingston) to bid for devolved powers from the Treasury.[690] This partnership was one of five across London that chose to work together to make the case for devolution to boroughs. There are numerous policy issues, such as housing numbers and the future of rail services, where these authorities are able to make common cause. Crossrail 2, which is being planned by the Mayor of London, would cross Merton: running in a tunnel from Wimbledon to Tottenham Hale, via Victoria and Tottenham Court Road. It would extend north to Alexandra Palace and Cheshunt (Hertfordshire) and south to Sutton, Kingston and Surrey.

Like Ealing, Merton is a political microcosm of the country as a whole. It is a changing, though settled, community that includes both affluent and more deprived areas.

NEWHAM

Newham was formed from the former county boroughs of West Ham and East Ham. North Woolwich (formerly part of Woolwich metropolitan borough) and a small section of Barking were added to the new authority. The name of Newham was chosen as a way of avoiding a struggle about adding an 'and' or, alternatively, coming up with a wholly new name. 'Newham' was a name that embraced part of both its predecessors. The council is one of two boroughs that have always been Labour-controlled. Even in Labour's *annus horribilis* of 1968, Newham remained

---

689 BBC News, 'Epsom and St Helier could be replaced under new hospital plan', 14 April 2015, http://www.bbc.co.uk/news/uk-england-32297664 (accessed 13 October 2015)

690 Louisa Clarence-Smith, '"Prawn cocktail approach" – Merton council leader to woo Treasury in south-west London devolution bid for jobs and homes', *Wimbledon Guardian*, 10 June 2015

Labour-controlled because of the use of the mayor's casting vote in a tied aldermanic election.[691]

The county boroughs of East Ham, West Ham and Croydon were among the least enthusiastic about reform of the councils outside the LCC's boundaries. Each had been a powerful all-purpose authority, free of the need to operate with an upper-tier county council running education, social services and transport. West Ham had a long municipal history, having been fully built up when the LCC was created in 1888. West Ham had benefited from legislation restricting noxious industry operating within London, which had had the effect of shifting manufacturing to the other side of the River Lee. The borough became a major centre of chemicals, pharmaceuticals and food processing. The construction of the Royal Docks further enhanced the area's industrial strength.

This strength turned to a weakness when, during the Second World War, the area became a target for Nazi bombers. Vera Lynn, the 'Forces' sweetheart', who was born in East Ham, came to embody resistance against the Blitz throughout Britain.[692] From the 1960s onwards, deindustrialisation struck London. Factories, the gas industry, docks and railways all declined.

This decline was precipitous and has shaped the area's subsequent development. There were 15,000 people working in engineering in Newham just before its creation.[693] In March 1968, the Jeyes Group, one of east London's best-known industrial enterprises, announced it was leaving two factories in Plaistow (and one in neighbouring Barking) after eighty years, with 900 jobs lost. In the same year, a further 140 jobs were lost at Yardley's box factory, and, a year later, 600 jobs were cut at Gallagher's cigarette factory, both in Stratford. But the biggest blow in terms of economic impact was when Beckton Gasworks shut down.[694]

---

691 Patrick Dunleavy, *The Politics of Mass Housing in Britain, 1945–1975: A Study of Corporate Power and Professional Influence in the Welfare State*, Oxford: Clarendon Press, 1981, page 208 (Aldermen were a small number of councillors elected by councillors themselves)

692 Sebastian Murphy-Bates, 'East Ham school celebrates 100 years of success', *Newham Recorder*, 16 June 2015

693 Information provided by London Borough of Newham

694 Ibid.

A rare countervailing investment was British Railways's announcement of a new continental railhead at Carpenters Road, Stratford, promising 300 new jobs. Tate & Lyle was one of the few companies to survive and prosper. Its factory at Silvertown has existed from the early days of Newham to post-industrial London, having originally opened at Silvertown in 1878.[695] The Tate & Lyle plant is one of the capital's most important, enduring, industrial icons.

The 1970s proved even bleaker for Newham and its industries with the final decline and closure of virtually all of the remaining docks in the borough. Physical decay did not only affect local companies; a study of education in the borough, written in the late 1970s, concluded:

> The general condition of the borough has affected the authority's fixed assets and the facilities through which their various local services are operated. Hospitals, schools, libraries, offices and other institutions of local government and services have been subject to the physical decay, which beset housing and industry in the area. This affected the quality of services the authority was able to provide, and compelled the local authority to consider the renovation and replacement of many of its older facilities.[696]

Newham was a classic 'inner city' authority. It had a long history of poverty and deprivation, but had fulfilled an important function for London as a whole, supplying labour and accommodating much of the city's less glamorous industry. The rapid economic decline between the late 1960s and early 1980s left the borough further impoverished and with a poor quality of life. Other authorities that shared similar characteristics, particularly Haringey and Brent, included substantial middle-class housing. Apart from a small part of Forest Gate, Newham was uniformly poor. Like neighbouring Barking, it had low staying-on rates for those above the school-leaving age.

---

695 Tate & Lyle, 'Henry Tate', 2015, http://www.tateandlyle.com/aboutus/history/pages/henrytate.aspx (accessed 15 September 2015)

696 Philip Tunley, Tony Travers and John Pratt, *Depriving the Deprived: A study of finance, educational provision and deprivation in a London borough*, London: Kogan Page, 1979, page 18

Housing stock had been subjected to a process of renewal in the latter years of East Ham and West Ham. The former authorities had resisted building high-rise blocks until government subsidies made them attractive.[697] West Ham built many towers. When Newham was created in 1965, West Ham's borough architect and planning officer were appointed to the new authority. The architect, T. E. North, wanted to extend system-built high-rise blocks across the new borough.[698]

East Ham's housing committee chair was unimpressed by West Ham's policy:

> I'm speaking on behalf of the people of East Ham when I say we don't want that kind of thing here [system building at high density]. I've fought this idea for many years and I would cry it from the rooftops if an attempt was made to make East Ham's development similar to West Ham's.

Of West Ham's tower blocks, he remarked: 'I was shocked to see the surroundings people will be expected to live in.' Ratepayer and Liberal councillors denounced West Ham's housing as 'a mass of pigeon holes' and 'a series of Dartmoor prisons'.[699]

The new borough was not discouraged from pursuing West Ham's approach. Patrick Dunleavy quoted Newham's own papers stating:

> The Newham Housing Project is considerably larger than the combined programmes of the two old boroughs, and the current four-year programme, as approved by the Minister of Housing and Local Government, is the largest of the 32 London boroughs … to cope with our expanding

697 Patrick Dunleavy, *The Politics of Mass Housing in Britain, 1945–1975: A Study of Corporate Power and Professional Influence in the Welfare State*, Oxford: Clarendon Press, 1981, page 230

698 Ibid., page 234

699 Ibid., page 235

programme it is essential, if we are to achieve our targets, that system building be continuously used in our programme.[700]

A new town was proposed for Beckton, with about 3,000 dwellings in 23- (revised later to sixteen-) storey blocks. The approach was highly industrialised and there was surprisingly little local resistance. For this massive project, resources proved insufficient and GLC support was sought. A joint agreement between Newham and the GLC was announced in December 1967.[701]

On 16 May 1968, Ronan Point, a 23-storey system-built tower in Canning Town, partially collapsed after a gas explosion on the eighteenth floor. Four people were killed and seventeen injured when the corner of the building collapsed, like dominoes, from top to bottom. The building had been completed just two months previously. Experts believed the accident was one for which no designer could have made allowances. Newham had followed official advice in constructing the tower, and was found not responsible for the disaster. However, the collapse produced an immediate outcry against tall, system-built flats. People in Beckton collected signatures in opposition to being moved into such buildings.[702]

Residents 'accepted that their homes would be pulled down ... and that their housing future would be determined by the local bureaucracy without consulting them',[703] and the council was hostile to opposition, being 'virtually never affected by genuine electoral competition, dominating and controlling an extremely weak interest-group process and run for very long stretches of time by the same small group of council leaders ... Even favoured and integrated groups ... were rigorously excluded from "political matters".'[704]

Newham's approach was relatively common in the 1960s and 1970s. Stephen Elkin, an American academic, writing in 1974 about developments at World's

---

700 Ibid., pages 237–8

701 Ibid., page 240

702 Ibid., page 244

703 Ibid., page 242

704 Ibid., page 335

End, Chelsea, and at St Giles concluded London politicians had little interest in public participation and interest groups. Professional decisions were empowered by disciplined party politicians and residents largely excluded.[705]

The imposition in 1981 of the LDDC to redevelop the derelict dock areas in Newham, Tower Hamlets and Southwark started a process that has affected Newham ever since. Despite opposition from the boroughs, the LDDC initiated a massive transformation of the area. The corporation is discussed in more detail in the Tower Hamlets section. Changes on the Isle of Dogs began to spread north and east to Canning Town and Stratford. The extension of the Docklands Light Railway allowed large tracts of former industrial land to be re-used for housing, eventually all the way to Beckton. The LDDC developed London City Airport on the site of the former Royal Docks.[706] In 1999, the Jubilee line was extended from central London to Canning Town, West Ham and Stratford.

An agreement was signed between the LDDC and Newham in 1987 to open up development around the Royal Docks to include 1,500 new homes for rent and a major shopping complex at Gallions Reach.[707] The LDDC worked with Newham to develop homes for sale at Beckton, which had previously been dominated by social housing.[708] Private house-builders had been little present in Newham before the LDDC's interventions. From this point, policy in the borough has been to create a more mixed population, including owner-occupiers and people with larger disposable incomes. Moderate and consistent leadership of the council allowed it to move relatively easily from the politically charged early 1980s to having a pragmatic approach to the docklands project.

The single biggest opportunity to face Newham since 1965 was London's successful bid to hold the 2012 Olympic Games. The GLC under Sir Horace

---

705 Stephen L. Elkin, *Politics and Land Use Planning: The London Experience*, Cambridge: Cambridge University Press, 1974, Chapter 5

706 James Bentley, *East of the City*, London: Pavilion Books, 1997, pages 55–6

707 Ibid., pages 91–2

708 Ibid., pages 107–8

Cutler had sought, in the late 1970s, to bring the games to London in 1984 or 1988, and had intended to use them as a catalyst for the regeneration of the Royal Docks.[709] But no bid was made, largely because of its expense. The successful 2005 bid led to the creation of a powerful Olympic Delivery Authority, and released upwards of £9 billion in regeneration, transport and other games-related public spending.[710] If transport improvements and other costs are added in, the total was even greater.

The main Olympics events took place on a site at Stratford railway lands, just north of the rail and Tube station. West Ham United will play at the Olympic Stadium, albeit after much controversy about the move from Upton Park.[711] From Newham's point of view, the regeneration undertaken was on a scale that might otherwise have taken decades. Within five years, a 2.5 sq. km zone of industrial dereliction was transformed into what has subsequently become the Queen Elizabeth Olympic Park. The area has been given its own post code, E20, which had hitherto been used by BBC soap *EastEnders*. There were also parts of the site in Hackney, Tower Hamlets and Waltham Forest.

From inner-east London's point of view, the key benefit of the games was the swift improvement and linking of areas such as Hackney Wick, Leyton, Maryland and Bow. Even before the games, Newham had been successful in attracting a massive Westfield shopping centre to what is now called Stratford City, which it is estimated will bring over 15,000 jobs to the area. There has been success in ensuring new employment has gone to local people.[712]

The arrival of Westfield appears to have improved trade in the old shopping centre at Stratford Broadway. Today, what had, for many years, been a large, polluted, ex-industrial site is now being used as a major new residential

---

709 Wes Whitehouse, *GLC – The Inside Story*, Sunbury: James Lester Publishers, 2000, page 107

710 National Audit Office, *The London 2012 Olympic Games and Paralympic Games: post-Games review*, 2012, London: TSO, page 23

711 John Dillon, 'Bitterness and envy from Chelsea, Arsenal and Tottenham won't change the fact that West Ham's Olympic Stadium move makes absolute sense', *Evening Standard*, 21 August 2015

712 Volterra, *Westfield Stratford City: The Inheritance before the Games*, 2011

and leisure neighbourhood. Benefits of this change at Stratford are being felt in Plaistow and West Ham, increasingly seen as residential locations for people priced out of inner London.

Newham has been run by Labour for the entire period from 1965 to 2015. In 2002, the borough voted to adopt a mayoral system of government. Sir Robin Wales, who had previously been leader since 1995, was elected mayor in 2002 and subsequently in 2006, 2010 and 2014. Under his leadership and that of his predecessor as leader, Stephen Timms, the council has pursued a form of redistributive pro-business redevelopment of what had previously been one of the poorest authorities in the country. Under both the 'council leader' and 'mayor' model of government, Newham has experienced powerful leadership. Timms, now the MP for East Ham, has built up huge votes and majorities in what is now one of Labour's safest seats.

Newham has transformed itself from being an area facing continuing economic decline and poverty to one that is increasingly linked into the post-industrial growth of inner and central London.

REDBRIDGE

R edbridge brought together three municipal boroughs formerly in Essex: Wanstead, Woodford and Ilford. Parts of the municipal borough of Dagenham and the whole of Chigwell urban district council were added. The name Redbridge was chosen as a compromise between the better-known districts that comprised the new authority.[713]

The western side of Ilford was close to East Ham and had been the eastern-most edge of Victorian London. Much of the eastern part of Ilford, notably around Gants Hill and Hainault, was developed rapidly immediately before and (by the LCC) just after the Second World War. Built-up London stops

---

713 Michael Hebbert, 'The Making of the Borough Map' in *London: A New Metropolitan Geography*, Keith Hoggart and David R. Green (eds), London: Edward Arnold, 1991, page 193

dead at the edge of the green belt in Hainault. Ilford council, responsible for a population of 180,000, had been sufficiently important to run its own tram services until they were taken over by the London Passenger Transport Board. The authority was an 'excepted district' for education purposes and ran services on behalf of Essex. The Royal Commission's original proposals for London boroughs would have left Ilford as a free-standing council.[714]

In Chigwell, which is part of Woodford, the London boundary runs through the middle of suburban streets. Indeed at the end of King's Avenue, at the Essex border, it runs through the middle of a semi-detached house. Woodford, where Sir Winston Churchill was MP until the end of 1964, and Wanstead contain a mixture of substantial older homes and inter-war semis. This part of Redbridge sprawls across into Epping Forest, and the built-up area runs almost continuously along the Central line to Theydon Bois and Epping. Anyone gazing at Underground train describers in central London will know by heart a number of Redbridge neighbourhoods, particularly the French-sounding Hainault. The Central line, including its spectacular 'Moscow Hall' Tube station at Gants Hill, is of enormous importance to Redbridge.

The new council chose to locate its headquarters in Ilford Town Hall, a Renaissance-style building constructed between 1899 and 1901. Plans to replace this grand edifice with a new one designed by Sir Frederick Gibberd (architect of Liverpool's Roman Catholic cathedral and the Regent's Park mosque) during the early 1960s had come to nothing. In the years immediately after 1965, a new £10 million civic centre was planned at Barkingside. Designed by borough architect Michael Booth, this new building was to be a low-rise pentagon, but was shelved because of financial difficulties.[715]

Redbridge in 1965 was a place that had, to a significant degree, been settled by residents moving away from inner London (as in the LCC housing at Hainault), or those who had chosen to live near but not in London. It was, and remains, a

714 *Royal Commission on Local Government in Greater London 1957–60 (Cmnd 1164)*, Report, London: HMSO, 1960, page 234

715 English Heritage, *London's Town Halls: The Architecture of local government from 1840 to the present*, Swindon: English Heritage, 1999, page 64

place of aspiration and upward mobility. Only about a fifth of the new borough was within the London postal area, and most people's addresses ended 'Essex'. The creation of Greater London meant that, as in a number of other boroughs such as Hillingdon and Bromley, the problems of 'London' were now shared. In these early years (1966–69), the council was only willing to make available up to forty homes for the GLC to nominate households into within its area. This total was tiny compared with the housing needed in the inner part of the capital.[716]

Another feature of Redbridge at this time was the attempt to construct major new roads, the so-called Ringways plan. The GLC's Ringway 2, part of the Motorway Box and built along the North Circular Road (A406), was to run north–south through Ilford, providing a link to the M11/M12 interchange at Woodford. According to the council, the A406 'acts as a physical barrier between Wanstead & Woodford and Ilford'.[717] Separately, a motorway (the M11) was to be extended to link the proposed Ringway 4 (similar to the M25) and Ringway 2 at Woodford. The A12, which came into London through the south of Redbridge, was to be developed to motorway standard through into Leyton and Stratford, thus linking Ringway 4 to Ringway 2 at Redbridge roundabout and then taking traffic towards Docklands.

The council, working alongside Patrick Jenkin (MP for Wanstead & Woodford from 1964 to 1987), opposed the piecemeal announcement of road schemes, the government's refusal to publish the costs, and the lack of compensation for the many householders affected by, particularly, the M11. Jenkin cited:

> Uplands Road in Woodford Bridge ... [where there were] houses with short
> back gardens, whose occupiers will find themselves within a stone's throw
> of a motorway on a 20-foot-high embankment with thousands of vehicles
> an hour roaring past and who will not get a penny piece of compensation.[718]

---

716 Gerald Rhodes (ed.), *The New Government of London: The First Five Years*, London: Weidenfeld & Nicolson, 1972, page 237

717 London Borough of Redbridge, *Artist Brief Public Art Commission South Woodford*, 2010, file:///H:/South%20Woodford%20Brief%20Final.pdf, (accessed 17 September 2015)

718 Hansard, HC Debates, Volume 781, London: HMSO, 3 April 1969, Columns 707–20

The council and the MP believed (rightly, as it proved) that the Ministry of Transport and the GLC were taking apparently unconnected steps that would leave Redbridge criss-crossed by motorway-scale roads. Such tactics were often used in the 1960s to minimise opposition to major highways.

The bridge that gave its name to the Woodford Bridge area was knocked down in the 1960s to accommodate road widening.[719] The construction of the M11 link road led to protests in Redbridge, in particular during 1993, when a tree was removed on George Green, east of Wanstead.[720] This part of the borough was left with cut-off streets just as Westway had chopped roads in half in North Kensington in the 1960s. Even today, some residential roads have the look of ones in Berlin divided by a large wall. Grass-roots protests against construction here and in Leyton attracted national attention, as the environmental consequences of new roads became ever-more contentious.[721]

Battles over roads were only one element in the borough's first decades. At that time, Ilford ranked as London's ninth biggest shopping centre, just behind Bromley and Romford, and bigger than Wood Green.[722] It was designated as a regional town centre by the GLC and was part of a de-concentration strategy pursued at the time to shift economic activity to sub-centres within outer London.[723]

In 1980, a town-centre action plan led to the development of Ilford's Winston Way, enabling the pedestrianisation of the High Road. Subsequently, Thurrock Lakeside, Bluewater in north Kent and, latterly, Westfield at Stratford have developed within easy reach of most east London and Essex shoppers. Each of these malls created major competition for Ilford's new

719 London Borough of Redbridge, *Woodford Bridge Conservation Area Draft Character Appraisal – May 2013*, 2013

720 Derek Wall, *Earth First! and the Anti-Roads Movement: Radical Environmentalism and Comparative Social Movements,* London: Routledge, 1999, page 76

721 Joe Moran, *On Roads: A Hidden History*, London: Profile Books, 2009, page 214

722 Barrie S. Morgan, 'The Hierarchy of Retail Centres', in *London: A New Metropolitan Geography*, Keith Hoggart and David R. Green (eds), London: Edward Arnold, 1991, page 127

723 Michael Hebbert,'Defining the Borough Effect', in *London: A New Metropolitan Geography*, Keith Hoggart and David R. Green (eds), London: Edward Arnold, 1991, page 201

centre, The Exchange, which was opened in 1991. However, The Exchange has been successful despite this growth of competition. The council sought to regenerate Ilford town centre during fifty years of rapid change in retailing and also developed the Kenneth More Theatre, which opened in 1975. Its long-serving manager and artistic director, Vivyan Ellacott, had local and national roles in the theatre.[724] Since the 2000s, large blocks of flats have been built in the town centre.

Ilford will be about twenty-three minutes from the West End when Crossrail opens in 2018. There will be stations at Seven Kings, Goodmayes and Chadwell Heath. The council has redeveloped Gants Hill, a local shopping area in Clayhall close to Valentine's Park.[725] The roads approaching Gants Hill roundabout are at a surprisingly grand scale, hinting at Parisian rather than London road standards. Three tall buildings have been added to the predominantly low-rise neighbourhood to strengthen the local economy.

Ilford was not only traditionally a major retail centre, but also Redbridge's main employment hub. The town's name was synonymous with photography. Alfred Harman set up a company that had an innovative way of developing photographs, and went on to be a world leader in photography. However, changes in the demand for film and cameras led the company to locate all its activities in Cheshire during the 1980s. The Ilford brand lives on. Plessey, the radio and TV manufacturers, had a factory in the area from the 1930s which, among other things, continued operations during the Second World War in the newly constructed Central line tunnels near Redbridge station.[726]

The largest groups of industries based in Ilford had been chemicals, engineering and plastics, sweets, paper novelties, water-softeners, blinds, breeze blocks, and bell fastenings. They were not concentrated in any one district.

724　Jessica Earnshaw, 'Life's a real cabaret for Ilford's Vivyan Ellacott', *Ilford Recorder*, 19 October 2012

725　London Borough of Redbridge, *Local Development Documents Local Development Scheme – 2013/2016*, 2013, file:///H:/Local%20Development%20Scheme%202013-%2016.pdf, (accessed 12 October 2015)

726　Sam Adams, 'Tube tunnels hid a wartime secret', *Wanstead & Woodford Guardian*, 27 March 2008

Older factories tended to be in or near the town centre. Later industrial development at Chadwell Heath was influenced by the growth of Ford's works at Dagenham. There was motor transport activity along Eastern Avenue.[727]

The scale of industrial employment in the borough, even in the south, was far less than in neighbouring Barking & Dagenham or Newham. Nevertheless, in common with other parts of London, the borough's industrial base was damaged by economic change in the 1970s and 1980s. However, Redbridge became the beneficiary of a substantial in-movement of ambitious immigrants from the inner boroughs. With good schools and housing, the several neighbourhoods within Redbridge became the destination of choice for many British-born and immigrant households looking for a well-connected home in an attractive neighbourhood.

As a result of forty or more years of such arrivals, Redbridge has become one of the most ethnically diverse areas of the UK. The borough has long had a substantial Jewish population and still does. European immigrants to the East End in the nineteenth and early twentieth centuries moved outwards as they became more prosperous. In the past twenty-five years, many migrants from south Asia, particularly from India, have made a similar move from Newham. Some immigrants now move to Redbridge, especially Ilford, as their first home in Britain.

The 2011 census showed the borough's non-white British population at 65.5 per cent, higher than the average for inner-London boroughs and way above the 20 per cent England and Wales figure.[728] Thirty-seven per cent of the population was born outside Britain. Redbridge is one of the most diverse places in terms of the different religions practised, also having a low proportion of its population claiming to have 'no religion'.[729] The borough's population

727 'The borough of Ilford', in *A History of the County of Essex: Volume 5*, W. R. Powell (ed.), London: British History, 1966, pages 249–66, http://www.british-history.ac.uk/vch/essex/vol5/pp249-266 (accessed 16 September 2015)

728 Office for National Statistics, '2011 Census: Ethnic group, local authorities in England and Wales', *Census 2011*, Table KS201EW

729 Office for National Statistics, *Religion in England and Wales 2011*, 11 December 2012, http://www.ons.gov.uk/ons/dcp171776_290510.pdf (accessed 5 March 2015)

is growing rapidly and will have needed over 10,000 additional school places between 2006 and 2014, with more required in coming years.[730]

Unlike a number of inner boroughs, Redbridge did not inherit or build large social housing estates in the 1960s and 1970s. Nevertheless, there are poor quality forty-year-old blocks at Claire House and Repton House in Clayhall, Ilford. They have been demolished and redeveloped by Swan Housing Association to provide additional homes.[731] South Woodford was, until 2004, home to the student residences of Queen Mary, University of London, but the distinctive tower blocks were demolished in 2007 and replaced with lower-rise privately owned flats.[732]

The politics of Redbridge has remained moderate and consensual through-out its existence. There was no ideological war during the 1970s and 1980s. The council was in Conservative control from 1964 to 1994 and again in 2002–09. Labour won control outright for the first time in 2014, suggesting a longer-term shift in local politics because of the area's changing population. Since 1965, Ilford's two parliamentary seats have proved marginal, though Ilford South has, over time, become a safe Labour seat.

Redbridge has been a successful leader in the development of its website, 'Redbridge i', launched in 2007. The purpose of Redbridge i was to allow public access to services and information. It has won national recognition and awards, with 85,000 people registered to it and over 3 million users per year. The council has established a budget consultation system which has been adopted by other authorities. Most council data is published and available to the public.[733] The Redbridge Music Service has arranged a biennial choral festival since 1975, while the authority collaborates with its neighbour Waltham Forest to run the North East London Music Education Hub.

---

730 Information supplied by London Borough of Redbridge

731 London Borough of Redbridge, 'Estate Regeneration' *Redbridge i*, http://www2.redbridge. gov.uk/cms/council_tax_benefits_housing/housing/housing_plans_and_policies/estate_ regeneration.aspx (accessed 7 March 2015)

732 London Borough of Redbridge, *Artist Brief Public Art Commission South Woodford*, 2010

733 Information supplied by London Borough of Redbridge

Redbridge has changed from being a classic London suburb to something closer to an inner-city authority. It is one of the most diverse places in Britain, with good schools and, in Ilford, a town centre that is growing upwards.

RICHMOND-UPON-THAMES

Richmond is the only borough that lies on both sides of the river. It was formed from three former municipal boroughs: Richmond and Barnes, which had both been in Surrey, and Twickenham, which was on the Middlesex side of the Thames. The council celebrated its fiftieth anniversary with a touring exhibition entitled 'Joined by the River'. The borough has 21 miles of Thames frontage, the longest of any borough.

In the early 1960s, as in many other boroughs, there was opposition to the merger of district authorities which were then in Surrey and Middlesex, and also to joining London. A 'Save our Surrey' campaign was launched, and there was particular aggravation in Twickenham over the choice of the name Richmond for the new borough.

Yet, Twickenham's York House became the main municipal building. The council chamber in Richmond Town Hall was hired out for meetings and the rest of the building was used as additional council offices, before being refurbished and modified as part of the Riverside development considered below. In 1987, the Central Reference Library, which previously had been housed with the lending library at Little Green, was opened on the first floor of the old town hall. The Local Studies Library was given its own space and a small museum dedicated to the history of Richmond.[734]

Richmond is home to the largest of all London's Royal Parks and is an important national nature reserve. Richmond Hill is a place described by Simon Jenkins as one that eighteenth-century Londoners visited 'to escape the fog and politics of

---

734 London Borough of Richmond-upon-Thames, 'The Old Town Hall, Richmond, Local History Notes, Richmond Libraries' Local Studies Collection, http://www.richmond.gov.uk/local_history_old_town_hall.pdf (accessed 3 September 2015)

London', and to which they brought poets, artists and essayists. These sophisticated visitors 'declared Richmond Arcadia, a landscape fit for Claude or Poussin'. Gainsborough and Constable painted there. The Thames has played a major part in the development of today's borough, with its unique qualities. Today, the river's curve below Richmond Hill, looking to Petersham Meadow, provides a view of 'ruminating cows, now under what amounts to a cow-protection order courtesy of the National Trust'.[735] Indeed, the Petersham view is preserved by law.[736] From King Henry's Mound, there is a protected view of St Paul's Cathedral in the City of London, over 10 miles to the east.[737]

Richmond is a relatively small but successful business location. The borough has also attracted inward investment because of its proximity to Heathrow, good rail links to central London, access to skilled labour and cheaper rental levels than in the city centre.[738] The authority has a high proportion of graduates within the local population, while in 2013, 96 per cent of the borough's schools were rated good or outstanding.[739] It has been popular with energy, retail, ICT, financial and professional services, and marketing companies.

Richmond, despite its leafy image, does have social housing, though all the authority's stock was transferred to a housing association in 2000. Ham Close estate, built by the borough in the 1970s, currently consists of fourteen blocks of flats, housing 192 properties in 8 acres of ground. The blocks do not exceed four storeys, and there are trees, as well as lawns and car parking, in the areas between the buildings. However, research by The Prince's Foundation suggested that there were problems with some of the housing, including poor

735	Simon Jenkins, *England's 100 Best Views*, London: Profile Books, 2013, pages 329–32

736	BBC News, 'Protected view unveiled to public', 14 June 2006, http://news.bbc.co.uk/1/hi/england/london/5079602.stm (accessed 3 September 2015)

737	'James Batten and St Paul's view', Friends of Richmond Park, 2015, http://www.frp.org.uk/news/269-james-batten-st-pauls-view (accessed 3 September 2015)

738	Roger Tym & Partners, *Local Economic Assessment Final Report*, Roger Tym & Partners and Renaisi for London Borough of Richmond-upon-Thames, October 2010, http://www.richmond.gov.uk/local_economic_assessment_rut_nov_2010.pdf (accessed 3 September 2015)

739	Greater London Authority, *The London Annual Education Report 2013*, London: Greater London Authority, 2013, page 10

insulation, damp, maintenance and lift problems. The area was also perceived to be cut off from the rest of the locality.[740] The report was concerned with developing a close understanding of residents' needs and aspirations, while attempting to encourage renewal and redevelopment. In comparison with the approach taken to many regeneration schemes in London, this study was clearly intended to be sensitive to local opinion.

Overall, Richmond has one of London's smallest social housing sectors, with about 12.5 per cent of all homes being owned by housing associations.[741] Over 99 per cent of housing association property in the borough meets the government's Decent Homes Standard, though the proportion of private sector homes failing to meet the standard is slightly above the national average.[742]

The council undertook a survey in 2010 to allow Richmond residents to identify what they considered to be their local neighbourhood. This 'all in one' research was used to draw up village areas within the borough. Boundaries were not prescriptive: villages were allowed to overlap and people could choose whichever area they most identified with and contributed to.[743]

The Royal Botanic Gardens at Kew is one of the world's leading botanical research centres and is funded by the UK government for its scientific and educational work. Kew Gardens, along with Richmond Park, Hampton Court Palace, Ham House, Strawberry Hill House, Garrick's Temple to Shakespeare, Kew Palace, the Palladian villa at Marble Hill and Richmond Riverside, are major London visitor attractions. Richmond, like Greenwich, is one of the few boroughs outside central London with a substantial tourism economy.

The large local leisure sector is enhanced by the presence of the Richmond Theatre and Twickenham, the home of the Rugby Football Union. The theatre, located adjacent to Richmond Green, was designed by Frank Matcham, who,

---

740 The Prince's Foundation for Building Community, *Vision for the Future of Ham Close Report*, London: The Prince's Foundation, October 2014, page 6

741 London Borough of Richmond-upon-Thames, *Housing Strategy 2013–17*, http://www. richmond.gov.uk/housing_strategy_13_17.pdf, page 4 (accessed 3 September 2015)

742 Ibid., page 8

743 London Borough of Richmond-upon-Thames, 'Village Plans', 2015, http://www.richmond. gov.uk/home/my_richmond/village_plans.htm, (accessed 3 September 2015)

though not qualified as an architect, was also responsible for the Karsino (also in Richmond), the Hackney Empire, the London Coliseum, the London Palladium, the Hippodrome and the Victoria Palace. A roll-call of other local theatres with names of previous boroughs were designed by Matcham in London, such as the Brixton Borough Theatre & Opera House, the Islington Marlborough, the Willesden Hippodrome, the Ilford Hippodrome, the Lewisham Hippodrome, the Chiswick Empire, the Finsbury Park Empire and the Winter Garden at Westminster have been demolished. Façades remain at Wood Green and Stratford in Newham.[744] The Richmond Theatre, with its preserved interior, is all the more important for this link to the history of theatre design. The borough council provided support for a programme of improvements in the early 1990s.

Twickenham, like Lords (Westminster), Wembley (Brent) and Wimbledon (Merton), is the home of one of the country's main sports. The ground has been substantially redeveloped since 1965, with permission from the council in 2002 to extend the capacity to 82,000, and for a Marriott hotel to be incorporated with the ground.

Teddington (also in the borough) and Twickenham have been home to famous film studios. Around the time of the 1965 London government reforms, iconic films such as *A Hard Day's Night*, *The Italian Job* and *Alfie* were made in the borough.[745] More recently, *Mandela – A Long Walk To Freedom* and *The Second Best Exotic Marigold Hotel* were partly made at Twickenham.[746] Teddington was used by Thames Television, the BBC and many other broadcasters to record national television programmes. *The Avengers*, *Minder*, *The World at War* and the *Benny Hill Show* were among the best-known outputs.[747]

744 Frank Matcham Society, 'Frank Matcham 1854–1920 List of Works', http://www. frankmatchamsociety.org.uk/matcham2.html (accessed 3 September 2015)

745 Rachel Bishop, 'After 99 years of movie magic Twickenham Film Studios put up for sale', *Your Local Guardian Richmond*, 17 February 2012, http://www.yourlocalguardian.co.uk/ news/local/richmondnews/9538838.After_99_years_of_movie_magic__Twickenham_ Film_Studios_put_up_for_sale (accessed 3 September 2015)

746 Laura Proto, 'Lights, camera and plenty more action at Twickenham Studios', *Richmond and Twickenham Times*, 6 March 2015

747 The Twickenham Museum, 'Teddington Studios', 2015, http://www.twickenham-museum. org.uk/detail.asp?ContentID=292 (accessed 3 September 2015)

The Richmond Riverside development in the mid-1980s neatly sums up Richmond's approach to development. The council wanted to improve the riverside, linking it to the historic town centre nearby. The architect Quinlan Terry was commissioned to propose a scheme that would conserve two historic buildings while creating a medium-scale commercial development. The results were highly unusual: an eclectic mixture of materials in Georgian, Baroque and Gothic styles, with terraced lawns leading down to the river.

Nothing quite like it has been constructed along the Thames at any point between 1965 and 2015. But it has been a successful urban project, showing that public acceptance of a 'picturesque neo-Classical disguise of a thoroughly modernist internal reality'[748] can confound architectural critics. Terry has also put forward proposals for a new 'groundscraper' to replace Hyde Park Barracks (Westminster), in the style of Baron Haussmann's Paris city blocks.[749]

Twickenham, as a separate municipality, had its own cultural scene, including the Luxor Cinema, at the junction of Heath Road and Cross Deep, which opened in 1929. Renamed the Odeon, the interior was refurbished and the seating reduced, but the exterior remained almost as it was originally designed. The cinema closed in October 1981 and was finally demolished five years later.[750] The cinema organ was removed, part of it being incorporated into one at the Odeon, Leicester Square. The centre of Twickenham, though smaller than Richmond town centre, has flourished. But the council has, since 2009, sought to redevelop and improve the area.[751] Quinlan Terry and his son Francis have been

748 Ken Allinson, *Architects and Architecture of London*, Oxford: Architectural Press, 2006, page 416

749 Robert Booth, 'Architects' vision of London takes inspiration from nineteenth-century Paris', *The Guardian*, 2 January 2015

750 London Borough of Richmond-upon-Thames, 'Luxor Cinema, Twickenham', Local History Notes, Richmond Libraries' Local Studies Collection, http://www.richmond.gov.uk/local_history_luxor.pdf (accessed 3 September 2015)

751 See London Borough of Richmond-upon-Thames, *Twickenham Area Action Plan*, Adopted July 2013, 2013, http://www.richmond.gov.uk/adopted_twickenham_area_action_plan_july_2013.pdf (accessed 3 September 2015)

commissioned by the council to produce designs for the future of Twickenham town centre.[752]

Richmond has been a Conservative borough for just over half of its life. Liberal Democrats overtook Labour in the 1970s to become the Tories' main contender. Labour now generally come a distant third (or even fourth) in elections, while the Greens have begun to build up a substantial vote in many wards. The Lib Dems controlled the council 1986–2002 and again 2006–10. The Conservatives then won it back. Unusually in London borough politics, the current leader, Nicholas True, is also a member of the House of Lords. Tony Arbour, a long-serving councillor in Hampton Wick, has a unique political record, having been leader of the council 2002–06, but is also one of the few people to have been both a member of the London Assembly and of the GLC.

Of all the post-1965 boroughs, Richmond is perhaps the one that has changed least since its inception. Its powerful and articulate residents have ensured councillors have preserved the feel and atmosphere of the area. There has been little change in the physical appearance of the area, with effective development control. Restrictions have been successful in preventing the construction of high-rise buildings. On the borders with neighbouring authorities, Richmond's low-rise policy contrasts with taller buildings across the boundary. The growth in population since the 1960s has been slightly above the London average, though Richmond is one of the least ethnically diverse boroughs in the city.[753]

SUTTON

Sutton was created by the merger of the Municipal Borough of Sutton & Cheam, the Municipal Borough of Beddington & Wallington, and

---

752 London Borough of Richmond-upon-Thames, 'World famous architects to propose designs for future of Twickenham town centre', Press Notice, 24 July 2015, http://www.richmond. gov.uk/world_famous_architects_to_propose_designs_for_future_of_twickenham_town (accessed 3 September 2015)

753 Greater London Authority, *2011 Census Snapshot: Ethnic Diversity Indices*, Census Information Scheme, December 2012, http://files.datapress.io/london/dataset/2011-census-diversity/2011-census-snapshot-ethnic-diversity-indices.pdf (accessed 3 September 2015)

Carshalton urban district council, all of which were districts in Surrey. The London border in the south of the borough was one of the most contested elements in reform of the capital's government in the early 1960s. The Herbert Commission's review area embraced a large chunk of suburban Surrey. The government's 1961 White Paper had proposed a far bigger authority, consisting of Banstead, Beddington & Wallington, Carshalton, Epsom & Ewell and Sutton & Cheam.[754]

After much lobbying and debate, Epsom & Ewell, Banstead, Walton & Weybridge and Esher all escaped the clutches of Greater London. As a result, Sutton's outer border in places such as Worcester Park and on the edge of Banstead is in the middle of a continuously built-up area. Much the same is true for Kingston, which means that the overlap between a part of London and the area's former shire county is greater at this point of the city's boundary than anywhere else, though something similar occurs on the Harrow and Hillingdon borders with the former Middlesex.

The borough describes itself as having 'a strong suburban heritage'.[755] 'Sutton used to be a collection of rural villages, linked to feudal and royal estates. The "village" feel remains, and people still refer to locations such as Carshalton, Cheam and Belmont as villages.'[756] No. 23 Railway Cuttings, East Cheam, was the fictitious home of Tony Hancock in the radio and television series *Hancock's Half Hour*. Other comedy series, including *The Good Life* and *The Fall and Rise of Reginald Perrin*, were also set in south-west London boroughs, reinforcing the area's reputation as the location of London's definitive commuter suburbs.

The council's civic centre in Sutton was constructed in the mid-1970s, creating new offices, assembly rooms, Sutton College of Learning for Adults, and a large public library. The council does not have a formal council chamber,

---

754 Gerald Rhodes, *The Government of London: The Struggle for Reform*, London: Weidenfeld & Nicolson, 1970, page 258

755 Information provided by London Borough of Sutton

756 London Borough of Sutton, *Core Planning Strategy*, December 2009, page 7, https://drive. google.com/file/d/0B2D4nIrCVaaSWDFaSUgtVjM5Rkk/view (accessed 5 September 2015)

with its meetings held in the ground floor of the library. The centre of Sutton has developed a large shopping centre and a number of taller buildings. The town is being redeveloped, including the decommissioning of a disused gas holder site and the demolition of buildings, including the Zurich tower, on the site. There will be nearly 200 new flats, a large new supermarket, a public square, trees and seating.[757]

The borough, like many outer-London authorities, has a number of parks and other green land. Overall, there are 420 hectares of such ground within eighty parks and other open spaces. There are two significant theatres in the borough: the Charles Cryer Theatre, Carshalton, and the Secombe Theatre in Sutton. The latter was named after former local resident and stage star Harry Secombe. In the 2010s, there was uncertainty about the future of the two theatres, though this was resolved in 2015 when (with the agreement of the council) they were taken over by the Sutton Theatres Trust.[758]

Notwithstanding its position on the affluent London/Surrey border, some parts of Sutton are, in the council's words, 'characterised by limited access to employment, social infrastructure and transport services including areas in the north of the borough, such as Rosehill, St Helier and the Wrythe and areas in South Beddington'.[759] Pockets of deprivation within an otherwise prosperous borough are significant. In 2009, Sutton had three areas among the 20 per cent most deprived in England: two in the Roundshaw area of Beddington and one in Benhill in Sutton. The most deprived neighbourhoods are all ones with high proportions of social housing.[760] Sutton has significantly fewer

---

757   Mike Murphy-Pyle, 'Major redevelopment of Sutton town centre to go ahead with backing from London Mayor Boris Johnson and Government', *Your Local Guardian*, 14 February 2014, http://www.yourlocalguardian.co.uk/news/11011584.Major_redevelopment_of_ Sutton_town_centre_to_go_ahead/ (accessed 5 September 2015)

758   Chris Caulfield, 'Dramatic rescue for Sutton's theatres as new 10-year takeover deal gets the nod', *Sutton Guardian*, 21 January 2015

759   London Borough of Sutton, *Core Planning Strategy*, December 2009, page 7, https://drive. google.com/file/d/0B2D4nIrCVaaSWDFaSUgtVjM5Rkk/view (accessed 5 September 2015)

760   London Borough of Sutton, *Economic Development Strategy 2010–2013 Draft*, 2009, page 6, http://sutton.moderngov.co.uk/documents/s12646/Economic%20Development%20 Strategy.pdf (accessed 5 September 2015)

people employed in higher occupations (such as managers, professionals and technical occupations) than the London average.[761] GDP per head is low by London standards.[762] It is a borough of reasonably affluent people, many of whom work to support the highly skilled London economy.

During the 1960s, Sutton built more social housing than many outer boroughs. Roundshaw, Durand Close and Corbet Close have all had to be regenerated in the period since 2000 because of the classic problems found in such estates. Roundshaw was built in the earliest years of the new borough on the site of the old Croydon Aerodrome. Roads on the estate include names related to the aviation industry, such as Lindbergh Road, Avro Way and Brabazon Avenue. The estate, which is compact, included underground garages and elevated balcony passageways. The housing, consisting of maisonettes and pre-cast concrete flats, was heated from a central communal boiler house.[763] Roe Way and Instone Close (a long, twelve-storey, block) were demolished in 2000.

Durand Close in Carshalton, also dating from the late 1960s and often featured on the television drama *The Bill*, consisted of twelve blocks of maisonettes and flats, sheltered accommodation for the elderly, an underground car park and other local facilities. It subsequently has been redeveloped.[764] Affinity Sutton, a housing association, and the council decided to decant residents from around 300 local authority properties at the Durand estate, then develop 260 homes for owner occupation and 214 new affordable homes. There will also be eighteen private rented-sector properties.[765]

Corbet Close in Hackbridge included long four-storey blocks with garages on the ground floor. While not on the scale of estates in inner London, Corbet

761 Ibid.

762 Ibid., page 8

763 London Borough of Sutton, 'Beddington Roundshaw', 2015, https://www.sutton.gov.uk/
     info/200168/libraries_and_culture/1360/beddington (accessed 4 September 2015)

764 Leanne Fender, 'Sad goodbyes as Sutton estate is bulldozed for revamp', *Sutton Guardian*,
     21 November 2009

765 'Regeneration Durand Close', Rydon, http://www.rydon.co.uk/what-we-do/regeneration/
     case-studies/regeneration/durand-close (accessed 10 September 2015)

Close was classic 1960s architecture with deck access and concrete features. It is to be replaced by new housing. Sutton has made a name for itself as requiring new developments, such as those at Durand Close and Corbet Close, to achieve high environmental standards.

Sutton worked with the Peabody Trust to develop BedZED at Hackbridge, the UK's largest mixed-use, carbon-neutral development. When it was built in 2002, it set new standards in environmentally sustainable building, and is seen as an international exemplar, with energy efficiency, including devices for water saving and photovoltaic solar panels to use heat and convert energy into electricity. BedZED is a mixed tenure development with two-thirds of the homes being 'affordable' or social housing, lower fuel costs, a healthy living centre, community facilities, a sports pitch, a 'village square', and a crèche. Materials for the development were locally sourced, while workspace was made available for local employment and enterprise. Locally available, renewable energy sources were provided.[766] Sutton sold land at below the market value in order to make the scheme viable.[767] BedZED is home to Bioregional, an environmental charity that works with Sutton. The scheme was where London's first car club was introduced.[768]

The borough has a relatively small economy compared to most boroughs. Employment is located in Sutton town centre, the Beddington and Kimpton industrial estates, a number of district centres and in places such as major hospitals.[769] Industrial and warehousing activity is concentrated in the borough's established industrial areas, three of which (Kimpton, Beddington and the Sutton part of Purley Way) are identified as Strategic Industrial Locations

---

766 Energy Saving Trust, *BedZED – Beddington Zero Energy Development, Sutton,* General Information Report 89, Housing Energy Efficiency Best Practice Programme, 2002, file:///C:/Users/TRAVERS/Downloads/22220_pdf29.pdf (accessed 5 September 2015)

767 'BEDZED (Peabody Trust)', Live Work Network, 2014, http://www.liveworknet.com/live-work-sec49-1.html (accessed 5 September 2015)

768 Information provided by London Borough of Sutton

769 London Borough of Sutton, *Economic Development Strategy 2010–2013 Draft,* 2009, page 7 http://sutton.moderngov.co.uk/documents/s12646/Economic%20Development%20Strategy.pdf (accessed 5 September 2015)

in the Mayor's London Plan. These areas are each close to key radial routes into London and out to the M25.

Sutton forms part of the Wandle Valley regeneration corridor, which historically contained a number of manufacturing and related activities. Substantial areas of industrial land remain, forming a ribbon of small- and medium-sized estates along the river corridor, with larger estates in the south-east of the area towards west Croydon. These industries

> comprise of a mix of traditional manufacturing, some 'dirty' industry (e.g. cement works and waste disposal), and areas of newer, high-tech manufacturing and creative industries. This industrial land use is a key source of local employment and is recognised as one of London's four important areas for economic growth.[770]

Sutton is also committed to improve the green environment along the Wandle Valley.

The council was selected in 2010 as one of four 'vanguard areas' for the government's Big Society initiative. The Big Society was, at the time, a Conservative policy designed to strengthen communities in such a way that voluntary organisations, co-operatives and mutually owned bodies would play a bigger role in delivering public services.[771] Sutton was selected because it was recognised as having an active voluntary sector and also the enthusiasm to pilot a policy that was being developed in advance of any certainty as to how it would operate.[772]

The politics of the borough are unusual: Sutton is a solid Liberal Democrat

---

770 Greater London Authority, *Appendix A South London Regional Park Opportunity Wandle Valley*, London Strategic Parks Project, 2006, page 77, http://legacy.london.gov.uk/mayor/planning/parks/docs/parks-studyA-text.pdf, (accessed 5 September 2015)

771 See Cabinet Office, *Building the Big Society*, 2010, https://www.gov.uk/government/uploads/system/uploads/attachment_data/file/78979/building-big-society_0.pdf (accessed 5 September 2015)

772 Allegra Stratton, 'David Cameron begins big sell of "big society"', *The Guardian*, 19 July 2010

bastion. At the 2014 borough elections, it was the only London authority to remain Liberal Democrat-controlled. In the 2015 general election, Tom Brake (Carshalton & Wallington) was one of just eight Liberal Democrat MPs to survive the party's catastrophic performance. Until 1974, Sutton had been a Conservative/Labour marginal borough, with a period of 'no overall control' from 1971 to 1974. Thereafter, the Liberal Democrats increased their vote share to the point that, in 1982, they overtook Labour. In every borough election since, the party has won the largest vote share and has controlled the council continuously since 1986. Labour, as in Richmond and Kingston, has suffered as a result of the Liberal Democrat surge and has not won a seat on the council since the 2002 elections.[773] The Conservatives have survived as the main opposition party and won the Sutton & Cheam seat from the Liberal Democrats in 2015.

A famous by-election occurred in 1972 when Sutton & Cheam was captured by Graham Tope for the Liberal Party from the Conservatives. The by-election took place at a time Edward Heath's government was unpopular. The 'swing' from the Conservatives to the Liberal Democrats was 33 per cent, one of the largest ever seen at a UK by-election. The Tories regained the seat in February 1974, but the by-election proved to be a building block in the longer-term growth of the Liberals, enabling them to win larger numbers of parliamentary seats. This cycle of renewed success for the party came to an end, disastrously, in 2015. But Sutton & Cheam, like the Orpington (Bromley) by-election in 1962, remains a totemic result for Liberal Democrats.

Tope then became leader of the council for thirteen years, before going on to sit on the London Assembly and in the House of Lords. Notable Conservative leaders have included Robin Squire, who went on to be MP for Hornchurch (in Havering). As leader, Squire resisted the then Labour government's demand to abolish grammar schools and move to a fully comprehensive schooling system. Grammar schools still exist in Sutton. Sir Godfrey 'Tag' Taylor, Conservative leader from 1965 to 1972, went on to chair the London Boroughs Association.

---

773 Greater London Authority, *London Borough Council Elections 22 May 2014*, London: GLA, 2014, page 163

Later, he chaired the London Residuary Body, which disposed of the assets of the GLC and the ILEA.[774]

Today, Sutton, led by Ruth Dombey, is the Liberal Democrats' remaining London redoubt, showing little willingness to be swayed by coalition-induced anti-Lib Dem sentiment. The local Liberal Democrats have even written a book about the longer-term phenomenon.[775] It is also an area of proud suburbia where, as in Kingston, London meets Surrey.

WALTHAM FOREST

Waltham Forest brought together three Essex municipal boroughs: Chingford, Leyton and Walthamstow. After some discussion about the possibility of calling the new authority Walthamstow (residents in Chingford and Leyton banded together collecting 15,000 signatures against this idea) or also Forestlea, it was decided to opt for a name that did not use the full names of any of its constituent districts. Waltham Forest was an ancient name for part of what is today Epping Forest. According to the council: 'From the end of the nineteenth century, the three areas had coalesced to form a significant dormitory suburb for workers in London, but they have kept their separate identities, and their histories can be outlined separately.'[776]

Like authorities such as Haringey and Merton, Waltham Forest is a borough with two distinctly different parts, reflected in voting patterns. The development of Leyton, Leytonstone and Walthamstow in the south of Waltham Forest created significant residential communities, predominantly living in long streets of terraced housing. The area was a 'suburban dormitory for clerks and workmen'.[777] These areas also saw substantial levels of

---

774 Information provided by London Borough of Sutton

775 Sutton Liberal Democrats, *A Flagship Borough*, London: Sutton Liberal Democrats, 2012

776 London Borough of Waltham Forest, *Waltham Forest Characterisation Study, Part Two: Borough-wide context*, page 20, http://www.walthamforest.gov.uk/documents/wf-characterisation-study-part-two.pdf (accessed 5 September 2015)

777 Ibid., page 22

industrial development. During the early twentieth century, these separate areas merged, with the gaps between them lost. Between 1918 and 1939, Chingford and Highham Hill developed rapidly to become a large suburban community on the northern edge of the conurbation. Residential densities are much lower in Chingford than in Leyton and Walthamstow, with many detached houses.[778]

As the boroughs got under way in 1965, councillors and officers sought ways to bring the different communities and local institutions together. LSE academics observed:

> The challenge of making local institutions feel part of the new borough was tackled differently from borough to borough. In Waltham Forest, assistant education officers were given an additional responsibility beyond their administrative ones. They were expected to spend half their time visiting schools and half the time in the office.[779]

The Lee Valley Regional Park and reservoirs make up a large proportion of the borough's western and southern boundaries. The regional park reaches from Ware in Hertfordshire to the Thames in Docklands. The Lee is an important open space link from the urbanised centre of London to the open countryside. The eastern edge of the borough is covered nearly in its entirety by Epping Forest, the largest public open space in the London area.[780]

The borough inherited a number of important buildings. Walthamstow Town Hall on Forest Road, built between 1938 and 1941, is a 'monumental building within an impressive formally landscaped setting' at the centre of a civic complex, which also includes the assembly hall and a courthouse, added

---

778 Ibid., pages 20–21

779 Gerald Rhodes (ed.), *The New Government of London: The First Five Years*, London: Weidenfeld & Nicolson, 1972, page 169

780 London Borough of Waltham Forest, *Waltham Forest Characterisation Study, Part Two: Borough-wide context*, page 26, http://www.walthamforest.gov.uk/documents/wf-characterisation-study-part-two.pdf (accessed 4 September 2015)

in 1971.[781] The Granada Theatre in Hoe Street, Grade II listed, was built in
1930 by architect Cecil Massey with extravagant Baroque and Moorish interiors
by the renowned Russian designer and director Theodore Komisarjevsky.[782]
Sidney Bernstein, the founder of Granada cinemas and Granada Television,
produced a number of films for Alfred Hitchcock there. After commercial
decline and then use as a church, the Granada was bought in 2014 by the Soho
Theatre, which plans to bring it back into use as an entertainment venue.[783]

Walthamstow Greyhound Stadium, an Art Deco structure dating from 1931,
is one of the few surviving dog tracks in the country, though it closed in 2008.
It, too, is Grade II listed. 'Affordable' housing is now being built on the site,
though the iconic frontage will be retained. Water House in Forest Road, the
childhood home of William Morris, is also listed.[784]

Waltham Forest saw an early influx of immigrants from India and Pakistan,
who were already present when the borough was created in 1965.[785] Although
an outer borough, Waltham Forest's strong links with Newham and the wider
east London industrial economy made it attractive to new migrants. Housing
was relatively cheap and there were opportunities to set up businesses. By the
time of the 2011 census, the borough was one of the most ethnically diverse
places in the UK, with 37 per cent born abroad and 62 per cent of the population being minorities.[786]

The borough's initial years coincided with the opening of the Victoria line.
London Transport, after a long period of expansion up to the outbreak of the

781 English Heritage, *London's Town Halls*, 1999, page 72

782 Bridget Cherry, Charles O'Brien and Nikolaus Pevsner, *The Buildings of England London 5:
     East*, New Haven and London: Yale University Press, 2005, page 760

783 BBC News, 'Walthamstow Granada cinema sold by church', 10 November 2014, http://
     www.bbc.co.uk/news/uk-england-london-29991794 (accessed 5 September 2015)

784 London Borough of Waltham Forest, *Waltham Forest Characterisation Study, Part
     Two: Borough-wide context*, page 23, http://www.walthamforest.gov.uk/documents/wf-
     characterisation-study-part-two.pdf (accessed 4 September 2015)

785 Francis Sheppard, *London: A History*, Oxford: Oxford University Press, 1998, page 346

786 London Borough of Waltham Forest, 'Data and Statistics', 2015, https://www.walthamforest.
     gov.uk/Pages/Services/statistics-economic-information-and-analysis.aspx#Population
     (accessed 6 September 2015)

Second World War, had built little thereafter. The Underground line from Walthamstow to Brixton provided a new, fast train service from north-east to south London. Blackhorse Road and Walthamstow Central found themselves less than twenty minutes from Oxford Circus. The first section to open was from Walthamstow Central to Highbury in September 1968.[787]

At one point, it had been proposed to run the line on to Wood Street in Walthamstow, to connect to British Railways services there.[788] However, the new line did not arrest the industrial decline of parts of Waltham Forest or its neighbour Haringey during the 1970s and 1980s. Indeed, the purposes of the line had far more to do with reducing road congestion in central London than with economic development. Nevertheless, by the 2000s, the service was allowing the borough to benefit economically from the link to the West End.

The area's economy included furniture, printing, rubber goods, clothing, and toy-making.[789] Leyton and Walthamstow were the main industrial centres, while Chingford remained largely residential. The London Motor Omnibus Company, established in 1905 in Hookers Lane, Walthamstow, later became the Associated Equipment Company (AEC) Limited, which built London buses until 1979. AEC designed the iconic Routemaster buses, some of which are still used on 'heritage' routes in London today.[790]

The London Rubber Company, Europe's biggest condom maker, was based in Waltham Forest until 1991. Other manufacturing included Philips records, Ford and Hawker Siddeley. Deindustrialisation affected the borough as it did all of east London: manufacturing activity declined from the late 1960s onwards, leaving empty factories and rising unemployment, particularly in

---

787 Michael F. Collins and Timothy M. Pharoah, *Transport Organisation in a Great City: The Case of London,* London: George Allen & Unwin, 1974, page 198

788 Ibid., page 195

789 'Walthamstow: Economic history, marshes and forests', in *A History of the County of Essex: Volume 6,* W. R. Powell (ed.), London: British History, 1973, pages 263–75, http://www.british-history.ac.uk/vch/essex/vol6/pp263-275 (accessed 31 August 2015); and 'Leyton: Economic history, marshes and forests', ibid., pages 197–205, http://www.british-history.ac.uk/vch/essex/vol6/pp197-205 (accessed 3 September 2015)

790 See Travis Elborough, *The Bus We Loved,* London: Granta Books, 2005, page 22

Walthamstow, Leyton and Leytonstone. Manufacturing is still present, nota-bly Allied Bakeries, Dunhill and Warren Evans.[791]

Waltham Forest is on the North Circular Road, which runs east–west across it and provides road links to Barnet, Brent, Ealing and Redbridge, as well as to the motorway system via the M11. The construction of the A12 (to link Hackney to the M11) through Leyton in the 1990s was highly controversial, with protests in both Leyton and Leytonstone.[792] Today, the A12 scythes through Leyton in a cutting, creating a dead-end outlook for residents of streets such as Colville Road and Grove Green Road. The same has happened in parts of neighbouring Redbridge. The A12/M11 link significantly increased traffic in Waltham Forest.[793]

In 1972, a large council housing estate was built at Cathall Road, Leytonstone. It consisted of two twenty-storey tower blocks and a huge maze of eight-storey flats. Cathall gained a reputation for crime and gang-related violence.[794] It has taken massive public investment, including the creation of a government-sponsored Housing Action Trust (HAT), to replace the slabs and blocks with better housing. The HAT also covered Oliver Close in Leyton and Boundary Road estate in Walthamstow. Unusually, tenants sat on the board of the HAT and have done so on the successor housing association.[795]

The Hornbeam and Redwood tower blocks at Cathall were demolished in 2002. They stood on the corner of Cathall Road and Hollydown Way and were cleared as part of as part of a regeneration scheme for the area. Elsewhere, some of the Beaumont estate tower blocks (built in the mid-1960s) have been demolished, and the Avenue Road development has been refurbished. The Leyton Grange estate has been modernised by London

791 Information provided by London Borough of Waltham Forest

792 Joe Moran, *On Roads: A Hidden History*, London: Profile Books, page 236

793 London Borough of Waltham Forest, 'Local Traffic Context', 2005, https://www.walthamforest.gov.uk/documents/2_local_transport_context-2.pdf (accessed 5 September 2015)

794 Paul Kassman, 'In the hood', *The Guardian*, 23 May 2007

795 Jo Rees, 'Top hat and tails', *Building*, March–April 2002, http://www.building.co.uk/top-hat-and-tails/1017031.article (accessed 5 September 2015)

& Quadrant Housing Association. Livingstone College and John Drinkwater towers have both also been demolished.[796]

Within fifty years, terraced houses were cleared to build tower blocks, which have then been demolished and replaced by low-rise brick housing in Leytonstone and elsewhere in the borough. This pattern is by no means unique to this corner of Waltham Forest, but Cathall, in particular, is a perfect example of the long cycle of clearance, estate building, re-clearance and estate rebuilding to be found in many parts of London since 1965.

Waltham Forest is located within what is now termed the 'London–Stansted–Cambridge corridor', a zone identified with continued potential growth.[797] Government funding has been made available to develop opportunities for intensification around Walthamstow, Leyton and Blackhorse Lane. The borough is also closely linked with Stratford and the Lower Lee Valley 'opportunity areas' in the Thames Gateway. The 2012 Olympic Games generated opportunities for development and regeneration in Newham, Hackney and Waltham Forest, providing resources for homes, jobs and infrastructure.[798] Leyton High Road was given a makeover that became national news ('more *Notting Hill* than *EastEnders*') in 2012.[799]

Town centres within Waltham Forest reflect long-term settlement and administrative patterns. The borough has four principal centres, at Leytonstone, Leyton, Chingford and Walthamstow. There are smaller sub-centres at Baker's Arms, Wood Street, Higham's Park and Chingford Mount. Walthamstow, which includes Europe's longest daily street market at Hoe Street, is the borough's largest retail and commercial location. The council has been leading

---

796 Leyton and Leytonstone Historical Society, '1965 to 1979 Housing', The History of Leyton and Leytonstone, http://www.leytonpast.info/page141.html (accessed 5 September 2015)

797 See 'London. Stansted. Cambridge. Consortium.', http://lscc.co (accessed 5 September 2015)

798 London Borough of Waltham Forest, *Waltham Forest Characterisation Study, Part Two: Borough-wide context*, page 16, http://www.walthamforest.gov.uk/documents/wf-characterisation-study-part-two.pdf (accessed 5 September 2015)

799 Rosie Taylor, 'The Olympic high street makeover: Just in time for the Games round the corner, shops get a new look that's more *Notting Hill* than *EastEnders*', *Daily Mail*, 17 June 2012

regeneration efforts around Walthamstow Central, including hotel and cinema developments. Chingford is different, with a traditional shopping centre that reflects its more established and affluent local population, including a range of smaller shops.[800]

If the Victoria line provided the borough's opening years with a new connection to central London, more recent public transport improvements have created an improved connection to the new orbital links around the city. The Gospel Oak–Barking line had long provided a dismal and little-used train service, shared with freight, with stations at Leytonstone High Road, Leyton Midland Road, Walthamstow Queen's Road and Blackhorse Road. Following the transfer of the service to TfL in 2005, new trains and higher frequencies have much improved the line. There are plans eventually to extend it to Barking Riverside.

In 2015, TfL also took over the national rail lines from Liverpool Street to Chingford and Cheshunt, including six stations in Waltham Forest. Like the Gospel Oak–Barking line, these services were poorly managed in comparison with the Overground and Underground. TfL is introducing new trains, staffed stations and a higher level of service.[801] Links from Waltham Forest to inner-west and east London have been much improved by the Overground.

Other recent change has included the renovation of the William Morris Gallery, which was named UK Museum of the Year in 2013. The council, led by Chris Robbins, appointed a growth commission, which reported in 2014, recommending that the borough should, among other things, work to 'stand out' in London by strengthening its identity, improving retailing streets and by developing business leadership in the borough.[802]

Waltham Forest politics has been moderate. Labour has had a majority in

800 London Borough of Waltham Forest, *Waltham Forest Characterisation Study, Part Two: Borough-wide context*, page 24, http://www.walthamforest.gov.uk/documents/wf-characterisation-study-part-two.pdf (accessed 5 September 2015)

801 Gwyn Topham, 'Clean, reliable and integrated: all change for neglected rail services in London', *The Guardian*, 29 May 2015

802 London Borough of Waltham Forest, *Waltham Forest Growth Commission 2014*, 2014, pages 10–12

every election except when the Conservatives won in 1968–71 and during a period of 'no overall control' from 1982 to 1986. The borough has a strongly Conservative north, but a (larger) Labour south. Chingford MPs have included Lord (Norman) Tebbit and Iain Duncan Smith.

Evidence of the independent-mindedness of the borough's voters was demonstrated immediately prior to the council taking office in April 1965. A by-election was triggered in Leyton in which Prime Minister Harold Wilson attempted to place Patrick Gordon-Walker (who had failed to win his seat in the 1964 general election) in a supposedly safe seat. The electorate had none of it, and the Tories triumphed.[803] Gordon-Walker was subsequently elected MP for Leyton in the 1966 Labour landslide.

During the life of the post-1965 borough, a number of luminaries have lived there. Baroness (Patricia) Scotland, who became the UK's first female Attorney General, grew up in Walthamstow, while footballer David Beckham and photographer David Bailey were both brought up in the borough. Alfred Hitchcock was born in Leytonstone.

Rapid social change is occurring today, with significant numbers of people who have been priced out of inner London moving to the borough. As in neighbouring Tottenham, gentrification is underway, and the Victoria line is bringing more affluent property buyers to Waltham Forest.

---

803 Keith Leybourn, *British Political Leaders: A Biographical Dictionary*, Santa Barbara: ABC-
     Clio, 2001, pages 132–3

PART III

CONCLUSIONS

CHAPTER 5

FIFTY YEARS:
AN ANALYSIS

After fifty years it is possible to look back and assess the complex and sometimes fragmented operation of London government, and the boroughs' successes and failures. As a prelude to drawing conclusions from the impact of the reforms brought about by the London Government Act 1963, it is important to analyse the major themes from the earlier parts of this book, in particular the borough-by-borough histories. The boroughs' separate stories together tell a greater truth about what has become, fortuitously, a remarkable metropolitan success story. Those who designed the post-1965 system of London government never saw themselves as the creators of one of the world's global mega-cities. But the arrangements they put in place led to such an outcome.

IMPACT OF HISTORY AND THE PROCESS OF
REFORM

The thirty-two boroughs that emerged from the process of reform bear some of the marks of the struggle to create them. In particular, the City of London's long-held position of maintaining its historic boundaries and exceptionalism had, for almost 150 years, ensured that units of government grew organically without a plan in the urban hinterland. By the mid-twentieth century, any idea there might be a powerful unitary government for all of built-up London had gone. Moreover, the gargantuan urban sprawl which occurred between 1918 and 1939 made it even less likely that a single authority alone could govern it. Further, the population of London was so great it was unlikely any British government would wish to invest too much power in one institution of government. By the 1960s, the fragmentation of London's governance was driven by history and political expediency.

The steps to reform were classically British. Years of expert lobbying and debate finally led to the creation of a Royal Commission. There then followed a White Paper, and lastly a parliamentary process. Herbert's fifty-one proposed boroughs became thirty-two. Parts of Surrey were removed from London as the legislation passed through Parliament. The outer boundary was, in many ways, an accident. Inner London kept a single education authority. Housing powers were vested with both the new GLC and the new boroughs. The reform was not so much a careful adjustment to the country's constitutional arrangements as, rather, a set of ad hoc and common-sense responses to a pressing need. Even then, the new arrangements survived only twenty-one years before they were radically reformed.

SETTING UP THE BOROUGHS

D ecisions were taken in the early days of the boroughs whose consequences can still be seen in the city's streets fifty years later. Choices made in the mid-1960s about logos and other 'identifiers' have, like the boroughs them-selves, proved resistant to changing fashions. Examples are Westminster's street-name signs, which have become a design classic for London as a whole, or Camden's 'linked hands' logo. Kensington & Chelsea has continued to use the former borough of Kensington's street-sign design, which makes them even more traditional. Because there are thirty-three separate local highways author-ities in London (thirty-four including TfL), policy on street signage started and has remained remarkably variable from council to council.[804] Many cities inter-nationally have a single style of sign and a single policy about location. The London boroughs' remarkably different approaches to this basic issue offers a simple way of understanding just how unusual the city's system of government is.

---

804 For a full analysis of the issue see Hugh Collis, *Where am I? Street-Name Signs in London*,
    London Transport Users Committee, May 2003

In their early years, the boroughs had to rationalise their buildings and decide where to put their headquarters. Some of the new councils added an annex to an existing town hall or civic centre, as at Ealing, Enfield, Greenwich, Hammersmith, Haringey, Havering, Kingston and Lewisham. Where such a bolt-on proved difficult, the decision was taken to create a modern complex, as in Bexley, Bromley, Hillingdon, Hounslow and Sutton. Croydon and Westminster bought conveniently located speculative office blocks. According to Michael Hebbert, two-thirds of the boroughs located the seat of local government in their dominant town centres.[805]

At least two of the new municipal buildings created by the new London boroughs became the object of controversy. In Hillingdon, a grand gesture was made. The council decided to construct a major new civic centre in Uxbridge and, as it turned out, disagreements about the building proved emblematic of a struggle between different interests in the borough. Labour wanted to urbanise the borough while the Conservatives preferred to preserve Hillingdon's suburban tranquillity.

The cost and splendour of the brick-clad chateau-style civic centre built in Uxbridge became national news. Hillingdon civic centre is one of the most important municipal buildings constructed in London since 1965. Only Kensington & Chelsea's (also brick-clad) headquarters is recognised as both 'of its time' and similarly architecturally striking. Both buildings cost significantly more than originally planned. As is sometimes the case, the controversy that surrounded the construction of such buildings is now forgotten, and the quality of the building is admired. The Hillingdon and Kensington & Chelsea civic buildings have prospered in a way that much social housing built across London a few years previously has not.

Many of the boroughs have built new town halls since 1965, particularly as regeneration schemes have allowed the creative use of land ownership and sites. Brent has moved into new offices by Wembley Stadium, Camden to St Pancras and Southwark to London Bridge from Peckham Town Hall.

---

805 Michael Hebbert, 'The Borough Effect in London's Geography', in *London: A New Metropolitan Geography*, London: Edward Arnold, 1991, pages 200–201

In each case, the new buildings are more like offices than conventional town or city halls. Whereas the parishes, district boards and metropolitan boroughs tended, like banks, to commission buildings whose architecture was intended to send a message about solidity and power, the most recent London council offices promote democracy, openness and accessible service. It was Shirley Porter, leader of Westminster, who introduced the 'one-stop shop' concept to local government.

The new boroughs were created amid the development of a new interest in public sector management. The Maud Report[806] proposed a more professionally run form of local government, and many of the new boroughs, which were large enterprises compared with most other councils in Britain, adopted new departmental structures and other arrangements designed to improve the quality of administration. The London reforms of 1963–65 became the template for the system of metropolitan local government adopted in 1974, following the report of the Redcliffe-Maud Commission, and, to some extent, for unitary authorities as they emerged subsequently.

Arrangements were put in place from the start of the boroughs to redistribute rateable resources from the richer central boroughs to the rest, although a similar arrangement had existed before the 1965 reform. The London Rate Equalisation Scheme operated until full equalisation was made possible by the introduction of a new grant regime in 1981.[807]

HOUSING

Both the GLC and the boroughs owned and maintained council houses and flats. The GLC had inherited the LCC's large housing empire, while the boroughs took over homes from the former metropolitan boroughs and other

---

806 Ministry of Housing and Local Government, *Committee on the Management of Local Government*, London: HMSO, 1967

807 Tony Travers, *The Politics of Local Government Finance*, London: Allen & Unwin, 1986, page 46

districts. Conservative control at County Hall generally led to council house sales and efforts to hand social housing to the boroughs. When Tory leader Sir Horace Cutler commissioned Sir Frank Marshall, former leader of Leeds City Council, to review the governance of London, Marshall proposed the GLC should give housing management and development to the boroughs.[808] Some housing was transferred, but it took GLC abolition in 1986 to deliver full responsibility for housing to the boroughs.

In the early years of the new councils, there was much enthusiasm within the inner boroughs to clear slums and to build modern housing estates. The new councils appointed borough architects to oversee the design of major developments. A number of these architects had trained at the Architectural Association, which was notable for exposing radical and innovative adherents to the theories of the Bauhaus and Le Corbusier. Many had worked with Sir Leslie Martin at the LCC Architects' Department.[809]

Lambeth appointed Ted Hollamby and Camden Sydney Cook. These architects believed in the capacity of well-designed buildings to change the lives of Londoners who had hitherto often lived in slum conditions. In Lambeth, Hollamby commissioned George Finch to design Lambeth Towers, Cotton Gardens and Brixton Rec. Lambeth Towers came complete with community facilities such as a doctor's surgery, nursery and older people's centre. This development is still in use, and broadly functions as planned. Camden, under the control of Sydney Cook, became a byword for low-rise, high-quality, modern architecture. Developments such as Branch Hill in Hampstead and, most famously, Alexandra Road, are, even today, seen as among municipal architecture's greatest triumphs.

Other council housing developments proved less successful. Indeed, many have been constructed and knocked down during the life of the London boroughs. The Ferrier estate in Kidbrooke (Greenwich) and Holly Street (Hackney)

---

808 Sir Frank Marshall, *The Marshall Report on Greater London, Report to the Greater London Council*, London: GLC, 1978, page 45

809 His influence on London public architecture can be gauged from: Peter Carolin, 'Obituary: Sir Leslie Martin', *Architects' Journal*, 3 August 2000

have been entirely redeveloped since their construction in the early years of the new authorities. Much has been written about the dire consequences of council housing estates built during the 1960s and early 1970s. Poor-quality construction, brutalist architecture, ill-thought-through layouts, cost-cutting and changes in residents' lifestyles are among the explanations put forward as to how idealistic public housing turned, in many cases, into a nightmare of vandalism, fetid lifts, boarded-up flats, poverty and social disorder. Anne Power explains that councils' letting arrangements and consequent social stigma had the effect of reinforcing the physical problems with estates: the most deprived people tended to be concentrated in the worst estates.[810]

A leading indicator of the need for change was provided by Ronan Point (Newham), whose collapse in 1968 signalled an end to this particular phase in the provision of social housing. It is easy today, with the benefit of hindsight, to understand what a disaster many high-rise towers and concrete housing estates turned out to be. But the boroughs and GLC sincerely believed they were involved in removing slums and replacing them with vastly better homes. A GLC film, made in 1967, captures the enthusiasm and optimism residents often felt for their new tower block flats. The council explains through a voiceover what the problem is; tenants are then allowed to say what they think. Even if such a film were mildly propagandist, the views are consistent with books written at the time:

> Official voiceover: 'But what about the future? Overcrowding in tenements and multi-occupied houses must be relieved and people with no real home of their own have to be decently housed as soon as possible. The building programme in London is being greatly accelerated, both by the boroughs and the GLC. By 1970, the GLC will be building 9,000 new homes a year. Industrialised methods will speed erection and the new homes will have bigger rooms, central heating and pedestrian walks, safely away from traffic...'
>
> First tenant: 'You see these open spaces, like the eighteen-storey

---

810 Anne Power, *Property Before People*, London: Allen & Unwin, 1987, page 119

blocks, and, ooh, it gives you such a different feeling. Although they're so tall, you've got the space around.'

Second tenant: 'I never thought I'd see such places as this. When I got married, I lived in Faraday Street in two rooms – being upstairs, I had to go down for the water, down for everything, down for your washing and all that. But when you come into a life like this, seems as if you're a princess.'

Third tenant: 'It's lovely being up here. It's a lovely view and quite quiet. I'll be eighty in January. I think this place saved my life, really...'[811]

Le Corbusier had died as recently as 1965, and the new borough and GLC architects would, for a brief moment, have felt that all their utopian efforts had been worthwhile. Londoners who had lived their lives in slums now occupied buildings with bathrooms, central heating and decent space standards. But, pretty well from this moment on, the rot set in. The 'industrial methods', homes 'away from traffic', 'pedestrian walks', the 'space around', and the 'quiet' all became elements of urban dystopia for hundreds of thousands of people.

Were the boroughs and the GLC to blame for the failures of the 1960s and 1970s? Today, it is easy to see why concrete slab blocks, elevated walkways and isolated towers would be problematic. Idealistic architects cannot have predicted the kinds of social change that occurred from the late 1960s onwards. At the time, councillors were attempting to clear what they saw as time-expired older housing, and to provide council tenants with decent, spacious homes, inside facilities and central heating.

But what went wrong, at least in some places, was the use of brutalist, inhuman architecture, a willingness to cut back on agreed building programmes, shoddy construction techniques and poor maintenance. Anne Power has pointed out that subsidies offered to councils had a profound influence on the drive towards demolition of older houses and on the kind of homes built

---

811 'Some Where Decent to Live', Greater London Council, Chess Valley Films, 1967, London Metropolitan Archives, https://www.youtube.com/watch?v=1A2wa9yeAKk (accessed 15 September 2015)

to replace slums: 'Not until the 1970s did subsidies substantially favour reha-bilitation over slum clearance and even then the financial incentives were often too marginal for structurally sound but badly run-down houses.'[812]

Different central government policies towards the rehabilitation of old houses and also towards the subsidy of particular kinds of new flats would have avoided many of the problems that were to emerge from the 1970s onwards. Ironically, the middle classes were using their own resources to resuscitate derelict and sub-standard housing in Islington, Camden and Lambeth and thus bring it back to life. If Whitehall had offered a different subsidy regime to the boroughs and the GLC, London would have been saved from many of the horrors that subsequently befell council housing and its residents.

Power believes that councils in London and elsewhere lost control of their housing:

> By the time social housing began to fall seriously from favour in the mid-1970s, the public landlord had almost lost control of estate management. Unpopular dwellings were coupled with a remote service that tenants could not identify with or locate. Meanwhile, housing staff found it increas-ingly difficult to deliver on anything but the narrowest part of the total service … mid-1970s local government was too complex to respond.[813]

This analysis was correct for a number of London boroughs, but not for all. The concentration of recently constructed housing estates in inner boroughs, in particular, made it inevitable that the most severe problems would emerge there. But even in inner London, not all boroughs 'lost control' of their hous-ing. The weak management that developed in a number of the radical, new left, administrations was a contributory factor. An unwillingness to pursue rent arrears or to tackle inadequate service standards undermined the capac-ity of some boroughs to maintain their housing stock.

---

812   Anne Power, *Property Before People*, London: Allen & Unwin, 1987, page 50

813   Ibid., page 236

In addition to the architecture and design of borough and GLC housing, there were political problems in the 1960s and 1970s that derived from the GLC's desire, supported by a number of boroughs within the former LCC area, to reduce densities in parts of the inner city, and move poorer residents to better homes in suburban areas. The government and the LCC had pursued policies of building new towns beyond the capital and other 'out of area' estates. The GLC attempted to relocate people from inner to outer London. Councils such as Hillingdon, Redbridge and Bromley had no need for slum clearance, nor did they wish to have the GLC building estates or, indeed, nominating over-many tenants into their areas.

Michael Hebbert described this phenomenon, echoing Anne Power's judgement about housing management:

> The GLC housing committee found itself blocked by outer London boroughs, forcing already densely populated inner boroughs to provide the sites for most of its output of 85,000 housing units in 1965–85 … Besides, County Hall acquired a poor reputation for the remoteness and inaccessibility of its housing management: playing the role of landlord to a dispersed stock of 240,000 rental dwellings had been no part of the Herbert Commission's vision for London government.[814]

From the beginning of the post-1965 system, there was tension between many outer boroughs and the GLC. When the council was Labour-controlled, Conservative boroughs found themselves resisting efforts to transfer people from inner to outer London. Some leading GLC members saw the resistance of the outer boroughs as demanding greater efforts to drive through new housing developments. During this period, the first seeds of GLC abolition were sown.

There is an additional aspect to housing. Social housing became an ideological battleground from the mid-1960s onwards. It still is. This issue is not one of the London boroughs' making, but it has affected the way social housing

---

814 Michael Hebbert, *London More by Fortune than Design*, Chichester: John Wiley & Sons, 1998, page 114

has developed. Today, many councils either operate largely through housing associations or through 'arms-length' management organisations. These latter institutions have been pivotal in bringing improvements to social housing. Ealing, unusually, brought its housing management back in-house in 2010.[815]

Borough involvement in social housing declined sharply after the initial enthusiasm for slum clearance and the construction of estates. During the 1980s and early 1990s, with the city's population falling or only rising slowly from a post-war low of 6.6 million, there were always housing shortages and homelessness, but not a 'crisis' of the kind that has emerged since London's population started to rise sharply in the later 1990s.

Population increases from that time onwards have gradually contributed to housing being the most politically salient challenge facing the city.[816] For many years, transport was the most pressing issue, but with Tube improvements, rail modernisation and Crossrail construction largely achieved, the capital's housing shortage now dominates the public debate. The GLA, through TfL, is responsible for transport, but the boroughs must deliver housing-stock increases, although within the terms of the Mayor's London Plan. Fifty years after their inauguration, the key issue for the boroughs is not a requirement to improve the quality of slum housing stock, but to facilitate the delivery of upwards of 50,000 new homes a year. Social housing has seen a revival in its popularity, if not in significant numbers. Need has moved from quality to quantity. Pressure on councils that do not deliver substantial numbers of homes will increase. As with the GLC in the 1970s, in such pressures lie the seeds of potential conflict between the boroughs and city-wide government.

By the 2010s, some authorities such as Camden and Hackney had started to act as developers of private properties so as to expand 'affordable' housing.[817] The experience of the 1960s and 1970s, compounded by the ideological strife

---

815 'Ealing to take housing management in-house', *Inside Housing*, 21 May 2010

816 Isabel Hardman, 'New poll puts housing and infrastructure top of Londoners' agenda', *Annual London Survey 2014*, Talk London, Greater London Authority, 3 March 2015

817 David Spittles, 'It's a game changer: Camden is first council to build homes to sell', *Evening Standard*, 19 November 2014

of the 1980s, has, it would appear, left most of local government wary of a return to earlier types of large, single-tenure developments. Instead, the boroughs are now experimenting with different forms of management, ownership and development. Less certainty has brought enlightened experimentation.

The coming of the GLA re-created a city-wide housing authority. But the Mayor of London is not responsible for building and operating social housing. Instead, City Hall has significant power by different means. It can 'call in' larger developments and, if the Mayor chooses, act as planning authority for such schemes. The Mayor's Housing Strategy determines major opportunities for housing development and Housing Zones within which there will be accelerated development. City Hall has assumed responsibility for allocating resources to support boroughs' 'affordable' housing developments.[818] The Mayor is committed to achieving major public sector land sales to assist in providing more homes.

The 2010 coalition government chose to implement its deficit reduction effort by making steep cuts to council expenditure so as to protect its own departmental programmes. London boroughs suffered some of the sharpest reductions.[819] But the coalition put in place new incentive regimes designed to encourage councils to build homes and increase economic development.[820] In parallel, councils were able to make a levy on development by means such as 'Section 106' deals and the Community Infrastructure Levy. Facing sharp reductions to their day-to-day budgets and to capital spending, London boroughs and the Mayor have turned to the construction of often densely packed housing developments to bring in additional resources.[821] Battersea/Nine Elms,

818 Mayor of London, *Homes for London: The London Housing Strategy*, London: GLA, June 2014

819 Report by the Comptroller and Auditor General, *Financial sustainability of local authorities 2014*, HC783, Session 2014–15, 19 November 2014, Figure 2, page 14

820 Paul Cheshire, Max Nathan, Henry Overman, *Urban Economics and Urban Policy: Challenging Conventional Policy Wisdom*, Cheltenham: Edward Elgar Publishing Limited, 2014, page 176

821 For a description of how Section 106 and CIL operate at a key London site, involving two boroughs and contributions for transport, housing, education, health and other provision, see Greater London Authority, 'Chapter 10 Section 106 and CIL', *Vauxhall Nine Elms Opportunity Area Planning Framework*, London: GLA, March 2012

planned jointly by Wandsworth, Lambeth and the Mayor, will see an extension to the Underground, 'affordable' housing, community facilities and much else funded by levies and taxation on new homes, offices and shops.

By 2015, the development of often massive clusters of new residential and commercial buildings is virtually the only way that London boroughs can generate additional resources for affordable housing and other new public provision. A measure of the importance of such developments can be seen in the yield of the New Homes Bonus (NHB), a grant rewarding the construction of new housing. In 2015–16, Tower Hamlets received £24.8 million, Hackney £14.8 million, Islington £13.8 million, Southwark £13.1 million, Newham £11.7 million, Lambeth £11.1 million and Greenwich £10.5 million. By comparison, major cities outside the capital, all with larger populations than any individual London council, received less: Birmingham £17.8 million, Leeds £13.6 million, Bristol £11.5 million and Manchester £10.3 million.[822]

The boroughs are now driven to build housing at a time when, luckily for them, it is possible to supplement their income in this way, as well as providing for the city's fast-growing population. Boroughs with more available land or more valuable sites will find it easier to take advantage of the various means of abstracting money from development. Thus, Waltham Forest and Lewisham each received more from the NHB than, for example, Reading or Slough. Development is now an incentive-driven generator of resources for London councils.

ROADS

R esponsibility for highways was split between the GLC, which ran major roads, and the boroughs, who were responsible for the 95 per cent of highways deemed 'local'. Such a split is unusual in major cities, which generally have a single authority in charge of all roads. In their early years, a number of the boroughs found themselves struggling to stop massive road schemes.

---

822 Department for Communities and Local Government, *New Homes Bonus Scheme, Grant Determination* (2015–16), April 2015

The GLC had plans for a series of Ringways: concentric rings of major roads, linked by other motorway-scale roads running outwards from the city centre. Had it been completed, the urban motorway system would have resembled a giant spider's web of highways and would have changed the city forever.

One of the linking roads was the Westway, which Kensington & Chelsea and other boroughs attempted to stop. The Westway cut a number of neighbourhoods in two and condemned the northern parts of Westminster and Kensington & Chelsea to years of chaotic disruption. Chunks of the Ringways or 'Motorway Box' can still be found in contemporary London. A section resembling Ringway 1 can be seen as the West Cross Route between North Kensington and Shepherd's Bush. There were huge protests against the Westway, including people putting up banners saying 'Get us out of this hell – rehouse us now' outside their windows.

As one expert commentator has observed of the Ringways system, which was so strongly promoted by the GLC:

> It would have affected life in the capital in every conceivable way, changing the way London looked and functioned. It would have changed the development of the city forever. It was far-reaching and visionary; planning on a scale rarely seen in this country. It was a transport scheme to end all transport schemes. And it was utterly unacceptable to the general public.[823]

Not all boroughs opposed all the roads. The Hayes bypass was long the subject of a lobby by Hillingdon council and local MPs, while Croydon has, for many years, attempted to have the A23 improved. Indeed, roads south of the river, apart from the M25, have not been constructed with the enthusiasm that the government and, for a while, the GLC managed in north London. In some ways, this disparity is a blessing, but, in a number of locations, it has left residents and businesses facing poor road and environmental conditions.

The boroughs and anti-roads campaigners eventually triumphed over the Robert Moses-style motorway construction which the GLC and the transport

---

823 'Ringways', cbrd.co.uk, http://www.cbrd.co.uk/articles/ringways

ministry wished to impose on London during the 1960s. Some of it was built, but much was not. Moreover, the mood changed. Borough councils now routinely close local roads to through-traffic. Many have imposed 20mph speed limits on their roads. Cyclists have been given increasing priority, including an innovative contra-flow policy introduced by Kensington & Chelsea,[824] which other boroughs, such as Camden, have followed. Parking policies have been imposed so as to keep non-residents out. Many street systems have been made complex to navigate, with one-way streets and closures, so as to discourage rat-running. Road space has been squeezed. Islington is enforcing a no-car-parking rule for new homes. A broadly anti-car ethos now prevails.

The effect of this policy has been to intensify traffic on the small number of GLA/TfL roads. Even the congestion charge, introduced by Ken Livingstone in 2003, has made no difference to traffic speeds. Boris Johnson appointed a Roads Task Force, which proposed, among other things, the possibility of burying some of the roads built during the 1960s, such as the Hammersmith Flyover and Brent Cross interchange, in tunnels.[825] Since 2000, the boroughs and the GLA between them have ensured that, as far as motor vehicles are concerned, London is a city of ever-declining road traffic and slower speeds.[826]

PLANNING

Many studies of planning in London and elsewhere consider the large, city-wide plans produced by metropolitan government. The Greater London Development Plan (GLDP) and the Mayor's London Plan are widely seen as explaining how the city might or should develop. While such strategic plans are important for the policy community, they have had less impact than,

---

824 Peter Walker, 'London trial to let cyclists pedal the "wrong" way on one-way streets', *The Guardian*, 17 September 2009

825 Tom Dines, 'TfL looks at road tunnels to ease congestion on London streets, *New Civil Engineer*, 25 July 2013

826 Transport for London, *Roads Task Force – Technical Note 9*, Roads Task Force Thematic Analysis, 2012, page 3

on the one hand, one-off policy interventions by central government and, on the other, fifty years of borough development control.

The GLDP might have turned London into a Los Angeles-style motorway city, but this endpoint was avoided. The plan assumed a metropolis whose population would continue to shrink, and within which London Docks would have survived. While there are remnants of the GLDP's proposals within contemporary London, the remains are few and far between. The London Plan has been more influential, particularly in its boosterist vision of rapid, globally driven, economic and population growth.

Far more important than the GLC and GLA's mega-plans have been decisions made by central government such as the abandonment of anti-London planning policies, the creation of the LDDC, the construction of the Docklands Light Railway, the extension of the Jubilee line, Crossrail and the decision to back the 2012 Olympic Games. The Thatcher government's abolition of the GLC left space for the Blair government's creation of the Mayor of London, bringing directly elected executives into British city-regional government. The Millennium lottery projects also left their mark. Whitehall has left a visible imprint on the capital.

The boroughs have had a profound effect on the city's development. Local plans have determined the rebuilding of town centres in Bexley (Bexleyheath), Bromley, Croydon, Hammersmith, Haringey (Wood Green) and Havering (Romford). Boroughs are today redeveloping Lewisham, Ilford (Redbridge), Sutton, Hounslow, Walthamstow (Waltham Forest) and Ealing. The City of London's decision to build high-rise buildings in the Square Mile has radically altered central London's look and feel. Tower Hamlets has, post-LDDC, followed the City and encouraged a growing cluster of skyscrapers. The availability of former industrial land along the South Bank has made it possible for Greenwich, Lewisham, Southwark, Lambeth and Wandsworth to give permission for dozens of riverside high-rise buildings. Yet Westminster and Kensington & Chelsea have largely rejected tall buildings. The London skyline in 2015 shows how different local policies can affect metropolitan development. GLC and GLA planning created a framework within which boroughs decide their own policy on tall buildings but, generally, boroughs (though occasionally the secretary of state) determine where towers are built.

The willingness of boroughs to accommodate net housing differs significantly. Judgements about how much land is available locally will be affected by residents' views about matters such as conservation, gardens, light, views, noise and traffic. There is a wide range of housing construction from borough to borough, with some delivering about 1,500 per year and others closer to 250.[827] Attitudes to heritage and conservation are locally determined. There are hanging baskets in the streets in Westminster's part of Fitzrovia, but not Camden's. Camden, by contrast, is less happy to accommodate cars in new residential developments. Councillors' local choice is real.

EDUCATION AND SOCIAL SERVICES

When the boroughs were created, the outer ones took over education from their former counties. In inner London the ILEA continued to run a single education service for the boroughs and the City. In the mid-1960s, the new Labour government required local authorities to prepare schemes for the reorganisation of schools along comprehensive lines. A number of (generally Labour-controlled) boroughs willingly moved to a system of comprehensive schools, as did the ILEA. Others, often Conservative-controlled, managed to keep their grammar schools, notably Barnet, Bexley, Bromley, Enfield, Kingston, Redbridge and Sutton.

Policies subsequently pursued by central government transferred advanced further education (mostly polytechnics) and then the remainder of further education to the control of government-appointed quangos. Since the passage of the Education Reform Bill 1988, schools have been reformed in a number of ways so as to give them greater autonomy. Local government's role has been much

---

827 Department for Communities and Local Government, live tables on house building, Table 253: permanent dwellings started and completed, by tenure and district, https://www.gov.uk/government/statistical-data-sets/live-tables-on-house-building

reduced. Grant-maintained schools, then academies, and latterly free schools have been introduced to operate outside council control. David Cameron suggested that the post-2015 government wished to transfer all schools away from council control.[828] London boroughs, in common with other councils, have seen their educational responsibilities dwindle over the past fifty years.

Social services, on the other hand, have proved to be one of the most complex and difficult of London borough responsibilities, particularly as London has changed so much since 1965. The capital's stock of relatively poor housing and significant levels of inequality have made the delivery of, particularly, children's social care a major challenge. Immigration from societies with different cultural histories has created additional complexity. In the early years of the boroughs, councils devoted significant efforts to creating mini welfare states. But problems thrown up by challenges such as new social behaviour norms, the decline of deference, the failures of newly constructed social housing and changing public expectations have together made social services more difficult to provide. The 'churn' in the capital's population makes it hard to monitor the movement of families. Social workers either intervene too little or too much. High-profile failures of social care have revealed weaknesses in public service integration and of proper bureaucratic practice. But they also exposed the near-impossibility of fulfilling public expectations that social services will follow, in detail, the private lives of thousands of families. There were wrong answers, but no simple correct ones.

THE CHANGING ECONOMY, REGENERATION AND A NEW MODEL OF LONDON GOVERNMENT

Between 1960 and 1980, London Docks declined from carrying their highest-ever tonnages to having virtually no business. Industry was shrinking, a problem made worse by the need to seek a government permit to develop any new factory in London. The Location of Offices Bureau, set up in 1963,

---

828 Rowena Mason, 'David Cameron: I want every school to become an academy', *The Guardian*, 15 August 2015

required official permission for the development of new offices in central London. Because of such policies and the development of new towns, London found itself facing rapid decline.[829] Peak-hour Tube and rail travel to central London began to fall,[830] which allowed the government to cut back on reinvestment in the Underground and other elements of the transport system. Such historic underfunding has been a problem for the capital ever since.

The metropolitan ring around London continued to grow during this period of London's decline. Planned dispersal policies and a desire to commute from the countryside had the long-term effect of further expanding London. Places such as the Chilterns, Hertfordshire and the London fringe of Kent and Surrey grew rapidly. Northampton, Peterborough, Crawley, Reading, Oxford, Cambridge and other prosperous centres within what planner Peter Hall termed the 'Greater South East' became parts of an even greater London. When the capital started to grow again from the late 1980s onwards, the scale and strength of this super-region was to become part of the city's 'Dark Star' attractiveness.

Much has been written about the change in London's economic fortunes in the period from the mid-1980s.[831] Its causes are uncertain, though they include natural changes in the city's demographics, Mrs Thatcher's economic policies, and wider changes to global economic forces, which, it is now argued, favour cities like London.[832] 'Big Bang' deregulation of financial services, the rapid development of banking, mass immigration, re-investment in the Underground and commuter railways, and inflows of foreign capital can be seen as both causes of and contributors to the turnaround.

829 Jerry White, *London in the Twentieth Century: A City and its People*, London: Vintage Books, pages 204–8

830 Department of Transport, *Central London Rail Study*, A joint study by the Department of Transport, British Rail Network South East, London Regional Transport, London Underground Ltd, London: Department of Transport, London Regional Transport and British Rail, January 1989, Figure 1, page 3

831 See, for example, Bridget Rosewell, *Reinventing London*, London: London Publishing Partnership, 2013 or Douglas McWilliams, *The Flat White Economy: How the digital economy is transforming London and other cities of the future*, London: Duckworth Overlook, 2015

832 A clear exposition of reasons for the success of London and cities like it can be found in: Edward Glaeser, *Triumph of the City: How urban spaces make us human*, London: Macmillan, 2011

The reversal in London's fortunes was not predicted. The boroughs have found themselves both benefiting from this resurgence and having to cope with demands for new infrastructure and public services. Primary schools in particular have faced pressure for many more places. Newham and Harrow were among the councils with the biggest gap between places and demands.[833] Gascoigne Primary School, in Barking & Dagenham, has become the largest in the country, with over 1,500 pupils.[834] Housing, social services and planning have all seen demand for increased provision as the population has increased. Tower Hamlets provides an example of the rollercoaster nature of demographic change. In 1939, the borough housed 490,000 people, before declining to about 140,000 in 1981. It then increased to 275,000 by 2015, and is projected to rise towards 350,000 by the end of the 2030s.[835]

The Central London Rail Study (CLRS), published in 1989, signalled an understanding inside government that the long-term decline of London's transport had become a problem. The Tube and buses were, by this time, bulging with new passenger growth. Apart from the original part of the Docklands Light Railway and an extension of the Underground to Heathrow, there had been little new public investment in the capital's transport system since the Victoria line had fully opened in 1968. The CLRS foreshadowed the extension via Southwark and Greenwich of the Jubilee line from Green Park to Stratford, new branches on the Docklands Light Railway, and the development of Crossrail.[836]

From the boroughs' point of view, another beneficial consequence of

833 Fiona Parker, 'London faces biggest shortage of primary school places', *Local Government Chronicle*, 8 April 2015

834 Nicola Woolcock, 'Britain's biggest primary school is expanding to take 1,500 pupils', *The Times*, 14 February 2015

835 Trust for London, 'Tower Hamlets', London's Poverty Profile, Trust for London/New Policy Institute, 2015, http://www.londonspovertyprofile.org.uk/indicators/boroughs/tower-hamlets (accessed 30 July 2015); also 'London's population high: Top metropolis facts, Duncan Smith, BBC, 2 February 2015, http://www.bbc.com/news/uk-england-london-31056626 (accessed 30 July 2015)

836 Department of Transport, *Central London Rail Study*, A joint study by The Department of Transport, British Rail Network South East, London Regional Transport, London Underground Ltd, London: Department of Transport, London Regional Transport and British Rail, January 1989

resurgence is that ex-industrial areas have become easier to re-use. In some areas, abandoned factories are now the source of new workspace for start-up companies in the tech industry. The Old Street roundabout, on the border of the City, Islington and Hackney, is today a cluster of tech companies. Stratford railway lands were the location of the 2012 Olympic Games and then subsequently accommodated flats, a university campus and a park. Battersea Power Station, the development of which defeated successive developers, is finally in the middle of a massive transformation. Old Oak Common, on the border of four west London boroughs, has been identified by the Mayor as requiring a mayoral development corporation in order to be redeveloped. All four of these regeneration sites are on or close to borough boundaries.[837]

Another step in the evolution of newly growing London was Tony Blair's New Labour landslide in 1997. Labour was committed to the re-creation of city-wide government in London, though Blair personally had come to the view that a directly elected Mayor of London should be introduced as the executive leader of the new GLA. In a referendum held in May 1998, every borough voted in favour of reform. The vacuum created by the abolition of the GLC left space for a Mayor and Assembly, which has subsequently been judged to be reasonably powerful, efficient and effective.[838]

One of the Mayor's most important roles was the requirement to create a London Plan.[839] The first and second Mayors of London each used the plan to set out a path for London's rapid growth, including additional housing, transport infrastructure and policies about tall buildings. Nicky Gavron, as Ken Livingstone's deputy mayor, promoted the idea of what became known as 'Orbirail', which eventually came to fruition in the early 2010s as a circular Highbury–Willesden–Clapham Junction–New Cross part of the Overground.

---

837 See, for example, Department for Communities and Local Government, *The Old Oak Common and Park Royal Development (Establishment) Order, 2015*, Urban Development, England, SI 2015 No. 53, London: TSO, 2015

838 Tony Travers, *The Politics of London: Governing an Ungovernable City*, London: Palgrave, 2004, pages 192–9

839 Mayor of London, *London Plan, Spatial Development Strategy for London*, London: Greater London Authority, February 2004

There have, from time to time, been differences between the Mayor's view of what was required for London as a whole and the desire of individual boroughs to determine their own destinies. As in the 1960s, some of the boroughs today favour a low-rise future with modest population growth. Other authorities use the financial and regeneration benefits of major developments to pay for services and facilities that would otherwise be impossible to fund. Haringey, Waltham Forest and Enfield are developing housing and employment along the Lee Valley in ways that will transform the fortunes of this formerly industrial corridor of the city. Boroughs such as Barnet, Ealing, Lewisham and Hounslow, which might have been seen as predominantly 'suburban' in the late 1960s, are now encouraging new residential developments that have a distinctly metropolitan scale and look. Inner London is moving outwards.

To develop big and densely packed sites, boroughs and the Mayor sometimes work together, though on other occasions they will find themselves in opposition. Financial incentives encourage development but require complex negotiations between boroughs and City Hall. The need to 'tax' new development is a significant new responsibility for the modern London borough.

The five Olympic boroughs, Newham, Waltham Forest, Hackney, Tower Hamlets and Greenwich, worked closely with successive mayors on the preparation of the 2012 Olympic Games. The Olympics opened up Leyton, Plaistow, Stratford, Homerton and Hackney Wick to the kind of improvement which had occurred in Islington and Camden during the 1970s and 1980s. Subsequently, the London Overground has connected Newham through Tube-style services around north London to Hackney, Islington, Camden, Brent, Ealing, Kensington & Chelsea, and Hammersmith & Fulham.

More widely, the Overground has altered the geography and economy of London in ways that would have been unthinkable fifty years ago.[840] Southwark, Lambeth and Wandsworth are linked in inner-south London. Many other boroughs, including Croydon, Waltham Forest, Haringey,

---

840 A leading estate agent's view of the impact of London Overground is revealing, see
     Hamptons, *Market Insight Going Overground*, London: Hamptons International, 2014

Harrow, Lewisham, Hounslow and Richmond, are on spurs off the central section of the Overground. Residents of outer London can now travel to each other more easily without visiting the city centre. The 'Ginger line', in addition to being a train service, has already become part of London's literary heritage.[841]

By the early 2010s, London's economic success was being challenged on a number of grounds. As in the 1950s and 1960s, some believed London's growth was at the expense of other parts of the country.[842] Others were more concerned about the unequal benefits derived by different sections of society.[843] But the fact that London paid more in taxation than was spent there by government has placed a limit on the extent to which any government would risk undermining the capital's success. Taxes such as income tax and stamp duty land tax produce a disproportionately high yield in London. A so-called mansion tax, proposed by the Labour Party during the 2015 general election, would have produced over 85 per cent of its yield in the capital, with Kensington & Chelsea paying 36 per cent of the UK total.[844] London is a golden goose and the boroughs its loving guardian.

DEMOGRAPHY AND IMMIGRATION

The decline and then growth of London's population since 1965 is a theme running through this book. Appendix 1 shows the boroughs' populations in 1961, 2011 and projections for 2031. Within the remarkable story of shrinkage followed by renewed growth is another one. In 1965, London

---

841 Iain Sinclair, *London Overground: A Day's Walk Around the Ginger Line*, London: Hamish Hamilton, 2015

842 See, for example, Ed Cox and Bill Davies, *Still on the Wrong Track: An Updated Analysis of Transport Infrastructure Spending*, Newcastle: IPPR North, 2013, page 18

843 See, for example, Daniel Dorling, *Injustice: Why social inequality persists*, Bristol: The Policy Press, 2011

844 Adam Palin, 'Mansion tax burden would fall predominantly on central London,' *Financial Times*, 9 April 2014

was still largely a city of white British-born people. There had been immigration from the Caribbean, India and Pakistan, but, in London as a whole, only 3 per cent of the population were from the new Commonwealth in the 1961 census.[845] The other major group of non-British-born residents had come from Ireland. For many years, the Irish were the single largest non-British population in London, with concentrations in Kilburn (Brent/Camden), Hammersmith and parts of Westminster.

There were occasional event-driven increases to the non-white migrant population; for example, the expulsion of Asians from Uganda in 1972, the arrival of Vietnamese 'boat people' at the end of the 1970s, the influx of asylum seekers from war zones in the 1990s and 2000s, and the subsequent expansion of the European Union (EU). Tony Blair's Labour government in 1997 oversaw the largest increase in international in-migration ever to occur in the UK. London, as has been the case historically, was the place many new residents chose to settle.[846] Efforts by the 2010–15 coalition and post-2015 Conservative government to reduce immigration have had little overall impact because of free movement within the EU.

When the boroughs were created, there were small concentrations of people born in Ireland, the Caribbean, India, and Pakistan, particularly in Lambeth, Wandsworth, Haringey, Hackney, Hammersmith, Westminster, Kensington & Chelsea and Hounslow. As immigration increased, ethnic diversity has appeared in all boroughs. The UK-born population of London has fallen steadily since 1965 from over 85 per cent in the 1971 census to 63 per cent in 2011. The white British proportion of the London population fell from 60 per cent to 45 per cent between 2001 and 2011.[847]

---

845 Tony Travers, 'The impact of migrants on London politics' in *Migration and London's Growth,* (ed.) Ben Kochan, London: LSE London, 2014, page 184

846 For a short history of the scale and origins of migration over time see Office for National Statistics, 'Immigration Patterns of Non-UK Born Populations in England and Wales in 2011', 17 December 2013, http://www.ons.gov.uk/ons/dcp171776_346219.pdf (accessed 30 July 2015)

847 London Datastore, Historical Census Tables, Table 29 and Table 31, http://data.london.gov.uk/dataset/historical-census-tables (accessed 30 July 2015)

This book is not about the remarkable changes brought about in London by immigration, but the patterns of settlement from place to place over time have had profound consequences for individual boroughs. Both the scale and speed of change could not have been predicted by borough leaderships. Barking & Dagenham saw its foreign-born population increase by over 200 per cent between 2001 and 2011, Greenwich by over 100 per cent, Havering and Hillingdon by 80–90 per cent. There were large percentage changes in Bexley, Waltham Forest, Redbridge and Newham, though all boroughs except Kensington & Chelsea experienced an increase in non-UK-born residents in excess of more than 20 per cent in this decade. In Barking & Dagenham, Bexley and Havering, the percentage increases were on a relatively modest base. Richmond saw a small percentage rise on a relatively small base, and is, with Kingston, among the boroughs least affected by international migration.[848]

The consequences of immigration and growing minority populations have included downwards pressure on wages, public service costs and occasional electoral responses.[849] One of the most marked impacts has been on the performance of London schools. According to Simon Burgess:

> [T]he basis for [London's improving and relatively better] performance is the ethnic composition of its school population. There is a straight-forward effect: the lowest progress group, white British pupils, make up 36 per cent of pupils in London and 84 per cent in the rest of England. London simply has a higher fraction of high-scoring pupils. This is not by chance of course; a key part of the London effect is its attraction to migrants and those aspiring to a better life. More speculatively, because of a more integrated school system and because of a larger population of non-white British pupils, more white British pupils have the opportunity

848   Anna Krausova and Dr Carlos Vargas-Silva, *Briefing London: Census Profile*, The Migration Observatory at the University of Oxford, 20 May 2013, http://www.migrationobservatory. ox.ac.uk/sites/files/migobs/Briefing%20-%20London%20census%20profile_0.pdf (accessed 31 July 2015)

849   See London School of Economics and Political Science, *The Impact of Recent Immigration on the London Economy*, London: City of London, 2007

for interactions in school with higher-scoring ethnic minority pupils than those outside the capital do.[850]

Other commentators have been less optimistic about the impacts of immigration. David Goodhart has argued that 'white flight' is an issue and has observed:

> [White flight] is a remarkably understudied phenomenon. This is perhaps because it is based on a notion of group identities and affinities that most liberal academics do not feel or understand and tend to stigmatise as 'racist', at least when expressed by white people. But one of the interesting things about white flight is that it has continued, and in the case of London apparently increased, at a time when racist attitudes have been in sharp decline.[851]

British government policies and attitudes towards immigration have changed over time. Moreover, the attractiveness of Britain as a destination for migrants has altered. At some points, the government has encouraged immigration and, at others, it has attempted to restrict it. Labour shortages, among other factors, have influenced policy.

London boroughs, more than any other group of local authorities (with the possible exception of places such as Slough, Leicester, Birmingham, Manchester and a number of smaller towns), have had to manage the consequences of UK government policy. While many of the impacts of immigration have been positive, it would be naïve to pretend there had not been costs. Little, if any, warning was given to councils about the possible consequences of mass immigration, either for public services or social cohesion. London boroughs and, more recently, the GLA have had to respond again and again to shifts in Whitehall

---

850 Simon Burgess, 'Understanding the success of London's schools', Centre for Market and Public Organisation Working Paper No. 14/333, University of Bristol, October 2014, pages 15–16

851 David Goodhart, 'London's "white flight" deserves attention', *Financial Times*, 26 December 2012

policy on immigration. A further change occurred in the autumn of 2015, with David Cameron's decision to accept up to 20,000 additional Syrian asylum seekers.[852] Local government's response has been rather more effective than national government's management of the UK border.

BOROUGH POLITICS

From the first elections in 1964, the boroughs have shown a wide variation in local electorates' willingness to vote Conservative, Labour or for other parties. For most of the time, and in most boroughs, there has either been a traditional Conservative v. Labour contest or a one-party state run by the Conservatives or Labour – such an outcome should have been expected in a city of many millions of people, including older, densely populated areas and newer, suburban, ones. The boroughs have developed their own political cultures: Conservatives in one borough can be different from Conservatives in another, even if neighbours. The same is true for Labour and the Liberal Democrats.

London boroughs have always used first-past-the-post voting within a national political system that substantially sustains two dominant parties. Barking & Dagenham and Newham have always been Labour-run, while Kensington & Chelsea and Westminster have always delivered Conservative majorities. Ealing, Hammersmith & Fulham, Harrow and Kingston have changed control on a number of occasions, while Havering has been under 'no overall control' for almost half its life. The table below shows the number of boroughs controlled by the major parties, or where there was 'no overall control', in each election from 1964 to 2014. With the exception of 1964, GLC and GLA elections have never coincided with borough ones. On only one occasion, 2010, did the London borough elections take place on the same day as a UK general election.

---

852 Matt Chorley, 'Britain to open the doors to 20,000 Syrians – but spread out over five years and ONLY from refugee camps in the Middle East', *Daily Mail*, 7 September 2015

Number of boroughs controlled by the major parties (or no overall control), 1964–2014

	1964	1968	1971	1974	1978	1982	1986	1990	1994	1998	2002	2006	2010	2014
Con	9	28	10	13	17	17	11	12	4	4	8	14	11	9
Lab	20	3	21	18	14	12	15	14	17	18	15	7	17	20
Lib/LD	0	0	0	0	0	0	2	3	3	2	3	3	2	1
NOC	3	1*	1	1	1	3	4	3	8	8	6	8	2	2

* Newham remained Labour-controlled by means of aldermen using their votes to choose a Labour mayor.

Source: Greater London Authority, *London Borough Council Elections 22 May 2014*, Figure 3, page xxix

Labour, despite their travails in the 1980s, have on average won control of rather more boroughs than the Conservatives, though in the period since 1964, there have been Conservative or Conservative-led governments at the national level for slightly longer than Labour ones, creating more 'mid-term' periods for Tories in London to fight against. But, if borough, GLC/GLA, parliamentary and European elections are analysed together, social and demographic changes appear to have tilted London towards being slightly more pro-Labour since the late 1990s than previously.[853] Nevertheless, London remains politically plural, with the possibility of a change in control in all but five or six boroughs.

The Liberal Democrats had a successful run from 1986 to 2006, but have fallen away latterly. The BNP won fourteen seats in the 2006 borough elections: twelve in Barking & Dagenham, one in Redbridge and one in Havering, though they were all lost in 2010. UKIP won twelve in 2014, with seven in Havering, three in Bexley and two in Bromley. Greens, though they scored vote shares of over 15 per cent in a number of boroughs in 2014, have found it hard to break through, winning only small numbers of councillors. In 2014,

---

853 Tony Travers, 'London – The election in the capital', *LSE General Election blog*, 3 April 2015, http://blogs.lse.ac.uk/generalelection/london-election-in-the-capital (accessed 30 May 2015)

they managed just four, though the single Green on Lewisham is the entire opposition to Labour.[854]

THE POLITICAL REVOLUTION OF THE 1980s

The economic decline of London and other cities had consequences for industrial relations and for politics. In 1968, the Conservatives swept to power in every borough except Barking, Newham, Southwark and Tower Hamlets. There was a huge cull of traditional Labour councillors. Three years later, there was a massive shift back to Labour, bringing many new and younger councillors onto the borough councils. In some authorities, the new left began to build up a power base. As Ken Livingstone observed of Lambeth after the Labour success of 1971: 'The 57–3 Tory majority on Lambeth council was transformed into a Labour majority of 51–9. The average age of the Labour group was halved and only eight Labour members had served on the council before.'[855]

The political and industrial struggles of the 1970s provided fertile grounds for radicalism. The election of Mrs Thatcher in 1979 initiated an all-out war between some on the left and the new, radical Conservative Prime Minister. London boroughs including Camden, Hackney, Lewisham, Islington, Brent, Haringey, Southwark, Greenwich and Lambeth found themselves subject to spending targets, grant penalties and rate-capping.[856] Direct-labour building departments had, under new legislation, to be exposed to private-sector competition. Many of the boroughs adopted radical policies, including decentralised

---

854 For vote shares, seats won and councillor numbers on individual boroughs for each year from 1964 to 2014, see the 'London Elections Reports' sections of the London Datastore website (http://data.london.gov.uk/elections). Detailed research on all London elections, including ward-by-ward results, has been undertaken by Michael Minors, Dennis Grenham and latterly Gareth Piggott. The London County Council, Greater London Council, London Research Centre and now the Greater London Authority have continued to publish this remarkable series of election data for the full fifty years of the boroughs' existence.

855 Ken Livingstone, *You Can't Say That: Memoirs*, London: Faber & Faber, 2012, page 78

856 Tony Travers, *The Politics of Local Government Finance*, London: Allen & Unwin, 1986, pages 150–77

sub-committees and the defence of services from cuts. As *London Labour Briefing*, the publication of the new left at the time, put it in 1982: 'One of our hopes for decentralisation of council services should be that it will help develop a political awareness among more people that the struggles of council workers and "the community" over cuts in jobs and services are a common anti-capitalist struggle against economic oppression.'

In response to rate-capping, efforts were made by several Labour boroughs to work together to refuse to set a rate, a tactic that, it was believed, would force the government to backtrack on cuts being imposed by Mrs Thatcher and her Environment Secretary Michael Heseltine.[857] The cuts were far smaller than the 30 per cent real-terms reductions faced by many London councils from 2010 to 2015. Other urban councils in Sheffield, Manchester and Liverpool were engaged in similar tactics. The GLC, from 1981 under a left-wing leadership, was signed up to the same policy.[858]

Eventually, opposition to rate-capping collapsed. One by one the boroughs found ways of justifying setting a rate or of allowing opposition councillors to set one. Most councillors did not wish to risk surcharge and bankruptcy at the hands of the district auditor, which is what happened to a number of Lambeth and Liverpool councillors.

This era was the time of 'creative accountancy'. A number of London boroughs and the GLC were adept at financial manoeuvres that, though lawful, came close to the edge of legality. Spending was moved from one year to another so as to minimise grant penalties and was shifted from revenue to capital accounts. Special funds were created. Councils sold off assets and then leased them back. An Audit Commission report on eight London boroughs concluded they had entered into so-called 'deferred purchase arrangements' to a value of £550 million.[859]

---

857 Ibid., pages 169–70

858 Stuart Lansley, Sue Goss and Christian Wolmar, *Councils in Conflict*, London: Macmillan, 1989, pages 34–44

859 For a full description of creative accounting at the time see Martin Loughlin, *Legality and Locality: The Role of Law in Central–Local Relations*, Oxford: Clarendon Press, 1996

A number of London councils became heavily involved in the swaps market, which gave local authorities flexibility in the management of their borrowings. Swaps allowed councils to generate extra income by speculating on interest rate movements. Hammersmith & Fulham, in particular, entered the swaps market during the mid-1980s. By 1988–89, at the height of its activity, the borough was responsible for 0.5 per cent of the entire world swaps market.

The district auditor appealed to the Divisional Court seeking a ruling that Hammersmith's capital market fund (i.e., its swaps activity) was contrary to law. The borough and others similarly involved suspended their activities in the swaps market and made provision for outstanding payments. The banks then issued proceedings to ensure they received payments due. As a result of the auditor's application, the banks decided not to proceed with writs against Hammersmith and a number of other councils. The councils were, as a result, protected against making potentially massive payments.

Policies pursued by radical, new left councils in London included a number of causes such as race equality and women's and gay rights, which have subsequently become mainstream across all parties in local and national government. 'Equal opportunities' were born at this time. But, in the 1980s, they stimulated the national media into a frenzied attack against the so-called 'loony left'. Progressive councillors were running ahead of public opinion though, by 2015, they can reasonably claim to have been proved right in their aspirations, if not in the way their message was delivered.

Many of the same authorities and councillors confused a more liberal attitude to people and rights with an over-relaxed attitude to good management and a lack of willingness to tackle failure, which undermined the quality of services, leading to the breakdown in some boroughs' housing, refuse collection and benefits services. Social care and education were badly affected. In Lambeth and Hackney, there were serious public-service failures, and it took new and determined leaderships many years to restore good government.

At the national level, the Labour leadership distanced itself from the views and actions of its more radical London councils. There were differences in approach between the agenda of London boroughs and the policies pursued by left-led metropolitan authorities. In the capital, concerns focused on rights, anti-racism and feminism, whereas in, say, Liverpool the focus was on a working-class struggle to build housing and stop de-industrialisation. The left's agenda in London looked odd to Labour activists elsewhere:

> The London left became lepers almost without friends. It was attacked by other sections of the left for wanting to deviate from class politics. According to Derek Hatton, former deputy leader of Liverpool council and a leading figure in the Trotskyist Militant Tendency, 'the London left are more concerned about black mayors and gay rights than about building homes' and 'more concerned that we called … a manhole cover a personhole cover, than they ever were about real issues'. 'People as a whole – especially older Labour voters', wrote a Scottish trade unionist, in a rank-and-file paper, 'become anti-Labour when they see councils in London … subsidising all kinds of odd activities'.[860]

While there is nothing new about factionalism on the left of politics, this differ-ence between London progressives and the social conservatism of the Militant Tendency ensured the Thatcher government was in an even more powerful position to crush it. Oddly, the legacy of 1980s London borough and GLC left-radical policies, while still occasionally accused of being 'political correct-ness gone mad', is visible in contemporary politics. The Labour Party's election of Jeremy Corbyn as leader in September 2015 provided voters with a sharp reminder of the politics of the past. In the 1980s, the party's national leaders had sought to rein in (what they saw as) local excesses. However, positions of Labour nationally and locally were reversed in 2015: London Labour coun-cils were pragmatic and moderate while the national Labour Party appeared to be adopting a new form of leftist radicalism.

Another consequence of the standoff between some Labour authorities and the government was the creation of the LDDC, imposed by Mrs Thatcher's

---

860 James Curran, Ivor Gaber and Julian Petley, *Culture Wars: The Media & The British Left*, Edinburgh: Edinburgh University Press, 2005, page 271

government in 1981 against the will of the local boroughs. At first, the local councils refused to co-operate:

> The experience in London [of the LDDC] was of a clash of interests, objectives and cultures; local government asserted planning, accountability and local needs and, in response, was effectively bypassed. However, LDDC was not the agent of a free-market approach but of a corporatist partnership with non-local business and central government involving public investment, subsidy and a form of planning.[861]

Over time, the LDDC began to work more consensually with Greenwich, Newham, Tower Hamlets, Lewisham and Southwark, particularly when Eric Sorensen became chief executive. Canary Wharf emerged as a symbol of the new London. If the LDDC had not been created in the fire of the struggle between the Thatcher government, local boroughs and the GLC, Tower Hamlets and the other local boroughs would today be different – and so would the London skyline.

The 1980s saw the emergence of new and radical Conservatives in a number of the boroughs. Wandsworth, under a series of Conservative leaders, developed a 'small state' and highly efficient version of local government. This low-cost model of local government has subsequently been much imitated. Although not particularly ideological in its inspiration, the Conservatives' opponents have long described Wandsworth as 'Thatcherite'. In Westminster, a new leadership was intent on imposing business principles on the council. 'One stop shops', which many councils now operate, were introduced. But its quest for efficiency led to the sale of three cemeteries, for £1, in such a way that maintenance contracts failed and the cemeteries had to be bought back at a higher price. This error was compounded by the 'homes for votes' scandal, which saw the council moving homeless tenants into asbestos-filled dwellings as part of what the district auditor described as 'gerrymandering'. This policy led to the surcharging of councillors.

---

861   Richard Batley, 'London Docklands: An Analysis of Power Relations Between UDCs and Local Government', *Public Administration*, Vol. 67, No. 2, page 186, June 1989

Most boroughs were untouched by virtually all this conflict and ideology. Residents of Croydon, Enfield, Barnet, Harrow, Richmond, Kingston, Hounslow, Merton, Sutton, Hillingdon, Havering, Bexley, Bromley, Barking & Dagenham, Redbridge, Waltham Forest, Newham, Kensington & Chelsea, Ealing and Hammersmith & Fulham would have lived through the 1980s without being aware (apart from what they read in newspapers) that London was in the grip of new and radical ideologies while locked in a war with central government. The compartmentalised nature of London's borough government means that the politics of any one council is unlikely to explain much even about its immediate neighbours' political life. None of the scandals of the 1980s and 1990s was about financial irregularity in the sense of councillors seeking personal financial gain: the scandals derived from different approaches to politics.

In several boroughs affected by the troubles of the 1980s, it required a number of years to re-establish effective administration. Lambeth, under aggressively moderate leadership, appointed a new chief executive with the explicit purpose of bringing about radical improvements to housing, street services and council-tax collection. Southwark similarly moved on from a period of complex collective leadership to the rebuilding of good government. In Hackney, there was briefly a Labour–Conservative administration to begin the process of service improvement. It appointed a tough managing director who had to work with senior councillors to tackle the challenge of chaotic management.

From this point on, the London boroughs, which had been affected by the struggles of the 1970s and 1980s, moved on to become among the best-run of all local government in England. Audit Commission performance rankings started to show councils such as Lambeth, Southwark and Hackney among the fastest improving anywhere. By the 2000s, London boroughs of all parties operated on the basis of tightly managed pragmatism. The ideological struggles of the 1980s, left and right, in many ways forged the pragmatic councils of the 2000s and the 2010s.

London borough Conservatives are now progressive on issues such as race and gender equality, while contemporary Labour councillors in London would never consider refusing to set the local tax as a protest against the Cameron government's austerity policies. What Labour boroughs often now do is generate resources for social programmes by developing land and assets as fast as possible. Indeed, by the 2010s, Labour councils were often more pro-development than Conservative ones: a remarkable turnaround compared with thirty years previously.

The ideological turmoil of the late 1970s and 1980s created conditions in which the GLC, established alongside the boroughs in 1965, was abolished. Bromley councillors, in particular, led the charge to abolish the GLC. Within three years of the Thatcher government's original announcement that the GLC was to be scrapped, it was gone. While Labour and even some Conservative politicians argued the abolition of the GLC would damage public services in London, the perceptible impact was slight. Simon James, writing four years after abolition, was able to observe:

> It would all be terrible; the city would grind to a standstill; the boroughs couldn't cope. Quite untrue. Many borough officers worked long hours and the transfer went rather well ... British local government is extraordinarily adaptable. At minimal notice its staff will cope with anything from flooding to licensing sex shops, not necessarily brilliantly but competently. And competence rather than brilliance is quite sufficient when you are numbering streets or disposing of household waste. The GLC's councillors should have foreseen this, since that same adaptability existed in equal measure among County Hall staff. As it was, Cassandra was confounded.[862]

Over time, other commentators recognised that a city such as London found it hard to function fully effectively without city-wide government. Even in the immediate aftermath of abolition, the boroughs found themselves with new responsibilities that saw them brought together by law for the purposes of service provision. Metropolitan government was, even in 1986, not dead.

---

862   Simon James, 'A Streamlined City: The Broken Pattern of London Government', *Public Administration*, Volume 68, Issue 4, December 1990, page 495

THE BOROUGHS AND THE INTERREGNUM

The boroughs and the City inherited many of the GLC's responsibilities. A new joint committee of boroughs, the London Fire & Civil Defence Authority, took over the fire brigade while another joint committee administered the GLC's large programme of grants to voluntary bodies. A third, the London Research Centre, assumed responsibility for statistics about greater London. There were several others, including a number of voluntary ones (overwhelmingly created by Labour authorities to continue ex-GLC policy work), which only a minority of boroughs took part in.

A measure of the underlying purpose of abolition was that the London Planning Advisory Committee (LPAC), set up to provide advice to ministers about London-wide planning, was chaired initially by a Richmond councillor, but given offices in Havering, almost 30 miles away. Planning was not intended to be a powerful, centrally driven, activity in the post-GLC world though, as it happened, LPAC went on to provide the intellectual basis for planning and development not only between 1986 and 2000, but also within the GLA. There were many other committees for all or part of London. The City of London, fulfilling an 'honest broker' role in these highly political times, agreed to run Hampstead Heath and a number of other former GLC responsibilities.[863]

The boroughs found themselves inheritors of parts of the GLC's empire. Some of the joint arrangements resembled the Metropolitan Board of Works which had been abolished almost 100 years previously. Nor were the new government-inspired committees and boards popular with the boroughs:

> London-wide voluntary committees of the boroughs are not new.
> For years, joint committees have run common services for children's
> homes, provided specialist social services courses and organized the
> boroughs' side of the Whitley councils. However, on GLC abolition, the

---

863 Michael Hebbert and Tony Travers (eds), *The London Government Handbook*, London: Cassell, 1988, has a full description of the post-abolition London arrangements

government expanded this practice from a few voluntary committees covering small areas of work funded by subscription to a proliferation of statutory boards with wide responsibilities, large budgets, many staff and precepting powers. Boroughs dislike these joint boards intensely: Labour and Liberal Democrats complain they provide limited strategic leadership or public accountability; Conservatives resent the survival of any pan-London body. All borough politicians fear these bodies' encroachment on the boroughs' independence.[864]

In April 1990, the ILEA was abolished. For the first time ever, the inner-London boroughs ran their own schools. Unlike GLC abolition, the process was less contested by the soon-to-be-abolished authority: ILEA worked to make the process as smooth as possible. In addition, the boroughs this time resisted new joint boards:

> [W]hen the inner London boroughs addressed cross-borough issues arising from ILEA abolition, the LBA boroughs refused point blank to set up any joint boards. A temporary joint committee representing the thirteen inner London boroughs was set up, christened the Inner London Education Advisory Committee, or ILEAC … they set up no less than twelve 'lead borough' arrangements under which one council took over a function and ran it as an agency, sharing costs with other subscribing boroughs. A few attracted subscriptions from all boroughs, like the careers service taken over by the City and the Centre for Young Musicians run by Westminster. However, most were supported by some boroughs only, such as the travellers' children education unit, the film and video library and the language and literacy unit.[865]

The London Residuary Body (LRB) was created by the government to parcel

---

864 Simon James, 'A Streamlined City: The Broken Pattern of London Government', *Public Administration*, Volume 68, Issue 4, December 1990, page 498

865 Ibid., page 500

up and sell off any remaining GLC (and then ILEA) services and assets. The leader of Croydon and also of the London Boroughs Association, Peter (now Lord) Bowness, was a member of the LRB board, which was chaired by Sir Godfrey Taylor, a former leader of Sutton. When the LRB had completed its work in the 1990s, any remaining functions were handed over to Bromley (GLC activities) and Kensington & Chelsea (ILEA).

After Mrs Thatcher resigned as Prime Minister at the end of 1990, John Major's government started a process of reconciliation with local government. In London, Labour councils pulled back from their confrontational stance and assumed a more traditional approach. Senior Labour politicians decided enough was enough. From now on, cleaning streets and repairing council housing was seen as a better route to popularity than an all-out ideologically based war with central government.[866]

The jumble of borough joint committees and other ad hoc arrangements that proliferated after GLC abolition led to creative searches for greater coherence and transparency. One proposal suggested bringing together the existing joint boards into one authority:

> Since their functions are for the most part technical – the [London Boroughs'] grants scheme is the obvious exception – they make up a fairly homogenous parcel of work. The Fire and Civil Defence Authority provides a ready-made administrative framework. Governments of different hue could cast its powers more or less restrictively as they choose. A Conservative government could justify the move as an administrative rationalisation, give it a suitably unglamorous name – the London Technical Services Board.[867]

Such a reform would have been a step back towards the MBW. Another

---

866 James Curran, Ivor Gaber and Julian Petley, *Culture Wars: The Media & The British Left*, Edinburgh: Edinburgh University Press, 2005, page 271

867 Simon James, 'A Streamlined City: The Broken Pattern of London Government', *Public Administration*, Volume 68, Issue 4, December 1990, page 503

proposal, from Westminster leader Dame Shirley Porter, suggested a minister for London. Tony Banks MP, previously a member of the Livingstone administration at County Hall, lobbied for a directly elected Mayor.[868] The Labour Party and the Liberal Democrats at this point argued for the restoration of a London-wide authority, although a streamlined version of the defunct GLC.

During the late 1980s, London found itself represented at international events by the LDDC, an appointed body for only part of the capital.[869] Michael Hebbert captured the spirit of the time: with no organisation able to step up and speak for London,

> the issue of representation refused to go away. Indeed, it was raised most insistently by the business lobby: in the competitive environment of the globalised economy, who would represent the capital in international gatherings? Who would receive overseas visitors? Who would bid for European funds, and solicit inward investment? Who would initiate a London bid for the year 2000 Olympic Games? (Answer, nobody: two rival bids based on Wembley and the Royal Docks cancelled each other out.) Property professionals, selling space in London, were vocal on the ... capital's need for a 'voice' in the specific sense of an agency to deal with inward investment.[870]

The Conservatives' 1992 manifesto promised to launch a new initiative for London-wide business promotion. The Major government brought about the creation of two organisations, London First and London Forum, which merged in 1993 under the name London First. Members of this new body included big companies (such as British Airways) with a commercial interest in London, the London Chamber of Commerce, the London CBI, property companies and sundry quangos. London First worked with the City of

---

868   Hansard, HC Debates, Volume 196, London: HMSO, 15 October 1991, Columns 284–92

869   Michael Hebbert, *London More by Fortune than Design*, Chichester: John Wiley & Sons, 1998, page 125

870   Ibid.

London, Westminster and LDDC on promotional campaigns and to lobby for major projects. It was at this point that the effort to deliver Crossrail began, though the government chose to go ahead with the Jubilee line extension to the Docklands.[871]

Another innovation at this time was the appointment of Steve Norris as Transport Minister for London, an explicit recognition that rail travel was of growing importance following consultations on the Central London Rail Study. Norris, a hyper-liberal Tory, was to be an important figure both in delivering major projects, but also in his capacity to build relations with the boroughs. He went on to be Conservative candidate for Mayor of London in 2000 and 2004.

Michael Hebbert, writing in the late 1990s, is critical of the 'basic problem of legitimacy', which surrounded London's patronage elites'. By this, he was referring to the government-encouraged boards, quangos and companies that had been brought together within London First. 'Unlike the growth coalitions of Manchester or Glasgow, they had no nexus in the local political class but were implanted by government. Whitehall did not intend them to function as lobby organisations.'[872]

The judgement today on London First and its activities is more positive. Its leading members, Alan Sheppard (of Grand Metropolitan) and Colin Marshall (of BA), were asked by the government to fill part of the vacuum left by the abolition of the GLC. They did so, acting with conspicuous sensitivity towards London's bruised political system. London First needed to get the government, the (by now) Labour-dominated boroughs and other business organisations to play ball. They succeeded, and London First, this time led by Baroness (Jo) Valentine, has continued to operate since London-wide government was restored in 2000.

Hebbert's point about legitimacy cannot be ignored. The government and the boroughs took steps during the mid-1990s to put in place a greater degree

---

871 Ibid., page 126

872 Ibid.

of public-sector involvement in London's representation and residual city-wide governance. John Gummer, the Secretary of State for the Environment, created the London Pride Partnership, involving the boroughs, London First and other business organisations, with the explicit remit of promoting the capital. Gummer styled himself 'Minister for London'. He was able to rely on officials from his own department and the Department of Transport, each of which had a London regional office that worked on planning, transport and related matters. In 1994, the Government Office for London (GOL) was created as part of an England-wide initiative to represent central government in the regions and vice versa.

GOL provided a stepping stone from the post-GLC abolition world to the GLA. GOL's first director, Robin Young, was appointed at a more senior civil service rank than the equivalent post in other regions. Young, working with another ex-DoE official, Liz Meek, was to be a leading player when Labour took office in 1997 in creating the legislative process that introduced the GLA. With Gummer as minister, GOL started major programmes near the Thames and, most influentially, the partial pedestrianisation of Trafalgar Square.

During the post-GLC period, the boroughs were not only running a number of city-wide services, but their own politics had calmed down to the point they were able to operate with a renewed single voice when dealing with the evolution of London First, GOL and newly created London ministers.

BOROUGH JOINT WORKING AND REPRESENTATION

The post-1965 boroughs created the LBA, modelled on a previous organisation that had represented the interests of the pre-1965 metropolitan boroughs. From 1965 until the political turbulence of the 1980s, the LBA lobbied on behalf of the boroughs and was formally consulted by central government on matters such as the local government finance system. Then, as relations between Labour and Conservative boroughs soured, the Labour councils split off and set up the Association of London Authorities (ALA). The Conservative and Liberal Democrat boroughs remained at the LBA, along with the City of London and Labour-controlled Barking & Dagenham. Indeed, Barking & Dagenham belonged to both organisations. Labour boroughs joined the new ALA with committees considering, among other things, policing, economic development, race and gender equality, health, welfare benefits and other issues the LBA did not wish to discuss.[873]

After several years of mutual suspicion, occasional meetings were held between the leaders of the two associations. Joint working groups sprang up on ILEA abolition, road planning, homelessness and concessionary fares. Yet they did not immediately re-unite. Simon James, who had been an officer at the LBA, wrote: 'Glasnost was one thing, perestroika another.'[874]

In 1995, when peace and rationality were fully restored, the LBA and the ALA merged under the politically sensitive leadership of Toby (now Lord) Harris, leader of Haringey. The new organisation was called the Association of London Government (ALG). It worked with central government and business organisations, such as the London Chamber of Commerce, the Confederation of British Industry and the newly created London First to create the 'London Pride Partnership' to promote the GLC-less capital. In 2006, the ALG was re-named London Councils. Today, the organisation represents all thirty-two boroughs and the City of London, and its membership includes the Mayor's Office of Policing & Crime and the London Fire & Emergency Planning Authority.

London Councils represents the boroughs and the City in dealing with central government, the GLA family, London's wider public services, businesses and others. It seeks to promote boroughs as leaders of integrated and cost-effective local provision and to help them to have the freedoms, powers and resources to deliver services to their residents, businesses and communities. London Councils runs a number of direct services on behalf of all of the boroughs, including the freedom pass, the independent parking appeals service and pan-London grants to voluntary organisations. It shares good practice

873   Simon James, 'A Streamlined City: The Broken Pattern of London Government', *Public Administration*, Volume 68, Issue 4, December 1990, page 501

874   Ibid., page 502

between boroughs, and houses activities such as support to London local government professional and political networks. The purpose of these networks is to drive better performance, to promote collaborative work on children's safeguarding, to act as the regional employer, and to improve young people's education and skills. London Councils also facilitates statutory joint arrangements for transport and grant-giving.

Another key role is providing a negotiating body to liaise with the Mayor and Assembly over London government issues, such as the capital's place in Whitehall's proposed 'city regional' government reforms, and also the future of local taxation. Senior London Councils members Jules Pipe (Hackney) and Theresa O'Neill (Bexley) and chief executives (Chris Duffield, formerly at the City of London, Nicholas Holgate, Kensington & Chelsea, and Martin Smith, Ealing) were also members of the London Finance Commission, appointed by the Mayor.[875]

A number of borough groupings for 'sub-regions' of London have emerged as a response to a wider, national debate about devolution to city regions.[876] Central London Forward succeeded the Central London Partnership in 2007 as a joint vehicle for eight city-centre boroughs. The South London Partnership, the West London Partnership and the North East London Strategic Alliance (NELSA) (a group of boroughs in the north-east of the city) fulfil similar functions in their parts of London. The scale of London is so great that groupings such as Central London Forward or NELSA are analogous in size to those that have emerged in Greater Manchester, the Liverpool City Region and Leeds City Region. How these sub-metropolitan groupings will develop in the longer-term is a fascinating question: they are different in kind and size from any previous London authority. They may take forward a larger scale of borough joint working or, alternatively, may shrink if and when central government's enthusiasm for 'city regions' wanes.

---

875 London Finance Commission, *Raising the Capital: The report of the London Finance Commission*, London: London Finance Commission/GLA, 2013

876 Mark Smullian, 'Clark seeks devolution plans from London borough groups', *Local Government Chronicle*, 10 June 2015

FIFTY GLORIOUS YEARS?

The boroughs, like all government institutions, have had better and worse periods in the decades since they were created. They have proved reasonably 'local' for residents and businesses within their areas, but big enough to tackle most public service issues. The GLC and GLA were created so as to deliver metropolitan, city-wide services that boroughs alone would have been unlikely to provide effectively. Not every year has been glorious in every borough, but the overall achievement has been sufficiently effective to avoid a major reform. By the standards of many British public institutions, this apparently understated achievement is remarkable.

THE STUDY OF CITIES

Academics from a number of disciplines study cities. Historians, political scientists, economists, planners, lawyers, sociologists and cultural theorists have all written extensively about aspects of urban areas. This examination of the London boroughs is a history rather than a theoretical examination of city governance. But it is important to consider, briefly, the way different disciplines have touched on the issue of government and the wider question of 'governance'. The latter term embraces a wider set of actors (such as business interests, non-governmental organisations and communities), not only those involved in the formal business of government.

Historical and political science studies of modern city government have generally looked at the development of urban government systems and those who influence them. The evolution of London's government has been examined in great detail by academics such as Laurence Gomme, William Robson, Gwilym Gibbon, Reginald Bell, Gerald Rhodes, Donald Foley, David Owen, John Davis, Ken Young, Patricia Garside, Nirmala Rao, George Jones and Jerry White. Their insights have included consideration of the struggle to develop metropolitan government during the nineteenth century, the growth of political parties, administrative systems and the cultural background to the evolution of the city's government.

There have been a number of more theoretical examinations of aspects of borough government at a particular point in time, including those by Patrick Dunleavy (of Newham's housing policy in the 1960s and early 1970s), Stephen Elkin (of politics and land use planning in boroughs including Kensington & Chelsea and Camden in the 1960s) and Andrew Glassberg (representation in Bromley, Tower Hamlets and Islington in the 1970s).[877] Glassberg produced the following borough 'councillor classification schema', which is still intriguing:

Borough councillor classification schema

		Scope of representation	
		Ward	Borough
Scope of ambition	Narrow	Classic parochials	Traditional rank-and-file
	Broad	'Ideology of localism' councillors	Traditional aspirants

Glassberg was attempting to categorise borough councillors into four broad groups determined by how far they saw themselves as being, for example, ward councillors primarily, with neighbourhood concerns being most important to them. These he described as 'classic parochials'. At the other corner of the table were councillors who were interested in borough-wide issues and who had ambition beyond the borough, who he called 'traditional aspirants'. Others were classified as 'ideology of localism' (primarily ward-based, but with a willingness to pursue such interests more broadly) or 'traditional rank-and-file' (borough political interests, often with strong party affiliations). While London borough politics has changed much since the late 1970s, Glassberg's analysis still has strength in understanding the kinds of borough councillor to be found in 2015.

---

877 Andrew D. Glassberg, *Representation and Urban Community*, London: Macmillan, 1981, pages 80–81

One attribute of cities that has changed significantly since the late 1960s has been the move from relatively simple 'government' systems to broader 'governance' arrangements. Kantor et al, in a book about city-region governance in London, New York, Paris and Tokyo, observed that:

> The traditional public administration model [of city government] saw the politician as exercising control through legislation and by being at the peak of a hierarchy of government ... Accountability systems stretched from voter, through politicians, to officials. Equity was achieved through one-person-one-vote, by administrative rules of fairness and the right to challenge through the courts ... Governance, with its bringing together in partnership of governmental and non-governmental forces, makes the simple prescriptions of public administration unsustainable.[878]

The growth of 'governance' has been attended by the evolution of growth coalitions in many big cities. London is no exception. Gerry Stoker has observed that local politicians have to act to

> facilitate the expression of voice in diverse communities and reconcile differences, develop shared visions and build partnerships to ensure their achievement. Leadership in these new circumstances is not about seizing control of the state machine; it is about building coalitions, developing networks, accountability and steering in a complex environment. Leaders are there to deliver a sense of direction or vision to communities, to support people as they struggle to find their own solutions and to bring the parts together in order to create the capacity to make things happen.[879]

---

878 Paul Kantor, Christian Lefèvre, Asato Saito, H. V. Savitch and Andy Thornley, *Struggling Giants: City-region Governance in London, New York, Paris and Tokyo*, Globalisation and Community, Volume 20, Minneapolis: University of Minnesota Press, 2012, page 48

879 Gerry Stoker, *Transforming Local Governance: from Thatcherism to New Labour*, Basingstoke: Palgrave Macmillan, 2004, page 139

This analysis is highly relevant to the case of London borough leaderships (as well as metropolitan government in London and other British city-regions) in the period from 1965 to 2015. In a system of governance as fragmented as London's this move to 'steering' government implies consequences for both government and economic development. Boroughs are part of the metropolitan growth coalition but also have their own, local, ones.

Borough leaders and mayors are now in the position of 'facilitating' the delivery of a part of 'global city' governance arrangement. Global cities have become an important reference point for contemporary academic understanding of cities and their development. Since the publication of Saskia Sassen's book *The Global City* in 1991, awareness of the importance and competitiveness of cities such as London, New York, Paris and Tokyo has grown significantly.[880] These cities are defined as being those with such attributes as international stock and trading exchanges, large numbers of company headquarters, political power, mass transit networks, hub airports and substantial cultural and media industries. Borough councils now find themselves as facilitators of government to parts of London as a global city.

Aspects of land-use planning and territorial resource distribution in large metropolitan jurisdictions have been analysed by legal scholars. The importance of planning and zoning policies has been considered widely, with growing acceptance that in rich and developed cities like London the impact of land-use rules is now a highly political and contested sphere of government.[881] London, unlike many American cities, has equalisation arrangements put in place by national government which to a significant extent avoid the 'hollowing out' and equity issues identified in the US literature about metropolitan government.[882]

But London, whose governmental arrangements have developed in a piecemeal way over many centuries, is probably in need of further theoretical

---

880 Saskia Sassen, *The Global City: New York, London, Tokyo*, Princeton: Princeton University Press, 1991

881 See, for example, Mariana Valverde, 'Seeing Like a State: The Dialectic of Modern and Premodern Ways of Seeing in Urban Governance', *Law & Society Review*, Vol. 45, No. 2, 2011

882 See, for example, Gerald Frug, *City Making: Building Communities without Building Walls*, Princeton: Princeton University Press, 2001

consideration. The 'bottom-heavy, two-tier system' described in this book is highly unusual. Comparisons and theoretical frameworks which are revealing about, say, cities in the United States or continental Europe may have limited application in the UK. There is scope for more detailed understanding of the ways in which the operation of London government provides evidence of the applicability or otherwise of new models of city government. This need will increase with the evolution of new city-regional governance models in England, Wales and Scotland.

CHAPTER 6

COUNTERFACTUALS

O ne way of exploring a number of the key impacts of the post-1965 system of government is to consider some variations that might have occurred if different choices had been made. Government systems have effects on land-use planning, the use of resources, and public services. To consider a number of these effects, this chapter briefly examines a number of 'counterfactuals' or 'what ifs'. Some of the conclusions may be contested, but they provide a starting point for debate.

IF DIFFERENT GOVERNMENT SYSTEMS FROM THE 1965 ONES HAD BEEN INTRODUCED

No reform in 1965

It had taken several decades to get to the point at which Henry Brooke, the Housing & Local Government Minister, announced the creation of the Herbert Commission. Had he not done so, it is unlikely Harold Wilson's 1964–70 government would have carried on with the reorganisation, as there appeared little political advantage to Labour. The moment might have been permanently lost. It was also possible, just, that Herbert would have decided that collaboration between existing authorities would have been sufficient to deal with the London government problem. If there had been no reform, or minimal change, in 1965, London government today would resemble the Paris arrangements. There would be a powerful 'city' authority for the inner London area, with a modest second tier. In the wider metropolitan area, there would be a large number of district and county authorities. Overall, there might be a weak regional entity. Intriguingly, the evolving 'Grand Paris' reform[883] has sought to move towards a system closer to London's arrangements.

GLC not abolished

The abolition of the GLC in 1986 was a remarkable act, given the council had been created only twenty-one years previously, and that its creation was the endpoint of decades of debate about the need for a unit of government for the wider metropolitan area. Even by Britain's standards, this period is a short life for an institution of government. The metropolitan counties, swept away at the same time, were just twelve years old. If Ken Livingstone had not become GLC leader and/or if Margaret Thatcher had not become Prime Minister, it is possible the GLC would still exist today. The council's demise was largely the consequence of Livingstone and Thatcher's cantankerous relationship.

If, like the boroughs, the GLC had lived on to its fiftieth anniversary, there would have been no Mayor of London and, perhaps, no directly elected mayors anywhere in the UK. County Hall would still be the home of London government, rather than a leisure complex. Boris Johnson would probably not have become leader of the GLC, though Ken Livingstone would have done.

From the boroughs' point of view, dealing with the GLC was a more complex and bureaucratic business than the current relationship with the mayor: the GLC had many more staff and could be slow in dealing with borough issues. The GLC had a staff (excluding the fire brigade) of 15,000 in its final year,[884] whereas the GLA has fewer than 1,000 staff. The minister responsible for the creation of the GLA, Nick Raynsford, made it clear in the government's consultation document that the new institution was to be small and efficient.[885] A single-person executive at City Hall makes relationships with

---

883 Sénat de France, 'Une comparaison des statuts de Paris, Berlin et Londres qui illustre les faiblesses de la capital Française', *Le Grand Paris: un vrai project pour un enjeu capital*, http://www.senat.fr/rap/r07-262/r07-26244.html (accessed 17 August 2015)

884 Greater London Council, *Budget 1985–86*, London: GLC, page 242

885 House of Commons Library, *The Greater London Authority (Referendum) Bill, Bill 61 of 1997–98*, Research Paper No 97/114, 6 November 1997, page 24

borough leaders relatively straightforward, albeit much of the day-to-day link-age is in the hands of London Councils and City Hall officers. Had the GLC lived on in its 1986 form, the boroughs would today be spending more time dealing with its planning and architects' departments, which were large and slow-moving, than they do with the GLA.

A single council for London – no London boroughs

It is fascinating to consider how different London would now be if the Herbert Commission and the Macmillan government had concluded that there should be a single metropolitan authority for the city. However, such a conclusion was unlikely, given the history summarised in Chapter 1 of this book. London gov-ernment developed piecemeal, while metropolitan institutions were from time to time overlaid on the wider built-up area of the city. Yet this bottom-heavy arrangement is unusual in similar cities in other countries. New York City is, to all intents and purposes, a single unit of government: its five boroughs have little executive power. Paris has twenty arrondissements, but the mayor and the city council are the substantive government institution. Berlin has twelve boroughs, but they are subordinate to the city senate.

So, what might have happened if the 1965 reform had created a single unit of government for Greater London? First, the GLC's suggested system of motorways would have progressed further. The Ringways proposed by the government and the new GLC were opposed by most boroughs. If there had been a single, city-wide government, it is almost inevitable that a larger proportion of these urban motorways would have been completed. Westway-style elevated roads would have swept into, and perhaps through, the West End. The Hammersmith Flyover and the Euston Underpass give a hint of the kind of 'death by infrastructure' roads London would have seen criss-crossing many neighbourhoods.

Second, there would have been more of the larger social housing estates favoured by the GLC. Big governments favour big projects, and, at the time the GLC was created, major slum-clearance initiatives were feeding large,

Whitehall-subsidised house-building programmes. Thamesmead is the most ambitious of the GLC developments, and it seems likely that, if there had been no boroughs, there would have been fewer, bigger, housing estates.

Third, Piccadilly Circus and Covent Garden would have been comprehensively redeveloped, and not in a good way. Westminster and Camden were powerful opponents of the grandiose plans put forward by the GLC, though it was the LCC which had started the Piccadilly Circus process.[886] The GLC would surely have got its own way if the boroughs had not been there to stop it. It seems likely that other major redevelopments would have been driven through by such a powerful single tier of city government. Indeed, this version of the GLC would have found it relatively easy to ride roughshod over neighbourhood and local opposition.

Fourth, a single tier of Greater London government would have been more central London-centric than the system put in place. By having thirty-three separately elected councils, as well as the GLC, boroughs were able to lobby for development in their centres. City leaders judge themselves by the prosperity and appearance of their 'downtown' area, so central London would have been important to the way the GLC might have viewed its successes and failures.

Fifth, borough boundaries would not have existed. As Michael Hebbert has observed, the post-1965 boroughs generally saw themselves as governmental islands and, for sensible electoral reasons, tended to develop the central parts of their areas. Boundaries at such places as the South Bank, Park Royal, Crystal Palace, Shoreditch and King's Cross had a significant impact on the propensity to develop them.[887] A single tier of government would have had no reason to take notice of such lines on maps.

Sixth, without the boroughs, the single pan-London authority would almost certainly have accepted the need for neighbourhoods and local communities to flourish as representative of areas Londoners identified with. London could

---

886 Simon Jenkins, *Landlords to London: The Story of a Capital and its Growth*, London: Faber & Faber, 1975, pages 256–60

887 Michael Hebbert, 'The Borough Effect in London's Geography', in *London: A New Metropolitan Geography*, London: Edward Arnold, 1991, page 206

have continued to be connected with its historical origins as a fragmented set of parishes and urban villages.

Seventh, if it had been decided to have only one tier of government, the ancient City of London would possibly have been absorbed into the new authority, although history suggests that somehow the City would have escaped this fate.

Eighth, a single tier of London government would have been able to develop and sustain a consistent policy about tall buildings. It is likely a Greater London government would have had two or three clusters of mega-structures, with one in the City and perhaps one at somewhere such as Tottenham Court Road, Victoria or Paddington. As it is, the thirty-two boroughs and the City have made their own decisions, and the result is predictably to scatter skyscrapers.

Finally, London super-government would have lurched more dramatically from policy to policy than the two-tier system. The boroughs have acted as a counter-balance on the GLC and GLA. Boroughs helped stop the destructive Ringways and the modernist redevelopment of Covent Garden. They helped kill off Ken Livingstone's proposed west London tram, and, day by day, have acted as the local voice in city-wide development.

Fifty-one boroughs

The Herbert Commission recommended fifty-one boroughs, including some places that ended up outside Greater London. Had there been a substantively larger number of London councils, some of the fragmentation issues explored above would have been exaggerated. The skyline would have been subject to even more scattered development. Local groups would have been more likely to find support in opposing metropolitan-scale projects, which might have slowed down the progress of GLC and GLA developments. There would have been more miles of boundary where development would have been limited. It is hard to imagine that calls for fewer boroughs would not by now have been heeded, and that there would not, therefore, have been a further reorganisation since 1965. It is possible a structural change of this kind would have sharply reduced the number of boroughs.

Five boroughs

Although no one was proposing as few as five boroughs in 1962–65, it is possible that, had there been a subsequent reform, it might well have led to five authorities. New York has five boroughs, a point regularly quoted in discussions about London. Ken Livingstone proposed a five 'pizza slices' option, though others wanted a powerful 'central' borough. A mega-borough for the city centre with a population of perhaps 2 million would have been more visible and powerful than the GLC and GLA. It is probably for this reason that Livingstone believed that wedges, each running from the centre to the periphery, would be a better option. But five boroughs, each of which would have had a population today of 1.5–2 million, would have been far from able to represent neighbourhood political needs. A five-borough model would have strengthened demands for a third tier of parish or community governance.

A central London borough

One of the proposals put forward during the passage of the London Government Act 1963 was for the creation of a single council for central London, including the City. Westminster, Camden and the City would have been substantially different places – indeed, there might have been another new borough for the northern parts of Westminster and Camden, embracing places such as Queen's Park, Maida Vale, Hampstead and Kentish Town. A single central borough would have meant Covent Garden and Fitzrovia were not cut in two by a borough boundary. Other natural communities might then have been bisected. The absorption of the City would have been the most radical element in such an authority. It is possible the borough of 'The City, Westminster, St Pancras & Holborn' would have maintained the City of London's ceremonial and philanthropic activities. But with a non-residential workforce of almost 1.25 million, the balance of power between residents and non-residents would have been a challenge.

If the central London authority had favoured tall buildings, central London might have developed one or two large clusters. If such an authority had opposed skyscrapers, it is likely central London would have been ringed by them, creating a new London Wall.

Greater South East regional authority created

A number of the planning experts who lobbied for a Greater London authority also wished to see a wider government for much or all of the south-east. Peter Hall, doyen of late twentieth-century town planners, predicted the issue would have to be revisited when he first published his book *London 2000*. Urban geographers and planners have generally seen London as an area of economic and social activity that extends far beyond the continuous built-up area of the city. It would have been possible that either a single 'Greater Greater London' council might have been created in 1965 or that, at some point, a modest 'Greater South East' region could have been superimposed on the GLC, the boroughs and surrounding areas. SERPLAN (the London and South East Regional Planning Conference) existed until regional development agencies were set up in the early years of Tony Blair's government. It provided planning advice for authorities in London and the south-east. During the life of the development agencies, there was a limited amount of joint working between London, the east and the south-east through an Inter Regional Planning Forum, though it lapsed when the RDAs were abolished in 2010.[888]

IF DIFFERENT POLICIES HAD BEEN PURSUED IN KEY SPHERES

No utopian housing estates

It was an accident of history that the 1965 reform coincided with a fashion for utopian social housing projects and radical changes in society. If the boroughs (though not all of them) and the GLC had not constructed system-built concrete towers and blocks, hundreds of thousands of people would have been spared the baleful conditions that followed during the 1970s, 1980s and

---

888 Duncan Bowie, 'The Challenges of London's growth: Strategic planning and the failures of governance in the Greater South East', University of Westminster, Paper prepared for Politics and Policy Conference, Bristol, 16 September 2014, http://www.westminster. ac.uk/__data/assets/pdf_file/0004/335398/Policy-and-Politics-2014.-FINAL-1.pdf (accessed 13 July 2015)

1990s. Nor would billions have had to be spent demolishing and replacing them. On the other hand, fewer people would have been re-housed from the appalling slums of the 1960s. What is now recognised is that the repair and refurbishment of 'slum' terraces would have been a better, cheaper and more humane option than tearing so many of them down.

The Ringways road system was completed

If the Ministry of Transport and the GLC had had their way, London today would have many more motorway-scale roads running right through to and across the city centre. The M1 would have been extended through Hampstead, Camden and on to Hyde Park Corner. Part of the LCC's proposed Motorway Box road system would have run east–west across Fitzrovia, roughly where Mortimer and Goodge Streets run. The GLC supported Ringways, including a North Cross Route that would have run through Harlesden, Kilburn, West Hampstead, Hampstead, Camden Town, Barnsbury and Islington, with a cut-and-cover tunnel through Belsize Park. There were equivalent routes to the south, west and east, which, with the north one, would have constituted Ringway 1. Ringways 2, 3 and 4 were further out from the centre.[889]

If most or all of the motorways proposed had been built, London today would have been a very different place. There would have been dozens of neighbourhoods cut in half, in the way North Kensington was. Central Hammersmith and Brentford, with the M4 carved through them, would have been representative of many parts of the city. There would have been 'spaghetti junction' interchanges in several parts of both inner and outer London. Pollution and congestion would have been worse or, alternatively, radical anti-pollution measures might have been triggered. What (largely) saved the city from this assault was the cost of delivering them coupled with growing opposition from boroughs and community groups.

---

889 For a helpful description see cbrd.co.uk, http://www.cbrd.co.uk/articles/ringways/
     background/postwar.shtml (accessed 18 July 2015)

No London Docklands
Development Corporation

The closure of the London Docks was one of the most dramatic industrial changes to affect London during the 1960s and 1970s. The GLC and the boroughs attempted to start the process of economic regeneration of the abandoned docks, though with few resources to do so. Mrs Thatcher's government decided to impose the London Docklands Development Corporation, with planning powers and Treasury money, to push through a liberal development regime on the area, albeit with massive State intervention. The Docklands Light Railway was built, Canary Wharf emerged and the Jubilee line was extended to the area. Today, the Isle of Dogs and the Royal Docks are a new city within London.

If the LDDC had not been created, the GLC and the boroughs would doubtless have continued their efforts to sustain manufacturing, build additional social housing and attract new employment suitable for ex-dockers. Assuming the rest of the London economy had prospered, it seems likely that Docklands would have become a large area of warehousing, light industry and other support functions for central London. Private housing and office developers would eventually have found their way to riverside sites and would have continued the Docklands-style developments which were under way in the late 1970s near the St Katharine Dock downstream of Tower Bridge. But there would be no Toronto-on-Thames cluster of towers at Canary Wharf. Most of the docks would either have been filled in or used for recreation. London City airport would have grown bigger because there would be no skyscrapers to avoid. Such a development might have made it more likely an estuary airport would have been built. With no Jubilee line at Stratford and no Docklands Light Railway, it is hard to see London holding the Olympic Games at Stratford. Wembley might have been the site for a lower-cost 2012 Olympics. Stratford railway lands would still be railway lands. There would be no E20 post code except in BBC's *EastEnders*.

IF DIFFERENT SOCIAL AND DEMOGRAPHIC CHANGE HAD OCCURRED

Population fell to below 6 million

At the time the boroughs and GLC were formed in 1965 the capital's population was dropping fast. Within twenty years it had reached 6.6 million. The GLC's demographers believed it was possible the fall would continue until the population fell below 6 million; if so, it might have levelled off somewhere between 6 and 5 million. London in the mid-2010s might have been a city not of 8.6 million but of 5.5 million.

A borough such as Barnet or Croydon would not have a population of 350,000, but closer to 200,000. Islington and Kensington & Chelsea might have only 100,000 to 125,000 residents. There would have been no need for the Jubilee line extension, no Crossrail, no Overground and little developer-driven regeneration. Tube and rail frequencies would have been cut and some lines would have closed. The Aldwych spur of the Piccadilly line and the Epping-to-Ongar section of the Central line were shut in 1994, even after the capital's resurgence had begun. It is possible the ends of a number of Tube lines (such as the Hainault loop) would have closed because of falling demand.

By the 2000s, there would perhaps have been a housing surplus with static house prices. More likely, the remaining homeowners would have bought far larger houses and consequently ensured that, as always in London, there was a housing shortage. It is also conceivable that large parts of ex-industrial London would have been turned over to open space. Areas such as King's Cross railway lands, Battersea and Docklands would have been left to greenery and wildlife. There would be no rush to build new residential skyscrapers, no pressure to build in the green belt and no concern about rich overseas buyers taking over the city. Milton Keynes would have been less prosperous, as might much of the inner south-east of England. Unemployment would have been higher and immigration far lower. Two-runway Heathrow would be sufficient for the country's airport needs. Overall, London would have been seen as having fulfilled the expectation of decline quoted on the opening pages of this book.

CHAPTER 7

CONCLUDING
OBSERVATIONS

Although it is half a century since the London boroughs came into existence, the sequence of events that led to their creation can be traced back over 1,000 years, and possibly 2,000. The earliest stage was the Romans' decision to create a settlement at a particular point on the Thames, and Anglo-Saxon re-settlement there. Institutions put in place by the Anglo-Saxons formed the basis for the City of London's contemporary government. Westminster developed separately within the oversight of the Royal Palace and the Abbey. As development spread outside the City, new, parish-based local government evolved. By the time this sprawl had grown into a continuous urban area of several million, Parliament acted to impose a metropolitan joint board to build infrastructure such as sewers and roads. By the end of the nineteenth century, London had a directly elected council and boroughs. As the continuous built-up area crept out to claim over 600 square miles of countryside, arguments grew for reform. In 1965, this wider area became the administrative area of London with an elected council and bigger boroughs. These latter institutions are considered in the pages of this book.

It is not easy to sum up thirty-two (thirty-three with the City) places as diverse as the London boroughs. This diversity has critical implications for the governing arrangements of the boroughs. They need structures that allow a variety of interests to be represented within relatively large municipalities. Strategic direction and executive leadership are generally provided in a collective collegial group accountable to these councils. But there is now some variety of executive arrangements, with twenty-eight (twenty-nine with the City) relatively 'traditional' government structures and four directly elected mayors. The city now has both multi-person and single-person (i.e. mayoral) government at the local level. The impact of these different systems is beyond the scope of this book, but worthy of research.

Writing in the mid-1970s, long-time London commentator Simon Jenkins concluded:

> [O]f all the institutions set up in the capital in 1964 the most successful
> have been ... the new London boroughs. While GLC and Whitehall
> bureaucrats bickered and battled their way from one strategic stale-
> mate to another, the boroughs were quietly making the best of their
> new powers ... the rapidity with which they established an identity of
> their own was remarkable ... Local government in London is borough
> government.[890]

In 1991, halfway from the mid-1960s to today, Michael Hebbert, an academic observer of boroughs, concluded:

> The borough effect is a straightforward expression of political geography.
> The units created by the reconstruction of 1965 had a new territoriality,
> distinct from their predecessors and competitive with their neighbours.
> Each arbitrary tract of built-up London defined in the reorganisation
> process became for borough leaders and their officers a 'field of vision,
> expectation and action'. Original marriages of administrative conveni-
> ence became ... real entities worth campaigning for, with boundaries
> that showed on council wall-maps like an island shoreline.[891]

Jenkins and Hebbert were correct. The post-1965 London boroughs, despite occasional policy and administrative failures, have got on with the business

---

890 Simon Jenkins, *Landlords to London: The Story of a Capital and its Growth*, London: Faber
& Faber, 1975, pages 234–235

891 Michael Hebbert, 'The Borough Effect in London's Geography' in *London: A New
Metropolitan Geography*, (eds) Keith Hoggart and David R. Green, London: Edward Arnold,
1991, page 199

of government. Simon James, quoted earlier in this book, noted 'competence rather than brilliance is quite sufficient' to deliver local government. Most of the London boroughs have developed into being better than just competent, particularly as they have faced a rapid increase in population at a time of substantial spending reductions. By 2015, London councils collectively were among the best in the country. Ironically, the pragmatism that dominates town halls in the mid-2010s is partly a reaction to the ideological turmoil of the boroughs' middle years.

The boroughs operate to some extent as 'islands' with the inevitable consequence that their boundaries are often places where either less desirable facilities are located or where it has proven hard to deliver coherent policy. One of the reasons the contemporary development of the south bank of the Thames resembles a gold rush is that this area, certainly from the Greenwich/Lewisham border to Wandsworth, represents the northern fringe of a succession of boroughs whose centre of democratic gravity is 2 or 3 miles away to the south. The riverside had traditionally been used as wharves or for light industrial purposes. The Festival of Britain was held there in 1951 because land was readily available, and the same was true for the National Theatre. However, apart from some office building in the 1960s, parts of this snake of land had become derelict by the 1970s. It was fiercely defended by local communities and remained underdeveloped, even though it was a short walk from the City and West End.

The LDDC started a process of regeneration at places such as Hay's Galleria and Butler's Wharf. Southwark planners, under Fred Manson, recognised the potential of Bankside, and pushed ahead with private investment within the council's plans for the area.[892] Tate Modern and Shakespeare's Globe moved in. Most dramatically, Britain's tallest building, the Shard, was constructed. With fast population growth, tightening housing demand and the boroughs' need for cash, super-charged development has taken root right along the south bank of the Thames. The inner-London stretch of the river will soon be lined

---

892 Nick Buck, Ian Gordon, Peter Hall, Michael Harloe and Mark Kleinman, *Working Capital: Life and Labour in Contemporary London*, London: Routledge, 2002, page 64

with skyscrapers, an accidental monument to London's economic history, but also to its structure of government.

Most of the tall buildings constructed in London since 2000 are for residential use. In 2014, New London Architecture (NLA) estimated that as many as 230 towers were planned for London. Architectural critic Rowan Moore argued that '"density" has been translated into height', and initiated a campaign to determine where height would be right and where it would not.[893] Peter Murray of NLA proposed a London Skyline Commission. The challenge the skyline protectors faced was that thirty-three councils independently make key decisions about planning, and therefore proposals for a single point of decision-making would inevitably take power and, more importantly, resources from the boroughs. In theory, the Mayor or the secretary of state could decide the location of towers, though this would lead to endless conflict with town halls. Moreover, as Rowan Moore recognised, two of the more controversial recent decisions giving the go-ahead to towers, a residential tower at Vauxhall and the 'Walkie Talkie' office building in the City, had actually been made by the secretary of state.[894] Peter Rees, former City of London chief planner, memorably observed: 'The greatest thing about London is that it's unplannable. The worst thing about it is that it's unplanned.'[895]

Given the failure of system-built high-rise social housing, the sudden appearance of a new wave of apartments in towers is a remarkable return to popularity for what was until recently a despised housing form. The boroughs, after their experience in the 1960s and 1970s, no longer see tower blocks as a desirable option for lower-income households. Thus, a remarkable change of fortune has occurred: high-income owner-occupiers (or those who rent from them) live in the new towers, while the lucky few who are allocated social and 'affordable' housing by councils tend to live in lower-rise flats or houses. In some

---

893 Rowan Moore, 'London is being transformed with 230 towers. Why the lack of consultation?', *The Observer*, 29 March 2014

894 Ibid.

895 James Pickford, 'City's former planning chief on why London is "unplannable"', *Financial Times*, 14 November 2014

areas, notably the Isle of Dogs (Tower Hamlets), large and tall private blocks are being constructed with residential densities at Hong Kong or Manhattan levels. These massive developments help pay for social and 'affordable' homes.

Housing policy more generally has seen remarkable change over fifty years, and a number of books have considered the issue. Many boroughs started their lives replacing slums with modern homes and then had to replace some of the newly built housing itself. Council house-building then virtually stopped, and housing associations became the providers of nearly all new social homes. The associations had a laudable role in regenerating a number of the less successful estates developed in the 1960s and 1970s. By the late 1990s, many boroughs were giving permission to build private housing developments, which included payments in support of social and 'affordable' housing. Private renting declined for many years after 1965, before picking up rapidly in around 2000.[896] By 2015, there were concerns about a number of housing issues, including a fall in owner occupation, a growing gap between population growth and house-building, and affordability. The purchase of new homes by overseas buyers received much press coverage, as did the prices paid at the top of the market.[897] Opinion polls showed that housing had become the most pressing policy issue for Londoners, overtaking transport.

Another longer-term policy change affecting housing policy was the Thatcher government's 'right to buy' initiative. In 2013, the Smith Institute estimated some 290,000 homes have been sold under the right-to-buy policy since 1980.[898] The policy was popular and many people were able to become owner-occupiers, who otherwise would not have done so. But there has been a consequence for the boroughs, as the city's population has risen. Karen Buck,

---

896 Kath Scanlon, Melissa Fernandez and Christine Whitehead, *A Lifestyle Choice for Families? Private Renting in London*, New York, Berlin and The Randstad, London: Get Living London, 2014, Figure 1, page 11

897 For differing views of the impact of overseas buyers, comparing those of former City planner Peter Rees with research published by Christine Whitehead, see James Pickford, 'City's former planning chief on why London is "unplannable", *Financial Times*, 14 November 2014

898 London Assembly, Housing and Regeneration Committee, Transcript of Item 6, 13 March 2013, Greater London Authority, 2013

MP for Westminster North, observed: 'People who can afford the private rents are not the same people who could afford social housing rents.' The combined effect of the right to-buy policy, London's rising population, and a shortfall of housing availability has seen councils paying rentals in former council homes to house those who are statutorily homeless.[899]

The boroughs have been leading players on the housing scene, but in roles that have changed over time. The conditions of London housing have improved beyond all recognition since 1965, when, in many parts of the capital, there were still thousands of homes without basic facilities such as bathrooms. From being the overseers of major building programmes and the purchasers of derelict street properties, borough councils have become experts in sales, regeneration and renewal. With London's population increase, boroughs became the primary movers in ensuring the planning system worked quickly to deliver more housing. Some are now moving into private development.

Changes to successive governments' housing policies and the complexities of subsidy arrangements have rendered the boroughs' role in delivering social and affordable housing a perpetual emergency rationing process. The vagaries of national policy initiatives have often had different effects in London from those experienced elsewhere. Some, such as the 2010–15 government's benefit reforms, were intended to do so. But, at any point, the boroughs (and the GLC/GLA) have found themselves first coping with national policy and then managing local housing. The result is visible throughout contemporary London.

The boroughs and the City really are thirty-three different places. The political and economic history of any one authority will not help much with an understanding of its neighbour, still less a borough 12 to 15 miles away. Conservatives vary significantly from borough to borough, as do councillors of other parties. Some boroughs, notably Tower Hamlets, Hackney, Newham and Hillingdon, have seen economic change on a spectacular scale over the past fifty years. Others, including Havering, Sutton and Bromley, have developed, but more gently. Westminster, uniquely, has seen a parish council re-emerge at Queen's Park. Inner London

---

899 Pete Apps, 'Right to Buy to Let', *Inside Housing*, 14 August 2015

has moved from being a place of conspicuous 'inner city' decline to being a glittering global entrepot. Outer London, by contrast, has fared relatively less well. Some of the decline previously seen only in the older, inner boroughs found its way to outer ones. The challenges facing the outer boroughs led Boris Johnson to create an Outer London Commission to explore policy options.

London in 2015 is more affluent and, in many ways, more settled than in 1965. Although the make-up of its population has changed enormously, London has gone from struggling with the 'orderly management of decline' to a need to accommodate population growth of over 100,000 per year. Throughout the whole of this period, the thirty-two boroughs and the City of London have swept the streets, emptied the bins, planned development and housed the homeless. There have been good times and bad, but after fifty years it is possible to look back and analyse what has been learned.

First, it is remarkable the boroughs have survived fifty years. Given the propensity of British governments to meddle and reorganise, the boroughs' relatively long life is a cause for surprise and delight. The GLC survived only twenty-one years and the ILEA just twenty-five. Many authorities outside London have been reorganised in the period since 1965. As elements in the city's local government, only the City of London, the Metropolitan Police and the London Fire Brigade are all older. The implication of the boroughs' relative longevity is perhaps that the boroughs were broadly the correct size to be both 'local' and yet powerful.

Second, the period of ideological war-of-all-against-all is not good for the boroughs, residents or businesses of the city. The years from about 1975 until 1990 were bad for London, even if the reactions to them have been moderation and pragmatism since the end of the struggles of the 1980s. The differences between Mrs Thatcher's government and the new left in London can be explained by changes to the city's industrial base and its population. But the results, at least in some boroughs, were not good for tenants, council staff or for the reputation of London government. Today's borough politicians operate against a background of knowing how much damage can be inflicted by the kind of strife witnessed in the 1980s. Pragmatism has succeeded ideology.

Third, London government has proved effective at recovering from a number of serious problems. Since 1965, the city has seen twenty years of population and relative economic decline followed by a remarkable resurgence. The first half of the boroughs' life was characterised by shrinkage in the city's population and its economic power. Most of the boroughs managed to continue to deliver effective services in this period and helped create the circumstances where people eventually wanted to move there in large numbers, often from overseas. Even the boroughs that suffered a period of weak government have shown how local politics can re-establish good government and then flourish. Since 2010, councils have had to manage rapidly declining resources. There has been no 'crisis' in London government (or outside the capital) of the kind witnessed in other, ring-fenced services such as the NHS. Over many centuries, London has shown itself capable of recovering from periods of decline to re-assert its economic strength. The post-1965 boroughs have, since 1985, presided over such a recovery.

Fourth, London's history suggests large developments and redevelopments are probably better left to private developers, albeit within firmly imposed rules and plans determined by the boroughs and the GLA. In the years immediately after 1965, the boroughs and the GLC undertook a number of large, comprehensive redevelopment schemes. Many of these projects did not turn out well. Indeed, it has taken years of regeneration and reinvestment to replace a number of failed 1960s and 1970s developments. This is not to say that London boroughs and the GLA should not plan for the redevelopment and improvement of tracts of the city. Rather, it appears that major development companies are more likely to have the skills and persistence to drive complex and often controversial schemes to successful completion.

Fifth, and not discussed hitherto, London's government needs greater fiscal autonomy. It is now widely accepted that England has one of the most centralised systems of taxation and public finance in the developed world. If the London boroughs and GLA are to prosper to their full potential, they need to have greater powers to determine both spending and taxation. The London Finance Commission outlined proposals for such a reform in 2013. These proposals have had the support of the boroughs and the Mayor, and at the Conservative Party conference in October 2015, the Chancellor announced significant devolution of business rates.

Sixth, the 'bottom-heavy two-tier system' of government is probably a good one to run a large city. For fifty years, the London boroughs have delivered municipal services. They have represented the most local level of government for a city of many millions of people. The Herbert Commission and the government judged the size of the boroughs correctly. Any smaller and they would have been under-powered; any larger and they might have been remote. Collectively, the boroughs spend twice as much as the GLA. For most people, 'the council' is the agency they expect to act when a solution is required to a local problem. This assessment is not denying a need for metropolitan government. London needs a city-wide, democratically elected transport, police, fire and planning authority.

Moreover, a two-tier system is now the established norm for London. Apart from the period from 1986 to 2000, there has been such an arrangement continuously since 1855. The geographical scale of London is such that a single government would inevitably be seen as too big and too distant. The much-defended 'borough' level, on the other hand, is too small to deliver many of the infrastructure-based services a great city requires. The London model would work well in many emerging global mega-cities.

The City of London can be seen as the origin of both borough and city-wide government. For many years, it was effectively both. Today, along with the monarchy, it represents part of the long-evolved, unique, institutional machinery of Britain. The City and the boroughs have developed together over fifty years into an essential part of London's patchwork of local government.

Does this system need further reform? Some voices in recent years have suggested there are too many boroughs, that the Mayor should be given greater powers over the boroughs, or that the boroughs should be fragmented into urban parishes. The issue of whether or not there are too many or too few boroughs needs to be seen against the backdrop of both the costs and benefits of potential reforms. Structural reorganisations of local government can rarely be proved to save money. The boroughs are already large institutions by the standards of municipalities in other countries. Is there any overwhelming case for fewer boroughs? The answer is 'no'. But that is not to say that, as spending constraints continue, there will not be a need for more joint working and combined administration.

On the other hand the balance of power between the boroughs and the Mayor may need to be changed. As London grows to become a city of 9 and then 10 million people, it will, from time to time, be necessary for the GLA to drive through developments boroughs do not want. The needs of London as a whole may have to be imposed on a particular area. But, in doing so, the Mayor will need to take great care: if the boroughs are unnecessarily aggravated, they will begin to agitate for reform – the lesson of the GLC's relationship with the boroughs. What happens in Greater Manchester and other major cities where council leaders and mayors work together in a form of joint leadership may yet influence developments in London.

For the time being, relationships between the boroughs, the City and the Mayor are broadly harmonious. The partnership of the Mayor and the boroughs will be important in meeting both the pressure on budgets and the infrastructure needs of London in the coming years. Devolution of powers and greater fiscal autonomy will require an agreement about a public service settlement which is convincing to central government. Greater Manchester has latterly prospered by successful joint working. London can do as well or better, proving, in a way that would have been thought impossible in the nineteenth century, that national, metropolitan and local interests can be successfully aligned.

As London grows, its government can capture the benefits of development to improve the lives of its people. For fifty years, the London boroughs have affected the lives of all the people of London. They continue to do so today. As we look ahead, it is likely the boroughs will continue to provide the fragmented, flexible, competitive, collaborative system of government they have done since 1965. Fifty years is a long time; though, in London's case, it isn't really so long. London will never be the good city of utopian hope. Rather, it will be a fortuitously successful city made up of its many constituent forces, most particularly the boroughs.

Writing in 1931, Hugh Green, town clerk of Finsbury, concluded an article about London government in the following way:

> [T]o all Londoners, whether by birth or adoption, and to all engaged in the government of London, I would say: guard you well your heritage and your charge. For what Londoner can look upon London and not love it? London! The mightiest and greatest city in the world, with its teeming millions, its immensity, its beauty! How we feel the throb of its life, the pulse-beats of its heart! How we delight in its pleasure and its gaieties, its river, its bridges, its buildings, its boulevards and parks! How we puzzle over its problems – its poverty, its slums, its sorrows! To preserve and foster its loveliness and influence; to redeem its faults, and ennoble its reputation amongst the peoples of the world; these are our tasks, we Londoners who work for London! Let us see to it that our task, so far as in us lies, fails not of accomplishment.[900]

So little changes, and yet so much appears to.

---

900 Hugh Green, 'How London is Governed', *Public Administration*, Vol. 9, No. 1, page 48

APPENDIX 1

BOROUGH POPULATION DATA

During 2015, London's population passed its previous highest total, which had been reached in 1939. In the period when final preparations for the 1965 reform were taking place, the city's population was about 600,000 below the pre-war peak. Between the early 1960s and the mid-1980s, it was to drop by a further 1,400,000 to a figure 2 million below the 1939 figure. GLC demographers believed the fall might continue until London's population was below 6 million. In the event, there was a turn-around in the mid-1980s and it is now almost certain the figure will exceed 9 million by 2020, then possibly rising to over 10 million during the 2030s.

Population projections are based on recent trends and population structures. As observed earlier in this book, the 1980s' levelling-off and increase were not predicted. It is likely that current projections for the 2020s and 2030s will not be correct, particularly at the individual borough level. But they give a guide to which boroughs are likely to grow fastest and to possibly what scale.

The table shows the 'highest ever' population for each borough, at the time of each population census, back to 1801. A number of inner boroughs (or, to be precise, their predecessor authorities jointly) reached their all-time high in 1901. Southwark, Tower Hamlets and Westminster had over half a million residents each, with almost 600,000 in Southwark and Tower Hamlets. Islington and Lambeth (in 1931) exceeded 400,000. A number of others, often in outer London, reached their all-time highest population in the 2011 census (and subsequently, each year).

	Highest since 1801	1961	Lowest since 1961	2016	2041
City of London	128,000 (1851)	4767	4246 (1971)	8,264	11,258
Camden	377,000 (1901)	294,440	161,098 (1981)	236,167	273,356
Greenwich	254,557 (2011)	229,810	207,650 (1991)	274,334	332,246
Hackney	389,000 (1901)	257,552	179,529 (1981)	265,688	309,964
Hammersmith & Fulham	307,391 (1931)	222,124	202,204 (1991)	185,962	214,676
Islington	436,000 (1901)	262,232	157,552 (1981)	219,596	246,546
Kensington & Chelsea	250,000 (1901)	218,528	125,892 (1981)	159,991	178,741
Lambeth	421,000 (1931)	341,626	244,143 (1981)	323,377	373,906
Lewisham	326,844 (1931)	290,582	230,488 (1981)	295,719	348,136
Southwark	596,000 (1901)	313,413	209,735 (1981)	305,494	349,118
Tower Hamlets	597,000 (1901)	205,682	139,996 (1981)	282,815	338,620
Wandsworth	388,000 (1931)	335,451	252,240 (1981)	323,794	377,395
Westminster	524,000 (1871)	271,703	163,892 (1981)	235,648	280,582
Barking & Dagenham	189,430 (1951)	177,092	143,681 (1991)	202,379	249,967
Barnet	356,386 (2011)	318,373	290,197 (1981)	381,441	457,693
Bexley	231,997 (2011)	209,893	214,355 (1981)	241,830	282,405
Brent	311,215 (2011)	295,893	243,025 (1991)	329,463	387,021
Bromley	309,292 (2011)	294,440	290,609 (1991)	325,530	382,131
Croydon	363,378 (2011)	327,427	313,501 (1991)	383,357	449,895
Ealing	310,690 (1951)	301,646	275,257 (1991)	354,758	416,678

	Highest since 1801	1961	Lowest since 1961	2016	2041
Enfield	312,466 (2011)	273,857	257,154 (1981)	331,360	395,115
Haringey	307,391 (1931)	259,156	202,204 (1991)	270,523	309,043
Harrow	239,056 (2011)	209,080	196,159 (1981)	253,880	311,871
Havering	247,696 (1971)	245,598	224,262 (2001)	248,641	304,389
Hillingdon	273,936 (2011)	228,370	231,602 (1991)	294,971	345,435
Hounslow	253,957 (2011)	208,893	198,938 (1981)	272,402	323,643
Kingston	160,060 (2011)	146,010	131,326 (1981)	169,449	190,334
Merton	200,140 (1951)	189,013	165,102 (1981)	209,197	243,150
Newham	448,000 (1921)	265,388	209,128 (1981)	330,819	390,710
Redbridge	278,970 (2011)	250,080	224,731 (1981)	301,431	382,475
Richmond	188,100 (1951)	181,052	157,304 (1981)	198,131	233,169
Sutton	190,146 (2011)	169,095	167,547 (1981)	201,385	240,247
Waltham Forest	286,000 (1939)	248,591	212,033 (1991)	278,758	345,535
Central	1,155,000 (1881)	740,705	455,583 (1981)		
Inner	4,560,000 (1911)	3,161,207	2,228,324 (1981)		
Outer	5,195,555 (2011)	4,835,887	4,380,274 (1981)		
Greater London	8,615,000 (1939)	7,997,094	6,608,598 (1981)	8,696,558	10,276,352
Total of highest-ever for each borough	10,451,000				

Sources: 'Highest', '1961' and 'lowest': Table 1, Population count, Historical Census Tables, London Datastore, http://data.london.gov.uk/dataset/historical-census-tables/resource/123f15f8-12e5-47e1-bf58-6dd16ab859af;

'2016' and '2041': 'GLA 2014 round of trend-based population projections – Results', GLA Intelligence, London: GLA, June 2015, http://data.london.gov.uk/dataset/2014-round-population-projections/resource/e52be3ef-b5d5-468a-adcb-0a4d6f1055d4#

NON-BOROUGH LONDON GOVERNMENT INSTITUTIONS

In the period since the Herbert Commission was created in 1957, a number of other local government institutions have been part of local government in London. This book is about the thirty-two boroughs created in 1965, but it is important to understand their operation against the backdrop of these other bodies. The most important ones are considered below.

London County Council (LCC)

The LCC had been created in 1888, partly in response to allegations of corruption at the Metropolitan Board of Works and also to give London a county as part of the reorganisation of local government which took place at this time. It was a pioneer in delivering social housing, hospitals and other welfare provision. In 1904 it assumed responsibility for education when the London School Board's powers were passed to it. Originally contested by 'Moderates' (Conservatives) and 'Progressives' (Liberals), it was controlled by Labour from 1934 until its abolition in 1965. Its most famous leader was Herbert Morrison (1934–40), who became a member of Churchill's War Cabinet. The LCC was arguably the most powerful local government entity ever to have existed in London. But by 1939, most of the built-up area of 'Greater London' was outside the LCC's boundaries and reforms to extend 'London' were proposed.

Greater London counties outside the LCC

As Greater London developed in the fields around the LCC area, the districts and counties within this growing metropolitan sprawl assumed increased importance as they became part of London's government. Middlesex, to the north and west of the LCC became almost entirely urban, while the London edge of Essex, Hertfordshire, Buckinghamshire, Berkshire, Surrey and Kent were increasingly covered in houses. There was no planning control until the 1930s, so farmers could sell fields for development as the Underground and railway companies extended their networks outwards. Efforts were made to co-ordinate planning and roads across the expanding metropolis, but to little effect. By the time the Herbert Commission was set up in 1957, many more people lived in these counties than within the LCC. But, of course, the political centre of gravity for most of them was still in county towns focused on what remained predominantly rural communities.

Metropolitan boroughs and other pre-1965 districts

Within the LCC area, district council services were provided by twenty-eight metropolitan boroughs and the City of London. The boroughs had been created in 1899 by amalgamating the parishes and district boards which existed previously.

County boroughs and other district councils within Greater London but outside the LCC

There were three all-purpose county boroughs within the urban area surrounding the LCC. Croydon lay to the south and West Ham to the east. Beyond West Ham was East Ham. The rest of the built-up area of Greater London within the counties listed above was carved into a series of municipal boroughs, urban districts and rural districts. A number of these authorities, such as Ilford and Ealing, had grown bigger (in population terms) than many of the metropolitan boroughs within London. Several of the more powerful districts ran education under powers delegated by their county councils.

Greater London Council (GLC)

The creation of the GLC, or more correctly of an institution of metropolitan government, was the main objective of the reform of London government between 1957 and 1965. Once it had been decided to create such a body it was inevitable that the boroughs and districts within it would have to be reorganised. No one ever suggested that the GLC, like New York City government, should be a single tier of administration without a 'local' level. The history of city government in London, described earlier, had been one where small units had emerged organically and where, on occasion, Parliament decided to impose a metropolitan board or council. Even when the London County Council was created in 1888 the urban area of the capital extended beyond the LCC's boundaries. By the 1930s, the London sprawl had reached deep into Essex, Surrey and, Hertfordshire and Kent.

The GLC was created in 1965 as the metropolitan authority for most, though not all, of the continuous urban area in Greater London. It was intended to be a 'strategic' institution, with power to plan across the 1500 sq. km (600 sq. mi.) of the capital. In its early years, the GLC promoted major infrastructure schemes, most importantly a system of concentric 'Ringways' which were intended to provide motorway-scale roads around and across the capital. Large new council housing estates were built in, among other places, Newham, Southwark, Lewisham and Thamesmead (on the Bexley/Greenwich border). In 1970, control of London Transport was transferred to the GLC, though Mrs Thatcher's government took it back in 1984. The Conservatives, under Sir Horace Cutler, pioneered right-to-buy council house sales. In 1981, Ken Livingstone became leader and there ensued a spectacular ideological conflict between the GLC (and a number of other councils) and central government. The GLC was abolished in 1986.

Inner London Education Authority (ILEA)

Inner London had had a single education service since the creation of a directly elected London School Board in 1870. As discussed above, the LCC had taken over from the Board in 1904 and was the local education authority for London. The Herbert Commission proposed that its proposed 'Council for Greater London' and the new inner-London boroughs should share responsibility for education, though the government decided to sustain a single education authority on the same basis as previously. ILEA (without a definite article generally pronounced 'ill-i-yuh') became a 'special committee' of the GLC, consisting of all GLC members for inner London, plus one from each of the inner boroughs and the City. ILEA was high-spending and progressive and thus regularly the object of criticism by Conservatives and conservatives. It survived the GLC's demise by four years, having become a directly elected stand-alone authority for four years from 1986 to 1990.

Greater London Authority (GLA)

After a fourteen-year 'interregnum', metropolitan government was restored to London on 1 April 2000. Tony Blair's Labour government published consultative documents and then held a referendum on whether or not to introduce a mayor and assembly for London. In the event, the residents of all thirty-two boroughs voted in favour of the reform. Paradoxically, the abolition of the GLC paved the way for the creation of a more powerful elected office and institution. The Conservatives, who had abolished the GLC, accepted reality and endorsed the new institution. The national Labour leadership held a contest to choose their initial mayoral candidate which used an electoral college that had the effect of precluding former GLC leader Ken Livingstone from being the candidate. Livingstone stood as an independent and won. The GLA, like the GLC, has responsibility for 'strategic' planning, transport and the fire brigade. In addition, the Mayor of London was given power to set the budget of the Metropolitan Police and to determine non-operational policy. Since 2000, the GLA has been given extra powers over housing, economic development, culture and health. Transport for London is by far the GLA's largest responsibility, though the overall GLA group budget is only half that of the boroughs collectively. As part of the 2000 reforms, a separately elected Assembly was also created to hold the mayor to account.

City of London Corporation

The City has all the responsibilities of a London borough, plus a number of other duties it has accreted over many centuries. The Corporation's origins, explained in Chapter 1, lie in Anglo-Saxon England, as chartered by the Normans. The City has its own police force and is responsible for a number of metropolitan open spaces such as West Ham Park, Epping Forest and Hampstead Heath. It also runs port health at Heathrow, London City Airport and the Thames from Teddington to Tilbury. The City's responsibilities also include a number of schools (academies and independent institutions) and the Guildhall School of Music and Drama. It also runs the Barbican Centre and funds institutions such as the Guildhall Art Gallery, Tower Bridge and the London Symphony Orchestra. It is responsible for the City Bridge Trust, which is the capital's largest grant-giving body.

For many years 'the City' has been synonymous with the financial services industry, much of which has its headquarters in the Square Mile (actually, 1.12 sq. mi.). The Lord Mayor of London, who (among other things) undertakes a substantial number of overseas visits representing business, is an annual, ceremonial, post.

Political leadership is in the hands of the Chairman of the Policy & Resources Committee. For generations, the City has hosted major banquets and diplomatic events in its gilded Mansion House. Its wealth, accumulated over centuries, is often the object of envy and has from time to time generated a desire to reform it, particularly on the Left.

The City's skyline is increasingly a cluster of differently shaped towers. As recently as the early 1980s there was just one skyscraper in the City, the NatWest Tower (now Tower 42). But the rapid development of Canary Wharf triggered a competitive response from the City which has led to the pro-skyscraper policy. Like the monarchy, the City of London has shown remarkable resilience and a capacity to adapt.

Transport for London/London Regional Transport/ London Transport

London Transport as, in a different form, it used to be called is probably the best-known transit corporation in the world. Originally a 'combine' of loss-making private Tube lines and profitable private buses, it became the London

Passenger Transport Board (LPTB) in 1933, though it was colloquially known as 'London Transport' (LT). Chaired by Lord Ashfield, its chief executive Frank Pick was the genius who commissioned much of the system's iconic design, including station architecture, Edward Johnston's classic typeface and dozens of advertising posters. Harry Beck's much-copied Tube map was designed while Pick was in charge. Pick also had the London General Omnibus Company's logo re-designed to create the definitive LT 'roundel'. The LPTB was a trust, powerfully influenced by Ashfield's charismatic leadership. In 1948, its role was taken over by the London Transport Executive, a nationalised industry. The LPTB provided services throughout Greater London and the inner part of the Home Counties. In 1970, London Transport became the responsibility of the GLC before being returned to nationalised control by Mrs Thatcher in 1984 as 'London Regional Transport'. LT's Tube and buses were brought together with a number of other responsibilities such as major roads and taxi licensing in 2002 to become 'Transport for London' (TfL), an agency of the Greater London Authority. TfL is, unusually by global standards, an urban transport authority whose political control is based within city government. In New York, for example, a state government institution is responsible, while transport in Paris is controlled by a national body. TfL has enormous influence on the daily life of London.

Metropolitan Police

The Metropolitan Police is London's longest-surviving institution of metropolitan governance. It was created in 1829 as a responsibility of the Home Secretary. Other police forces in Britain, when created, were responsible to local police authorities. The 'Met' as it is widely known, has long had responsibility for a district far bigger than the LCC and was thus a 'Greater London' institution long before the GLC or the GLA. It has evolved from a traditional 'Dixon of Dock Green' force of friendly bobbies-on-the-beat into a complex modern organisation dealing with global crime and terror threats to London. The Met has from time to time had problems with corruption and also in its relations to some minority communities, though more recent commissioners have, haltingly, brought about improvement. In addition to its duties as the London police force, the Met is also responsible for Royal, diplomatic and terrorist policing across the country.

When the GLA was created in 2000, the Metropolitan Police budget was made a responsibility of the Mayor, with oversight by the Metropolitan Police Authority (MPA). Subsequently, the MPA was replaced by the Mayor's Office for Policing and Crime which now sets the direction and budget for the Metropolitan Police Service on behalf of the Mayor. The City of London has its own, separate, police force. Policing of the Underground and the railway system is the responsibility of the British Transport Police.

London Fire Brigade

Although not as long-established at the Metropolitan Police, the London Fire Brigade (LFB), formed as the Metropolitan Fire Brigade in 1866, is almost as old. It was the responsibility of the MBW, LCC and then the GLC until the latter's abolition in 1986. For the next fourteen years, it was controlled by a joint committee of the boroughs, who constituted the London Fire and Civil Defence Authority. It then, in 2000, became part of the GLA group under the control of the London Fire and Emergency Planning Authority. The LFB has a totemic London identity, partly deriving from the Blitz when, as part of the National Fire Service, the Brigade fought to control the bombing which so affected the city, particularly the docks.

London Development Agency

The Labour government elected in 1997 created a regional development agency (RDA) for each region of England, modelled on the Welsh and Scottish development agencies. When the GLA was formed in 2000, the London Development Agency (LDA) was set up alongside TfL, the Metropolitan Police Authority and the London Fire and Emergency Planning Authority as one of the Mayor's 'functional bodies'. The LDA had responsibility for regeneration, economic development and business support. The 2010 coalition government abolished the RDAs, including London's. The economic development functions previously in the hands of the LDA have passed to the City Hall administration and, in part to a new London Enterprise Panel.

Whitehall

The central government department with responsibility for London government has changed in terms of its name and configuration on several occasions since the Herbert Commission was announced in 1957. Henry Brooke, who announced the creation of the Commission, was Minister of Housing & Local Government (MHLG), a post in a department both of which existed until 1970. Responsibility for London and local government then passed to the giant Department of the Environment (DoE), which brought together all the MHLG's responsibilities, plus environmental protection and transport. This configuration existed till 1997, though transport was removed during this period. DoE was succeeded by the Department of the Environment, Transport and the Regions from 1997 to 2001, reuniting local government, planning and transport. The environment was then removed, leaving a Department for Transport, Local Government and the Regions (DTLR) for 2001–02. Then, the Office of the Deputy Prime Minister (ODPM) was formed, to include local government. ODPM existed from 2002 to 2006. It was succeeded by the Department for Communities and Local Government.

In 1994, a 'Government Office for London' (GOL) was created as part of a wider change to create 'Whitehall in the regions' outposts. In London, the reform suggested John Major's government was moving away from the absolutist position struck by Mrs Thatcher in 1986 and was allowing a metropolitan administrative unit to be re-created. The first director was Robin Young, a high-flyer of a more senior rank that the directors of other regional offices. GOL was responsible, working to minister Nick Raynsford and lead official Liz Meek, for the passage of the legislation which introduced the GLA. The Government Office for London was abolished, with those for all other regions, in 2010.

The London boroughs have had to interact with no fewer than six different Whitehall configurations within fifty years, including a seventeen-year period when there was a separate, overlapping, Government Office for London. This administrative churn is a telling indicator of the way British government is conducted.

Interregnum bodies

In the fourteen-year gap between the abolition of the GLC and the creation of the GLA, a number of organisations contributed to the government of London. The London Residuary Body (LRB) was created in 1985 to prepare to take over functions and assets of the GLC which could not immediately be passed to the boroughs or to Whitehall and its agencies. It handled the process of transferring and selling off ex-GLC services and property until only an irreducible, tiny, number were left to transfer to Bromley as the last resting place of the GLC. The LRB undertook a similar role in relation to the ILEA before handing its residual activities to Kensington & Chelsea.

When the GLC was abolished, the boroughs took over a number of city-wide services. To do this, a number of 33-authority joint committees were set up. A 'London Co-ordinating Committee' (ironically, another 'LCC') was formed to initiate the process of forming post-abolition government. Principal among the new committees were the London Fire & Civil Defence Authority (LFCDA), the London Planning Advisory Committee (LPAC), the London Boroughs Grants Scheme (LBGS), the London Research Centre (LRC) and the London Waste Regulation Authority (LWRA). Other joint committees such as the London Boroughs' Children's Regional Planning Committee had existed before abolition. London boroughs and the GLC had been members of the London and South East Regional Planning Conference (SERPLAN), which continued after the end of the GLC.

In the immediate aftermath of abolition, a number of Labour boroughs set up new institutions such as Greater London Enterprise (GLE), the London Strategic Policy Unit and the Technical Services Joint Committee in an attempt to continue elements of a 'GLC in exile'. GLE prospered and expanded in the years after abolition while few of the other bodies set up by the Labour councils lasted for more than a year or two. A number of government-appointed bodies were also created as a result of abolition, notably the South Bank Board and the Traffic Control System Unit (TCSU). The South Bank continues to operate as a separate entity, while the TCSU was transferred first to the Department of Transport, then to the City of London and then on to TfL.

Of the city-wide joint committees created after 1986, the most influential were LPAC and the LRC. LPAC, with Havering as the lead borough and chaired by Sally Hamwee (Richmond) then Nicky Gavron (Haringey), used its position to publish policy papers and to influence the debate about London as its population and economy grew in the years after abolition. In 1991, it published 'London: World City', a report which framed a debate about the future of the city in a way which influenced subsequent thinking and, after 2000, the London Plan. The LRC, with Islington as lead borough, took over the GLC's research and intelligence function and maintained statistical series such as those on the city's demography and elections. This continuity proved of enormous importance. The LBGS took over the GLC's controversial programme of grants to voluntary organisations with remarkably little dislocation or fuss. Indeed, given the trauma of GLC abolition the boroughs, working jointly through 33-member committees, proved remarkably adept at managing metropolitan services.

APPENDIX 3

ABBREVIATIONS FREQUENTLY USED

AGMA	Association of Greater Manchester Authorities
ALA	Association of London Authorities
ALG	Association of London Government
DCLG	Department for Communities and Local Government
DJC	Docklands Joint Committee
DoE	Department of the Environment
GLA	Greater London Authority
GLC	Greater London Council
GLDP	Greater London Development Plan
GOL	Government Office for London
HMSO	Her Majesty's Stationery Office
ILEA	Inner London Education Authority
LBA	London Boroughs Association
LC	London Councils
LCC	London County Council
LDA	London Development Agency
LDDC	London Docklands Development Corporation
LFB	London Fire Brigade
LFCDA	London Fire and Civil Defence Authority
LFEPA	London Fire and Emergency Planning Authority
LGA	Local Government Association
LPAC	London Planning Advisory Committee
LRB	London Residuary Body
LRES	London Rate Equalisation Scheme
LRT	London Regional Transport
LSB	London School Board
LSE	London School of Economics
LT	London Transport
LU	London Underground
MBW	Metropolitan Board of Works
MHLG	Ministry of Housing and Local Government
MOPAC	Mayor's Office for Policing and Crime
MPA	Metropolitan Police Authority
MPS	Metropolitan Police Service
ODPM	Office of the Deputy Prime Minister
SERPLAN	London and South East Regional Planning Conference
TfL	Transport for London
TSO	The Stationery Office
UCL	University College London

APPENDIX 4

BOROUGH LEADERS AND CHIEF EXECUTIVES

LEADERS 1964–2014

Barking and Dagenham
1964–72: Ted Ball
1972–86: Joe Butler
1986–98: George Brooker
1998–2009: Charles Fairbrass
2009–14: Liam Smith
2014–: Darren Rodwell

Barnet
1969–73: Alan Philip Fletcher
1973–76: Andrew Pares
1976–91: Leslie Pym
1991–94: Roy Shutz
1994–2002: Alan Williams
2002–05: Victor Lyon
2005–06: Brian Salinger
2006–10: Mike Freer
2010–11: Lynne Hillan
2011–: Richard Cornelius

Bexley
1964–66: Jim Wellbeloved
1966–68: Peter Maxwell
1968–71: Frederick Brearley
1971–74: Peter Maxwell
1974–78: Julian Tremayne
1978–94: Leonard Newton
1994–96: Donna Briant
1996–98: Kathryn Smith
1998–2002: Michael Slaughter
2002–06: Chris Ball
2006–08: Ian Clement
2008–: Teresa O'Neill

Brent
1964–65: Reg Freeson
1965–67: John Hockey
1967–68: George Marshall
1968–71: Alderman Edwin
1971–77: P. Hartley
1977–78: James Goudie
1978–81: John Lebor
1981–83: Tom Bryson
1983–86: Martin Coleman
1986–88: Merle Amory
1988–90: Dorman Long
1990–96: Bob Blackman
1996–2001: Paul Daisley
2001–06: Ann John
2006–10: Paul Lorber
2010–12: Ann John
2012–: Muhammed Butt

Bromley
1971–72: H. W. Haden
1972–76: Dennis Barkway
1976–81: Simon Randall
1981–96: Dennis Barkway
1996–97: Frank Cooke
1997–98: Michael Tinkner
1998–2001: Chris Maines & Sue Polydorou
2001–03: Michael Tickner
2003–04: Russell Mellor
2004–: Stephen Carr

Camden

1964–68: C. J. Ratchford
1968–70: Geoffrey Finsberg
1970–71: Martin Morton
1971–73: Millie Miller
1973–75: Frank Dobson
1975–82: Roy Shaw
1982–86: Phil Turner
1986–90: Anthony Dykes
1990–93: Julie Fitzgerald
1993–2000: Richard Arthur
2000–2006: Jane Roberts
2006–10: Keith Moffitt
2010–12: Nasim Ali
2012–: Sarah Hayward

City of London

1984–92: Peter Rigby
1992–97: Michael Cassidy
1997–2003: Judith Mayhew
2003–08: Michael Snyder
2008–12: Stuart Fraser
2012–: Mark Boleat

Croydon

1964–67: Albert John Dunn
1967–70: Digby Milward Weightman
1970–76: Albert John Dunn
1976–79: Peter Bowness
1979–80: Stanley Elliott Littlechild
1980–94: Peter Bowness
1994–96: Mary Walker
1996–97: Geraint Davies
1997–2000: Valerie Shawcross
2000–2005: Hugh Malyan
2005–06: Tony Newman
2006–14: Mike Fisher
2014–: Tony Newman

Ealing

1964–68: William Hopkins
1968–71: Robert Hetherington
1971–75: John Telfer
1975–78: Michael Elliot
1978–81: Beatrice Howard

1981–83: John Wood
1983–86: Ken Kettle
1986–89: Len Turner
1989–90: John Cudmore
1990–91: Martin Mallam
1991–94: Graham Bull
1994–2005: John Cudmore
2005–06: Leo Thomson
2006–10: Jason Stacey
2010–: Julian Bell

Enfield

1964–66: Ted Graham
1966–68: Eric Smythe
1968–87: Alan Young
1987–88: John Lindsay
1988–94: Graham Eustance
1994–99: Jeff Rodin
1999–2002: Doug Taylor
2002–10: Mike Rye
2010–: Doug Taylor

Greenwich

1964–66: Ronald Stucke
1966–68: Thomas Smith
1968–69: William Manners
1969–71: Charles Miles
1971–74: John Cartwright
1974–82: Arthur Capelin
1982–87: John Austin Walker
1987–89: David Picton
1989–92: Quentin Marsh
1992–2000: Len Duvall
2000–2014: Chris Roberts
2014–: Denis Hyland

Hackney

1964–68: Martin Ottolangui
1968–70: C. H. Hegerty
1970–71: D. H. P. Bridgehouse
1971–81: Martin Ottolangui
1981–82: John Kotz
1982–85: Anthony Kendall
1985–86: Tony Milwood
1986–90: Andrew Puddephat

1990–95: John McCafferty
1995–96: Nick Tallentire
1996–2001: No leader
2001–: Jules Pipe

Hammersmith and Fulham

1965–66: John F. Heaks
1966–68: Anthony Chapman
1968–71: William Smith
1971–73: Alfred Little
1973–78: Barry Stead
1978–79: Stuart Leishman
1979–85: Kim Howe
1985–86: John Putnam
1986–88: Gordon Prentice
1988–91: Mike Goodman
1991–96: Iain Coleman
1996–2005: Andrew Slaughter
2005–06: Stephen Burke
2006–12: Stephen Greenhalgh
2012–14: Nicholas Botterill
2014–: Stephen Cowan

Haringey

1964–67: John McIlwain
1967–68: Sheila Berkery-Smith
1968–71: Peter Rigby
1971–73: Sheila Berkery-Smith
1973–80: Colin Ware
1980–82: Robin Young
1982–83: Angela Greatley
1983–84: George Meehan
1984–87: Bernie Grant
1987–99: Toby Harris
1999–2004: George Meehan
2004–06: Charles Adje
2006–09: George Meehan
2009–: Claire Kober

Harrow

1964–68: Charles Jordan
1968–71: Edward Buckle
1971–74: Cyril Harrison
1974–77: Harold Mote
1977–79: Edward Buckle

1979–84: Brian Clark
1984–87: Donald Abbott
1987–91: Ron Grant
1991–94: Donald Abbott
1994–96: Chris Noyce
1996–97: Andrew Wiseman
1997–98: Chris Noyce
1998–2002: Bob Shannon
2002–04: Archie Foulds
2004–06: Navin Shah
2006–08: Chris Mote
2008–10: David Ashton
2010–12: Bill Stephenson
2012–13: Thaya Idaikkadar
2013–14: Susan Hall
2014–: David Perry

Havering

1964–71: Jack Moultrie
1971–74: Michael Ward
1974–77: Jack Moultrie
1977–78: William Sibley
1978–84: Jack Moultrie
1984–90: Roger Ramsey
1990–96: Arthur Latham
1996–97: Louise Sinclair
1997–98: Wilf Mills
1998–2002: Ray Harris
2002–04: Eric Munday
2004–14: Michael White
2014–: Roger Ramsey

Hillingdon

1965–68: Alfred Beck
1968–71: W. Darrell Charles
1971–73: Alfred Beck
1973–78: John Bartlett
1978–84: John Watts
1984–86: Norman Hawkins
1990–92: Andrew Boff
1992–94: Richard Barnes
1994–97: Chris Rogers
1997–98: Paul Harmsworth
1998–2000: Richard Barnes
2000–: Ray Puddifoot

Hounslow

1964–68: Alf King
1968–71: D. C. L. Usher
1971–86: Alf King
1986–87: John Grigg
1987–91: David Wetzel
1991–99: John Chatt
1999–2002: John Connelly
2002–04: John Chatt
2004–06: Colin Ellar
2006–10: Peter Thompson
2010–14: Jagdish Sharma
2014–: Steve Curran

Islington

1964–68: David Gwyn Jones
1968–71: Michael Morris
1971–72: David Gwyn Jones
1972–82: Gerry Southgate
1982–92: Margaret Hodge
1992–94: Derek Sawyer
1994–97: Alan Clinton
1997–2002: Derek Sawyer
2002–06: Steve Hitchins
2006–09: James Kempton
2009–10: Terry Stacy
2010–14: Catherine West
2014–: Richard Watts

Kensington and Chelsea

1964–68: Anslow Wilson
1968–78: Malby Crofton
1978–89: Nicholas Freeman
1989–2000: Joan Hanham
2000–2013: Merrick Cockell
2013–: Nicholas Paget-Brown

Kingston upon Thames

1972–74: C. M. Cotton
1974–83: Mike Knowles
1983–85: David Edwards
1985–86: Frank Hartfree
1986–87: Chris Nicholson
1987–88: Steve Harris
1988–90: Frank Hartfree

1990–94: Paul Clokie
1994–97: John Tilley
1997–98: Derek Osbourne
1998–2001: David Edwards
2001–02: Kevin Davis
2002–03: Roger Hayes
2003–13: Derek Osbourne
2013–14: Liz Green
2014–: Kevin Davis

Lambeth

1973–78: David Stimpson
1978–86: Ted Knight
1986–88: Linda Bellos
1988–89: Dick Sorabji
1989–93: Joan Twelves
1993–94: Steve Whaley
1994–2000: Jim Dickson
2000–2002: Tom Franklin
2002–06: Peter Truesdale
2006–12: Steve Reed
2012–: Lib Peck

Lewisham

1964–68: Fred Winslade
1968–71: Norman Dinsdale
Banks
1971–84: Andy Hawkins
1984–85: Ron Stockbridge
1985–88: Dave Sullivan
1988–93: Steve Bullock
1993–95: Margaret Moran
1995–98: Jim Mallory
1998–2002: Dave Sullivan
2002–: Steve Bullock

Merton

1964–65: E. K. Clarke
1965–71: Vincent Talbot
1971–74: Dennis Hempstead
1974–75: Vincent Talbot
1975–80: Allan Jones
1980–88: Harry Cowd
1988–90: John Elvidge
1990–91: Geoffrey Smith

1991–97: Tony Colman
1997–99: Mike Brunt
1999–2000: Philip Jones
2000–2001: Peter Holt
2001–06: Andrew Judge
2006–10: David William
2010–: Stephen Alambritis

Newham

1964–77: Samuel Boyce
1977–85: Jack Hart
1985–90: Fred Jones
1990–94: Stephen Timms
1994–95: John Isted
1995–96: Mike Brown
1996–99: Robin Wales
1999–2007: Dave Burbage

Redbridge

1964–72: R. A. Dalton
1972–74: A. J. Escott
1974–75: J. W. S. Telford
1975–79: K. Webb
1979–85: K. J. Salter
1985–88: J. A. Ramsden
1988–91: John Lovell
1991–94: Ronnie Barden
1994–99: Liz Pearce
1999–2000: Keith Axon
2000–2002: Mohammed Javed
2002–03: Keith Axon
2003–04: Allan Burgess
2004–05: Elaine Norman
2005–06: Laurence Davies
2006–09: Alan Weinberg
2009–14: Keith Prince
2014–: Jas Athwal

Richmond upon Thames

1964–78: H. Hall
1978–80: J. K. Barker
1980–83: K. J. Morell
1983–2001: David Williams
2001–02: Serge Lourie
2002–06: Tony Arbour

2006–10: Serge Lourie
2010–: Nicholas True

Southwark

1964–65: Ronald William Brown
1965–68: A. J. Kemp
1968–82: John O'Grady
1982–84: Alan Davis
1984–86: Tony Ritchie
1986–90: Annie Matthews
1990–93: Sally Keeble
1993–97: Jeremy Fraser
1997–2000: Niall Duffy
2000–2002: Stephanie Elsy
2002–10: Nick Stanton
2010–: Peter John

Sutton

1964–73: Godfrey Taylor
1973–76: John Charles Cox
1976–80: Robin Squire
1980–86: Dr Trafford
1986–99: Graham Tope
1999–2002: Mike Cooper
2002–12: Sean Brennan
2012–: Ruth Dombey

Tower Hamlets

1964–74: John Orwell
1974–84: Paul Beasley
1984–86: John Riley
1986–87: Eric Flounders
1987–88: Chris Birt
1988–90: Brenda Collins
1990–91: Eric Flounders
1991–94: Peter Hughes
1994–95: John Biggs
1995–97: Dennis Twomey
1997–98: Michael Keith
1998–99: Julia Mainwaring
1999–2001: Michael Keith
2001–05: Helal Abbas
2005–06: Michael Keith
2006–08: Denise Jones
2008–10: Lutfur Rahman

2010–11: Helal Uddin Abbas
2011–: Lutfur Rahman

Waltham Forest

1964–68: Herbert Palethorpe
1968–71: Tom Brandon
1971–82: Bill Pearmine
1982–86: Gerald King
1986–90: Neil Gerrard
1990–92: Clive Morton
1992–94: Evan Jones
1994–98: Huw Morgan-Thomas
1998–2003: Tony Buckley
2003–09: Clyde Loakes
2009–: Chris Robbins

Wandsworth

1964–66: S. Wellbelove
1966–68: S. Sporle
1968–71: R. Ash
1971–72: I. McGarry
1972–73: F. Sims & I. McGarry

1973–76: I. McGarry
1976–78: J. Tilley
1978–79: A. Belton & D. Mallam
1979–83: C. Chope
1983–92: Paul Beresford
1992–2011: Edward Lister
2011–: Ravi Govindia

Westminster

1964–65: David Cobbold
1965–69: Gordon Pirie
1969–72: A. C. Barrett
1972–76: Hugh (Guy) Cubitt
1976–83: David Cobbold
1983–91: Shirley Porter
1991–93: David Weeks
1993–94: Simon Milton
1994–95: Miles Young
1995–2000: Melvyn Caplan
2000–2008: Simon Milton
2008–12: Colin Barrow
2012–: Philippa Roe

CHIEF EXECUTIVES 1964–2014

Barking and Dagenham

1964–74: Keith Lauder
1974–79: Stanley Watson-Barker
1979–92: Dudley Farr
1992–2000: William (Bill) Smith
2000–2004: Graham Farrant
2004–05: John Tatum
2005–10: Rob Whiteman
2010–11: David Woods
2011–12: Stella Manzie
2012–: Graham Farrant

Barnet

1964–75: R. H. Williams
1975–90: Ernest Michael Bennett
1990–2000: Max Caller
2000–2001: Rita Dexter
2001–09: Leo Boland
2009–13: Nick Walkley
2013–: Andrew Travers

Bexley

1964–72: Clive Dennis
1972–75: Ernest Michael Bennett
1975–95: Terrence Musgrave
1995–2003: Chris Duffield
2003–08: Nick Johnson
2008–: Will Tuckley

Brent

1964–74: R. S. Forster
1974–80: Kenneth Betts
1980–86: Michael Bichard
1986–95: Charles Wood
1995–98: George Benham
1998–2012: Gareth Daniel
2012–: Christine Gilbert

Bromley

1964–71: Thomas Fagg
1971–79: Percy Bunting

1979–95: Nigel Palk
1995–2000: Michael Blanch
2000–2007: David Bartlett
2007–15: Doug Patterson

Camden
1964–78: Brian Wilson
1978–90: Frank Nickson
1990–96: Jeremy Smith
1996–2003: Steve Bundred
2003–12: Moira Gibb
2012–: Mike Cooke

City of London
1964–74: E. H. Nichols
1974–82: S. Clayton
1982–91: G. W. Rowley
1991–96: Sam Jones
1996–99: Bernard Harty
1999–2003: Tom Simmons
2003–12: Chris Duffield
2012–: John Barradell

Croydon
1964–82: Alan Blakemore
1982–90: Frank Birch
1990–93: Roger Jefferies
1993–2007: David Wechsler
2007–13: Jon Rouse
2013–: Nathan Elvery

Ealing
1964–70: E. J. Cope-Brown
1970–81: Peter Coomber
1981–82: Alan Groves
1982–83: R. J. Chalkley
1983–86: Brian T. Collins
1986–87: R. J. Chalkley & John Leadbetter
1987–94: Judith Hunt
1994–2005: Gillian Guy
2005–10: Darra Singh
2010–: Martin Smith

Enfield
1964–74: Cyril Platten

1974–77: W. Day
1990–92: Brian McAndrew
1993–95: Maralyn Arnold
1995–2002: David Plank
2002–03: Donald Graham
2003–: Rob Leak

Greenwich
1964–70: R. L. Doble
1970–78: R. Doble
1978–84: D. Brokenshire
1984–88: Alan Glover
1988–97: Colin Roberts
1997–2001: David Brooks
2001–: Mary Ney

Hackney
1964–77: L. G. Huddy
1977–81: Dennis Wood
1981–85: Brian Blackler
1985–89: Pamela Gordon
1989–95: Jerry White
1995–99: Tony Elliston
1999–2000: Sarah Ebanja
2000–2005: Max Caller
2005–07: Penny Thompson
2007–: Tim Shields

Hammersmith and Fulham
1964–74: Carey Randall
1974–76: Reginald Ward
1976–87: Anthony Allen
1987–91: Tony Eddison
1991–92: Drew Stevenson & Heather Rabbatts
1992–93: Peter Derrick
1993–98: Neil Newton
1998–2002: Richard Harbord
2002–12: Geoff Alltimes
2012–14: Derek Myers
2014–: Nicholas Holgate

Haringey
1964–67: K. W. Robbins
1967–75: Brian Cooper

1975–89: Roy Limb
1989–2000: Gurbux Singh
2000–2005: David Warwick
2005–06: Max Caller
2006–10: Ita O'Donovan
2010–12: Kevin Crompton
2012–: Nick Walkley

Harrow
1964–66: D. H. Pritchard
1966–74: Stanley Lancaster
1974–79: Raymond Hill
1979–87: D. Adams
1987–2002: Tony Redmond
2002–06: Joyce Markham
2006–13: Michael Lockwood
2013–: Paul Najsarek

Havering
1964–70: John E. Symons
1970–73: J. Symons
1973–76: R. Tridgell
1990–96: David R. Bradley
1996–2003: Harold Tinworth
2003–07: Stephen Evans
2007–: Cheryl Coppell

Hillingdon
1964–82: George Hooper
1982–92: Paul Johnson
1992–97: Chris Rippingdale
1997–98: Glenys Andrews
1998–2006: Dorian Leatham
2006–12: Hugh Dunnachie
2012–: Fran Beasley

Hounslow
1964–74: D. Mathieson
1974–75: Brian Algar
1975–92: Roger Jefferies
1992–97: Bob Kerslake
1997–2000: Derek Myers
2000–2001: Chris Langstaff
2001–10: Mark Gilks

2010–11: Michael Frater
2011–: Mary Harpley

Islington
1964–72: F. L. Croft
1972–84: H. M. Dewing
1984–96: Eric Dear
1996–2002: Leisha Fullick
2002–08: Helen Bailey
2008–11: John Foster
2011–: Lesley Seary

Kensington and Chelsea
1964–68: J. Waring Sainsbury
1968–75: L. E. Holmes
1975–79: R. Stillwell
1979–90: R. S. Webber
1990–2000: Alan Taylor
2000–2013: Derek Myers
2013–: Nicholas Holgate

Kingston upon Thames
1964–74: J. Noel Martin
1974–77: J. Bishop
1977–80: John Ashbourne
1980–82: R. Tarr
1982–87: George Hollis
1987–92: Robert McCloy
1992–95: Timothy Hornsby
1995–99: Bernard Quoroll
1999–: Bruce McDonald

Lambeth
1964–70 John E. Fishwick
1970–80: F. Dixon-Ward
1980–90: John George
1990–93: Herman Ouseley
1993–95: Henry Gilby
1995–2000: Heather Rabbatts
2000–2001: Heather du Quesnay
2001–05: Faith Boardman
2005–06: Andrew Webster
2006–: Derrick Anderson

Lewisham
1964–71: Alan Milner-Smith
1971–76: John French
1976–82: Frank Birch
1982–89: John Harwood
1989–94: Terry Hanafin
1994–: Barry Quirk

Merton
1964–74: Sydney Astin
1974–81: Alan Robinson
1981–91: William McKee
1991–92: Richard Davis
1992–96: Heather Rabbatts
1996–98: Sue Charteris
1998–2003: Roger Paine
2003–04: Richard Rawes
2004–: Ged Curran

Newham
1964–70: G. E. Smith
1970–74: G. Smith
1974–77: J. Warren
1990–93: John Samuel
1993–96: Drew Stevenson
1996–99: Wendy Thomson
2000–2007: Dave Burbage
2007–08: Chris Wood
2008–10: Joe Duckworth
2010–: Kim Bromley-Derry

Redbridge
1964–71: K. F. B. Nicholls
1971–80: A. McCarlie Findlay
1980–93: G. U. Price
1993–2000: Michael Frater
2000–: Roger Hampson

Richmond upon Thames
1964–70: W. H. Jones
1970–80: A. Goode
1980–88: M. J. Honey
1988–99: Richard Harbord
1999–: Gillian Norton

Southwark
1964–69: F. Dixon Ward
1969–70: E. J. Pitt
1970–81: S. T. Evans
1981–84: A. G. Corless
1984–85: J. B. Parker
1985–94: Anna Whyatt
1994–2005: Bob Coomber
2005–12: Annie Shepperd
2012–: Eleanor Kelly

Sutton
1964–81: T. M. H. Scott
1981–90: Alan Taylor
1990–2001: Patricia Hughes
2001–05: Joanna Simons
2005–10: Paul Martin
2010–11: Ian Birnbaum
2011–: Niall Bolger

Tower Hamlets
1964–86: Jack Wolkind
1986–87: Daniel Regan
1987–88: Charles Lea & Alan Tobias
1988–90: John McBride
1990–91: Tom Herbert & Keith Ivory
1991–94: Albert Golding
1994–95: Sylvia Dean
1995–99: Sylvie Pierce
1999–2000: Eleanor Kelly
2000–2006: Christine Gilbert
2006–07: Ian Wilson
2007–09: Martin Smith
2009–11: Kevan Collins
2011–12: Aman Dalvi
2012–: Stephen Halsey

Waltham Forest
1964–73: Edna A. Cann
1973–90: Leonard Knox
1990–2000: Alan Tobias
2000–2004: Simon White
2004–07: Jacquie Dean
2007–08: Roger Taylor

2008–10: Andrew Kilburn
2010–: Martin Esom

Wandsworth
1964–68: D. C. Kerr
1968–69: B. A. Payton
1969–77: Norman White
1977–80: Lionel Akid
1980–84: Fred Haynes
1984–87: Albert Newman
1987–2011: Gerald Jones
2011–: Paul Martin

Westminster
1964–77: Alan Dawtry
1977–83: J. David Whittty
1983–87: Rodney Brooke
1987–88: Rodney Brooke and Bill
Phillips
1988–91: Bill Phillips
1991–94: Mervyn Montacute
1994–99: Bill Roots
1999–2007: Peter Rogers
2007–13: Mike Moore
2013–: Charlie Parker

Listed here are the names of the leader (or equivalent) and chief executive (or equivalent) in each borough from 1964 to the present.

Up until 1974 the chief officer is generally a town clerk, and from 1974 onwards a chief executive, following the convention adopted by the majority of boroughs. Where boroughs have at times operated a committee system without a leader, the chair of the policy and resources committee or equivalent is listed, in place of the leader.

The information has been sourced from historic London Councils directories, records held online by the GLA, and records at the London Metropolitan Archives. London Councils contacted boroughs directly for assistance in completing the records, although not all names could be located. The political control of each council is available on the London Councils website at http://boroughs50.londoncouncils.gov.uk/almanac/.

Wherever possible, entries reflect the position from the annual meeting of the council of that year. Therefore, a leader listed as having served from 1964 to 1968 will have served from the annual council in 1964 to the annual council in 1968.

INDEX